D0207505

Beggar Thy Neighbor

M.Jackson Inv.t   Boitard Sculp.t

The Prodigals Nurse; or Modern Heir.

From Parents & from Friends set free,   To Nurse, th'Us'rer, he applies, —
Young Squander comes the Town to see :   Who neer for Cent per Cent denies. —
Debauch'd by Party and by Whores, —   Learn Hence, ye Rakes! when old Ones gone
Dad stops his Hand in paying Scores .   Th'Estate ye have is not your own .—

Publish'd according to Act of Parliament May   1750.

Beggar Thy Neighbor

A History of Usury and Debt

Charles R. Geisst

PENN

UNIVERSITY OF PENNSYLVANIA PRESS

Philadelphia

Copyright © 2013 University of Pennsylvania Press

Published by
University of Pennsylvania Press
Philadelphia, Pennsylvania 19104-4112
www.upenn.edu/pennpress

Printed in the United States of America on acid-free paper
10 9 8 7 6 5 4 3 2 1

Library of Congress Cataloging-in-Publication Data
Geisst, Charles R.
  Beggar thy neighbor : a history of usury and debt / Charles R. Geisst. —
1st ed.
     p. cm.
  Includes bibliographical references and index.
  ISBN 978-0-8122-4462-5 (hardcover : alk. paper)
  1. Usury—History.   2. Usury—Religious aspects—History.
3. Usury laws—History.   4. Debt—History.   I. Title.
  HB551.G45 2013
  332.8'309—dc23
                                                          2012022355

Frontispiece: Louis-Philippe Boitard, *The Prodigals Nurse; or Modern Heir*
(1750). Engraving. Library of Congress Prints and Photographs Division,
Washington, D.C. 20540 USA. The lines beneath the image read: "From
Parents & from friends set free, / Young Squander comes the Town to see; /
Debauch'd by Party and by Whores, / Dad stops his Hand in paying Scores /
To Nurse, the Us'rer, he applies, / Who nee'r for Cent per Cent denies. / Learn
Hence, ye Rakes! when old One's gone / Th' Estate ye have is not your own."

Contents

Introduction

After the discovery of America, capital was in demand, and men were ready to pay interest on it. Then the theologians were obliged to review their teachings. If it had come to this, that money must be had, and men would pay interest on it, ecclesiastical ethics must be revised.
—Richard Henry Dana, 1867

Seven years before the assassination of Julius Caesar, an acrimonious dispute broke out between Marcus Tullius Cicero, at the time the provincial governor of Cilicia, and Marcus Junius Brutus, a young provincial Roman administrator. The elder statesman chided the younger man for using his administrative post in Cyprus to earn ill-gotten gains at the expense of the local people. Cicero received reports that Brutus had been lending money in Cyprus at four times the maximum rate stipulated by Roman law. To make matters even worse, he did it anonymously through an agent who did not mind using strong-arm tactics to collect the debts. When Cicero brought the matter to his attention, Brutus ignored him and continued to lend money. When he finally returned to Rome, he did so a wealthy man.

The problem caused Cicero to coin a name for the practice which became a cornerstone of Roman law. The story was told innumerable times over the next eighteen hundred years. The Roman historians dutifully recorded it and Adam Smith alluded to it in the *Wealth of Nations*. According to Roman law, simple interest was permitted but compound interest was anathema. Compounding had been used in many ancient civilizations, but the Romans eventually made it illegal. By doing so, they also established a tradition that would create much confusion in the centuries to follow. They did not make all interest illegal, only compound or "accumulating interest."

Prohibitions against excessive interest, or more properly usury, have been found in almost all societies since antiquity. Charging interest on loans is the oldest financial practice. It has also been decried almost from the beginning as predatory, with the lender seeking to take advantage of the borrower. Whether loans were made in cash or in kind, unscrupulous lenders were said to be practicing a beggar-thy-neighbor policy by ensuring that the borrowers were disadvantaged to the point of losing their collateral or in extreme cases even losing their freedom or families. Charging simple interest was barely condoned, but charging compound interest was unscrupulous, immoral, and rapacious. It was also practiced with near impunity.

The problem was clear in the ancient world but became obscured over time. Over the centuries, usury prohibitions became part of civil law, and that unwritten law of nations generally referred to as the natural law. But it was still practiced widely and openly by the accursed moneylenders who quickly became part of legend and literature. This uneasy combination of theory and practice is partially responsible for the uneven patterns of economic development found in Europe from the decline of Rome to the Reformation. In the early Middle Ages especially, all interest was considered usury by the church. Compound interest became "Jewish interest," suggesting that it had dark, magical, non-Christian qualities that could be used for expropriation by the lender, considered a societal outsider.

Through its long history, interest and usury have gone from being anathema to being big business in the contemporary world, but they remain at least partially illegal in many jurisdictions. Many American states still retain laws against criminal interest, or loan-sharking. At the same time, it frequently is ignored in the same places with impunity and only becomes the center of attention in poor economic climates or in times of capital shortage or high inflation. Perhaps that is why it has remained part of the universal canon of proscribed practices. Usury prohibitions firmly are part of the natural law tradition, in that natural law specifies what cannot be done. Since the fall of Rome, there have been more centuries characterized by what is known as capital shortage than there have been of periods of sustained growth and general prosperity. It is not a coincidence that the outcry against usury has been most shrill during those difficult times.

Today, usury is considered excessive interest, but that definition is relatively new in historical terms. Originally, *usura* was interest and its actual rate differed from place to place. The debate over it was intense. Excessive interest in many ancient societies was interest on interest, or *usurae usararum*, which added to the principal of an unpaid loan. In the ancient world and

Middle Ages especially, this was anathema. The tribal tradition of the Hebrews prohibiting Jews from lending to each other at interest was cited by medieval churchmen as the major Old Testament source for proscribing all interest, not just simple interest. The great irony was that Jews were exempt from lending to gentiles and accepted as moneylenders by the church in the Middle Ages. That loophole allowed them to compete with the Lombards and Cahors who were allowed to lend at interest.

In medieval Europe, these groups were the main moneylenders before the arrival of the Jews. Curiously, none was condemned for it and the Lombards were responsible for the development of the money markets in the fourteenth century. The Italian bankers in particular became financiers to monarchs and princes as far north as England. Their experiences with Edward III in particular were unpleasant, but their skills were highly sought after in countries where the treasuries were either low on cash or management skills. Despite the general ban on interest, the moneylenders were tolerated and even occasionally put the feet of monarchs to the fire when the interest bill was overdue. Jewish lenders usually were less fortunate. This apparent contradiction can be explained by a combination of tradition, religion, and law. The Lombards were the barbarian tribe that conquered Rome in the sixth century; the Cahors were the descendants of the Visigoths who settled in France. Neither group had any provisions against interest or usury in their laws because both came from societies that originally used barter or payment in kind rather than money. Natural law in the late Roman Empire assumed a commonality among civilized societies, but that did not include barbarians. Neither group had a tradition against usury; each continued to pursue its newly acquired money-lending skills without interruption. No loud objection was heard until the Lombards were conquered by Charlemagne in 800, but by that time their tradition was established.

The barbarian invasions also relegated much of Roman law to the shadows of history until the general revival of learning in the twelfth century. When many books that had been missing for centuries reappeared, those of Aristotle became the main reference for many churchmen, including Thomas Aquinas. This complicated matters for moneylending because the Scholastics accepted Aristotle's dictum that money was sterile, having no intrinsic qualities other than being used as a medium of exchange. It could not beget itself and therefore usury was not useful. Unknown (or ignored) was the discovery of Justinian's *Code* in 1130. In it, the prohibition against *anatocismus* (Cicero's term) and *alterum tantum* (doubling a debt by interest charges) could be found. Today those practices collectively are known as compound interest. Normal rates of interest were tolerated, but adding interest to outstanding principal was banned. But medieval church law would not even admit to ordinary interest despite the distinction between the two in Roman law.

Compound interest would not become a math exercise until the Middle Ages when the Italian mathematician Fibonacci discussed compound interest questions and puzzles. Because of the usury prohibition, he carefully avoided discussions about loan values and instead focused on future value problems, an issue medieval philosophers were not acquainted with and did not discuss. He posed questions about the future value of a unit of currency and, most famously, how many rabbits would be the result of an original pair, assuming continuous rabbit compounding. But he avoided the usury issue, as did his equally famous countryman Luca Pacioli two centuries later when he discussed double entry bookkeeping for the first time. Fibonacci did, however, tackle the problem of debasing a currency, a politically correct topic in the thirteenth century for kings and princes.

There is a great temptation to criticize various usury and interest ceilings as being inconsistent over the centuries. The medieval church adopted a ban on usury, similar to the one in the Muslim world, only to see it circumvented with great frequency between the twelfth and nineteenth centuries. Different commentators had sundry opinions on the subject, but all agreed that interest needed to be controlled. Even Adam Smith, considered the father of free market economic theory, favored a ceiling on interest. But as usury and interest approached the nineteenth century, it becomes more clear that there was a great deal of consistency in the way they were treated, given the differences in cultures and political motives of those opposed to them. The tendency to abuse one's position as a lender was recognized by most commentators regardless of their political or moral position.

The term "beggar thy neighbor" today is used to describe an international trade practice where one nation attempts to establish advantage over its trading partners through restrictive trade practices or policies. This derives from a mercantilist idea that owed its origins to an era when colonial powers exploited their far-flung colonies and ensured that they exported more than they imported. Before the mercantilist period, however, the term was associated more simply with borrowing and lending. The Shylocks of the world exploited the Antonios, seeking to extract their pound of flesh, when Christian principles demanded fairness and lenient lending policies. Equity and Christian charity suggested that lenders should treat borrowers as brothers, members of the same community. The idea was practiced only rarely.

Shylock stood apart from that community; his religion and tradition were different; he was allowed to lend to non-Jews, a well-known, widely circulated biblical fact. Coincidentally Portia, who successfully defended Antonio against Shylock in Shakespeare's court, was also the name of Brutus's second wife, which was probably not a coincidence since Shakespeare was well acquainted with Roman history.

The lending tradition became a nasty circle of recrimination and counter-recrimination that lasted for centuries. Lenders and early bankers, whether they were Jews, Lombards, Cahors, or the Templars, realized that their financial expertise and alien status in many European societies made them subjects of envy, derision, and ultimately retaliation from many hard pressed sovereigns. As a result, many of them charged compound interest to compensate for their business risk or disguised interest charges as hidden, discounted fees. The risks they faced were more than simple counterparty risk because they could be expelled from their homes, sent to the Inquisition, or expropriated. The fact that many well-known bankers in northern Europe prior to the Renaissance came from distant locales attests to the fact that foreigners were often sought as lenders precisely because borrowers could default on loans to them without much fear of reprisal.

The history of usury usually has been divided into a general discussion surrounding borrowing and lending on the one hand and the legal treatment of usury by various societies on the other. Since the early years of the Roman monarchy, through the republic and ending with the empire, Rome always had what is known as statutory usury. Laws governing interest were embodied in the law, at first in the *Twelve Tables* and then later in Justinian's *Code* and *Digest*. The latter incorporated the writings of many prominent rhetoricians and philosophers, so together they were an excellent compilation of the major ideas on usury in Rome for the previous centuries. These laws, different in scope and sophistication, actually specified the maximum rate of interest that lenders could charge borrowers. They did not ban lending rates but only sought a level of interest that was considered practical and viable. To borrow an idea from Adam Smith, the more prosperous and wealthy a society, the lower was its rate of interest.

It has been suggested that the history of usury is nothing more than an exercise in intellectual history. Accordingly, usury is an idea with a long history, riddled with enigmas and inconsistencies, that exists mostly in the minds of economic historians. That is true but it ignores the subtext, which has proved to be one of the most powerful notions in all societies for three thousand years. As part of general natural law, it reflects societal notions of fairness and equity that have transcended ancient, medieval, and modern societies. The power of interest, and especially compound interest, cannot be understated. Usury and interest have been condemned together for centuries, although it is not always clear whether critics distinguished, or even understood, the differences between the two. Compound interest has commanded little discussion by itself until recently. John Maynard Keynes recognized the problems compound interest would cause for Germany in paying World War I reparations. Albert Einstein reputedly called it the eighth wonder of the world for its ability to produce future values far in excess of present value. The English clergyman Richard Price tried to use compound interest to retire the sizable British national debt in the eighteenth century. American lenders are now required to state the annual percentage rate they charge customers on unpaid balances, but the rates themselves have been left untouched by federal regulators. In the early 1980s, several large American banks went to great lengths and expense to establish credit card facilities in states with no functional usury laws in order to avoid potential prosecution for charging high interest rates, ratcheted even higher by daily or monthly compounding.

There has been a clear distinction between misgivings about usury and the law of usury. The misgivings certainly have been more colorful. Dante relegated usurers to the inferno while numerous writers cited scripture to illustrate the pitfalls of lending money. In early nineteenth-century Ireland, the Reverend Jeremiah O'Callaghan refused the sacraments to a dying man until he recanted his alleged usury, an incident that eventually got the priest banished to the wilds of northern Vermont. When the Catholic Church finally reconsidered its ban on usury, it did so quietly through a letter by the pope to the Italian bishops in the eighteenth century, not through a papal encyclical as would have been expected. One hundred years later, the ban would politely be ignored. After centuries of condemnation, the lure of fixed income investment returns finally became too great to resist.

Despite the colorful vignettes, it has always been easier to denounce the practice than actually pass a useful usury law. When the British government finally abolished its usury laws in the early nineteenth century, many of the arguments in the debate later surfaced in the United States. Banning usury was bad for business and therefore the usury laws should be abolished. No one could forcibly argue against the point, but no one could totally agree either given the abuses to which lenders often subjected borrowers. Advocates of maintaining a ban often cited the Old Testament and it became a major source of speech material for legislators in the nineteenth century.

While much of it sounded like hell, fire, and brimstone, the laws that subsequently followed sounded very tame in comparison. Usury laws lived on in the United States for another one hundred years. The fact that a major credit crisis followed within a few decades did not seem to faze proponents of leverage and free market interest rates who apparently were not aware that the South Sea Bubble, the crash of 1929, and most of the American panics of the nineteenth and twentieth centuries all were caused by excessive borrowing and high leverage that spilled over into the equities markets.

American usury laws, established during the colonial period, underwent a slow transformation. Since most of the meaningful laws were state rather than federal, they would change individually or in small groups rather than all be changed in one fell swoop. Pressure to change began before the Civil War when the economic debate shifted to competition from matters of justice or equity. The movement reached fruition in the late 1920s, and states began to raise their usury ceilings. This was another way of saying that they should be abolished. If lenders were allowed to charge higher rates, in the 30 percent range in many states, then loan sharks would be put out of business. This was particularly significant because loan sharks were a major source of consumption loans and a significant social problem because of the blatant usury they practiced. The sharks ran the gauntlet from unregistered lenders charging less than 100 percent interest to organized crime, which charged 1,000 percent or more. But the statewide movement to raise usury ceilings encountered several obstacles. The move toward higher ceilings was curtailed by the Great Depression and World War II. It also was a contributing factor to the crash of 1929 and the Depression, causing a slowdown in consumption because of the higher rates at a time when lower rates definitely were needed.

The twentieth century in particular proved a watershed for interest. Most of the mysteries of compound interest have become more clearly understandable since Isaac Newton demonstrated the first interest rate calculation, showing a formula for effective compound rates in the early eighteenth century. Credit card companies and other consumer lenders then discovered continuous interest, the most frequent method of compounding a nominal rate. While the calculations are now understood by a larger segment of the population than ever before, the basic facts about compound interest that distressed previous generations remain the same. Loans made for consumption quickly become onerous when interest is added to the existing principal amount, the original and timeless practice of "accumulating interest." For that reason, many European societies enacted sumptuary laws for over a thousand years. People were willing to borrow in order to purchase items that allowed them to aspire above their station in life, a practice those in power deemed inimical to the common good, so consumption was often banned. Laws prohibiting the wearing of fur collars or fancy ribbons may seem quaint and repressive today, but by banning them many governments were attempting to dissuade those in the lower classes from consuming by borrowing. Unlike contemporary societies, they were intent upon removing the means of becoming overextended through loans, not simply extending lending facilities to as many as possible and then letting the market decide who was successful and who was not. The users of credit were targeted, not the producers. The usury laws already on the books were not working well enough to protect the populace at large, according to this reasoning.

Despite the long and arduous opinions about interest, borrowing, and usury over the years, interest has made most of modern life manageable for vast portions of the populace in the developed world, a statement that could not have been made three hundred years ago. Early, speculative instruments called tontines were first proposed in the seventeenth century and annuities and life insurance resulted, having developed along with the government bond markets. Long-term investment planning became possible for the first time on a large scale. Real property became more scarce as European populations grew larger, so passing financial assets from generation to generation and ensuring income in later years became crucial to overall economic growth. By the end of the Napoleonic Wars, it was possible to live comfortably in England without having wealth tied to land, as had been the case for centuries. Fixed income investments and life insurance provided the means to living better than one's ancestors.

The number of financial debacles and panics also increased as a result, many of them caused by excessive leverage and inflated asset prices. Recent financial crises have demonstrated that the credit markets are central to understanding the asset markets. Despite the techniques and ingenuity of modern finance, when centuries-old maxims concerning debt, repayment, and the dangers of excessive consumption are violated, the same happens in the twenty-first century as did in the first: borrowers are impoverished and lenders become reluctant to make other types of productive loans that contribute to economic growth.

Brutus found it lucrative to become a lender in Cyprus because Roman law allowed higher interest rates in lending in the provinces than in Rome itself. When Citibank moved its credit card operations out of New York in the early 1980s to avoid the local usury laws, it sought the same sort of flex-' ibility from a state that would tolerate its activities in return for creating local jobs. This practice recently became known as "regulatory arbitrage": the process of dumping one regulator in favor of another that is more lenient and accommodating. The catchy phrase obscures the fact that it is the lending activities that should be under scrutiny. Less known about Brutus is that his agent locked the recalcitrant borrowers in a closed room and denied them food and drink until several of them died of hunger. Today, hard-put borrowers are extended more credit to tide them over until they face personal bankruptcy, an idea that has only been in existence since the nineteenth century. Before that, bankruptcy meant prison for the defaulted borrower and even his entire family.

A notable dissent to Western finance has emerged from the Islamic world within the last thirty-five years. Building on the general ban on interest found in its holy writings, Islamic law (*sharia*) has joined forces with modern structured finance to develop what has become known as Islamic finance: the design and implementation of financial instruments that are compliant with the Koran and *fatwas* of Islamic scholars. All financial instruments and investments must comply with a strict code of ethical behavior that assiduously avoids interest or even the hint of it. This new market runs parallel to the development of microlending, a worldwide movement to extend working capital and very small business loans to the poor that began in Bangladesh. In its original form, microlending also embodied Islamic principles although at the opposite end of the financial and social spectrum from the model oriented on the City of London. No one ever considered lending to the poor on a massive scale before. The closest attempt was in the city-states of northern Italy in the late Middle Ages through institutions called *montes*. The only surviving *monte* is today one of Italy's larger banks. Twenty years after being founded it almost collapsed after making a loan outside its original lending model. The loan made to Christopher Columbus was written off as unpaid, making it the most memorable loan default in history.

Charging interest, usury, and excessive leverage are common today, but in the twentieth century new financial techniques were developed that helped produce great prosperity while posing enormous risks at the same time. When securitization became popular in the mid-1970s, it led to a revolution in lending practices that helped democratize credit. Being able to pool loans and get them off a balance sheet allowed lenders to relax banking standards that had been in place for generations. Looser standards meant that more people were able to obtain mortgages than in the past, leading to the inevitable housing bubble that burst in 2007 and 2008. The idea of lending became decoupled from the responsibility of behaving as a prudent lender. Loans were understood as fungible and marketable. Extending credit and then off-loading it to investors in a securitized bond was easier than simply saying no to a poorly rated borrower in the first place.

The same technique also led to the widespread use of credit cards, distributed without much regard for the ability to repay, which naturally suited the card lenders. Applying diversification principles normally associated with securities investing, credit card lenders were able to justify extending credit to marginal borrowers and even the poor on the assumption that the higher rates charged to those borrowers would enhance the returns on the pools of loans they sold through securitization. Like other lenders employing techniques relying on heavy leverage, their defense ultimately was that only a cataclysmic event would undo their financial structuring, something that had only a 1 percent chance of happening in any event. Forgotten was the point that excessive reliance on these techniques increased those chances exponentially.

Looking back on the history of interest and usury, it is tempting to think that recent lenders and financial engineers either forgot or never knew the tradition preceding them and were destined to make the same mistakes repeatedly. When Mexico required a massive financial restructuring in the late 1980s, however, it was accomplished using a financial practice that originated under the Tudors four hundred years before. The term "defeasance" was not even found in the dictionaries when it was used again recently. Cicero's term for compound interest (*anatocismus*) disappeared from English usage in the nineteenth century, although it still survives in other places that use elements of Roman law. As debt crises become more common, the debate about interest and usury will continue because the predatory element in lending still exists. The more onerous term "debt" has been used less in marketing financial products, suggesting that "credit" was a reward for the borrower rather than a caveat. The packaging is different, but the results are much the same when limits are exceeded.

No one today will agree with the Scholastics that interest is inherently unjust and should be banned, except those in the Islamic world. Without credit facilities, modern capitalism would not have developed. But the temptations that finance presents have always been present, regardless of time and place. Charging high rates of interest was easier than productive work, as generations of Italian bankers and English merchants, including Shakespeare's father, discovered. The arch opponents of usury recognized the fact. In the sixteenth century, Thomas Wilson, a prominent writer and opponent of usury in Tudor England, tried to affect the outcome of a debate in Parliament about usury ceilings. He admitted, "I have been a doer in this world these 30 winters, and as fresh an occupier as another, and yet never found I better or more assured gain than by putting out my money for gain, the same being always the best and easiest trade in the world."

The most recent twist on lending and interest rates came in the years preceding the credit market crisis of 2007. For generations, borrowing for consumption had been strictly separated from borrowing for residential real estate or for productive purposes. New financial developments obscured the differences when the home equity loan was introduced. This second mortgage allowed homeowners to "unlock the equity" in their homes, to borrow a catchphrase from the real estate industry, and use the cash in any way they saw fit. Often, the money was used for consumption because the interest rates were low when compared to credit card interest. When the mortgage crisis began, home values declined and consumer spending dropped sharply, leading to a severe drop in real estate assets values and forcing many borrowers into foreclosure and personal bankruptcy.

In many ways, the home equity loan, a simple financial product, helped underscore the developments that had been made in lending. It also helped underscore the weaknesses in lending procedures that ignored consumer debt in favor of real estate. Once the two became intertwined, the debt revolution that began eighty years before turned full circle. Homeowners were increasing consumption to almost 80 percent of the gross domestic product from the 67 percent that had been in place since the 1920s. Once consumers used their homes as collateral for their spending habits, they began engaging in a form of "cannibal consumption," devouring what equity they held in their homes in favor of increased spending. The results demonstrated that axioms about borrowing in excess of the ability to repay were not simply old fashioned rules that could be violated willy-nilly.

Usury prohibitions were part of the natural law tradition in Europe until the Enlightenment, when they were assumed to have faded from view because of the writings of Hugo Grotius and other jurists who demonstrated the finality of reason over moral sanctions and the vestiges of canon law. That judgment was premature because the usury laws persisted for several more centuries and still can be found in discussions of interest and unfair lending practices. Theories about free markets and competition have relegated them to a backseat in public policy positions, but the idea of usury still is alive and well. Discussions about limiting maximum rates of interest are still discussed. The notion proves as powerful as ever despite attempts to ignore it. Excessive interest still is a thorny problem. Paraphrasing Justice Potter Stewart, usury can be difficult to define, but one usually knows it when one sees it.

Chapter 1

Saints and Sinners

God, nature, reason, all scripture, all law, all authors, all doctors, yea all councils are against usury. Philosophers, Greeks, Latins, Lawyers, Divines, Catholics, Heretics, all tongues, all nations, have thought usury as bad as a thief.
—Roger Fenton, 1612

Collecting interest traditionally was considered the world's second oldest profession until the Industrial Revolution. It was lumped together with other socially unacceptable practices as inimical to the common good and a perversion of the idea that man should help his fellow man. Along with prostitution, arson, and murder, it was considered an execrable crime under religious law, although it was more gingerly tolerated in the secular world. In the Middle Ages, usurers were often relegated to the seedier sections of towns, segregated much as prostitutes were in red light districts. Theory and practice concerning interest often diverged widely, but generally the more religious the society, the stronger the prohibition against it.

Originally, usury and interest were considered the same practice and were not differentiated in a systematic way. Biblical references were to usury alone, meaning interest, but later distinctions were made between interest and excessive interest. As will be seen, however, usury has always been considered excessive interest, whatever the basic rate of interest may have been. Until the Enlightenment, the two terms were interchangeable, with usury being the operative—and pejorative—term. As the use of Latin declined in Western Europe, the term "interest" evolved in the vernacular but was never able to shake its medieval connotation. For almost a thousand years it was understood to be something not conducive to economic well-being.

Interest became known by its Latin name, "usury," or *usura*, meaning to charge a high or exorbitant rate of interest. In the Middle Ages, the term became *usuria*, from which the modern spelling derives. This negative connotation of the practice of usury is the one that has survived the ages because charging interest at a reasonable rate has always been considered standard business practice despite church prohibitions against it in the medieval world. But as in all commercial practice, the question of how much interest was considered fair versus usurious was never settled in a satisfactory sense because of the fragmented nature of ancient societies, characterized by different religious traditions. The absence of a uniform marketplace for credit also meant that interest rates varied widely, and wildly, from place to place.

Mixed with the straightforward definitions of interest and usury were ideas of fairness or justice, which gave moneylending strong political connotations as well. Ordinary interest was as common as it is today, although when economies began using money as a medium of exchange the debate quickly began over what was normal and what was excessive. Calculating it was difficult under barter economies because interest was usually paid in kind. If a merchant lent a farmer a sack of seed, what was considered normal interest? How much had to be paid back and in what commodity? Was the crop harvested from the seed more or less valuable than the seed? These questions were solved on the local level. In general, interest charges on nonmonetary items were not considered usury in the strict sense of the word. But when money became more widely used, ethics entered the discussion. Usury was any amount paid on money loans above the principal amount originally lent. Since moneylending was considered the product of idleness, high rates were frowned upon. Again, the same problem persisted. What was considered high?

In its simplest form, interest charged on a loan for consumption purposes was considered unjust, presumably because the person borrowing the money did not have the means to live without borrowing. Any usury in this case was considered exploitative. This notion is the oldest and can be found in the Old Testament. Most ancient and medieval commentators and writers used Deuteronomy as their main source for condemnations of usury. It stated, "Thou shalt not lend upon usury to thy brother; usury of money, usury of victuals, usury of anything that is lent upon usury" (23:19). Continuing, it stated, "Unto a stranger thou mayest lend upon usury; but unto thy brother thou shalt not lend upon usury, that the Lord thy God may bless thee in all that thou settest thine hand to in the land whither thou goest to possess it" (23:20). "Brother" was not meant to be a general term, however; it was much more specific. A brother was a member of one's own tribe. In other words, Jews could lend to gentiles and collect usury but could not do the same to fellow Jews. This has been referred to as the "Deuteronomic double standard."[1]

Other biblical references stated the same principle. Leviticus 25:36 said, "Take thou no usury of him, or increase: but fear thy God; that thy brother may live with thee." But the passage in Deuteronomy became the standard that would be cited for generations as the biblical prohibition of usury of any kind. The standard was indeed a double standard only because there was evidence that Jews did in fact lend to other Jews. Josephus claimed that a lender should be satisfied with the gratitude of a needy borrower rather than expect usury in return for a loan. Early loan contracts demonstrate that, admonitions aside, lending at usury occurred despite the warnings of the prophets. Interest was set at 12 percent among the Hebrews. A similar rate structure was found in many ancient cultures. When Nehemiah was the provincial governor of Judea between 444 and 432 B.C., he declared the 12 percent rate to be used to settle disputes, a practice that would endure for over two thousand years.[2]

A similar admonition can be found in Psalms. "He that putteth not out his money to usury, nor taketh reward against the innocent. He that doeth these things shall never be moved" (25:5). These statements, especially the one concerning lending to members of one's own tribe, were perhaps the earliest foundation of a cottage industry that would be known throughout the ancient and medieval worlds. In order to conform to Deuteronomy, Jews could only lend to gentiles and a tradition began that survived for centuries. They became associated with lending and suffered both the fruits and the consequences of their activity. As they later discovered, rulers in Europe often required their services desperately but often cited church law forbidding usury when it was time to repay. Citing religion was a powerful reason for not repaying a loan since secular law traditionally did not condemn usury.

A distinction between usury and interest was made very early. Generally, loans were made to someone in distress, a member of one's own clan in need. If interest was charged at all, it had to be minimal, simply in order to cover the costs of the lending in today's language. What the minimum rate of interest should have been was almost never stated, however. Usury entered when the lender was thought to be trying to take advantage of the borrower's situation, forcing him to ruin or some other compromising position. Thus, usury was equated with conduct unbecoming a member of one's own tribe or clan and was roundly condemned. The punishments could vary but ostracism and banishment were common. In the ancient and medieval worlds, they were applied to lenders and borrowers alike. Punishments for borrowers reneging on debts were also harsh, if they could be proved to have done harm to the lenders. Lenders carried the onus of having to prove that injury had been incurred and that they were not practicing excessive interest.

A major problem in discussing interest and usury, especially in the period before the Roman Empire, was determining exactly how interest was calculated. Reading present practice backward suggests that the concept and calculations of interest rates have not been constant and have indeed changed over time. Some of the extant material strongly suggests that interest was calculated on a monthly, and simple, basis. The annual rate, or the total interest bill, was simply the amount charged per month times the number of months the loan was extended. Loans (*mutuum* in Latin) that appeared to have high rates attached to them were medium-term loans for periods longer than a year. The exact repayment terms were not standard due to the absence of an organized banking system in the ancient world and varied from lender to lender. In contemporary language, the sources for loans were private, meaning that funds came from wealthy individuals and merchants.

In Roman law, the code known as the *Twelve Tables* (*Duodicem Tabularum*) was the most noteworthy attempt to codify usury for both patricians and plebeians. Patricians were the usual lenders to plebeians, who often objected vehemently to the rates charged. Roman history was replete with attempts to ban or control lending rates. Drawn by a council known as the Decemviri in 450 B.C., the law stated, "No person shall practice usury at a rate of more than one twelfths."[3] This meant that the legal rate of interest was set at 8.33 percent per annum, conforming to the Roman calendar of twelve months established by King Numa in 695 B.C. It has also been understood as a rate of 1 percent per month, as Montesquieu later interpreted it in the eighteenth century. But that may be overstating the case slightly since most loans were meant to be for one month on average. The rate of one-twelfth was derived from agriculture. It represented one ounce in a pound of crop, with payment due on the first of each month. Interest was stated on an annual basis, with no compounding.[4] If it was compounded, it was called *anatocismus anniversarius* (annual compounding). A subsequent change raised the lending rate to 12 percent (*usurae centesimae*) in the later years of the republic and first years of the empire and it remained the same for about a century before being revised several times, finally being reaffirmed by Constantine in the fourth century A.D. But while the rate of interest was relatively low, the penalties for not repaying a loan remained harsh. The code continued: "When debt has been acknowledged, or judgment about the matter had been pronounced in court, thirty days must be the legitimate time of grace. After that, then arrest of debtor may be made by laying on hands. Bring him into court. If he does not satisfy the judgment, or no one in court offers himself as surety on his behalf, the creditor may take the defaulter with him. He may bind him either in stocks or in chains; he may bind him with weight not less than fifteen pounds or with more if he shall so desire."[5] Other interpretations of the law suggested that creditors could have insolvent debtors tied and then carved into pieces to satisfy the lenders. Other accounts had creditors selling debtors' children into slavery.

Although lending rates were set and remedies provided for violations, the laws were not universally followed by any means. Cicero, while provincial governor of Cilicia, related that Marcus Junius Brutus did a tidy money-lending business in Cyprus, lending at 48 percent rather than the 12 percent official rate, using an intermediary to hide his identity from the Roman Senate. Roman law forbade lending money in the provinces at high rates, but the law was harder to enforce than it was at home. Even at home, disputes over usury were not settled amicably. The historian Appian recalled a case in Rome in 89 B.C. where a dispute between debtors and their creditors was taken to a praetor (magistrate). The debtors claimed that an old law, preceding the *Twelve Tables*, forbid taking usury of any sort and they refused to pay their creditors. Unable to reach an amicable agreement, the praetor allowed the parties to pursue the case in court. The lenders became exasperated at the thought that they could lose due to an older law and killed the praetor in the Roman Forum. The Senate offered a reward for the identity of the killers, to no avail.[6]

Simple interest presented social and moral problems, but compound interest was roundly condemned. *Usura* was simple interest, but *usurae usurarum* (usury on usury) was compound interest. In Roman law it was also known as *anatocismus*, a term Cicero introduced into Latin from the Greek (meaning "interest again") around 51 B.C., and it found its way into legal usage and judicial practice before being officially banned several centuries later under Justinian. But simply being interest on interest was not enough to get it banned; the consequences were unpalatable. *Anatocismus* created additional interest that was added to the principal of a loan. Therefore, the addition of the extra interest put the borrower more deeply in debt than had been the case before compounding.[7]

Anatocismus was the general word used for compound interest. Its deleterious effect was known as *alterum tantum*, or "twice as much." Interest was considered excessive when the rate applied doubled the principal amount to be repaid at the end of the loan term. This was the most precise term used to denote a rate beyond which practical everyday usury should not venture, despite the official 12 percent rate. If a borrower was charged at the official 12 percent rate and he paid no interest monthly as usually stipulated, the loan amount would double in six years. If 48 percent was charged, the amount would double in one and a half years under the same conditions. Adding unpaid interest to principal was not unique to the Romans; it was also found in ancient Hindu society. The general assumption is that *alterum tantum* and *anatocismus* were both generally disregarded by the time of Ulpian in the third century and only Justinian's *Code* made them legally operative again.[8]

The two terms demonstrate that the Romans developed an early range of lending rates, similar to those that would be used centuries later. Twelve percent was the official rate below which no one would lend while the upper end of the band was capped by *alterum tantum*, literally the rate that would double the principal amount. While the upper limit was high, it nevertheless attempted to define a usurious rate that clearly would prove disastrous for the borrower. It also demonstrated that the official rate was routinely violated. If understood in this manner, it also gives some insight into the origin of the well-known mathematical rule called the Rule of 72, which clearly shows how many years it will take to double an amount. All a borrower or lender needed to do was to divide 72 by the interest rate charged. The answer was the number of years necessary to double the amount of money involved.

If that amount occurred within a brief time, from one to two years, it would clearly be in violation of the spirit of lending. But even under *anatocismus* it was not considered improper for the lender to take the additional interest received from a borrower and lend it to another; the prohibition extended only to adding it to the original borrower's principal. Using compound interest meant that a borrower could owe more interest than principal on a loan through compounding if the rate was high enough and the repayment period long and this was why *anatocismus* was frowned upon and eventually banned. The ban did not, however, do away with the practice. Compound interest, especially semi-annual compound interest, clearly existed and was first mathematically implied in the work of Fibonacci in the early thirteenth century, but the actual calculations were not clear.

Regardless of how interest was calculated, the fact that it was always used in business transactions runs somewhat counter to the general religious prohibitions. But a clear distinction had to be made between interest charged on money loans and other forms of payment in kind. Money interest was usually considered the most odious. It was the result of idleness on the part of the lender and desperation on the part of the borrower. A money-lender lent a sum to a borrower and demanded to be paid in money or in kind, quite often the latter. Regardless, usury was considered a wasteful practice according to most ancient and medieval writers. No value was created and nothing useful accomplished except to enrich the lender. The notion was characteristic of a hand-to-mouth economy where farmers and city-dwellers existed on a day-to-day basis with little savings or accumulated working capital. The idea remained static while commerce developed over the centuries, slowly demanding larger and larger amounts of capital to be invested in business enterprises.

Other than biblical and Roman sources, Aristotle was considered the philosophic authority on interest, especially among ancient and medieval churchmen. Plato mentioned usury rarely, stating that, "No money is . . . to be lent on interest. The law will not protect a man in recovering either interest or principal."[9] But there is a sizable time gap because Aristotle's writings were lost in Europe after the fall of Rome and only were reintroduced by Arab scholars in the eleventh century. After the reintroduction, Aristotelian thought became widely used by the Scholastic philosophers in the thirteenth century, the most notable being Thomas Aquinas, who, along with other medieval writers and canonists, considered Aristotle to be "the Philosopher." Aristotle explored usury in a different vein. Rather than expressing his dislike of the practice in tribal or commandment form as the Old Testament sources did, he approached it philosophically. Usury was considered a practice that was inequitable to the borrower because it had the ability to beggar him. Usury was the most unnatural form of acquisition: "the art of the petty usurer is hated most, and with most reason; it makes a profit from currency itself, instead of making it from the process which currency was meant to serve."[10] To Aristotle, money was barren and intended only to be a medium of exchange, not something that could be deployed to earn its own rate of return. If it were used to facilitate exchange of goods and services, its use was valid. If it were lent to earn usury, it was unjust and barren and the lender was nothing more than a thief. When a loan was made, no usury was to be expected. This is not to say that money was not lent at interest in ancient Athens but only suggests that the opinion makers of the day, whose influence would extend for centuries, considered it a banal practice that would impoverish the borrower while enriching the lender.

There was also a moral and socioeconomic framework that accompanied usury laws in many ancient societies, including Greece and Rome.

These were the sumptuary (consumption) laws, aimed at controlling the consumption of the lower classes who wanted to emulate the nobles or ruling class. The laws stipulated the amount of certain luxury items an individual could own. The first Roman sumptuary law was the Lex Oppia, enacted in 215 B.C. It dictated, among other things, the amount of ornamental gold a woman could own as well as the materials that could be used in dressing gowns and the like. The traditional view of sumptuary laws was that they were used to keep the non-noble classes from assuming ideas above their station. Only noblemen could dress like noblemen; tradesmen or the masses were prohibited from doing so. But consumption of fine goods also had a great deal to do with borrowing money since many of those seeking to emulate rich public figures often needed to borrow in order to do so. While the sumptuary laws were no more effective than usury laws in many cases, they did demonstrate that there was a concern about indebtedness for consumption purposes that many feared would divert valuable resources from productive purposes, especially during times of financial crisis. The Lex Oppia was passed during the Second Punic War with Carthage, although it was relaxed after the eventual Roman victory. As the usury laws, the sumptuary laws often faded from view only to reappear at a later date.

Origins in Canon Law

Since Aristotle was not translated into Latin until the thirteenth century, it is difficult to say how much of his theory, if any, was known to early churchmen prior to the fall of Rome. But the extant materials provided a solid basis to proceed against usury even without him. Armed with the Old Testament and Roman law as authoritative sources, the early church began to codify bans against usury in early canon law. There is no substantial mention of the practice in the New Testament, except for a passage in Matthew (16:28) that mentions 12 percent monthly interest as prevalent at the time, despite what later church writers would claim. The early church fathers paid close attention to the Old Testament texts and especially Deuteronomy.

The first significant council of the church mentioned usury specifically along with a host of more important doctrinal matters. The Council of Nicaea in 325 A.D. embodied the old prohibitions against usury, although it necessarily limited the ban to usury committed by a churchman, not an uncommon practice in the ancient world. It stated, "Since many enrolled among the clergy have been induced by greed and avarice to forget the sacred text, 'who does not put his money out at interest,' and to charge one percent per month on loans . . . they shall be deposed from the clergy and their names struck from the roll,"[11] meaning that they were subject to banishment from the church. This was Constantine's reiteration of the rate of usury proscribed by the *Twelve Tables* and subsequently modified.

The canon went on to state that the same punishment would apply to anyone charging 50 percent or more on a loan. From the text, one may assume that 1 percent per month was the average rate of interest at the time and that 50 percent was the average total interest bill, normally taking slightly more than four years to repay a loan. The implication was that charging less than 1 percent was acceptable, probably recognizing the average rates charged in the marketplace at the time. This simple statement also suggests that usury then was interpreted as it is today: that is, an excessive rate of interest, something more than the normal, acceptable rate.

The council was better known for affirming the concept of the Trinity in the face of the Arian heresy, so any other canons included were to be taken very seriously. This meant that clergymen would be booted from the church if found in violation. What is not clearly stated concerns loans made by clergy for less than the prevailing rate. Clearly, interest rates that high were usurious in either the ancient or modern worlds. This canon began an almost fifteen-hundred-year ban on usury that would be invoked with some curious applications in the centuries to follow. However, it would take almost five hundred more years to extend the ban to layman officially.

When the usury prohibition was included in the Nicene canons, it acquired doctrinal status. Clearly, charging usury on money loans was a social practice that normally would be expected to change over time, but after Nicaea it became far more than just a church condemnation against unsavory economic procedure. Because it had first been mentioned in the Old Testament and dovetailed nicely with the early church's interpretation of scripture, this social practice now had been elevated to the level of doctrine. But as one of the first major church councils, Nicaea also had the effect of civil law in the eyes of Roman civilians. Although jurists would not admit that the divine law as interpreted by Rome was actually superior to civil law, they did recognize that civil law that ran counter to it was wrong.[12]

In 345 the Council of Carthage extended the ban on usury to laymen. The proscription was repeated in 789 at the Council of Aix.[13] The church outside Europe was beginning to disintegrate because of barbarian and then Muslim invasions, thus the reiteration was necessary because Carthage was no longer in the Christian world. Similarly, the Council of Aix occurred after the barbarian invasions in Gaul and reaffirmed the earlier principles that later would be reiterated by Charlemagne. As the Western Empire crumbled, the differences between *usurae* and *usurae usararum* seem to disappear and both emerged under the single term *usurae*.

The ban on usury as practiced by churchmen also was found in the writings of Pope Leo the Great, who reigned from 440 to 461. Leo's writings were considered equal to, if not exceeding, the Nicaean doctrine partly because of his stature as one of the greatest popes of antiquity. He was best remembered for saving the Roman Empire from Attila, by meeting the Hun chieftain in northern Italy near Mantua and persuading him to negotiate with the emperor rather than invade Rome. In doctrinal matters, his writings carried heavy weight. His decree *Nec Hoc Quoque* forbade clerics to practice usury and also stated that laymen who practiced it were guilty of "shameful gain." Although the direct power to extend the ban to laymen was lacking, the continuing attack had its desired effect. Usury now was on par with murder and adultery and was destined to remain so for centuries. The theory behind it was simple yet captivating. Usury was an example of man's usurpation of time, a realm where divine law prevailed. Human practices were secondary to religious doctrine and would have to bend.

The principle underlying the ancient and medieval concept of usury was time. In the modern world, most would agree with Benjamin Franklin's basic dictum that "time is money." But in the later Roman Empire and the Middle Ages, the concept was very different. Until the Renaissance, time was considered as belonging to God; it was a gift bestowed on mankind. Put another way, it was common property, something that could not be sold by an individual to another. Charging for its use was immoral, an idea first attributed to William of Auxerre, a predecessor of Thomas Aquinas. Man could not charge for that which God had given. Since the Roman Church was the single keeper of God's word in the West until the Reformation, the deal was closed. Creating something out of nothing was God's work, not that of a financial sorcerer. Usury was a crime against God and the church and would not be tolerated. This overlooked the fact that church institutions collected and paid interest, often quite profitably.

More importantly, charging for the use of time was tantamount to theft. Early Christian theology stressed the importance of sharing wealth with the community rather than accumulating it for its own sake. In a moral tale from Acts 5:2, a woman and her husband, members of the early Jerusalem church, sold land and did not share the proceeds with the needy, keeping the proceeds for themselves. When confronted by Peter, they both lied about the transaction. They then mysteriously died within three hours of their transgression. As a result, "a great fear came upon the whole church." Some later medieval tales told of statues falling from church roofs as usurers tried to enter places of worship where they clearly were unwelcome. Church teaching held that wealth was to be shared, not accumulated for its own sake.

Equally important for the practice of usury was the *Codex Theodosianus*, or *Theodosian Code*, written in the late fourth century, compiling all the codes written during the reign of Constantine. The code excluded all heretics and schismatics from privileges of the citizenry following the new official religion of the empire, the Catholic faith. It also prescribed that they be subject to various fines. While aimed at Manichean heretics who denied the Trinity, it was clear that anyone, including Jews, not following the faith would be subject to certain civil sanctions. As canon law developed, an "otherness" would come to characterize Jews and other moneylenders who did not follow the precepts of the church. This separateness marginalized their status in society, often making them dispensable after having proved to be indispensable at other times.

Because of the Jews' knowledge of money and lending, their reputation among the populace only fanned suspicion. Their role as the killers of Christ was well bandied about in the folklore of the Middle Ages and other heinous crimes were attributed to them as a result. Whenever public indignation was inflamed, especially during the Inquisition, their livelihoods and safety became endangered. More than one Jewish merchant was brought before the Inquisition, charged with infanticide or some other equally detestable act, usually when it suited the accusers financially.

In order for usury to remain banned after Nicaea, it would have to establish a foothold in Roman law in the new millennium. Two hundred years later, three compilations of law appeared during the reign of the eastern emperor Caesar Flavius Justinian. A group of lawyers commissioned by the emperor began an extensive review of existing law and rewrote much of it to conform with the period. There were three individual projects, the *Code*, the *Digest*, and the *Institutes*. In the *Institutes*, the concept of usury is found under the general context of "usufructs," meaning to enjoy the fruits of another's property or labor. Generally, this concept was used in willing money or property to one who was not the legal heir of the property holder. The *Institutes* was the textbook portion of the three projects, the most comprehensive set of Roman laws yet written. It was completed in 534 and was written as a guide to legal terms for law students and had a far-reaching effect upon generations of legal theorists and practitioners. It was written after Constantine allegedly had recognized Christianity as the official religion. It describes a usufruct as "the right of using and taking the fruits of property not one's own, without impairing the substance of that property."[14] While this sounds like a general acceptance of usury as a legitimate activity not counter to the law, it qualifies the practice by stating that taking compensation in the form of usury is permissible as long as it does no harm to the underlying asset or collateral. The code is in keeping with the ancient and medieval caveat that any interest collected could not do harm to the borrower or somehow imperil his person or belongings. In the ancient and medieval worlds, interest could be paid only if it did no harm. Otherwise it was illegal. In contemporary terms, the payment could not bankrupt the borrower.

As a result, rates of usury differed, depending on the borrower. Individuals borrowed at 6 percent while business borrowers generally borrowed at 8 percent. The rate varied, depending on community practice and ultimately tribunals decided upon the proper rate under the circumstances.[15] Rates varied depending upon the use of the money, but in all cases *anatocismus* was prohibited. Compound interest certainly was practiced, but it was barred from loan contracts (*mutuum*) as a way of protecting borrowers. This was not new to the *Digest*. The work compiled under Justinian included earlier law from the Eastern Empire known as the *Constitutions of Leo*. Named after the eastern emperor Leo I, this set of codes clearly forbade the practice of *alterum tantum*. It did, however, permit a simple interest rate of 4 percent. In prohibiting compound interest, the *Constitutions* described a case where two grandsons filed a petition with a court to be relieved of their grandfather's debt, incurred some years before. The grandfather had borrowed a sum and his sons had paid back an amount to the lender's heirs, which was in dispute. The grandsons claimed that double the amount borrowed had already been paid as well as an additional amount, while the lenders heirs claimed they still had an outstanding balance. When the case was decided in the borrowers' favor, the ruling stated, "Therefore our laws do not require more than double the principal to be paid . . . they will be entitled to recover the note . . . bearing interest, in order that the debt may not be collected more than once."[16]

The admonitions of Cicero had found a place in the civil law. But that did not mean that compound interest officially was proscribed in Europe because the *Code* was the body of law in the Eastern Empire and it is not clear whether it was understood outside Constantinople. It was not discovered in the West until 1130 when the Calabrians invaded Sicily under Roger II. The manuscript then was officially "re-discovered" and sent to Florence for safekeeping.[17] By the time it reappeared, a substantial amount had been written about usury that did not distinguish between *usura* and *usurae usararum*.

Prohibitions against usury remained intact for churchmen until the ninth century. General political disorganization in Europe at the time meant that the ban was confined to churchmen as previously stated in Nicaean doctrine and the writings of Pope Leo, but when the Holy Roman Empire was formed, politics again entered the discussion. Declaring the Roman Empire to have moved to what later medieval writers called the "Germanic" kingdoms, Charlemagne established the legitimacy of his own throne by naming it the Holy Roman Empire; the old Roman empire reborn and ruled by Christian monarchs. By 800 the Eastern Empire in Constantinople had become a separate entity, no longer considered the true empire by those in Western Europe. Constantine had established Christianity as the official religion of the empire and Leo had saved Rome from the scourge of Attila, but political organization was only beginning to reestablish itself. Charlemagne seized the moment to establish a combination of the two old powers, the church and the state. Assuming the mantle of emperor put him in the position of pronouncing on sacred affairs as well as secular ones. Naturally, usury was included.

In consolidating political power, Charlemagne moved into Italy and defeated the Lombards, the German tribe that had occupied northern Italy since the reconquest of Justinian deteriorated in the sixth century. The Lombards were not originally Christians and embraced Arianism when they entered Italy, in antithesis to the established doctrine of the Roman Church. They then began to codify their laws after experiencing the highly organized codes of Justinian and Theodosius. Their treatment of lending was surprisingly liberal, perhaps because their relatively unsophisticated society was not based on a money economy and was relatively primitive when compared to Rome.

According to the Lombard laws, if "anyone borrows money from another man on agreement, and if within five years the creditor demands his money and the debtor does not have that with which to pay, then the agreement shall be renewed up to ten years. If within ten years, the debt is demanded and not repaid, and he [the debtor] delays up to twenty years, then if the debt has been demanded either by the prince or by the judge of the district and the agreement is proved, the debtor or his heirs shall pay." But then the onus shifted. "But if the agreement was not renewed twice in the ten years and the prince or the judge had not made the demand clearly within the twenty years, we order that the creditor be silent afterwards and he shall have no right of bringing charges against his debtors unless he was in captivity."[18] This humane treatment of debtors may well have been influenced by the sophistication of Roman law and it was certainly more forgiving than the laws before Justinian.

Charlemagne extended the ban on clergy practicing usury to laymen as well. Using previous decretals, by the eighth century collectively known as the *Hadriana*, as precedents, Charlemagne extended the ban on usury to laymen in his capitularies. The *Hadriana* was assembled by his friend Pope Hadrian I and presented to him before he died. Because Charlemagne was the most formidable ruler in Europe, his writings and the church councils of the period also bolstered the ban in canon law. But Charlemagne's thoughts on usury were taken in a wider context. When he assumed power, his biographer Einhard noted that there were different laws among the various tribes falling under his newly established power and the capitularies were a convenient method of uniting these disparate laws under one uniform code including usury. The effect on collecting interest was significant, however. A church synod held in Pavia in 850 took the next step in the long process by prescribing excommunication for laymen practicing usury and calling for restitution to borrowers after the deaths of the usurers from whom they had borrowed. Clearly, Charlemagne's influence helped begin the long period in which the ban on usury became a serious impediment in the development of Western commerce.

Subsequent church writings about usury began to equate it with theft. These writings began to appear about the same time that trade was revived in Europe and the timing could not have been worse for commerce in general, although it was that revival that may have prompted the new twist on usury in the first place. St. Anselm of Canterbury, Anslem of Lucca (both Italians), and more notably Peter Lombard all wrote of usury as theft in the late eleventh and early twelfth centuries, paving the way for a strong position in later church councils. Prior to the twelfth century, the church's position against usury had its strongest effect. But the revival of commerce and the profits to be earned by moneylending would prove too great an allure for the new merchant class to ignore, leading to the development of the late medieval and early Renaissance banking houses.

Moneylending became more popular as merchants amassed wealth through their normal activities and discovered that usury earned often was a greater source of profits than their own merchant activities. The wealthier classes acquired more free time in which to put their money to use. Ancient Greeks called this the acquisition of leisure, a sign that society was progressing. Even more leisure time was created by providing financial services than actually laboring at a living, a phenomenon as recognizable in the medieval world as in the modern. Not since the height of the Roman Empire had so many merchants found themselves free to expand into new areas. The papacy would not be pleased by these events because they ultimately proved a threat to its authority.

Medieval Pawnbroking and Financing

As lending increased during the Middle Ages, those who made their living simply by lending money became known as "manifest usurers." This was the type of usurer who made a living simply by lending money and collecting interest. These lenders clearly charged a fee for their shameful services without equivocation, often doing business under a particular logo such as a pawnbroker's sign. In the ancient and medieval worlds, much personal lending was done through pawnbrokers, whose trade has remained remarkably consistent over the centuries. But the profession was never considered reputable and often was conducted in separate parts of towns and cities reserved for Jews, pawnbrokers, and prostitutes. The pawnbroker sign, universally characterized by the three hanging golden balls, became the symbol for usury in the medieval world.

Pawnbrokers usually required collateral for a loan, much as they do today. Medieval chroniclers delighted in telling stories of borrowers being charged high rates of interest and still losing their collateral when they could not repay the loan. Pawnbrokers served all levels of society, from common people to royalty, but the poor and the lower classes were the main clients. Most pawnbrokers, but not all, were Jews and the rates charged could easily be defined as usurious even by contemporary standards, often exceeding 50 percent per annum. Many pawnbrokers specialized in making what has become known as consumption loans. These loans were made mostly to poor people who had fallen on hard times and needed cash to survive, raised mainly by pledging whatever sort of collateral they had. These clearly were not loans for working capital since the money was not used for a productive purpose. Pawnbrokers flourished in Europe, generally being recognized as necessary for survival. And their success spawned a new type of financial institution, especially in Italy, that would help revolutionize personal financing and help it become more humane.

Ironically, the recognition of the need for sources of working capital, especially among citizens of the Italian communes, came from a religious order. The Franciscans recognized the need for pawnbrokers. If pawnbroking could be conducted at reasonable rates of interest rather than at usury, then a valuable service could be provided to the masses that used the system for loans. Pawnbroking functioned as the lender of last resort in a world with few banks and no financial institutions serving individuals. As a result, in the early fourteenth century a Franciscan, Durand of St. Purcain, devised a new twist on the older form of state borrowing in the Italian communes by suggesting that there should also be a state lender in addition to the private. Traditionally, in some city-states, merchants and wealthy citizens were required to make loans to the sovereign at a rate of about 5 percent, effectively providing cheap money for the princes who ruled the region. The idea of a public lender simply turned the notion upside down. These lenders could make loans to the masses at a nominal rate of 5 percent or less, avoiding any implication of practicing usury. Collateral would be required, but the process would be cheaper and more forgiving than that of the professional pawnbroker or moneylender.

The state borrowers were originally called *mons* while the new public lenders became known as *montes*. In the latter part of the fifteenth century, they evolved into what became known as the *montes de pietatis*, literally mountains of pity. The Franciscans quickly ran afoul of the papacy, which was intent on maintaining the prohibitions against usury despite the economic and social developments made during the fourteenth and fifteenth centuries. Power was devolving away from the church and the papacy would be quick to react. Most of the *montes* remained lenders to the poor, but some later evolved into banks.

Another important development for commerce was the growing acceptance of bills of exchange. These instruments became especially important in international trade where foreign exchange was involved. A party in one country could obtain a bill to pay a party in another without having to transport valuable currency across boundaries. The bill took its place and could be redeemed by the second party in its own country at a moneylender or bank that recognized it as a viable instrument. Once bills became popular, trade between countries increased, leading to the increasing productivity and commerce between parties that may have otherwise avoided trading with each other due to transportation and currency risks. While the bills did not alleviate currency risk, they did make it more acceptable to trade with foreigners, also opening Europe to ideas and influences from the Middle East.

In the tenth and eleventh centuries, commerce began to revive in Western Europe. The phenomenon was both the cause and a result of the Crusades. The First Crusade, called by Pope Urban II, began in 1096 and culminated with the capture of Jerusalem in 1099. One of its major effects was a renewal of contact between Rome and the Eastern Empire in Constantinople as well as new contacts made with the Arab world. In this new international atmosphere, Jews played a crucial role in commerce between the three different cultures. Having a peripatetic history, the Jews did not have the luxury of becoming embedded in any particular society and as a result remained international in their outlook. Moneylending had always been a specialty, but it did not yet play the prominent role that it would in the twelfth and thirteenth centuries, leading to their expulsion from many kingdoms and principalities.[19]

Jews had competition as lenders in Europe during the Crusades. While not all usurers were Jews, they were *all* considered Jews by borrowers, especially kings and princes. Many moneylenders came from the Lombard region of northern Italy, southern France, and the Low Countries. In southern France, the Cahors provided the service, and the Lombards later migrated north to the Low Countries. The term "lombard" became a standard term for moneylender or pawnbroker. In a similar vein, more than one sovereign referred to lenders generally as "my Jews," regardless of religious affiliation. English law referred to them as the "king's Jews" prior to the thirteenth century. This "otherness" helped keep moneylenders at arms' length from their clients, a useful distance when expropriation became politically expedient. Although the ethnic element is certainly clear, the term "Jew" also became a surrogate for lending in general. In the Magna Carta, signed by John at Runnymede in 1215, there are two chapters, or clauses, specifically referring to Jews and lending. Concerning dying in debt, it stated, "If one who has borrowed from the Jews any sum, great or small, die before that loan be repaid, the debt shall not bear interest while the heir is under age . . . and if the debt fall into our [king's] hands, we will not take anything except the principal sum contained in the bond."[20]

The Cahors were descendents of the Visigoths, living in what became southwestern France. Unlike the Lombards, their tribal code, known as the *Forum Judicum* (*Visigothic Code*), specified the maximum rate of usury that could be charged on a loan. In a manner strikingly similar to the *Twelve Tables*, it stated:

> Where anyone loans money at interest, he shall not have a right to demand more than three *siliquæ* per annum, for every *solidus*; the debtor shall pay one *solidus*, as annual interest, for every eight *solidi*, and the creditor may claim from the debtor the principal and the aforesaid interest. If the creditor, by a written agreement, should extort from the necessities of the debtor a sum, as interest, in excess of the above amount, the contract, being contrary to law, shall be invalid. But if any one should thus violate the law, and should receive the sum which was agreed upon in writing, the usurious interest shall not be returned.[21]

This set the maximum rate of interest at 12.5 percent (one in eight) and the rate could not be violated even by written contract, an indirect acknowledgment that many Visigoths were not literate. While the date of the code extended over several hundred years, it was clear that the rate of interest conformed roughly to the *Twelve Tables* rather than Justinian's *Code* because of its relatively high rate and similar, if not precise, language. The fact that the Cahors became notorious moneylenders in France clearly breaks with the code but attests to the fact that not all ancient interest rate ceilings were acknowledged. Technically, the Cahors of France were outside the traditional Visigoth domain of Spain in the latter years of the Western Empire so they could claim that they were only adopting Brutus's principle of lending at the local, prevailing rates of interest.

Originally, both the Lombards and the Visigoths were Arians and did not convert to Catholicism until they became more settled in their respective domains. As such, they did not acknowledge the Council of Nicaea or the Nicene Creed, the same council that proscribed usury for churchmen. In addition to being barbarians in Roman eyes, they were also heretics, so it was not unusual that they fell outside the orbit of the church during the formative period of natural law theory. They adopted moneylending with a natural flourish. The descendents of both barbarian groups were in direct competition with the Jews after the eleventh century. In England, Edward I forbade Jewish usury in 1275 and expelled Jews from England in 1290. Expulsion of the Jews was becoming more commonplace in Europe, with France expelling a large population a hundred years later. Spain later provided perhaps the best-known expulsion in 1492, expelling its population as the kingdoms of Castile and Aragon were united. When the Jews were expelled, Lombards usually took their place for lack of any other group with the necessary resources. Moneylending certainly was a risky profession. In order to reflect the risk of lending to princes, most lenders charged them interest at rates higher than those charged ordinary businessmen. Loans to princes ranged from 15 to 80 percent during the fourteenth century while commercial loans ranged from 5 to 25 percent, amply illustrating the risk attached to princely sums.[22] Doing so only infuriated monarchs even more, convincing them that confiscating the property of the moneylender was actually just. Being peripatetic was both a blessing and a curse for many moneylenders since they were considered politically expendable.

The Renaissance of the Twelfth Century

During the twelfth century, a revival of trade began in Europe that brought traders into better contact with the Eastern Empire and the Muslim world. This has become known as the renaissance of the twelfth century because it signaled a general rebirth of trade and learning. But as far as usury was concerned, there was nothing new in the way in which it was interpreted during the century. Denunciations against it became stronger despite the fact that trade was changing the political and economic face of Europe.

Usury already was well defined by the church in the twelfth century but came into clearer focus in the compendium of canon law known as Gratian's *Decretals* (*Decretum Gratiani*). Although the historical evidence is sketchy, Johannes Gratian was thought to be a monk who taught at the University of Bologna, although his first name is not known with certainty.[23] Little actually is known about him other than the compendium. His masterwork and commentaries covered a vast amount of previously declared canons. Compiling them usefully into a large text was a great benefit to students of canon law. The compendium appeared around 1140 and included Gratian's own definition of legal terms. He also went to great lengths to research the sources of the various canons and ranked them in the order of their gravity and importance. In a sense, he was following in the steps of Justinian by producing a code that would later prove invaluable to students and churchmen.

The *Decretals* became part of the curriculum at many universities and centers of learning in Italy where canon law was studied, especially at the University of Padua, one of the leading centers for the study of law and Aristotle. The work led to a general revival of Roman law in the twelfth century, although not all European countries would fall fully under its influence. The prohibitions against usury were prominent in the *Decretals* and survived as a part of doctrine even though medieval trade was reviving and growing. Paying interest to investors and depositors was necessary because without it there would have been no compensation for risk. Interest was vital to lending during the Middle Ages despite the religious prohibitions. How it was accomplished became more and more ingenious as time passed.

Parts of the *Decretals* treated the relationship between borrower and lender in traditional medieval fashion. Usury was allowed when the counterparty was an enemy. Justice was suspended between belligerents and if the law recognized the right of a man to kill an enemy then there was no reason why usury could not be tolerated under such circumstances. Generally, the borrower became a vassal of the lender for the time that the debt remained outstanding. When the debt was paid, the servile relationship ended.[24] The exceptions and nuances of the attitudes toward usury amply displayed the intricacies of canon law and often also illustrated the inconsistencies that could be reached by attempting to apply syllogistic logic to commercial affairs. Nevertheless, the church now had its own codified version of canon law, which complemented the Justinian *Code*.

A more practical approach was taken a century after the *Decretals* appeared. In a well-known medieval study of Justinian's *Institutes* and *Code*, Azo of Bologna stated that although usury clearly was against the law of God, it had to be interpreted liberally and tolerated "on account of the actual necessities of the world."[25] Although the two spheres of law seemed incompatible, even canon lawyers recognized that the two could exist side by side if the civil law did not blatantly violate church law. This was particularly important after the first millennium because during the early twelfth century a new form of business organization began to develop in Europe. The *compagnia* began to supplant the older Greco-Roman form of enterprise known as the *societas* as the preferred form of partnership organization. It was more flexible than its older counterpart. In the *societas*, a partner's equity could be either labor or capital and each partner was equally at risk for the partnerships' liabilities. If the partnership failed and debts could not be paid, the penalties were often severe. Under the *compagnia*, the amount of capital contributed by partners was more sophisticated. It consisted of earnings retained by the partnership, additional paid-in capital, and deposits made by other investors. The deposits paid interest but were disguised as "discretionary payments" made by the partnership to avoid the ban on usury.

Another clever method of avoiding charges of usury was to ensure that the repayment of a loan or contribution was more than the principal originally lent without any discussion of interest. Other methods included borrowers making "gifts" to lenders and setting erroneous dates for payments that would be deliberately missed so that a penalty could be properly assessed by the lender.[26] These increased sources of capital made the partnership more flexible and allowed it to attract outside investors who were vital for expansion. In most cases, the *compagnia* was similar to the *societas* in that most of the partners were family members or closely associated with the other partners in some way. The penalties for business failure were still severe and could easily include imprisonment or even having the bankrupts sold into slavery.[27] Knowing your partner well was a prerequisite for conducting business.

Usury prohibitions were affecting the language of business organization but were not impeding commerce despite the church's pronouncements. Church law recognized this and attempted to deal with the matter of partnerships. In the thirteenth century, Thomas Aquinas stated that "he who entrusts his money to a merchant or craftsman, by means of some kind of partnership, does not transfer the ownership of his money to the latter, but it remains his; so that the merchant trades with it or the craftsman uses it at the owner's risk; hence he may lawfully claim a part of the gain arising therefrom, as being his own property."[28] This interpretation made one of the partners an agent rather than a principal to a business transaction, a concept alien to established practice at the time.

The penalties for defaulting on a loan varied from place to place, and could lead to enforced restitution, imprisonment, or having the debtor sold into slavery. But one common relief was found in many jurisdictions traditionally associated with political refugees rather than fiscal ones. Places of sanctuary began to appear, normally in churches or on sacred ground, allowing debtors to find relief from their creditors. Declaring sanctuary was not without its problems for the debtor, however, since his goods were unprotected once he sought sanctuary and could be seized by civil authorities at the behest of his creditors. Sanctuaries became well known and frequently used, especially in London, although not all churches qualified since once a debtor claimed sanctuary he was stuck in that abode until he decided to come out. Naturally, those places offering the best accommodations won the day. Several locales in the city became popular among debtors. One was the Collegiate Church of St. Martins le Grand, founded in 1056 for expressly that purpose. It remained in existence until the dissolution of the monasteries by Henry VIII almost five hundred years later. Another was the sanctuary associated with the Carmelites called White Friars (after the order's robes), which was located next to Middle Temple and founded by Patrick Grey in 1241.

By the twelfth century, it had become clear that interest was being charged overtly on commercial and personal transactions and that it was separated from usury by both effect and intent. Interest had to do no harm to the borrower, meaning that he would be able to repay a loan in a timely fashion without depriving himself or putting himself into penury. The loan needed to be for a productive purpose as well and technically had to be lent by someone whose main business was not simply lending, this in order to avoid the charge of manifest usury. As commerce and industry began to increase, an outright church ban on loans would have meant a ban on business and economic growth itself. So the argument continued to center on excessive interest charged by socially undesirable moneylenders and its potentially damaging economic effects.

The church councils convened in the twelfth century all were unequivocal about usury: it was condemned in no uncertain terms. It was not coincidental that the increasingly strident denunciations came during a time of economic revival since interest rates in Western Europe were on the rise. Demand for loans increased the rate charged for them across all types of lenders, from loans made to princes and kings down to loans made to businesses and individuals for personal use. In England, personal loan rates ranged from 40 percent to 120 percent, while in Italy rates for business loans were in the 20 percent range.[29] The personal loan rate was higher and the loans often were made by pawnbrokers who demanded collateral in return for cash. The increased demand made moneylenders increasingly important and endangered at the same time. The church disapproved of them because of their acquired power.

The Second Lateran Council of 1139 condemned usury in harsh terms. "We condemn that practice accounted despicable and blameworthy by divine and human laws, denounced by Scripture in the old and new Testaments, namely the ferocious greed of usurers; and we sever them from every comfort of the church."[30] Called by Pope Innocent II, the council took a dim view of other social practices of the time, including the sport of jousting, which it termed "abominable," and denied a Christian burial to any knight who died as a result of injuries sustained in a tournament. The same punishment was meted out to arsonists and other penalties were prescribed for anyone who laid hands on a cleric. Usurers were in danger of having the sacraments denied to them, and anyone, including priests, who failed to take notice risked church penalties.

Clerics who overlooked the ban on the sacraments could also face the wrath of the church for doing so. They could be excommunicated for burying the miscreant, although social pressures led some to take risks with a burial. In one case, a usurer died and his friends insisted that he be buried properly, although the local priest initially demurred. The body was placed on a donkey, and the priest proclaimed that "wherever the donkey takes it, be it a church, a cemetery, or elsewhere, there I will bury it." The priest was in luck because the donkey headed straight for the burial ground where thieves were interred and heaved the usurer off his back into a pile of dung.[31]

At the Third Lateran Council called by Pope Alexander III in 1179, usury was addressed directly and again those who practiced it were made subject to a potential ban from the sacraments. The language used in the canon also was of interest because it gave an indication of the prevalence of usury at the time. "Since in almost every place the crime of usury has become so prevalent that many persons give up all other business and become usurers," the council concluded that only a ban on them receiving the sacraments could be a viable preventative. But the street did not run two ways. "No priest shall accept their alms," the canon concluded, meaning that a usurer could not buy his way back into good grace.[32] Illicit gain could not be laundered back to respectability since it was sinful originally and remained so.

Despite the large body of writing and laws condemning it, usury remained illegal only under canon law. Despite Charlemagne having extended it to laymen, business was still business in the lay world, although most secular rulers paid lip service to church doctrine somewhat gingerly. The Third Lateran Council acknowledged, "Nearly everywhere the crime of usury has become so firmly rooted that many, omitting other business, practice usury as if it were permitted, and in no way observe how it is forbidden in both the Old and New Testament."[33] The most severe penalty against it was excommunication for usurers. While the penalty may not have bothered everyone spiritually, it carried serious social and economic overtones even for non-Christians. Those excommunicated were put at a distinct disadvantage among their peers and found that certain economic and social doors were closed to them. As a result, excommunication was more serious than it would otherwise appear and had to be taken seriously by even the nominally faithful.

As the church extended its power over the empire and secular rulers, excommunication became a convenient tool through which to express its political will. One hundred years before the Third Lateran Council, the young Holy Roman Emperor challenged the authority of Pope Gregory VII, the former monk known as Hildebrand. Henry challenged the pope's authority only to find that he was excommunicated from the church, which would have proved a valid excuse for princes to rebel from his authority. The language of the pope was explicit and contained more than a simple admonition against disobedience. "I now declare . . . that Henry, son of the Emperor Henry, is deprived of his kingdom of Italy and Germany," he wrote in 1076. As a result, Henry traveled to Canossa in the Alps in 1077, where the pope was staying, and stood penitentially outside his residence in the snow until Gregory forgave his sins and restored his standing in the church. The spectacle of an emperor having to do penitence in such a manner was one of the medieval world's most enduring images and made a strong impression on the faithful and non-believers alike.

Within their own realms, kings were able to confiscate the property of the excommunicated under their jurisdiction. Although a direct legal link between church and secular law was tenuous, the religious codes formed the basis of the secular law and that was enough to provide the basis for the confiscation of property.[34] The convenience factor was also present. The property of excommunicants proved too tempting a lure to ignore for sovereigns constantly in need of money. Expropriation became a convenient method of raising money in the Middle Ages and helped contribute to the longevity of the usury laws.

In the early twentieth century, the Swedish economist Gustav Cassel characterized the logic employed by medieval churchmen in their condemnation of usury as either sophistry, the "worst degeneration of human thought," or an "appeal to authority, the suppression of thought."[35] Sophistry was perhaps the most barbed criticism one could level because it referred back to the eloquent but empty argumentative techniques of those ancient Greek rhetoricians collectively known as Sophists. The concept found no better application than in the pronouncement about usury in the canons of the Fourth Lateran Council in 1215, called by the most notable medieval pope, Innocent III, which stated that "the more the Christian religion is restrained from usurious practices, so much the more does the perfidy of the Jews grow in these matters, so that within a short time they are exhausting the resources of Christians."[36] Jews were required to make satisfaction to borrowers or the secular authorities and to dress differently from Christians so that they could easily be distinguished. The church was adopting a more strident position against Jewish usurers, anticipating Thomas Aquinas, whose own views helped solidify the idea. The council also proclaimed that in addition to dressing differently Jews were not to hold public office since they used such offices to conceal their "contempt for Christians." This method of distinguishing Jews through their dress became a common medieval practice to single out the usurer and non-believer.

The first English statute discussing usury appeared in 1235. Passed during the reign of Henry III, the Statute of Merton prohibited usury from being charged to a minor who had inherited from his father, until he reached the legal age. There was a general assumption by legal scholars long after the fact that the statute applied mainly to Jews, who had become moneylenders in England by the thirteenth century. The assumption was that since Edward the Confessor had prohibited usury before the Norman Conquest of 1066, then the law only applied to Jews because Christians were not practicing usury, an assumption that may not have been correct.[37]

At the First Council of Lyons in 1245, the more practical, and revealing, side of usury was discussed. Acknowledging that many churches had fallen into debt over the years, the council ordered new pastors or administrators to take an immediate inventory of all church possessions within one month of assuming their new offices and report the findings to their immediate superiors. They were then to pay off all usurious debts by selling the movable assets of the church if necessary in order to make the churches solvent again, and they were forbidden to enter into any new mortgage arrangements that might lead to the forfeited ownership of church lands in the future. This was perhaps the first time that canon law dealt with such practical matters arising from usury. However, within a short time, monarchs would find an even better way to free themselves from previously incurred debt.

On the other side of the coin, many churchmen openly practiced usury and many saw it as a source of funds for their own clerical activities. The practice was widespread but apparently not centralized or coordinated in any particular way. The bishop of Paris once was consulted by a usurer about saving his soul before it was too late. Instead of suggesting restitution, as church policy suggested, the bishop instead suggested that the usurer donate his ill-gotten gains to the church so that the cathedral of Notre Dame could be built. When St. Bernard saw the gothic masterpiece, he exclaimed, "Wealth is drawn up by ropes of wealth . . . thus money bringeth money."[38]

The First Council of Lyons also took up the practical matter of the Crusades. Jerusalem again had fallen to the Muslims in 1244, prompting Louis IX of France to prepare the Seventh Crusade in 1248. In order to help in the effort, the council offered enticements to potential combatants. Anyone volunteering to fight in the Holy Land was to be freed from his debts and the payment of interest until his return. Secular rulers were to protect their subjects from paying interest to Jews by forcing the lenders to postpone interest until the faithful either returned from the crusade or were dead. The council was clear that "such a benefit seems not to entail much loss, inasmuch as it postpones the repayment but does not cancel the debt."[39] This pronouncement was in keeping with the idea that the payment of interest should not be injurious to the lender or the borrower. The Crusade did not end well for Louis, however. He was captured by the Muslims and subsequently freed, eventually organizing the Eighth Crusade in 1270. After landing his troops at Tunis in North Africa, he soon died after plague broke out among his troops, only adding to the cumulative woes of the Crusades in general.

The canons of the First Council of Lyons were affirmed at the Second Council of Lyons in 1274. A particular medieval practice was also brought to light, which demonstrated how the church sought reparations from what the council called "notorious usurers." Those who practiced usury often left wills that provided for restitution after their deaths to their borrowers. Why such clauses appeared in wills was as much practical as religious. If restitution were made, the church would not deny a proper burial and the usurer's family would not be stigmatized. Breaking canon law was one thing, but there was also the matter of eternal damnation. Restitution was the absolution a usurer needed to ensure a peaceful, eternal rest. Most importantly, this provision brought usury within the jurisdiction of the ecclesiastical courts, which soon would have a virtual monopoly on the testamentary business.[40]

An example of such restitution can be found in the *Dialogue of the Exchequer,* a description of the finances of England written in Socratic dialogue form around 1170. In response to a question distinguishing between public and private usury, the exchequer responds:

> The Royal Authority would not do a Christian-like action was it to proceed thus against a clerk [cleric] or layman who had offended [by practicing usury], while he was living, for there is time to repent. But when he is dead, all his goods become the King's. It remains to show what is public, and what is not public, usury. We call that public and common usury when, according to the manner of the Jews, anyone takes more by agreement of the same species of money than he lent . . . We do not call that public, but damnable usury, when anyone takes a church or an estate for what is lent, and receives the profits of them till the principal is paid off.[41]

But that was not to suggest that restitution became the order of the day in the medieval world: far from it. Stories abounded of the fate of usurers and their allies who did not make restitution. One writer, Stephen of Bourbon, recalled a story of what happened to the friends of a usurer who decided to go against his wishes and not make restitution to his victims after his death. "They were to return the property he had acquired from others, and he required an oath from them. They took the oath, which they accompanied by imprecations. One of them called down upon himself the sacred fire . . . and said that it should burn him if he did not fulfill his promise. The other did the same, invoking leprosy. But after the usurer's death, they kept the money, and fell victim to their imprecations. Under the pressure of their torment, they confessed."[42] Unfortunately for them, their afflictions were irrevocable.

One of the most important dates for the practice of usury occurred in 1202. A well-traveled Italian named Fibonacci wrote a book entitled *Liber Abaci*, or the *Book of the Abacus*. This was a treatise devoted to the introduction of Arabic numbers into Europe, a method of calculation generally unknown until that time. Traditional European practice involved math using Roman numerals, a system that had serious drawbacks for calculations involving more than simple arithmetic. The book covered such topics as the use of decimals, the introduction of square roots, the rules of proportion, the use of whole numbers and fractions, and the many applications of these calculations. One of the applications was interest rate calculations, a topic that was not standard despite the centuries of condemning usury.

Fibonacci was born Leonardo Pisano, the son of an Italian diplomat, around 1170. Although "Fibonacci" literally translated can have several meanings, "blockhead" and "loafer" were the two most commonly accepted nicknames. However, the young man proved to be anything but a fool. After being introduced to the Hindu-Arab numbering systems while visiting his father, a Pisan diplomat, in North Africa, he wrote his book and published it in longhand manuscript form in 1202 because the printing press had not been invented yet. The work quickly caught the attention of medieval mathematicians, especially those at the court of Frederick II, the Holy Roman emperor. Responding to questions posed by Frederick's advisers, Fibonacci demonstrated to the royal audience how many rabbits could be expected to breed in a year after a pair was left alone (377 pairs).[43] The answer so impressed the court that Frederick became his patron and his book's success was assured. The result was a revolution in mathematics as practiced in Europe and a revealing look at what was known about interest at the time.

The revolution owed much of its impetus to the adoption of Arabic numerals in Europe, replacing Roman numerals after around 1150. Without the flexibility offered by the new numerals, interest rate calculations and the math tricks Fibonacci used to gain converts to his cause would have been much more difficult if not impossible. The calculations described in the *Book of the Abacus* became standard in apprentice schools of the Middle Ages where young men learned commercial arts and business. Many are mathematical solutions to practical questions. One of the more intriguing involves a compound interest problem. Fibonacci asks a simple moneylenders' question. If a man has one denaro and expects it to double every five years, how many will he have at the end of one hundred years? As he noted, the money will double every five years, so in one hundred years it will double twenty times. Without using an equation, he was able to show the future value of 1,048,876 denari by simply compounding the sum in longhand.[44] In contemporary terms, the future value was compounded at 14.355 percent to arrive at the same sum but, in an interesting wrinkle, it can only be achieved by semi-annual compounding: that is, 1 denaro (present value) compounded for two hundred periods at 7.1775 percent. Clearly, medieval businessmen understood compound interest and the Fibonacci calculation is the first known written example in Western Europe.

Another wrinkle is that the rate of interest is not mentioned, only the desired result. In this example, the well-known financial mathematical rule of 72 can be employed to arrive at the desired rate.[45] Using 72 as a standard numerator, 72 divided by 14.4 percent equals five periods, the time the money needs to double. But Fibonacci did not mention the compound rate, only the answer. It is not difficult to appreciate the sort of calculations necessary to arrive at future value in this case since the value has to be determined by continuously multiplying the present value until the answer is reached. In place of a rate of interest being quoted, the objective was stated.

A major question is raised when Fibonacci's use of compound interest is found in the future value calculation. The idea of interest on interest clearly was known and used, but its origins are murky. Even Fibonacci does not mention semi-annual compounding directly; he simply uses it in this example. The notion of interest on interest violated the usury prohibitions by being the result of idleness, or taking advantage of the borrower by the lender, so mentioning it as an accepted method of calculation would have been misplaced in the face of church authority. More importantly, using examples of compound interest was the moneylenders' method of combating the enemy of value in the Middle Ages—debasement of currency by sovereign princes short of cash.

An indication of this can be found in Fibonacci's use of the denarius as a currency in his examples. It was the currency of the Roman Empire until replaced by the antoninianus around 215 A.D. when the emperor of the same name, better known as Caracalla, issued it to fund a pay increase for his legions. Successive emperors beginning with Nero regularly debased it until it was eventually replaced. In his book, Fibonacci devotes considerable time describing "alloying monies." While a mathematical exercise, it also amply demonstrates how to debase a currency to get desired results. Otherwise, it seems a strange addition to a practical work of math. Compound interest was one method of combating this problem for the individual with money for investment. The frequency of the compounding would compensate the investor for the debasements that invariably occurred in the ancient and medieval worlds. For example, Fibonacci's original problem above would yield future dinari worth 669,138 compounded annually. The additional 379,738 are realized simply because of the semi-annual compounding, a fact not lost on medieval businessmen living under princes constantly strapped for cash.

Fibonacci's interest rate calculations were based on the Julian calendar and were the standard in Europe until the sixteenth century, when the Gregorian calendar was adopted. At that time, interest calculations had to be changed slightly to accommodate the new year, and that prompted the first interest rate tables to be published. But that would not diminish Fibonacci's contribution to mathematical sciences and actuarial calculations. And the same Arab influences that sparked his imagination and prompted the other books he wrote on similar topics also affected a radically different group of adventurers who would achieve the distinction of becoming the first cross-border bankers in Europe.

God's Bankers

The church-state conflict also heated up in the early fourteenth century and it was to have an indirect effect on the origins of banking during the late Middle Ages. The church-state conflict can best be seen in the papal bull *Unam Sanctam*, issued by Pope Boniface VIII in 1302. Citing the spiritual and temporal realms, he concluded, "If, therefore, the earthly power err, it shall be judged by the spiritual power . . . but if the supreme spiritual power err, it could be judged solely by God; not by man."[46] This stark declaration of papal power essentially made Philippe IV of France and Edward II of England vassals of the pope; Philippe was also Edward's father-in-law.

Boniface's strong stand led to one of the low points in the history of church-state relations. Incensed by the pope's stand, Philippe had the pope kidnapped and he died a short time later. The king's supporters had Clement elected pope and the papal court was removed to Avignon, where Clement became known as the first pope subjected to the "Babylonian captivity" of the papacy, which lasted for more than one hundred years. Given this state of affairs, it was clear that Clement would do the king's bidding regarding one of the church's most visible institutions. It also meant that usurers were facing a period of increased danger, with needy sovereigns using church law when it suited them to confiscate the property of moneylenders. When the spiritual power of the papacy was combined with armed force, the results were disastrous for the growing financial classes.

The Crusades became a watershed for lending and banking in one other respect. The international reach of the Jews was greatly exceeded by another group that took up international banking on a scale not seen before, becoming a major lender in Europe. As long as the Crusades were in operation, this group retained its preeminent position. But after the wars ended, these nouveau riche bankers became just another minority who became pawns in the larger game of church-state power politics in the fourteenth century.

Founded around 1119 in the newly conquered Jerusalem, the Knights Templars were a monastic, militant order organized by two French knights, Hugh des Payens and Godfrey of St. Omer. They were established about the same time that the Poor Brethren of the Hospital of St. John, or Knights Hospitallers, were founded by Raymond du Puy. The Templars were housed by King Baldwin II of the Latin Kingdom of Jerusalem at his own expense. Their original brief was to protect pilgrims making the trip to Jerusalem from Europe. Their name derived from the lodging that Baldwin gave them: they were housed in his palace in the remains of the Temple of Solomon, of which only the Wailing Wall survives today. Those original accommodations were to become the source of legend for centuries after their official demise as an order recognized by the church.

The Templars were formally recognized by the church at the Council of Troyes in 1128 and their rules of conduct were drawn up by St. Bernard of Clairvaux, closely following the Cistercian order. Originally known as the Poor Soldiers of the Temple, the Templars were originally a mendicant (begging) order and adhered to the rigid code with great fervor. Their order required obedience and celibacy and when combined with their growing military prowess, they developed an almost legendary reputation in Europe. Their lodges, or temples, became scattered throughout Europe, mostly in

England, Spain, and France, and to a lesser extent Germany. From their earliest days, they established an elaborate fundraising network using the temples as their bases. Their ability to collect money became equally legendary and their reputation grew quickly as a powerful order of monastic knights dedicated to the recovery of Jerusalem, prompting the Fourth Crusade. This network became one of the first banking networks in Europe and the Templars excelled at moving funds around Europe quickly. Bills of exchange, drafts, and foreign currency became easier to deal and the order reaped the rewards for its efforts.

The international dimension of the Templars' organization was not without its drawbacks, however. After the fall of Jerusalem, during the pontificate of Clement V, they moved part of the Jerusalem operation to the south of France, making Philippe IV (the Fair) visibly nervous. Like the other military orders serving in the Holy Land, they were blamed for the loss of Jerusalem by many critics in Europe. The French king had established a reputation for poor administration, although he had successfully cowed the papacy into submission after the kidnapping of Boniface VIII. Philippe had already confiscated the property of Jews living in France in order to maintain his large bureaucracy and free-spending lifestyle. The Templars were a sophisticated military organization essentially organized outside the traditional lines of feudalism in Europe. As an order of knights, they had the ability to declare war and make peace treaties but were not required to fight on behalf of any prince since they owed no secular power allegiance.[47] They owed fealty to no one save the pope, a trait that would only add to their woes since the Avignon captivity had just begun. While rumors greatly exaggerated their wealth and numbers, they became victims of their own legend and were an enviable source of funds for financially incompetent monarchs such as Philippe. Once they established themselves firmly on French soil it was only a matter of time before the lure of their wealth would be too great for him to ignore.

In England, the Templars built their first lodge in Holborn in London before moving to a site on Fleet Street in 1185. All the churches were built in a round style, on the model of the temple in Jerusalem. Today the site houses one of the three Inns of Court, the Middle Temple. As the order grew rapidly, it became an entrenched part of the English establishment, with close ties to the exchequer and the crown. The London operation greatly benefited Edward II, who relied on the Templars for financing and advice, especially since Edward I had expelled the Jews just a few years before. The temple in London became a depository for the monarchy and for wealthy merchants, many of whom left substantial sums with the order. The site was considered a safe place to leave funds because it was sacred, that is run by a monastic order. King John deposited the crown jewels as well as important records in the Temple. Edward I made deposits, and more frequently withdrawals. The knights also were frequently used by the crown to collect revenue and transport it safely. Funds raised for the Crusades especially fell under the Templars' care, although not always successfully. One knight was discovered embezzling money from funds designated for a crusade in the late twelfth century. He was spared by the king, although the order dealt with him more severely.[48] And funds deposited in the temple in London were not inviolate from the monarchy, which often seized funds for its own use. Edward II could not afford to pursue the Templars because his own interests were integrally tied to their welfare, at least initially. But more Templars resided in France and it was there that their problems began.

The French monarch coveted the Templars' wealth, but in attacking them he also would undermine the network of international banking they created. Although the Templars were bankers, they specialized in bills of exchange and bank drafts, not lending money directly. A bill of exchange drawn on the London temple could be presented in Paris and the proceeds paid in local currency. The knights made their money from the profit on the foreign exchange transaction, not by charging usury on the principal amount involved. By doing so, they avoided any potential charge of usury since profiting from the foreign exchange part of the transaction was tolerated by canon law. The Scholastic churchmen who served as the guardians of the canon law were mostly favorable to the practice and that served as precedent for the future. It also explains why the Templars were not eventually charged with usury when the order came under attack and their wealth was confiscated.[49]

The Templars were born of the politics of the crusading period and subsequently found themselves in the middle of the battle for political power in the late thirteenth century and the early fourteenth. The Middle Ages were filled with papal-political confrontations like the one between Gregory and Henry at Canossa, and the papacy won the battles in almost all cases. In addition to the polemical literature arguing for the supremacy of the pope, Rome also had the infamous donation of Constantine on its side when arguing for the political primacy of the pope in Rome. Attributed to the emperor, the document purported to give the Holy See the reins of political power as Constantine willingly gave his empire to the church: "Therefore, we have seen it to be fitting that our Empire and the power of the kingdom should be transferred and translated to the eastern regions . . . we decree that all things which we have established by this our holy Imperial edict and by other divine decrees shall remain uninjured and unbroken until the end of the world."[50] Although the donation was proved to be a forgery by Lorenzo Valla in the fifteenth century, it was considered part and parcel of church history at the time and only confirmed, at least in Rome's eyes, the supremacy of spiritual power over worldly. But the humiliation of Boniface by Philippe had changed the balance of power in favor of monarchy and now the popes were serving at the pleasure of the French.

Philippe finally ordered the arrest of the Templars in France beginning in 1307. Their property was seized and they were remanded to Dominican inquisitors for interviews. One hundred thirty-eight Templars were arrested, including their preceptor Jacques de Molay. De Molay and the king were friends; the Templar preceptor once had served as the godfather to the king's son. Most were tortured and about half of them succumbed and confessed to various crimes, including idolatry and unnatural acts. One of the charges reputed that novices were required to kiss the buttocks of their superiors in an initiation ceremony. The Inquisition's torturers proved highly effective in extracting confessions and some prisoners died of wounds received. Despite all the charges, mostly trumped up by churchmen loyal to Philippe, the Templars were not charged with usury despite their extensive banking operations.[51] The reasons for charging them with unnatural crimes and idolatry rather than usury are not clear, but Philippe clearly sought their wealth and making a charge like usury may have seemed a bit obvious. As noted, dealing in bills of exchange was not considered usurious at the time in any event. Technically, usury would not be declared heretical until the Council of Vienne several years later and the other charges were more likely to stick at the time. Philippe also put severe pressure on Clement V, who complied by attempting to move against the Templars in other jurisdictions by pressuring monarchs to follow Philippe's suit.

Edward II demurred, replying that he could not act against the Templars. In any event, English law would prove the Inquisition powerless because England already had banned the use of torture in civil law by the time the Templars were accused of heresy by the Inquisition. Without the threat of force, the Templars were safe from coercion in Britain. Edward also tried to convince the kings of Castile, Aragon, Naples, and Portugal not to pursue the Templars, but he fought a losing battle. Clement prevailed by demanding that Edward acknowledge and apply ecclesiastical law over English law. Edward finally ordered the arrest of the English Templars and seized their property in 1308. Inquisitors used torture in England for a brief time in order to make the knights compliant, although many fled the jurisdiction before being handed over to the inquisitors. Their property was expropriated and the knights were confined to religious houses.

The Templars were dissolved in 1312 by the papal bull *Vox in Excelso* (*Voice in Heaven*) in which Clement stated that he thought the Templars were guilty of the charges brought against them, although they proved difficult to document. Clement's reasoning was to become one of the low points for the medieval papacy and was decried for centuries after, but the Templars' fate had been cast almost twenty-five years before when Philippe declared all of their holdings void, although he never implemented his decision at the time. Their wealth was too great a temptation to be ignored by an impecunious king and his papal ally.

As a direct result of the conflict with the Templars, Clement voided all secular law tolerating usury at the Council of Vienne in 1311. The council was called primarily to deal with the Templars and its language showed the connection between the knights and the money-lending problem that caused concern and conflict within the ranks of the church. "We, therefore, wishing to get rid of these pernicious practices, decree with the approval of the sacred council, that all the magistrates, captains, rulers, consuls, judges, counselors or any other officials of these communities who presume in the future to decide . . . that usury be paid or, if paid, that it may be not fully and freely restored when claimed, incur the sentence of excommunication," the council proclaimed. But the council also took the practice of usury into uncharted waters. It also announced that anyone who fell into the trap of proclaiming that usury was not sinful was subject to an even greater punishment, stating, "We decree that he is to be punished as a heretic; and we strictly enjoin on local ordinaries and inquisitors of heresy to proceed against those they suspect of such error as they would against those suspected of heresy."[52] Once the specter of heresy and the Inquisition had been invoked, prosecutions against suspected usurers would become more harsh.

The back of the Templars had been broken by Clement and Philippe, although de Molay was still alive after the Council of Vienne finished its work. He had avoided serious punishment in 1307 by admitting to one of the Inquisition's lesser charges, a practice common for some who had been charged with heresy.[53] In 1314, he and Geoffroi de Charney, another high-ranking Templar, were declared relapsed heretics and burned at the stake in Paris.[54] Like many other Templar executions, the fires burned slowly so that the Inquisitors sent a strong public message. The Templars were dissolved as an order, although more than half their number were already dead. Their wealth, originally intended to benefit Rome, was seized by Philippe. The finances of his kingdom improved dramatically, albeit temporarily, after the Templars were rounded up. One of the more intriguing episodes of the Middle Ages had come to an abrupt and bloody end. Usurers and moneylenders throughout Europe had good cause for dread. After the expulsion of the Jews from France and England, the papacy and its major allies had conspired to expropriate one of their own extremely popular institutions.

The abrupt end of the Templars had a positive side by necessitating the rise of other lenders and bankers, leading to the establishment of an early banking system in Europe. Merchants in the Italian communes began to branch out, lending money in addition to their normal businesses. In Siena in the early thirteenth century, merchant families like the Bonsignori and the Tolomei established themselves as bankers in the wake of the Templars by lending money to the papacy. The same was true of the other Italian city-states. In Florence, the Peruzzi and Scali families became established, although it would not be until the fifteenth century that the Medici Bank was established in Florence, eclipsing the others in stature and importance. Banking was not without its risks, however, since lending to sovereigns in general was riskier than lending to established merchants.

Although catastrophic for the Templars, the affair marked the beginning of a decline in papal power and the influence of the Inquisition, which was effectively employed by many secular rulers to consolidate their own power. Most importantly, practicing usury now was officially declared heretical and as such was subject to the forces of the Inquisition. But the irony of the short history of the Templars was not lost on moneylenders and early bankers. Originally conceived as a mendicant order, the Templars had grown wealthy and influential by begging for alms, becoming wealthy, and continuing to accept donations while becoming the first transnational banking force in Europe. A mendicant order had evolved into moneylending and trade financing. What once was recognized as beggary could not exist if it preyed on its neighbor for profit in the name of alms. The ancient concept of universal brotherhood still was alive and being practiced, although moneylenders had cause to wonder who benefited the most.

One medieval financing technique was developed in the late Middle Ages and would evolve over the centuries and emerge as a money market instrument hundreds of years later. The lending technique known as "dry exchange" made its appearance with Lombard bankers and became known as a loophole to avoid charges of usury when the church ban was at its height. It involved a borrower and a commercial lender exchanging bills of exchange internationally, denominated in more than one currency. A bill would be drawn on one lender and then presented to its branch or agent in an overseas location, each cancelling each other except for the exchange element. Since money did not cross borders the exchange was considered dry.[55] If drawn properly, the lender would benefit and profit from the exchange rate difference while seemingly not receiving any interest on the advance. The exchange of bills was considered a legitimate banking transaction, although another form—fictitious exchange—was not. The church officially declared dry exchange usurious during the pontificate of Pius V in 1571.

Views of Aquinas

Despite the later influence of Aristotle on the church concepts of usury, Plato was the main source of philosophic interpretation for most medieval thinkers until the late twelfth century. Fragments of Aristotle's works were known in the West, but the greater body of his writings only became known through the Muslim philosophers Avicenna and Averroes, both of whom had become known to European writers by the later twelfth century. Although the Crusades failed to establish Christian influence in the Middle East, they did help East and West establish trade and some cultural contacts, leading to the rediscovery of many of the Greek writers and philosophers. The most influential of Aristotle's works, the *Politics*, was one of the last of his works to be translated from the Greek by William of Moerbeke, a Dominican and a friend of Thomas Aquinas, in 1260. Until it was incorporated in church thought by Aquinas, the prohibitions against usury lacked a sound philosophic basis. But once it could be shown that usury had been denounced by Aristotle, the practice then had both theoretical and doctrinal authority working against it.

All the discussions and proscriptions against usury amassed over the centuries finally came to be enshrined in doctrine in the writings of Aquinas, the foremost Christian thinker to discuss usury in the Middle Ages. Thomas followed Aristotle's pronouncements closely, also adhering closely to the concept of justice that necessarily surrounded "the Philosopher's" politics and ethics. To Aristotle, usury was a practice surrounding the organization of the household. It was a domestic matter, crucial to the development of civil society. Justice demanded that a lender not attempt to seek unfair advantage from a borrower but extend him a helping hand in accordance with justice that applied to both parties. This notion was not merely home economics to Aristotle but the basis of all social arrangements. The principles that prevailed in the household prevailed in the larger society. Justice began at home. If matters of simple economics were not inherently just, then the concepts would be useless in society at large.

Like many medieval clerics, Thomas Aquinas was born into a well-to-do family in 1225. His father, Landulph, the Count of Aquino, placed him in the care of Dominicans for his early education but did not support Thomas's decision to join the order at the age of fifteen. His family was reputed to have gone to great lengths to keep him from the church, including hiring a prostitute to entertain him, but he was resolute and joined the order in spite of their protests. The Dominicans sent him to study at Cologne under Albertus Magnus, where he earned the sobriquet "dumb ox," although his brilliance soon became evident. He also studied at the University of Paris and earned the title of church doctor. At Paris, he became friendly with the French king Louis IX, with whom he often dined. He also became an accomplished preacher and was sent to the Second Council of Lyons by Pope Gregory X, but he died en route in 1274, leaving his magnum opus, *Summa Theologica*, unfinished. Enough of the work had been completed, however, to become the definitive work in church theology.

In his doctrinal magnum opus, Aquinas conveniently summed up most of the arguments against usury advanced over the centuries. Basically, most arguments defending usury centered on the idea that paying it was voluntary, so collecting it was not unjust but natural. Aristotle had rejected the notion that reciprocity itself was enough to explain the basic idea of interest and Thomas followed suit. He followed Aristotle's dictum about lent money being essentially barren. "To accept usury for the loan of money is in itself unjust; because this is selling what does not exist, and must obviously give rise to inequality, which is contrary to justice," he wrote in *Summa Theologica*.[56] But simply being unjust would not suffice; usurers had to make restitution for their sins. "Just as a man is bound to restore other things unjustly acquired, so he is bound to restore money received through usury."[57] The doctrines of previous church councils were now embodied in a single document that was to have great importance in the following centuries.

The use of money, according to Thomas, was simple and had not changed since Aristotle fifteen hundred years before. "The proper and principal use of money lies in its consumption or expenditure in the business of exchange."[58] What is not clear from this is how wealth was to be accumulated and maintained. Presumably, it would be earned and kept through acquisition of goods or land but never invested in the modern sense for that would require a rate of return, implying something beyond the basic rate of interest. While that may sound like a major shortcoming in Thomas's system, it actually was more complicated.

Thomas was not totally impractical about commercial life. Recognizing that commerce certainly existed and that usury was charged in daily transactions, he applied another of Aristotle's ideas to the amount that could be charged for goods, including the lending of money. This was known as the idea of the "just price." A good could not be sold for more than its basic value, the "price that it is worth to its possessor." At the same time, the price charged should do no harm, either to the buyer or the seller. When it does not, the price is just. "And thus a thing may lawfully [be] for more than it is worth in itself, though not more than it is worth to its possessor."[59] The concept revolved around justice in business transactions, but exactly how these considerations could be given value was another problem.

If a thing was to be sold at a price that it was worth to its owner, then the owner needed to do a calculation that today is known as opportunity cost. If a good was worth 10 percent more to its owner than its stated price, he could justifiably charge 10 percent more in selling it. If land sold brought in rents of 10 percent more than its value, the selling price could legally be adjusted to reflect the income received. Beyond that point, however, the arguments were less strong because the methods for adopting and evaluating value were crude. What was just to one party could easily be unjust to another and without a standard marketplace to sort out the price the price remained moot. At the back of these arguments, however, the power of the church was substituted for the marketplace.

But interest does not seem to play a role in medieval calculations of opportunities. Today, bonds are sold and the buyer pays accrued interest, acknowledging that the seller is to be compensated for the loss of opportunity until the next interest payment date. In the medieval world, the idea of using interest rates seems not to have played a role, at least not to churchmen. Value was not measured by interest and charging for time was not a viable concept. Time still belonged to God (or the church in his absence) and time could not be measured in monetary terms. Therefore, interest could not be admitted as a standard way of measuring it.

Aquinas also tackled the description of usufruct in Justinian's *Code*. In the *Summa*, he cited the *Institutes'* treatment of usufructs as acceptable practice. According to his interpretation of the Roman law, the code accepted usury because it was classified as a "quasi-usufruct," meaning that it had been accepted by human (not divine) law until that time, not because it was necessarily considered just but because it prevented lenders from disadvantaging borrowers. The Roman law embodied basic notions of justice, but they were not extensive or conclusive: "We ought not to lend or do any other good deed on account of hope in man, but on account of hope in God."[60] By implication, interest itself was not the problem, only the collection or charging of usury, which violated all of the Aristotelian standards. Aquinas singled out this passage because of the overall importance of Justinian's *Code* to the development of law in the Middle Ages. The code was still so powerful that Dante assigned the emperor a place in paradise while roundly relegating usurers to a place in hell.

By adding the political to the ethical, Thomas put a tight lock on the practice of usury, which would put the church in a theoretical bind for centuries because his writings were considered among its highest philosophical and theological teachings. He did admit, however, that while lending money at usury was unlawful, borrowing it was not, if the borrower put the money to good use. The door was left open for moneylenders operating ethically. Unlike Aristotle, however, Thomas's views were permeated with political and moral overtones indicative of the thirteenth century bias against non-Christians. The separateness of usurers and Jews would find a home in his thoughts on the treatment of non-believers despite the fact that all were assumed bound by church law in the same manner. Aquinas had some relatively harsh things to say about Europe's growing numbers of moneylenders and the theological and political parts of his writings cannot easily be separated from his views on the treatment of Jews.

There was still a political background to Aquinas's writings, closely paralleling the religious nature of the Middle Ages. By implication, it would seem that Jews escaped the prohibitions against usury because of the passage in Deuteronomy that stated that they could lend to those outside their own tribe. Thomas made no exceptions, however, claiming that Jews were bound in the same way as Christians. Universal brotherhood was advocated as the way around the biblical loophole. The brotherhood of man prohibited usury; all men belonged to the same tribe. This would extend the church's dominion to the Jews and other non-believers as well.

Despite this comment, Jews still practiced usury and their ranks among the moneylenders were growing. Although the history of usury in the Western tradition begins with the comments about it made in the Old Testament, Jews were not the principal moneylenders in Europe until the thirteenth century. By the time of Aquinas, their reputation as bankers had already been established and he knew well that doctrine and practice would diverge. Moneylending would continue since it was necessary as the population of Europe grew. Other passages from the *Summa* are not as unequivocal about the Jews' exemption from Christian law. Jews were permitted to lend money to avoid an even greater evil—that of being forced by necessity to allow Christians to practice usury. Canon law was divided on this issue, but reality prevailed and Christians were "saved" from having to engage in such an odious practice.[61]

Some of Aquinas's straightforward comments on Jewish usurers also can be found in a letter he wrote to the Duchess of Brabant in which he outlined his ideas on the treatment of Jews by a sovereign. Her husband had recently died and had left orders to confiscate the property of Jews in the duchy upon his death. She wrote to Aquinas for assistance in the matter. The results would not please Jews in the slightest. Answering her question about "whether at any time, and if so, when it is permissible to exact tribute of the Jews," he responded that "sovereigns of states may treat their [Jews'] goods as their own property; with the sole proviso that they do not deprive them of all that is necessary to sustain life."[62] This sounded harsh but was logical according to the Aristotelian comments about usurers. Anyone who earned usury from others was not entitled to the riches they accumulated and the wealth became eligible for confiscation. But the confiscation could not leave the usurer penniless any more than it could leave a borrower in bad financial shape. Thomas also was in favor of forcing Jews to make restitution to those from whom they had exacted usury and also favored levying heavy fines upon them when caught in the act. The only solace to Jews in this case was that the same penalties were recommended to all who practiced usury, regardless of creed.

Aquinas was not particularly original on this point but was only following standard practice at the time. One hundred years before, several Cistercian monasteries were built in northern England with funds supplied by a moneylender named Aaron of Lincoln, one of England's wealthiest Jewish financiers. Upon Aaron's death, Henry II kept most of Aaron's lands and fortune intact for himself, but after a loss of a substantial part of his capital Henry found himself with debts inherited from the fortune of £20,000, almost half the Angevin annual revenue.[63] Within several years, under Richard I, a massacre occurred at York where much of the Jewish wealth in northern England was confiscated. By the time of Aquinas, the Edict of Expulsion had been signed by Edward I, who was always short of cash, and the Jews were formally expelled.

On the practical side, all the church pronouncements about usury and other infractions made the job of a confessor difficult. The Fourth Lateran Council in 1215 made at least an annual confession obligatory. What was to be the penance for a usurer since there were apparently many degrees of the sin? In the fourteenth century, after formal confessions became commonplace in church practice, many confessor's manuals began to appear; they were intended to guide priests hearing confessions of penitents. In addition to the usual litany of sins violating one of the commandments, usury also found its way into the manuals as an offense requiring serious penance. One well-known manual, the *Ayenbite of Inwyt*, a Kentish translation of a French manual produced a century earlier, gave priests a thorough grounding in usury so that the proper penance could be prescribed in the confessional. The manual described seven types of usury, conforming to traditional Thomist and Aristotelian categories. One type, however, indicates that compound interest was understood at the time, even if in a rudimentary sense. It also acknowledges the practice of disguising usury by adding it to the debt itself. It read: "What is worse, a creditor will sometimes demand payment several times in the year, to raise the rate of usury, even at each term he receives a gift; and he will often turn the interest into the principal debt."[64] The entire discussion of usury was dominated by the concept of fair price and the various ways by which usury was often exacted by the unscrupulous. One of the most detested types was "that of those who lend a little to their poor neighbors when they are in need, on condition that they shall work for them, and get out of them three pennyworth of work for every penny they have lent."[65] In the confessional at least, the church still held to the Old Testament view of usury as pure exploitation. While appearing coincidental to the development of views on usury, a standard penance for admitting usury proved to be a powerful means of distributing doctrine in the Middle Ages. The *Ayenbite* was only one of hundreds of manuals produced by the church to help provide some standard for confession and repentance. Clearly, usury was on the target list of mortal sins requiring a uniform response, especially since it was a growing practice by Christians as well as others.

Thomas's views on the topic were indicative of the times and not considered unduly harsh. The tribal notion concerning usury still was alive and well. Clergy could not practice usury because, in modern terms, it would have been a conflict of interest to do so against the faithful. Jews did not fit into the scheme of things, so they were begrudgingly allowed to practice usury by secular rulers, most of whom were constantly in need of money for defense. For those among the Christian tribe practicing usury, the church had its remedies, which sovereigns often seized with gusto, although secular law did not proscribe the taking of usury. Because of this incongruity between church and secular law, the church, mainly through Aquinas's writings, elevated usury to a level far above that of a serious but simple mortal sin. It became a violation of natural law as well.

Usury and Natural Law

Other than being roundly condemned, usury did not evolve substantially over the centuries. As a practice, it was simple and prohibitions against it were equally simple, not requiring much sophistication. However, during the early Middle Ages the church made a stronger case that elevated usury above a simple mortal sin onto a level that suggested that it had an aura of universality about it that far exceeded anything the average moneylender ever imagined.

As the church acquired increasing power prior to the fourteenth century, it threw a large blanket over the practice of charging usury in an attempt to curtail its use and exercise power over usurers. By the time Thomas Aquinas wrote his *Summa*, usury had evolved into a transgression against divine law, now equated with natural law. By the late thirteenth century, natural law had come to prohibit usury. According to church theory, the previous biblical and patristic sources already had concluded that it was more than just another corrupt practice like jousting or prostitution. *Ius naturale*, or natural law, prohibited usury, making it a sin against humanity and the church because it represented the interpretation of God's word on Earth.

In the Middle Ages, three types of law were acknowledged—*ius naturale, ius gentium*, and *ius civile*. In addition to natural law, the other two were the law of nations and the civil law. Natural law was the universal embodiment of principles held everywhere; it was law derived from abstract reason. These principles were constant and standard, never changing. The law of nations was law that different nations shared in order to facilitate relations between them, or what would today be called international law. Civil law was the law of a particular state. There was a hierarchy among them, a totem pole that suggested that the law of nations and civil law had to be consonant with the natural law. If that condition could be achieved, it would lead to what was known as harmony or unity in the Middle Ages.

The case for usury being a transgression against natural law was strong but not quite as strong as the prohibitions against murder, incest, theft, and rape, which were normally included among its more egregious violations. The biblical and canonical writings proscribing usury were not quite universal. The prohibition against usury in Deuteronomy was only against Jews practicing it against Jews, not gentiles. In the Nicaean canon and the writings of Leo I, the prohibition was against churchmen practicing it. The *Twelve Tables* allowed interest and many ancient societies had different types of interest rates for different sorts of borrowing. The situation began to change in the ninth century when Charlemagne extended the usury ban to laymen as well as churchmen. Thus, until that time, a case had been made for usury to be a violation of civil law or, at the margin, the law of nations. Until Thomas Aquinas, the violation had not yet reached the status of natural law understood as equal with divine law although it nevertheless was found in most societies.

This can also be seen in the *Institutes* and the *Code* of Justinian. Universally admired and accepted during the Middle Ages, the code had been the source of much Western European law. It was also universally recognized as the greatest source of natural law yet propounded because of its universal and elegant statement of principles.[66] It was the universality of Roman law that made it the best expression of the natural law ever written. Aquinas agreed that it was but only to that point in time. He accepted that part of it dealing with usufructs but noted that the discussion had been accepted only by human law until the time it was written. The *ius civile* always had to bend in the face of divine law once it had been properly interpreted. Divine law—the law of God interpreted by the church and the same as natural law—could not tolerate the distinction that the writers of the code made because it was not comprehensive enough. Tolerating usury in any form was practical on the one hand but impious on the other. As a result, Thomas made a case for usury being against the natural and divine law, although he acknowledged that even the greatest source of natural law seemed to tolerate it under certain circumstances. The natural law did not have to be watertight as long as it was universally accepted.

The process did not begin with Aquinas but with Gratian's *Decretals*. Gratian distinguished between two types of law—natural law and custom. "Natural law is what is contained in the Scriptures and the Gospel," he noted.[67] Natural law had a biblical origin, which dovetailed with the church's position. Since usury was prohibited in the Old Testament and had been incorporated into canon law, there was little doubt that violating it was a crime against the natural law. When Clement V had usury equated with heresy at the Council of Vienne, his position was on solid ground if somewhat extreme. Without the influence of the Templars, perhaps usury would not have been linked with heresy and the Inquisition. But commercial life was prospering during the fourteenth century and the development of banking and the papacy's constant need for funds necessitated a moratorium on blanket condemnations of bankers.

The Thomist interpretation also paralleled developments in Islamic law, which equally prohibited usury. The second book of the Koran contained strong language prohibiting usury, admonitions so clear and emphatic that they had a deep influence on commerce in the Islamic world. It states: "O ye who believe. Devour not usury, doubling and quadrupling (the sum lent)." As one commentator noted, collecting usury was common in the Arab world before the advent of Islam. Samuel Pufendorf, writing centuries later, best described the practice by saying that, despite the Koranic ban, "the Moors borrow money to carry on trade, and allow the creditor half the gain; but if the principal happen to be lost, the debtor refunds that only."[68] But after the teachings of Mohammed were promulgated, the Arab practice changed considerably and usury was prohibited and everyday trading and commerce had to be redefined so that they did not collide with the Koran. This ban on usury generally would help make the universal nature of usury bans stronger, appearing to foster the argument that the ban was indeed included in *ius gentium* and making a strong case for it to be included in *ius naturale*, but it is not clear whether the Islamic position was known to Gratian or Aquinas. Over the centuries, the Islamic attitude toward usury changed remarkably little.

After Aquinas, little needed to be said officially about usury. The topic was only addressed sporadically in the wake of the *Summa*. The strident denunciations of the early Middle Ages and the ancient world became somewhat muted, especially after denying usury was declared heretical. Having attained the status of doctrine enshrined in natural law, usury was no longer on the front burners in church councils. But the untenable position of being able to accuse many businessmen and bankers of heresy and potentially bringing them before the Inquisition would eventually erode the prohibitions against usury and a small portion of the church's authority as well, especially since interest was now being openly taught to prospective business students employing Arabic numerals and the decimal system.

Aquinas's main contribution to the theory and practice of interest was to keep usury on the front burners as an illegal and immoral practice and embed it in the natural rights theory so prevalent in the Middle Ages. Regardless of how much the church importuned against usury and manifest usurers, commercial life proceeded (albeit slowly) in the medieval world and credit facilities developed, despite the warnings and occasional forays against moneylenders of different stripes. The bankers of the Renaissance would have a materially different view of time than the church traditionally expounded. Gradually, time was becoming measured in money. Whether it was being compounded was another question.

Chapter 2

Embracing Shylock

> The necessity of carrying on business with borrowed money became more and more frequent as trade developed during the latter part of the Middle Ages. Thus the Canonists saw themselves forced . . . to invent distinctions between those forms and the "usura," the payment for the mere use of money.
> —Gustav Cassel, 1903

Official attitudes toward usury changed remarkably little in the late Middle Ages and the early years of the Renaissance. It still was considered an execrable sin against humanity although in reality it was being practiced by all and sundry in the commercial revolution in Italy and the rest of Europe. The papacy had become the first financial regulator since usury was under its power, but it exercised that power very selectively, begrudgingly acknowledging interest as necessary for business. Yet with the rising commercialism came discussions about money and usury that were not evident in previous centuries. The revival of learning during the quattrocento opened new dimensions concerning the nature and uses of money and the interpretations were no longer exclusively negative. The sterile concept of money was changing.

As more ideas circulated on interest and usury, it became clear that attitudes were in a state of flux. The use of money carried with it more than one potential sin. In addition to usury, debasement of coin, monopoly, and simony now were included. Devaluation of money by princes and the selling of church offices became the hot topics of the day. Simony would become one of the pivotal issues of the Reformation and while usury remained in the limelight as always, it was not quite the burning issue it had been in the time of Aquinas. Some of the new ideas about money also helped cast light on the earlier usury debate, helping later generations understand the nature of the problem.

An eloquent defense of money came from the Italian writer Bernardo Davanzati in 1588. In an oration delivered at the Academy of Florence, he praised money as "an excellent invention, and an Instrument of doing infinite good; if any makes ill use of it, 'tis not the Thing but the Person that is to be blamed and punished." If money was used for evil purposes, more needed to be known about its intrinsic qualities. One of those qualities was the quantity in circulation. Bankers and politicians realized that being able to count that amount carefully would provide a safeguard against many sovereigns' favorite method of funding the national treasury. Inflation, or what Renaissance writers called debasement, was the prime economic topic of the period. The supply of money in a principality was understood to be static until the Renaissance. Since each Italian principality had its own money, this was not a primitive notion but one existing in a very real but limited universe. When gold and silver from the Americas found their way into Europe, prices began to rise as Spain imported more from its trading partners, who in turn raised prices as a result. Davanzati asked, "If that same quantity of Silver be at present in 109 pieces, which used before to be in a hundred only, must not 109 be now paid for that which formerly cost but a hundred?"[1]

In the early years of the Roman Empire, when divine law had a profound impact on civil life, usury was considered a violation of the law because only God had the ability to tinker with time, not man. When one man charged another usury, he was usurping a power reserved only for the almighty. But the Renaissance notion that the supply of money was linked to the amount of goods produced in society demonstrated that an increase in the amount of goods required more money. Without the equivalent increase, what later became known as inflation would be created. Before the importation of gold and silver from the Americas, prices were assumed to be more stable unless a sovereign undertook currency debasement, a somewhat frequent occurrence.

While attitudes toward excessive interest remained remarkably constant through the late Middle Ages, they nevertheless were being paid lip service while business continued to expand. Fibonacci's discussion of compound interest in his *Book of the Abacus* serves as something of a crucible in the history of finance because it was a reminder that interest was discussed and calculated in relatively sophisticated terms. Although usury was railed against by ancients and medievals alike, it was practiced widely and became one of the great cultural paradoxes of the ancient and medieval worlds. To paraphrase the popular religious phrase, man could not serve two masters.

In theory, his allegiance was owed to the church, not a creditor, especially if the latter was a Jew or from another unpopular lender.

One fact about medieval and ancient discussions of interest was that no stated rate of interest was ever discussed, only the number of units to be paid back. While modern interest is discussed by the rate charged and the frequency of compounding, the concept appears to have been known to early mathematicians or bankers but not clearly mentioned. Returning to Fibonacci's original problem, one unit invested at 14.355 percent interest compounded semi-annually over a five-year period results in a future value of 2 units. Compounding was never mentioned in his discussion nor was the rate of interest. Another question is whether the rate of 14.355 percent was usurious, although that is cleverly sidestepped by the omission. While the usury debate is easier when the rate is stated in percentage terms, it is much more difficult when interest is stated in terms of the desired outcome on the part of the lender. Paraphrasing his example, if I lend a unit and want two units in return in a five-year period, is that usury? The only method the medieval churchmen and bankers had to solve the problem was to admit that it was more demanding than, say, one and a half units in return. Without using percentage rates of interest, the problem remains in limbo. Why would one borrower receive the 14 percent rate while the other a lesser one? Credit risk was not discussed by writers so the whole process seems subjective at best. Risk in the Middle Ages was assessed by judging the borrower's character or familiarity to the lender. Whoever was charged more naturally would cry usury at the apparent indignity.

If interest was charged by a professional lender, or "manifest usurer," the medieval answer was that the rate was usurious regardless of the implied rate. In contrast, if it was a rate of return on a profitable partnership venture, the answer was not as clear. Who paid the return? If it was extracted by lending to another, then usury was involved. If it came from a maritime venture where the exchange of goods was involved in a profitable business transaction, the water was murkier because it was a more complicated transaction and would involve more scrutiny to determine its moral qualities. Transactions of that sort never came under close scrutiny by church authorities unless they became a matter of litigation. Even then, the parties involved had to be careful not to appear to have violated church law.

But it would be unreasonable to assume that business was conducted for more than two thousand years without some idea of credit risk. Perhaps the best example is still the first. Deuteronomy states that Jews could not charge other Jews interest, only non-Jews. A contemporary way of reading that passage suggests that non-Jews were considered more risky to lend to than members of one's own tribe, so usury was permitted. Jews all fell under the same legal codes while non-Jews did not. In a tribal society, the implication was that non-members had to be charged a fee for what would be considered largesse within the tribe itself.

Usury therefore could be a subjective charge. If a standard concept of credit risk was lacking and stated rates of interest had not yet been introduced, then one man paying two units could claim usury if another paid only one and a half. A simple case of inequitable treatment could be made in Aristotelian terms since justice apparently had not been served. When compound interest entered, the case for usury became even more dramatic because it was well understood that interest paid more frequently was even more unjust. The idea of grossing up a compound yield was unknown in percentage terms. It would not be until a more standard set of interest rate calculations was introduced that usury would become more clearly understood not as simply interest alone but compound interest expressed in frequency terms. And even when that sort of progress had been made, the medieval notions about interest still would linger well into the nineteenth century.

Money was attracting attention as a necessary tool of the state in the late Middle Ages. While this may seem somewhat obvious, it was only when money began to be understood as a legitimate method of facilitating trade that it could be universally accepted and interest understood as a method of facilitating business. During the period 600–1,000 A.D., when many money economies collapsed after the decline of Rome, a return to a barter system made many discussions of usury in money terms superfluous. But late medieval writers did not write discourses on money per se; instead they wrote about its place in the state. One of the favorite metaphors used was its role in the *body politic*. Gradually, the state was becoming understood as an organic creation, not simply a construct of laws designed to rule. The state was a live organism with government as its head and the masses as its body. Money was seen as its blood. This idea was originally expounded by Marsilius of Padua and Nicholas of Oresme in the fourteenth century. While neither was an economic thinker in the modern sense of the word, their organic theories of the state did prompt the notion that money was its life blood. The French Estates General adopted the notion by 1485, stating that "Money is in the body politic what blood is in the human body."[2]

The idea of likening money to the blood of the state was best expressed by Bernardo Davanzati. In his speech before the Academy of Florence in

1588, he discussed the origin and use of money, stating that "it may easily be conceived that every state must have a quantity of money, as every body a quantity of Blood to circulate therein."[3] He also noted that the quantity should not be held only by the rich for risk of cutting off the circulation to the lower classes. And neither should the coins in circulation be debased by monarchs constantly in need of revenue. A healthy body politic needed all of its parts working well to avoid sickness. Davanzati's remarks shed light upon economic thinking at the time, as simple as it may have sounded. His main concern in the address was the inflation caused by gold and silver in the decades following the Spanish discoveries in the Americas. Rising prices presented a problem to the church and its attitude toward usury. If prices rose, would interest follow? What would then become of the usury prohibitions if the economic climate created changes because of exploration not experienced before?

Double Entendre

The activities of princes also played a crucial role in the development of usury in the late Middle Ages and the early Renaissance. In addition to subjugating the papacy, Philippe the Fair also became one of the best-known debasers of currency. Besides being poor credit risks, kings and princes could not be trusted with preserving the value of money in the royal coffers. Usury slowly was entering a new phase that would take the bite out of its sinfulness.

Nicholas of Oresme, a prominent French churchman of the fourteenth century, stated in his *Treatise on the First Invention of Money* (circa 1360) that usury was only the second worst thing that could be done with money. The first was altering it, not by physically changing or forging its value but by debasing it or replacing it with other currencies as some medieval monarchs had done. Monarchs and princes often were among the worst enemies of value when discussing the concept of money. In addition to expelling Jews from their domains, they often debased money, rendering it worthless and impoverishing their subjects, who were often heavily taxed at the same time. While Jews and the Templars often were the bogeymen in the history of medieval usury and banking, monarchs were usually the instigating force behind most monetary problems.

The Fifth Lateran Council, held between 1512 and 1517, was the last church council to discuss usury, almost as if nothing was left to say about the practice in church doctrine. Specifically, it addressed the *montes*, which by the late fifteenth century had become highly popular in lending to the poor despite earlier church protests. The council addressed the charge that the state-run organizations were charging interest, doing harm to the poor whom they served in the process. Somewhat surprisingly, the council took a liberal view of the benefits the *montes* provided, concluding that they were an asset to the church and the poor. "They ought not to be condemned in any way. Rather such a type of lending is meritorious and should be praised and approved. It certainly should not be considered usurious," the council concluded.[4] But the reasons behind this support were purely practical rather than doctrinal and indicate that centuries of commercial development finally were having a positive effect on the church. Calling them credit organizations, the council concluded that usury was not an issue as long as the interest paid was being used to cover the costs of lending by the *montes* and not causing the borrowers harm. In contemporary terms, the *montes* were considered not-for-profit institutions, but at the time they operated as low-interest pawnbrokers. This was one of the early instances where financial practice forced a regulatory body to admit that a previously forbidden practice had become common de facto practice.

One of the *montes* located in Siena, today known as Banca Monte dei Paschi de Siena, was founded in 1472 in keeping with the tradition of lending to the poor. Twenty years later, it stepped outside its original mandate by making a loan to Christopher Columbus for his voyage of 1492 and lost the money it lent to him. It was not clear what made the pawnbroker overstep its bounds at the time, but the demand for banking services, and higher rates of return, quickly affected the *montes* in the northern Italian city-states.

The increased interest in mathematics and learning led to advances in the development and sophistication of commercial practices. Fibonacci's writings were often used in trade schools in Italy, but many commercial practices were not yet standard. That began to change in the late fifteenth century with the publication of a mathematical work that was to have the most profound change on the way business had been conducted since the Roman Empire. As with many profound business changes, the process began simply.

The publication of the first acknowledged accounting method in the late fifteenth century was a milestone in business history. For the first time, accounts could be presented in a uniform and integrated manner, reflecting a more accurate picture of costs and profits. Although the publication of the double-entry method of accounting (where all bookkeeping entries must have corresponding debits and/or credits) had a simple purpose, the idea originally was presented by a mathematician rather than a manual writer or a businessman. While a simple idea, it evolved along with math theory and was considered highly innovative at the time because it opened the most successful accounting practices to the general merchant classes.

The first formal exposition of double-entry bookkeeping was published by Luca Pacioli, an Italian mathematician, in 1494. He was born in 1445 and educated at the University of Padua. His first job was as the tutor to the children of the wealthy Venetian merchant Antonio Rompiasi. In addition to teaching, he also helped his employer in his business, gaining valuable insight into everyday commercial affairs. After leaving his employment, Pacioli entered the Franciscan order as a friar and began teaching at several universities, most notably at the University of Perugia. In 1494, he published his first major work, the *Summa de Aritmetica, Geometria, Proportioni, et Proportionalita.* The book was written in Italian rather than Latin so that its readers would be businessmen. The *Book of the Abacus* of Fibonacci was a strong influence on Pacioli's work, which also helped to preserve some of the earlier work for posterity.

Pacioli devoted a section to the description of the Venetian system of accounting that he used previously. As he stated, "This treatise will adopt the system used in Venice, which is certainly to be recommended above all the others." He discussed how to calculate a firm's profitability, earning him the laurels in the accounting community of the future. The work was far from purely practical, however. Throughout the text, Pacioli continually discussed profits and the need to believe in God, so his writings on the subject were not purely secular. This was no doubt done to avoid thornier questions about usury and its role in profits. Unlike later treatises on interest and accounting, Pacioli avoided usury in his writings. He was keen on describing the energy businessmen need in order to be profitable, an example of a fifteenth-century management book. His affinity to businessmen was clear when he wrote, "In the great republics, nothing was considered superior to the word of the good merchant, and oaths were taken on the word of a good merchant."[5]

Following Pacioli, French commercial practices during the sixteenth century also were aided by the proliferation of commercial texts, designed to aid the businessman and his apprentices in the ways of finance. Despite the official church position, ten of fourteen commercial "arithmetics," as these manuals were known, aided readers in computing interest. Disguising the term interest as profit or merit, the manuals also discussed compound interest, meaning the amount charged at the end of the loan's term along with the repayment of principal at redemption. Compound interest was referred to as "Judaic interest" by some, indicating that a good Christian would not charge his fellows on a compound basis. Regardless of interpretation, however, the method for calculating was standard; it attempted to determine how much profit could be made without referring to the stated rate of interest. One example from 1565 asked: "A man has put 1,000 livres at profit, which at the end of six months have earned him 350 livres. He would like to know how much he would earn in 11 months if he lent 4,500 livres at the same profit."[6] (The answer is the 4,500 livres plus 2,887 livres interest for a total of 7,387 livres). Regardless of the religion of the lender, the rate was usurious; 70 percent per annum simple interest in this example. But stated as a profitable return, it was commendable.

Although the introduction of double-entry bookkeeping traditionally is attributed to Pacioli, the method had been used by businessmen outside Italy in one form or other for centuries. The practice was mentioned one hundred years before Pacioli by Chaucer. In the *Canterbury Tales*, a monk named Sir John borrows a sum of money from a merchant, who is exuberant about the loan. The monk made restitution but in a circuitous manner, through the merchant's wife. From the "Shipman's Tale":

You were so kind to me the other day,
Lending me money; all I have to say
Is many, many thanks! God give you life!
But I returned the money to your wife
—The sum you lent—and put it in your till
At home. She'll know about it all, she will,
For it was all arranged by double entry.[7]

Clearly, Chaucer had tongue in cheek when writing this, but he did show that the term was used, although he turned it into a double entendre. More to the point, during Chaucer's time, borrowers and lenders often kept a tally stick, which was broken in half when a loan was incurred and put back together again when the loan was finally paid off. That could account for the concept of double entry used by the Monk here, but Pacioli's use of the term is a more sophisticated version of the tally stick, used extensively by the exchequer in England to keep a tab on taxes due.

Pacioli later went to work for Ludovico Sforza, the Duke of Milan, at what was quickly becoming the most erudite and sophisticated court in

Europe. At Milan, he met Leonardo da Vinci and the two quickly became friends and collaborators. In 1509, he published his *Divina Proportione,* three books that investigated the "golden ratio." The work incorporated original ideas of Euclid and was illustrated by Leonardo. The golden ratio gained wide acceptance during the Renaissance as a tool for architecture and design and was keenly endorsed by da Vinci. Closer to business practices, it also could be found in a Fibonacci sequence of numbers. Eventually, Pacioli returned to his hometown, where he died in 1517. Throughout his career, he remained a synthesizer, not contributing as much original work to mathematics as others but providing better explanations than many of his predecessors and contemporaries. The collaboration with Leonardo is one example, although he remains best known in business for his technical description of double-entry bookkeeping.

Banking was developing rapidly in Italy as a result of these innovations since the collapse of the Siena banking houses, demonstrating yet again that dealing with money was growing in popularity even if it was sinful. The Medici opened branches of their Florentine bank in many Italian cities as well as in London, Bruges, and Geneva, helping pave the way for indigenous institutions to appear in those places at a later date. And many writers began offering theories about how to understand the role of money in society. Although their ideas were very basic, they helped cast some much needed light on the vehemence with which usury had been discussed since the days of the Roman Republic.

Origins of Modern Insurance and Annuities

Commercial developments such as the growing use of bills of exchange certainly helped international trading transactions, but endemic risks still persisted, making some business transactions extremely risky. One of the riskiest was shipping, especially between international ports. When coupled with church prohibitions against usury, these risks had far reaching effects on commercial activity. Usury had especially profound effects on trade through marine partnerships.

Shipping activity traditionally was conducted through contracts binding the financiers of shipping ventures with those actually conducting the shipping itself. If usury practically collided with contractual partnership arrangements then economic development would be impaired. The longer, and riskier, the maritime venture the less probable it was that the venture would be undertaken for fear of financial ruin on the part of the parties involved. And failure of all parties involved would expose the partners to potential charges of usury.

Until the early fourteenth century, partnerships remained the traditional means of sharing risk in business adventures. What later would be known as insurance had not yet made its appearance in European commercial practice, although its need was becoming more and more urgent. Ironically, the first insurance contracts acknowledged that usury bans were a problem and purposely used vague, ambivalent language to structure a partnership arrangement that effectively circumvented the paying of interest.

In order to keep within the ban on usury, marine contracts, or *mutuum nauticum*, usually called for a partnership between creditor and debtor, or banker and shipper. These practices were in keeping with the common collusive practices among borrowers and lenders to avoid usury. If a contract was broken in some way, the debtor was responsible, but the language of these contracts was constructed so that there was no specific mention of responsibility in the event that there was *no* occurrence. Therefore the loan could be paid in silence, not violating usury law as a result. Contracts discovered dating from 1343 and 1347 in Italy attest to this purposeful ambiguity of language.[8]

This built-in loophole to the contracts inadvertently provided for one of the early forms of financial innovation and led to the development of the insurance contract. It would also pave the way for the transoceanic explorations that would begin in the next century. The loophole seems to have been known in the thirteenth century. Aquinas previously stated, "I answer that it is wholly sinful to practice fraud for the express purpose of selling a thing for more than its just price, inasmuch as a man deceives his neighbor to his loss."[9] Citing Cicero, he declared that deception should be eliminated from contracts and that prices in them should not be bid up or down. Illegal contracts promoting fraud were one matter, but the idea of avoiding the church's laws concerning usury had to be much more flexible. But viable insurance contracts would not have evolved without partners recognizing that they had equal stakes in ventures and could not simply act as agents as Aquinas suggested.

Ironically, one financial product that enjoyed a renewed popularity in the Middle Ages escaped the usury discussion, mainly because of its importance politically. Annuities became increasingly popular as a method of raising money, but since the borrowers were not the poor annuities stood a much better chance of gaining widespread acceptance. Annuities escaped the usury prohibitions for two reasons: they were established financial contracts and satisfied the Roman legal definitions of usufruct.

The idea of a loan repaid as a fixed payment over a specific number of years is one of the oldest, if not the oldest, financial product in history. There is evidence of annuities being paid in ancient Assyria, Babylon, and Egypt and the practice continued well into the Roman Empire and the Middle Ages in Europe. A borrower, usually a city-state, would borrow a lump sum from a lender and agree contractually to repay the loan at a specific rate over a set number of years, or for the lender's life. The loan was supported by the revenues of the borrower, usually the harvest of tillable land, taxes, or fees that it charged. It was not an example of lending to the poor or for consumptive purposes. Since the revenue stream was a product of the fruits of the property secured it fulfilled the law of usufruct. In Justinian's *Institutes*, usufruct of money was perfectly legal: "If a usufruct of money be given by legacy, that money, on being delivered to the legatee, becomes his property, though he has to give security to the heir that he will repay an equivalent sum on his dying or undergoing a loss of status."[10]

Annuities became a common method of secured borrowing. The Italian city-states used them to raise money for various purposes, Henry I of England used one to raise an army, and some German principalities banned them because they were too lucrative for the bankers who arranged them. In contemporary terms, the older form of annuities was actually a series of payments similar to the interest on a revenue bond. In the Middle Ages, their most common purpose was to finance wars. Although interest was frowned upon because of its exploitative nature, mortgaging the realm or the castle was considered an acceptable way of raising an army, especially if it was to do God's work.

The Romans produced financial tables apparently designed to help the payers of annuities determine how many payments they would have to make to their lenders depending upon their ages. The best-known table was one produced by Ulpian around 225 A.D. It appears to be a life expectancy table and it is assumed that it was used to determine a person's life span using sixty years as a benchmark. It is assumed that the table had something to do with annuities paid by the empire to former members of the legions, some of whom retired in their late forties and were supported by Rome. But the calculations had their own long life span, as they were still being used in the nineteenth century by the Tuscan government in northern Italy for official purposes.[11]

The Rise of the Medici Bank

While banking practices were well established in Europe at the beginning of the fifteenth century, banking organizations remained balkanized. Bills of exchange and money-lending facilities were well entrenched because they circumvented the bans on usury. Bankers evolved from the merchant classes and many remained merchant bankers, a term that survives today. While banking was widespread, it was dominated by the Italians, who remained Europe's best-known and skillful financiers.

After the fall of the Templars, banking was in the hands of small Italian merchant banking families that supplied the papacy, Europe's largest and most complex institution, with the funds it continuously demanded. Many of the smaller banking houses did not survive the advent of the fifteenth century intact, however. They were too small to survive political and social upheavals such as a regime change or Europe's major catastrophe in the mid-fourteenth century—the Black Death. The plague had severe repercussions on the availability of credit in Europe. It, together with Edward III's actions during the Hundred Years' War with France, altered banking practices for over a century. In Florence alone, over eighty banks existed in 1338. By 1350, the number had dropped to fifty-seven. The original eighty still had not returned by the end of the century.[12]

Many of the Italian banking houses established overseas branches and had operations in England and other locations scattered throughout Western Europe. They also established themselves in the Levant (Middle East), retracing the steps of the Templars two hundred years before. But the Bonsignori banking house in Siena, the center of Italian banking at the time, failed in 1298 and the center of financial power shifted to Florence. There, three Lombard banking families dominated the business—the Peruzzi, the Bardi, and the Acciaiouli. The Bardi were particularly wealthy, reputedly having assets equal to the annual income of Edward III of England, who was a major customer. All three established offices abroad, including London. But paying interest on deposits and lending at higher rates was not a main source of revenue because of the ban on usury. They, like their successors, made most of their profits on what today what is known as "fee banking." Rather than lend at higher rates than those paid for deposits (spread banking), fee banking involved charging a flat fee for a foreign exchange operation, bills of exchange, or gold transactions rather than appear to be charging usury. The practice was well established and accepted by Rome, which had little choice but to pay the fees associated with its various transactions since the papacy's need for money was continuous. The Holy See received revenues from a variety of sources and needed exchange facilities to convert revenue or make subsidies to its various constituents.

One of those sources was the Jewish banking community that had resided in Italy since the thirteenth century, mostly in Rome and the other large cities. The bankers had enjoyed the protection of the papacy over the years, but the relationship was not always comfortable. Nevertheless, the Jewish bankers felt secure enough lobby the Holy See on occasion when its vested interests in the community were threatened. The relationship was most amicable when Martin V was pope from 1417 to 1431 despite the anti-Jewish fervor of the Franciscans and the Inquisition.[13]

While the banking houses did good business with the Vatican, the same could not be said about their relations with some notorious sovereign borrowers. Both the Bardi and the Peruzzi were forced into bankruptcy because of their dealings with Edward III of England during the course of the Hundred Years' War with France. Their wealth made them reputable bankers but also vulnerable at the same time. In order to pursue his military campaigns against the French over the disputed French throne, Edward sought any source of funds that would provide him with more ammunition against his enemies. He forbade the export of England's major product—wool—to its main buyers, the Flemish cloth makers who relied upon it as the main source of their own trade. In 1336, he began using sacks of wool produced in England as collateral for loans that he intended to use in the war. He also attempted to grant wealthy English wool producers a monopoly in the trade in exchange for financial considerations. None of the plans worked out successfully and Edward found himself in the red by about £70,000. Soon, it was clear that his options were running out and that the only avenue left open was the one used by monarchs many times before.

After the two Italian banking houses had supported his administration for over a decade, Edward finally defaulted on their loans in 1346. At the time, he owed approximately £50,000 to the Bardi and an additional £20,000 to the Peruzzi, enormous sums at the time, equivalent to millions of ducats in Italy.[14] The cost of fighting the Hundred Years' War with France convinced Edward that the Italians were expendable and after imprisoning representatives of both banks in the Tower of London, he expelled them from England, ending their unprofitable saga. When the Florentine "big three" had disappeared by the end of the fourteenth century, a gaping need appeared in the banking business, which was quickly filled by one of Florence's best-known families.

In 1397, the Medici bank was established in Florence by Giovanni di Bicci de Medici. Giovanni was a Roman banker who moved his operations north to Florence. The banking company was later operated by his much better known heirs, Cosimo and Lorenzo. Although the bank existed for almost one hundred years, it failed along with the family political fortunes in 1494. But during that relatively short period of time, the Medici bank became the largest institution of its type. It was able to do business successfully with the papacy and many influential merchants in Europe, with a well-established branch network in Italy and elsewhere on the Continent. Clearly a moneylender, it operated in much the same manner as its successful predecessors while not appearing to charge usury. Rather than make loans outright, the Medici, as the Templars, the Bardi, and the Bonsignori before them, developed an elaborate network for bills of exchange that disguised interest as "profit and loss." The amount of interest charged was factored into the costs of the bills, thus avoiding any charge of usury.

By following this established pattern, the Medici banks appeared not to be making loans but rather acting as fee bankers. They also acted as pawnbrokers on occasion, although not to poor individuals desperately in need of cash. Giovanni di Bicci made a loan to the original Pope John XXIII (an antipope) and held the pope's bejeweled miter as collateral.[15] It was later claimed by his successor, Martin V, also a good client of the family bank. While strenuously avoiding usury, the Medici were not able to avoid the scrutiny of Florentine politics, which viewed the family's great wealth with a combination of suspicion and awe. The Medici financial power would last only as long as the prevailing political power permitted. By the fifteenth century, financial and political connections to the papacy were not enough to secure safety.

During the Renaissance, Italian bankers made lavish donations to the church, mainly for the restoration or building of churches and cathedrals. The largesse came mainly from a desire to ward off accusations of usury. Art and architecture benefited greatly from the church's usury doctrines, although the admitted reason for the gifts was for the greater glory of God and the church. Cosimo de Medici paid for the restoration of a monastery in return for a papal bull absolving him of past sins in a clear attempt to absolve himself and his heirs of any potential charge of usury.[16] Similar donations occurred throughout Italy during the fifteenth century, providing impetus for the building and art boom of the Renaissance. Since Notre Dame in Paris had been built with donations of moneylenders, the church wisely recognized where it could obtain financing for higher purpose.

The network of Italian bankers that developed during the late Middle Ages and the Renaissance led to the development of a money market in Europe. Bills of exchange were used extensively in cross-border trading and the bills were presented for payment along with a need for foreign exchange transactions between buyers and sellers. The foreign exchange side of the deals required bankers to be adept at exchange and a market quickly developed around these instruments. Most of the major Italian urban centers were banking centers along with Bruges and London and they quickly became known as money markets. Rome was a special case because the Roman Curia, the administrative arm of the church, was the major client of bankers, and the Medici among others assigned bankers to the Curia who moved with the pope on his travels, usually within Italy.[17] If a banker could not be mobile then he could not do business with the papacy.

Despite its success, the Medici bank did not have a long life. The bank disappeared in 1494 after thirty years of poor financial performance. After the death of Cosimo de Medici in 1464, the family (and Florence) was ruled by his son Piero de Medici until 1469 and then by his grandson Lorenzo until 1494. The bank's misfortunes were caused by a severe economic slowdown, the worst it and Florence had suffered since the Black Death took its toll a century before. Between 1422 and 1470, the number of banks doing international business in Florence fell from seventy-two to thirty-three. By 1494, only six survived.[18] Many of the firms with which the bank did business failed during the slowdown and neither Piero nor his son was up to the task of reviving its fortunes. The bank reached the height of its short-lived powers under Cosimo, although Lorenzo, dubbed Lorenzo the Magnificent, was the best known of the Medicis politically. But none of the successors was properly trained in banking and misused the bank's considerable powers to make more enemies than friends.

Adding to the commercial problems of the time was a change in the political climate in Florence. In the early 1490s, the city was dominated by the hellfire and brimstone preacher Giorlamo Savanarola. The radical priest preached a simple and effective no-nonsense form of Catholicism that predated the Reformation by twenty-five years. Savanarola had little use for bankers and the financial shenanigans of the papacy and Florence fell under his spell in the later days of Medici rule. The simple Christianity he preached appealed to many in Florence due to the poor economic climate. And he would have nothing to do with the Medicis either, eschewing them for prayer and his own type of firebrand preaching. Finally, when he was at death's door, Lorenzo called for Savanarola. The priest could not deny a dying man, and Lorenzo made peace before he died. Perhaps he was still mindful of trying to clean the slate before death, as so many bankers before him had done.

Lorenzo was succeeded by his son Piero. During his short rule, the Medici were expelled from Florence and had to wait almost eighteen years before returning. Faced with an invading French army led by the young king, Charles VIII, Piero fled Florence in 1494 rather than submit. The family's assets were seized and the bank dissolved. After almost a century of success, the most successful banking network Europe had yet seen was gone. But the model was not forgotten. Many northern European states realized that they could not thrive when their bankers were foreigners. As a result, the lack of credit facilities led many small merchants in Holland and England to begin advancing loans to customers, getting them into the usury business. The results would be mixed, but the ball finally had begun rolling toward the development of rudimentary national banking systems.

Changing Tides

The Renaissance spirit led to further questioning of the old ideas of money and usury. In the past, Scholastics and other writers were happy to argue salient points about doctrine with others but usually managed to do so within the confines of accepted argumentative boundaries. That began to change publicly during the sixteenth century when the boundaries began to crumble.

After Luther pinned his theses to the door of Wittenberg cathedral in 1517, attitudes toward interest and usury began to change. The pace of change was slow, however, demonstrating that the long history of usury was imprinted indelibly on churchmen's minds and would not give way easily. The usury conversation soon was due to become more vocal and rude. Luther resembled the church fathers in his discussion of usury, but those who inherited his reforming zeal did not. The now familiar thesis of Max Weber that the Reformation bore the seeds of modern capitalism was proved correct, but attributing the birth of the economic phenomenon to the mid-sixteenth century was still a stretch of the imagination. The origins could be seen in the writings of the Protestant reformers but so too could the lingering hangover of past centuries.

Because of the break with Rome, the way was paved for reformers to question the validity of banning all interest. Both Luther and Calvin were concerned more with what they saw as abuses within the church such as simony but still were attracted to the usury debate because it was clear that interest was an integral part of commercial and religious life. Luther did not condone interest without qualification, however. In fact, his position was more that of a traditionalist than a reformer. In a tract he wrote on usury, he adopted the traditional Deuteronomic position and also subscribed to Aristotle's notion that money was sterile. In order to be tolerated, interest would have to be used for productive purposes. The debtor had to pledge collateral that could be used to help pay off the loan. The debtor also had to be allowed to dictate terms of repayment. If these conditions could be met, then a low rate of nominal interest from 5 to 7 percent could be charged justifiably.

While these conditions were commensurate with the Christian notions of justice and equity, they were not necessarily at the heart of capitalism. Early capitalism did not find a champion in Luther, only a begrudging acknowledgment. In an illustration on the title page on one of his tracts on the subject, a peasant was depicted returning a goose he had borrowed along with the eggs it had laid, suggesting that a lending agreement of some type was in force.[19] The question raised by this illustration was why the peasant borrowed the goose in the first place if he returned all the eggs to the lender. The assumption was that he returned the goose with the eggs it laid because that was the full value of the goose for the time it was borrowed. Presumably, no interest was charged on the goose itself. Max Weber called Luther's numerous statements against usury "from a capitalistic view point, definitely backward."[20]

In an early pamphlet, anonymously written in 1521, the contemporary German business view of usury was demonstrated, showing both sides of the debate in everyday language. In a conversation between a burgher and a peasant, the burgher explains to the peasant how he lends, demanding collateral, and how he seizes the property if the borrower defaults. The peasant replies that he thought only Jews practiced usury. The burgher quickly sets him straight. "Usury? Who is talking about usury? Nobody here practices usury. What the debtor pays is interest. Interest, not usury." After the peasant objects, the burgher and a priest who has joined the discussion make the point again, more emphatically. The peasant was equally emphatic in his reply. "Interest indeed. You baptize two children . . . Now you ask me what are the two, I answer: they are children. It's the same with lending money at a profit. Baptize it as interest or anything else, it's still usury whether you or the Jews do it."²¹ Clearly, both the burgher and the priest are accused of lending money at usury.

Calvin, on the other hand, was more liberal than Luther and espoused the ethic that Max Weber would proclaim to be at the heart of capitalism. He rejected the Aristotelian notions about sterile money and accepted the idea that receiving interest could be productive if it were invested in income-producing land. He gave the following example, replete with an implicit rejection of usury as being against natural law:

> A rich man, *A*, well endowed with landed property and other
> income is short of ready money. Another man, *B*, is not as rich as *A*
> but has an abundance of liquid money. *A* asks *B* for a loan of money.
> *B* could easily buy the land for himself or he could have the land
> bought with money hypothecated [mortgaged] to him until the debt
> is repaid. Suppose instead of that he contents himself with the
> interest, the fruit of his money, is that to be condemned when the
> harsher contract is reckoned fair? That would be nothing else than
> playing with God, a child's game.²²

In other words, the loan is the easier way to achieve the end, so why should interest be condemned when mortgaging off the land would be more troublesome and have more potential serious consequences. The ancient notion of tinkering with God's gift of time also is alive and well in this passage but is no longer considered a transgression as it was in the Middle Ages.

Unlike Luther, Calvin broke with the Deuteronomic position. In a reply to an inquiry about interest, he wrote, "If we wholly condemn usury, we impose tighter fetters on the conscience than God himself." He considered the ban prohibiting Jews from lending at usury to other Jews a matter of ancient Jewish policy rather than a universal spiritual law.²³ While he affirmed that times had changed and that usury now had to be acknowledged, the golden rule must be acknowledged at the same time. When charging interest, the lender had to do to the borrower as he would have had done to himself. In other words, charge a reasonable rate that would do no harm to the borrower. On this point, the two reformers agreed.

Calvinists interpreted this acceptance of reasonable interest begrudgingly. In the Netherlands, Lombard bankers who charged high rates of interest, around 30 percent, were refused communion and their wives were asked to save their husbands from sin. Many of the reformed churches refused donations from bankers under any circumstances, claiming the funds were tainted. Yet reformed Christianity made a valuable point. Usury was high interest for consumption loans. The valid charging of usury involved interest on a productive loan where the borrower made a profit with the lender's capital.[24] This was the essential concession made by the reformers that produced the spirit of capitalism.

The period around 1545 witnessed an intense political debate over the nature of usury that would have legislative consequences in England. The Protestant break with Rome would have practical applications in business. Encouraged by the break, the English parliament tackled the issue of usury at the behest of Henry VIII. It took several measures to help commerce develop and bring some sense to the usury debate. A parliamentary act of 1545 established 10 percent as the legal rate of interest during his reign. Anyone charging more was to be fined treble the interest.

The statute of 1545 supplanted the common law notions of usury and helped define it for future generations in Britain. The moral arguments against it were strong, but the clear law helped reduce much of the background noise that had surrounded the issue since the early Middle Ages. But the act originally was short-lived and was replaced by another act in 1552, which rescinded the 10 percent rate and made interest illegal again during the reign of Edward VI. After an uncomfortable hiatus, the 10 percent rate was restored by the Act of 1571, which also stated that all contracts calling for more than the legal rate were rendered null and void. The teachings of Calvin could be heard in the discussion. During the debate on restoring legal interest, one member of Parliament noted that although he personally thought usury a sin, "yet it was to be punished here on earth according to the good or bad, or according to the greater or less hurt which growth thereby." A colleague put it more succinctly: "God did not absolutely forbid usury, which surely as if it had been utterly ill, he would have done."[25]

The new law prompted many court cases in England testing the new usury limits. The jurist Sir Edward Coke sat for some of these cases and commented, "To them that lend money my caveat is, that neither directly or indirectly, by art or cunning invention, they take above ten in the hundred, for they that seek by sleight to creep out of these statutes, will deceive themselves, and repent in the end."[26] However, some lenders were able to skirt the statutes and collect more by arranging for repayment on a delayed basis.

In the case of the Tudors, debasement was also an issue alongside that of usury. Henry had debased the pound of its sterling content while at the same time attempting to limit interest rates. Allowing rates exceeding the official limit would undermine the debasement policy, upsetting early monetary policy. Henry followed in many medieval sovereigns' footsteps in this respect, although the limit on usury ceilings is usually hailed as a step in the direction of justice rather than bowing to bankers and moneylenders. Debasement was the common method used for creating more money, but Henry did not have to go into debt personally as some of his predecessors had done.

The new law reestablished usury as legal, with limits. Anyone lending at less than 10 percent was also to be penalized by being required to forfeit the smaller amount. But in all cases, the 10 percent rate still was not stated in the modern sense; 10 percent was "ten pound in the hundred," not its Latin equivalent of 10 percent (in full, per centum). In any event, the law brought some revenue to the crown. In 1578, a commission reported that some £6,600 was due to the crown in fines from offenders.[27] Informers also did well, collecting their portion of the fines as fees for disclosing usurers since it was common practice to compensate them for information.

Since the Plantagenets, sumptuary laws often were passed in England, dictating dress and possession of fine goods ordinarily used only by nobility. Several were passed during the reigns of Edward I and Edward III. Another was passed during Elizabeth's reign in 1574 and is noteworthy because of the comment made by the queen when delivering the proclamation. She said, in part, that many frivolous people "and others seeking by show of apparel to be esteemed as gentlemen, who, allured by the vain show of those things, do not only consume themselves, their goods, and lands which their parents left unto them, but also run into such debts and shifts as they cannot live out of danger of laws without attempting unlawful acts, whereby they are not any ways serviceable to their country as otherwise they might be."[28] Her concerns would be echoed time and again by many at court and by commentators, including Adam Smith two hundred years later.

One lender caught in the middle of the sixteenth-century usury conundrum was John Shakespeare, the father of the playwright. A wool trader, he also dabbled in lending, as did many small merchants in England at the time. The Bard therefore had some firsthand experience with the practice before writing *The Merchant of Venice*. His father's experience with lending was uncomfortable, as he had been accused of usury on several occasions and brought to court at least once. In 1570 John, from Stratford-upon-Avon, was accused by two informants of usury. In one case, he exacted interest of 20 percent for a loan made in 1569 (£20 on a loan of £100) and in the other 25 percent (£20 on a loan of £80). In both cases, he was charged with usury under the Act of 1552, in which usury of any sort clearly was illegal. A year later, the charges would still have been valid because the rate was higher than the 10 percent mandated by the Act of 1571. Informants in the Tudor era regularly hoped to receive about one half the penalties charged to the miscreants when usury was successfully proved in court. Shakespeare, however, only went to court in one of the two cases and settled the claim without a trial.[29]

His son's account of interest has become much better known. In *The Merchant of Venice*, all the traditional attitudes and ideas about usury are on full display. Having approached Shylock (a Jew) about a loan, Antonio (the merchant) listens to Shylock's terms and readily agrees, fully realizing that they could potentially be harsh. Shylock demands strong terms for what he considers personal injustices suffered at Antonio's hand in the past. Says Shylock to Antonio:

> *This kindness will I show.*
> *Go with me to a notary, seal me there*
> *Your single bond; and, in a merry sport,*
> *If you repay me not on such a day,*
> *In such a place, such sum or sums as are*
> *Express'd in the condition, let the forfeit*
> *Be nominated for an equal pound*
> *Of your fair flesh, to be cut off and taken*
> *In what part of your body pleaseth me.*[30]

Readily agreeing, Antonio could not foresee the future financial problems that would cause him to renege on his debt. Later, as Shylock prepares to enforce his bond and take his pound of flesh, Portia's defense saves the day. As she (in disguise) argues, Shylock has the right to exact his bond, but according to the law he must do so without shedding one drop of blood. This clearly was a traditional reference to the idea that lending should do no harm. Frustrated, Shylock realizes that he has been bested and withdraws. Regardless of the travails of his father, Shakespeare adopted the traditional definition of interest without introducing the golden rule. Luckily for Antonio, tradition held sway. But the blood analogy is evident here as well, although not in the sweeping sense of the medievals. For Shakespeare, spilling Antonio's blood would have been Shylock's downfall. In that sense, blood was equated with risk and the risk clearly was not worth assuming by the moneylender.

In the more formal world of law, a sweeping refutation of the Scholastic ideas on usury came from Charles Dumoulin, a French jurist of the sixteenth century. Born in 1500, he studied law at Poitiers and Orleans before writing his magnum opus, *Commentarium in Consuetudines Parisienses*, published in 1539. Writing under the Latinized version of his name, Carolus Molinaeus, he also published the controversial *Tractatus Contractuum et Usurarum* (*A Treatise on Contracts and Usury*) in 1546. In it, he refuted most of the notions of the church fathers on usury, setting off a fierce controversy in the process. Many of his comments were blunt and expressed doubt about the expertise of the church fathers, especially Aquinas. Four years before writing the work he began following the teachings of Luther and Calvin, abandoning the Catholic Church in the process. He had little use for traditional doctrine and his acceptance of usury was a prime example. Molinaeus wrote that tolerating usury was as necessary as tolerating the use of money. But the crux of the matter was the purpose for which usury was charged. In one particularly infuriating statement, he scorned the Scholastics and acknowledged the idea of credit risk all in the same utterance: "The scholastic doctors, not only theologians but canonists and jurists . . . do not consider usury or what is meant by laws limiting usury. But they are wholly mistaken, as a result both of ignorance of the law and lack of practical experience. For who ever contracted for usury for the mere service of lending, and not as a compensation for loss to be incurred or gain to be prevented, or in order to participate in the gains which the debtor expected to make?"[31]

On one level, the remark is typical of the age; it is a typical Renaissance attitude reflecting a concern with the present and a refutation of the past. Personally, Molinaeus was able to make such statements without reservation because he held himself in particularly high esteem. He reputedly said, "I yield to no one nor is anyone able to teach me." He spent time in prison for remarks made in a treatise written lambasting the Council of Trent in 1564. He also produced a commentary on Gratian containing notes hostile to the pope. The writings made him even more unpopular with the Catholic Church. Finally, he was reconciled with Rome on his deathbed in 1566, following the time-hallowed tradition of many bankers desirous of hedging their bets on the afterlife.

On the opposite side of the coin, a strong condemnation of usury came from a well-respected author and civil servant in the mid-sixteenth century despite the liberalization of the usury laws. Thomas Wilson, a graduate of Eton and King's College, Cambridge was an accomplished writer and diplomat who penned a serious tirade against usury. Born in 1525, Wilson left England for Italy during the reign of Mary because he was politically opposed to the reinstatement of Catholicism. While in Italy, he was denounced as a heretic and persecuted for his political beliefs. Refusing to return home when ordered by the government, he was imprisoned for a year by the Inquisition. Upon his escape from a Roman prison, he studied law at Ferrara and received a degree before returning to England in 1560 after an absence of five years.

After returning to good standing with the government, he served in various capacities for the crown. He served in the judiciary, and in Parliament on several occasions, joined various diplomatic missions, and was ambassador to the Netherlands. His most famous book, *A Discourse upon Usury*, was completed in 1569, and clearly was intended to influence the debate in Parliament about reinstating the legal rate of interest at 10 percent. The book became a standard reference on the subject for generations and overshadowed his other works, among them a book on logic. His rigorous condemnation of usury as excessive interest was distinguished from normal market rates of interest with which he had become familiar in the Antwerp money market. These distinctions between usury and interest set the tone in England for debate. Wilson sounded as if he were among the old guard in defending society against the evils of usury. Even the method employed in his discourse was neoclassical. The book was written in dialogue form, reminiscent of Plato and Cicero, with long discussions by the principal interlocutors. But his conclusions were much more modern.

Wilson's argument dovetailed with an expanding English economy under the Tudors that was seriously in need of more sophisticated banking facilities than were present at the time. English exports increased dramatically during the second half of the sixteenth century, land was being enclosed and escalating in price, tin mining in the southwestern part of England was increasing, and fabric making was becoming the principal manufacturing industry. As a result, the need for capital, both short- and long-term, was increasing and the nascent English banking business was emerging to serve these needs. The term "banker" emerged during the early sixteenth century, describing the process of lending money at interest, but it still was practiced by a wide variety of merchants, demonstrating that the English banking business was a cottage industry rather than the more sophisticated type developed by the Italians.[32]

Wilson's distinction between interest and usury, which was indicative of the trend developing in the business ranks of the day, was straightforward. Acts of Parliament already drew this distinction and discussion would provide the basis for the future distinction of usury as being excessive interest that exists to this day. According to Wilson, "Usury and trewe interest be things as contrary as falsehood is to trewth. For usury contayneth in itself inequalitie and unnatural dealinge and trewe interest observeth equitie and naturall dealinge."[33] The practical way to join both sides would be to legalize interest and have its maximum rate set by the state, as the Act of 1571 did. Anything above and beyond the official rate would be considered usury. Wilson's discussion of usury became a standard reference and was mentioned time and again as the interest rate ceilings in Britain were lowered in subsequent years.

The late sixteenth century saw many traditional condemnations of all forms of interest, mainly on the Continent. The Benedictine Alphonsus Vilagut published his *Tractate on Usury* in 1589 in Venice and it detailed a thorough condemnation of usury in all its forms. Describing usury as any amount in excess of the original loan, he denied usurers the sacraments, a church burial, and even absolution for their sins. Only bishops could decide whether to accept donations from the estates of usurers; priests were excluded from the process. Not to be outdone by Vilagut, sixty years later in Venice Onorato Leotardi wrote an anti-usury tract with the same title, this time equating usurers with murderers. Theft was not their only sin.

The consideration of all interest as usury lived on in England despite the act of Parliament and Wilson and prompted a debate that spanned three decades in the seventeenth century. The outcome helped further erode the medieval notions and was lively although it involved sparring by what seemed at first as unlikely combatants.

A spirited defense of prohibiting usury was made in 1612 by Roger Fenton. The argument was more medieval than modern in his own day, being based mostly on scripture and former church councils to prove the point that usury was illegal and immoral. He commented that "the Council of Vienne under Clement the 5 condemned all for Heretikes who held usury to be lawful." He acknowledged that Calvin's position on usury "will relive us very little even when he is most favorable." Luther was closer to his position among the reformers. The distinction between usury and tolerable interest was not made clear, but Fenton did admit that the Elizabethan interest ceiling was the rule of the land in 1612 and that "the law of our country doth not tolerate any [usury] at all and therefore by his [God's] rule it is not lawful for us to take any usury at all."[34]

In Fenton's opinion, the Elizabethan statute was too humane concerning usury while the complete prohibition under Edward VI was more to the point. Another of the dozens of proofs he offered is that the "heathen writers, who never heard of Scripture against usury," like Aristotle, also found it intellectually wanting and condemned it. But his comments showed ambiguity about interest. The ten in a hundred ceiling of Elizabeth did not persuade him that only interest above 10 percent was considered usurious; all interest was usurious, regardless of the law of the realm. While in keeping with the long tradition of equating all interest with usury, the implication that the Elizabethan statute still was basically (and morally) wrong invoked a response from another well-known writer of the period not normally associated with matters of economics.

A damaging rebuttal to the older interpretation came thirteen years later from Robert Filmer, a writer best known for his later defense of monarchy in *Patriarcha*, a book that became reviled as one of the last defenses of strong monarchy in an age leaning strongly toward republican government. His defense of usury came in his *Quaestio Quodlibetica* which sided squarely with merchants and traders who practiced and paid usury in the course of everyday business. Using an argument in the style of medieval disputation, Filmer tackled assumptions made by detractors of usury, including Fenton, to determine whether they were correct. Claim that usury was necessary for trade and business, he maintained that only harsh, or "biting usury" to use a common phrase of the period, was unjust and should be condemned.

More powerfully, Filmer tackled the question of usury and early English state annuities. The correlation was simple. Without interest, the care of orphans would be a problem for the state. Interest made annuities possible; without them the expense would have been overwhelming, or the service not provided. Despite problems arising out of administering estates for orphans, the good outweighed the problems presented. "And further cannot policy provide for the good of orphans without such private and public mischiefs as arise out of usury."[35] Leaving aside moral and theological arguments, this was one of the first public policy considerations in response to the condemnation of usury.

Filmer sharpened his attack on the anti-usury positions and Fenton in particular, describing his antagonist as being somewhat fuzzy about the definition of usury and its uses. In doing so, he helped define future arguments more clearly. Definition had been a problem for interest and usury for centuries and Filmer detected the problem in Fenton. "Neither does he so much describe actual usury only he tells us of diversity of descriptions of others but never lets us know which he approves."[36] Filmer went on to show the benefits that usury produced but stopped short of giving a comprehensive, useful definition, a characteristic common at the time. He was happy to refute the condemnation, leaving a more modern definition still wanting.

Part of the refutation was political. Filmer was a royalist whose *Patriarcha* showed the origins and virtues of monarchy passed from generation to generation. Fenton had showed some disrespect for the monarchy in his comments about the collision of the interest rate ceilings of the Tudors and the morality of usury laws. Acceptance of usury as reasonable interest was equated with efficiency and usefulness and therefore with monarchy. By implication, this would make Filmer's political ideas unpopular in years to come, but they were in keeping with the early Protestant tradition. Luther also detested usury in line with his dislike of the papacy and all of its financial felonies, such as usury but mainly simony.

Usury was given additional credence by Francis Bacon. Bacon left Cambridge as a student during Elizabeth's reign because he was disenchanted with Aristotelian method that dominated the university at the time. It would be years before he began producing his major works on observation and the scientific method, the *Advancement of Learning* and the *New Method*. In the interim, he was a courtier and occasional lawyer. Well connected by birth, Bacon served both Elizabeth and James I, although he and his brother Anthony encountered financial difficulties on occasion and were forced to seek the help of usurers. His brother's financial plight was said to be the basis of Shakespeare's Antonio in *The Merchant of Venice,* suggesting to some that it actually was Bacon who wrote the Shakespeare plays. Bacon's attitude toward money was distinctly modern. He claimed, with the aplomb of an English country gentleman, that "money is like muck, not good except to be spread."

His own experience with usurers made his comments about it and usurers quite practical. "Since there must be borrowing and lending, and men are so hard of heart as they will not lend freely, usury must be permitted." Before banking developed in England, usury played a vital role in business. "Some others have made suspicious and cunning propositions of banks . . . and other inventions; but few have spoken of usury usefully."[37] What made Bacon's thoughts on usury unusual was his idea of two established rates of interest: one at 5 percent and the other higher, to be lent to merchants and businessmen. Those lending to businesses at the higher rate needed to be licensed because they were clearly exceeding the general rate. While the idea was more flexible than some of his contemporaries' thoughts, the suspicion of official banks reflected a general distrust of the idea in England at the time.

Equally if not more indicative of the emerging attitudes toward usury were the writings of another person with a scientific background rather than a legal or theological education. Despite the continuing controversy and theories, one particular development did more to advance the legitimacy of interest than most others of the sixteenth century. In 1582, a Dutch engineer and mathematician published the first interest rate tables. By doing so, he made public calculations that bankers had kept under lock and key for decades for fear of divulging the tricks of their trade. The calculations also opened the door for the marketing of long-term debt contracts that would help revolutionize financing.

Breaking the Banker Cabal

Simon Stevin was born in Bruges in 1548. Much like Pacioli, he worked in business as a bookkeeper in Antwerp before working in the municipal government of Bruges as a tax collector. In 1583, he moved to Leiden, entering the university at the age of thirty-five after he already had established a scientific reputation. After publishing many books on diverse subjects, he established an engineering school at the university at the behest of Prince Maurits, a friend and benefactor, who originally got to know him because of his engineering skills. But it was one of his early works that would have a profound impact on the way business was done. In 1582, one year after the death of Thomas Wilson, Stevin published his *Tables of Interest*, making public the interest rate calculations that Italian bankers had kept secret for years, partly to keep the church from seeing the effects of compound interest.

Italian and Dutch bankers had used interest rate tables for centuries but were not enthusiastic about making them public. Stevin provided a valuable service by publishing them so that anyone familiar with basic arithmetic could determine the effects of interest. It was not a coincidence that his tables were published in the same year that the Gregorian calendar was adopted. The new calendar effectively dropped ten days from the existing Julian calendar, altering the calculation of annual interest when comparing it to countries that did not adopt the new calendar. The older Julian calendar used by Fibonacci and others had 365¼ days in each year. Over time, it began to drift from the solar year by slightly more than eleven minutes. By 1580, that meant that the spring equinox was falling almost ten days earlier than it should. The new calendar corrected the problem and was quickly adopted by most Catholic countries in Europe. Britain and its American colonies did not adopt the Gregorian calendar until 1752, however. Some commercial problems arose in Europe during the years that the dual systems were used. Compound interest over time would differ depending on the number of days used in a year.

Once Stevin had let the proverbial cat out of the bag, interest rate tables began to be produced for businessmen. His tables were a combination of discount (present value or PV) tables and the future value of annuities, ranging from 1 percent to 20 percent. Over the next two hundred years, many more practical tables and devices would appear, called "reckoners." These practical tables were designed to be used in everyday commerce and came in a variety of forms. The tables and reckoners helped to establish a standard for computing interest charges, although the church's official stand on usury had not changed. But the very fact that tables were being produced indicates that fear of the church had given way to a more practical acknowledgment that business was business. Even the Protestant leaders of the sixteenth century came to an accommodation over usury, although not without some tortuous thought.

One of Stevin's most important contributions to practical math was the introduction of decimals. Without decimals, compound interest tables could not be fully developed and used effectively. Stevin's use of decimals would not immediately be clear to readers today because of the notation he employed, but he certainly made an enormous impact on financial mathematics with their introduction. The factors in his tables lacked a dot in front of the present values so the PVs look like nothing more than a column of random numbers. But they are the same factors found in contemporary present and future value tables. An example of his tables is found in the Appendix.

The contrast between Stevin and Wilson could not have been more stark in terms of style. Wilson's argument was dominated by moral and religious overtones while Stevin had the benefit of mathematics on his side. Since Stevin's tables listed values for interest as high as 20 percent, it is obvious that Wilson would have considered that usurious. They both served their respective governments in Holland at the same time, but it is not clear whether Wilson knew of Stevin or his work. Both, however, were aware of the price inflation caused by the import of gold from the Americas into Europe by the Spanish. The mere fact that things cost more than they did in the past amply demonstrated that the use of money could no longer be considered free, practically if not morally.

Following in the steps of Simon Stevin, William Webster published the first set of interest rate tables in England in 1620. Annuity calculations were part of the book, made necessary both by Stevin's tables and the growing popularity of annuities at the time. Even though England was free of the restraints of the Catholic Church, the presence of the usury laws legislated by Parliament can be found. Unlike Stevin, Webster did not use a rate higher than 10 percent in his tables because of the Elizabethan rate ceiling. In the third edition of his book in 1634, he lists interest calculations at 10, 8, and 6 percent respectively, although 6 percent would not be adopted until 1660. Eight percent had been adopted under James I in 1620 (see the Appendix for an example).

One of the more lively discussions about price inflation came from Jean Bodin, the noted French political theorist. Best known for his *Six Books of the Republic*, published in 1576, he wrote a short treatise about the price inflation in Europe eighty years after the discovery of America. Trained as a lawyer, Bodin approached politics in a theoretical and systematic manner. His ideas about inflation infuriated more of his readers than his ideas on politics, which eventually became sympathetic with monarchy after initially espousing popular government. As far as he was concerned, inflation was caused by mismanagement of resources, both by the Spanish and the French monarchies. Concerning the Spanish, he stated unequivocally, "Now the fact is that the Spaniard, who gets his subsistence only from France . . . goes to the ends of the earth to seek gold and silver and spices to pay us with." This was to be compared with the northern Europeans, especially the English, who were able to mine their own mineral resources without much difficulty.[38] Europe was suffering already under the surge in prices caused by inflation. The import of gold and silver into Spain from the Americas increased Spanish imports and had an indirect effect upon manufactured prices in the rest of Europe, especially in those countries trading with Spain.

Bodin also gave a good indication of why Philippe the Fair was so desperate for Templar wealth two hundred fifty years before. According to his account, "Philippe the Fair, grandson of Saint Louis, in the year thirteen hundred, so debased the silver money that a *sold* of the old money was worth three of the new."[39] In this respect, he echoed the concerns of Nicholas of Oresme and Davanzati who were more concerned with the debasement of money than the usurious activities of lenders. In the minds of early writers on democracy and popular government, usury and monarchy were slowly becoming irrelevant to the dictates of the modern world, especially if past abuses were used to gauge their efficacy.

Despite the fact that prices rose because of the import of gold and silver, interest rates north of Spain did not rise appreciably in the sixteenth century and were actually lower than they were in earlier centuries. In the sixteenth century, loans to individual princes ranged from 6 to 18 percent as compared with 15 to 80 percent in the fourteenth century. Loans to states remained in the 6 to 15 percent range for the same two-hundred-year period, although they did rise when the Italian city-states went to war with each other during the fifteenth century.[40] This suggests that rising inflation was not reflected in interest rates. The usury problem was creating a related problem because an adjustment could not be made to deposits paid by banks or to loan rates charged by bankers. A new source of wealth would be needed to infuse the European economies with fresh revenues before inflation began to erode the standard of living they had been able to achieve despite periodic wars and the continuing attitude toward charging interest.

The "Miracle of Holland"

The Protestant reformers' challenge to usury was complemented by the writings of the Dutch lawyer Hugo Grotius, who was born about a year after Stevin published his interest rate tables in 1582. Highly precocious, Grotius entered the University of Leiden at the age of eleven and graduated in three years. Three years later, he accompanied a Dutch diplomatic mission to France and during his stay was awarded a doctor of laws degree from the university at Orleans. The French king feted him as the "miracle of Holland." Grotius turned to a career in law and began writing legal texts. One in particular, his *Introduction to Dutch Jurisprudence*, became a standard text in law schools for over 150 years and was in use in South Africa until 1901. But he is best remembered for his writings on international law, which had the effect of opening the discipline to a new dimension and putting usury further on the back shelf.

Grotius's classic *The Rights of War and Peace* became one of the most read treatises on law and rivaled Blackstone's *Commentaries* in importance outside common law countries. Grotius's basic theme was that nations violating the international legal order could be punished militarily by others in accord within the accepted laws of war. In outlining the various types of law, including natural law, Grotius maintained that his ideas were wholly consistent with being a Christian. And his treatment of usury proved to be a death knell for the pietistic treatment of usury and usurers. Using a lawyer's penchant for simple fact, he refuted Aquinas and the church fathers by implicitly acknowledging the value of debt capital. Concerning usury, he stated flatly that "those human laws, which allow a compensation to be made for the use of money or any other thing, are neither repugnant to natural law nor revealed law." Recognizing credit risk, he added that "in Holland, where the rate of interest upon common loans was eight percent, there was no injustice in requiring 12 percent of merchants; because the hazard was greater." If the rate, however, exceeded the risk, then the lending became "an act of extortion or repression."[41] The idea of formal credit risk entered the usury conversation.

Equally important was the decoupling of usury laws from "higher laws," especially the Thomist version of natural law, which equated it with the eternal law of God. This was one of the first serious attempts to show that charging interest was not against common practices in civil society, which formed the basis of Grotius's own version of the natural law. It was nothing more than a natural compensation for the risk assumed by lenders. Grotius sought to make charging truly excessive interest nothing more than a civil misdemeanor. This certainly was not the death knell for traditional views of all interest as usury, although it provided much more flexibility in interpretation.

Being aware of the Deuteronomic interpretation of usury, he continued that the prohibition against Jews taking interest only from other Jews was political and not a moral precept. Since Jews were allowed to charge gentiles for the use of money, the passage only proved that usury was not illegal. This was a purely legal interpretation of the Old Testament prohibition rather than a religious one and would further help erode the authority of biblical precedents that had been relied upon for centuries. Equally, he dismissed the Romans in similar fashion: "But what Cato, Cicero, Plutarch and others allege against usury, applies not so much to the nature of the thing, as to the accidental circumstances and consequences with which it is commonly attended."[42] Simply, the Romans during the republic did not make their case convincingly enough, although later generations embellished the notion.

While Grotius was able to divorce usury from its natural law–eternal law connection, he was not totally successful in divorcing it from its established position in contemporary natural law theory. Usury prohibitions remained firmly in place in the seventeenth century while interest and compound interest remained embedded in business practice, continuing the centuries-old tension. Grotius was not alone in his acceptance of usury. One of his contemporaries did even more to help destroy the old bugaboo about lending by becoming involved in a bitter public controversy.

Comments on Grotius were common in the seventeenth century. Some of the more incisive came from Samuel Pufendorf, the German philosopher and legal theorist who abandoned the study of theology for law. His important works began to appear after 1670. Discussing Grotius's understanding of usury, he wrote in his own book on natural law that "Grotius rejects the name of usury, but allows the thing. For, says he, there are some things which look like usury but are parts of another nature: as the amends that ought to be made a creditor for the loss he is at being out his money, and the regard that ought to be had to the gain he might have made of it." The idea that opportunity gains and losses should be calculated in considerations of loans was a more incisive way of saying that usury existed so there was no practical reason to ban it anymore. Continuing, he asked, "Who would not laugh at those who pretend that they don't take usury for their money, but only what they themselves might have made of it?"[43]

Claudius Salmasius wrote a book entitled *On Usury* in 1638 that helped pave the way for better-known economic thinkers to follow. He assumed that economic activity was legitimate, not simply necessary, and should be encouraged. Interest was vital for commerce and lending also should be encouraged. Even more shockingly modern was his assertion that interest rates would be low if bankers were allowed to compete for business rather than sidestep the usury laws that existed. The competition would cause them to offer the lowest rates possible in order to win business. This was one of the first clear indications that economic thought was moving beyond discussions of debasement of currencies and biblical interpretations of usury to a standard driven by competition and banking practices.

Salmasius was the Latinized name of Claude Saumaise, a French scholar born in Burgundy in 1588. He studied in Paris and at the university in Heidelberg, where he read the classics and devoted himself to Protestantism. His early academic career was notable for editing earlier anti-papal writers before producing his best-known scholarly book, a critical edition of the Roman historian Pliny. He then accepted a teaching post at Leiden. Most of his work was scholarly criticism, which made the book on usury almost a natural for him, although he was widely denounced for writing it by traditionalists. The book did convince the Dutch church to admit moneylenders to holy orders, helping to end the centuries old ban in that country.

Salmasius was involved in a nasty pamphleteering battle with John Milton over the role of Charles I of England, who was deposed in 1649. According to rumor, Salmasius accepted a stipend of one hundred pieces of gold to condemn the regicide of Charles. Milton, on behalf of Oliver Cromwell and the anti-royalists who deposed and beheaded the king, argued effectively against Salmasius. In 1651, Milton wrote a Latin verse against him, in which he opined: "Who made Salamasius so glib with his Hundred and taught the magpie to try our words? His teacher in this art was his stomach and the hundred Jacobuses that were the vitals of the purse of the exiled king [Charles II]," [44] implying that Charles II paid him off. Milton won the day with his arguments against monarchical government and Salmasius receded from view along with his liberal theory on usury. The seventeenth-century tussle over the proper form of government helped obscure the usury debate to an extent, leaving further secularization of interest for another day.

When the writings and work of Stevin, Grotius, and Salmasius were combined, it was clear that the Dutch contribution to the usury debate of the sixteenth and seventeenth centuries was considerable. While Luther and Calvin may have set the ball rolling toward a refutation of usury, it was the secular writers, adept in math, law, and the classics who gave the early reformers considerable momentum as the Protestant ethic began to pick up steam. Stevin's ability in math and his publication of the first interest rate tables had the same effect that many financial innovations and revelations would have in the future: the once obscure and mythical would become common knowledge and help destroy the old bugaboos about interest myths in the process.

The Expansionist Reaction

Increased commerce was responsible for changes in attitude toward usury over the years. A curious fact remains that those advocating usury came from both sides of the political spectrum, both early democratic thinkers and royalists. Many remained firmly in the royalist camp while advocating legitimate interest as a means of lubricating the wheels of government and business. Advocates of popular government saw it as a way for the populace and the non-noble classes to achieve a better life.

This was not an inconsistency but reflected the predominant economic philosophy of the day. Since the late Renaissance, European governments actively pursued mercantilist policies that emphasized exports over imports and the search for gold bullion. Wealth was measured in the metal and economic policies centered around it, especially after the Spanish had imported so much of it after the discovery of the Americas. When it became apparent that gold had become the universal measure of wealth, economic policies were dedicated to obtaining as much of it as possible. This required trading nations to emphasize international trading since a positive balance of trade and expansion was required. Liberalization of the usury laws went hand in hand with mercantilist policies.

Governments became painfully aware of this over the centuries. Trading was preferable to confiscation because stealing wealth from members of one's own society through debasement had never proved to be a viable economic policy in the long run. In the Renaissance view, net exporting nations were the wealthiest. The idea also required a policy of aggressive exploration and expansion, sometimes with unintended consequences. Governments would go to great lengths to pursue mercantilist policies. Imports had to be balanced by domestic production or the results would be catastrophic. Bodin's criticism of the Spanish was perhaps the most succinct example. Importing gold was enviable, but when it was used to buy basic goods and manufactures from others the only effect it had was to force prices up across the board. In order to survive without causing a reaction in domestic prices, governments had to apply their mercantilist policies adeptly.

One particular characteristic of mercantilism did not sit well with republicans and advocates of popular forms of government. Many monarchical governments practicing mercantilism granted monopolies to merchants or trading companies. In return for the exclusivity, revenues would increase to the crown. This was an example of the prerogatives exercised by sovereigns, even if they were somewhat limited by parliaments. The process held considerable prestige for those granted the exclusiveness and represented great potential revenues for kings, who were as strapped for cash in the seventeenth and eighteenth centuries as they had been in the past.

As a result, many advocates of liberalizing the usury laws were also monarchists of varying degrees. Getting rid of usury was a worthy goal since it would help lubricate the wheels of mercantilist economic policies. The classic example of early mercantilism was found in the attempt to create new wealth through exploration when Elizabeth I chartered the East India Company in 1599. The company was the first joint stock company dedicated to exploration beyond Europe. It began operating in 1600 and developed two distinct classes of shareholders. The first class consisted of shareholders who had purchased stock that cost between £500 and £2,000 in order to sit on its General Court, which was involved directly with the company's affairs. From within this group came the directors, the ultimate authority in the company. The second class of shareholders consisted mostly of noblemen and wealthy individuals who were attracted by the possibility of reaping large dividends. This joint stock company would be recognizable today, although at the time it would help deal a serious blow to usury prohibitions.

The capital of the company actually was a mix of equity and debt. Maritime insurance contracts and low-interest debentures were used in order to raise capital. The interest rate on the debentures after the company's first voyages was lower than the Tudor 10 percent limit since official English interest rates were lowered after 1624 to 8 percent, falling to 6 percent after 1651.[45] Debt and insurance contracts could be used in financing along with stock because rates were, and remained, low. Shareholders were accustomed to receiving dividends on their holdings of around 20 percent on average for a successful voyage. In addition, the stocks doubled in price so shareholders had a distinct advantage over debt holders during the early years. The English crown also became an investor in the company when James II subscribed to £7,000 in 1687.

In its early days, the company organized separate stock ventures for individual voyages. Between 1600 and 1612, it conducted twelve expeditions in the Levant and the Far East. After 1612, the company actively sought a route to the Orient through a northern passage in order to circumvent the treacherous and time-consuming passage around the Cape of Good Hope. The first twelve voyages were organized as sole ventures, with stock being sold to investors at £100 nominal per share. Each voyage was capitalized between £40,000 and £80,000 and was liquidated upon completion, at a gain or loss to the shareholders. All but two of the original twelve voyages proved highly profitable, registering gains of almost 200 percent in several cases.[46] Clearly, the use of the joint stock company obviated the old need for disguising the role of lenders and any subsequent discussions of usury.

One of the early directors of the company was Thomas Mun, who was elected in 1615 and held the post until 1641. Mun became a trader in early adulthood and accumulated extensive business experience in the Middle East and Italy. In 1630, he wrote what would become known as the best-known mercantilist tract of the day, *England's Treasure by Forraign Trade*, although it was not officially published for twenty years. By treasure, he meant what today is known as a positive current account balance. He stated the basic mercantilist principle very simply: "The ordinary means therefore to increase our wealth and treasure is by *Forraign Trade*, wherein we must ever observe this rule; to sell more to strangers yearly than we consume of theirs in value."[47] Wealth would be created by the surplus, but not necessarily by having a monarch accumulate large cash surpluses. Mun noted that kings with surpluses had a tendency to wage war on others.

The emergence of the joint stock company, adding a new wrinkle to financing, helped to erode the medieval notions of usury. Interest slowly was becoming acceptable in theory as well as in practice, helped by the fact that interest rates in Western Europe were relatively low during the seventeenth century. Usury certainly was not forgotten and would continue to be a topic of often heated, and legislative, discussion until the twentieth century. As Karl Marx later noted, historically, reasonable interest aided economic growth. Capitalism's greatest critic recognized the changing psychology of post-Reformation business practices well before it was fashionable to speak of the Protestant ethic in the development of capitalism.

Widows and Orphans

Simon Stevin's interest rate tables also gave a glimpse into a financial practice already quite old in the sixteenth century. His entries for the future value of annuities were practically based. Annuities had been sold in Europe to investors seeking a steady income stream since the Middle Ages. But like other practices using interest rates, annuities were characterized by a lack of hard information about the annuities themselves other than the fact that they paid their recipients an income for a set period of time, usually years. Stevin's contribution to the topic in his tables was the disclosure of the rate of interest used to compound the amounts.

In the Middle Ages, annuities were known as "census." States, groups of noblemen, and other established organizations would sell a census to an individual for a lump sum, agreeing to pay a set income for a specified number of years. Usually, the income paid was derived from property, so discussions of usury normally were avoided. Ordinarily, the amount paid out periodically was fixed rather than variable and could be paid out for periods of life or shorter periods. Given the propensity for war and political upheaval, the longer annuities were riskier but were sold on an equal basis with the others. The Vatican considered annuities legitimate forms of investment and the popes Martin V and Calixtus III approved them in 1425 and 1455 respectively.[48] Often monasteries invested their large gifts in the same manner as wealthy individuals. Often lacking banking facilities they could trust, investing with a state or nobleman was one of the only viable long-term forms of investment that did not expose the investor to business risk directly. Annuities grew to become the first widows and orphans investment.

On the other side of the coin, annuities were the first attempt at raising long-term capital in Europe. As early as the fourteenth century, Bruges adopted a plan where estates of orphans were invested in annuities provided by the city government, supplying them with a steady income until they were of legal age.[49] They then received the principal amount back and were free to use it as they wished. The plan was humane and also very wise financially. The payback period depended upon the age of the orphaned child and what was considered the legal age for inheriting money. The time period could be estimated and the annuity designed to operate efficiently. But longer-term annuities presented a problem to the borrowers since the payback periods were wider and could depend upon a variety of circumstances surrounding both the buyer and the seller.

Annuities became more popular in the seventeenth century in England and Holland and soon became the favorite method of raising government funds before the bond markets developed. Their increased popularity was aided by developments in statistics and probability theory. Before the seventeenth century, what today would be called actuarial assumptions were made based upon tables developed by the Roman jurist Ulpian around 225 A.D. They contained no analysis based upon what was later known as probability theory, developed in the seventeenth century by Edmund Halley, John Graunt, and William Petty. They were assumed to be based on simple observation of life spans. During the intervening centuries, no further attempts were made to correct or challenge Ulpian, despite the vast changes in average life spans and other demographic factors affecting life in Western Europe.

Developing probability theory was crucial for financial development in Europe. How annuities could be offered without an intelligent reference to the average life span of the buyer (or how long he would live if the payout was a life annuity) suggests that the annuities were not successful for the most part, especially longer-term ones. In the absence of actuarial science, annuities' success could be attributed to low interest rates. In many cases, annuities based upon land revenues were rarely higher than deposit rates offered by bankers or governments. Holland especially offered low annuity rates for recipients. That made for good business practice. The higher the rate offered on an annuity payout, the riskier it became for the borrower so rates were low, reducing their risks along with the return to the recipient. Charges of usury also were avoided, since the income stream produced was derived from productive property.

England lagged behind Holland in offering long-term annuities, but when it did adopt them it did so with a flourish. English banking also lagged that of the Dutch and the Italians until the reign of the Stuarts, but it finally began to catch up in the later seventeenth century. The Glorious Revolution of 1688 ousted James II and brought William of Orange to the English throne. Coming from the Low Countries, William also brought with him advisers well acquainted with the art of long-term financing. The English treasury began offering annuities. As long as the government or other entity offering these benefits could be trusted to survive, the market for long-term financial products flourished. When England boasted that it had not been invaded since 1066, it was not just a matter of national pride. It also proved to be a good marketing strategy for annuities.

In contemporary terms, long-term interest rates paid on the annuity streams were actually lower than short-term interest rates. Investors buying annuities received a lower rate of return than did those who lent shorter term. This inversion of the modern risk-reward relationship may be explained by the fact that an annuity issued by a state not totally dominated by one-man rule, with an element of parliamentary government and prospects for smooth transition, had a better chance of being paid in the event of a regime change than did one bought from a government dominated by an autocratic or tyrannical monarch with little democratic apparatus to support him. Even William of Orange initially had a difficult time selling annuities as long as there was a chance the Stuarts might return. Once that possibility faded from view, the prospect for annuity sales brightened considerably.

For the most part, the term structure of interest rates in Europe from the Roman Empire through the seventeenth century mostly was negatively sloped. This helps explain in macro terms why the Italian banking houses could enjoy such success only to be followed by such dismal failure. In order to gain a maximum profit, despite the warnings about usury, they allied themselves with kings and princes who were not among the finest credit risks although they could afford to pay high interest rates. Low interest rates traditionally were associated with political stability while usury was found when political conditions were more volatile, which proved to be the case during most of the Middle Ages and the early Renaissance. In biblical Jewish society, the idea of brotherhood and continuity of belief led to the prohibition of Jews charging each other interest. Clearly, when Jewish merchants and pawnbrokers loaned to kings and princes, the situation changed considerably and interest rates reflected that. As peripatetic merchants throughout their history, Jews naturally demanded a rate of return commensurate with the risks that they would be defaulted upon or even expelled from their homes. The same sort of situation can be found in all lending activities. Uncertainty is the breeding ground for high interest rates.

Despite Shakespeare's clever demonstration of the traditional attitudes toward usury in *The Merchant of Venice*, most of Europe was beginning to embrace Shylock openly by the end of the seventeenth century. The fact was that moneylenders had been embraced, if not publicly, since lending began. The distinction between reasonable interest and usury had been well established. The old usury prohibitions were undergoing changes, but they were not yet forgotten. The spirit of capitalism was becoming the dominant force in business and would transform the mercantilist system of trading into a dominant force for three centuries. When confronted with the nasty choice in the play of taking his pound of flesh only if it drew no blood, Shylock wisely demurred, recognizing the futility of demanding payment contrary to tradition. The intended harm was averted. One hundred fifty years later, Portia's defense certainly would have had to be more technical. Unfortunately for Antonio, bankruptcy laws had not been devised in sixteenth-century Venice. If they had, he would have been protected from his creditor without fear of bodily harm.

When trade began to increase substantially in Europe and mercantilist policies were practiced, the beggar-thy-neighbor concept as it is currently understood took over from the earlier notion that charging usury to one's neighbor caused poverty, or worse. The idea had now become institutionalized and could be seen in official national policy rather than simply being attributed to questionable lending practices. The older interpretation of the term did not die, however, but remained alive in the usury debate, which would never abate entirely.

Chapter 3

Protestants, War, and Capitalism

Since the time of Henry VIII, the wealth and revenue of the country have been continually advancing, and in the course of their progress, their pace seems rather to have been gradually accelerated than retarded.
—Adam Smith, 1776

Following the Reformation, faith-based prohibitions against usury and interest began to crumble in the wake of increased commerce and exploration, although they maintained their emotional and moral appeal for centuries to come. But practicality slowly began to win the usury debate and capitalism emerged from the shadows of church dogma.

The contributions of the Dutch to a more liberal interpretation of interest and usury cannot be overstated. On a practical level, Stevin's interest tables made the secrets of bankers accessible for the first time. On a higher level, Grotius helped divorce usury from its Thomist connotations while still managing to keep it under the rubric of natural law. The combination of the two was a new dynamic helping to energize early capitalism and moneylending. Lenders were now seen as an integral part of commerce rather than standing slightly apart from it. It was now possible to talk about money as a topic rather than speak softly in hushed tones, admitting it only as a necessary evil. Even the term capitalism itself is defined in compound interest terms: using money to make more money.

Although attitudes toward usury among some early Protestant reformers were not materially different from those of the Catholic Church in the sixteenth century, demographic factors began to take the sting out of the term "usury." The reformers acknowledged the difference between usury and legitimate interest while the Catholic Church continued to condemn usury in general even as it unofficially recognized the needs of business. But a growing European population and a need for capital for expansion and exploration soon became more important than moral condemnations of money. Once the plagues that devastated the population began to recede, society became more stable and the need for resources and manufacturing increased geometrically. England's population reached pre-plague levels by 1550, just about the time that usury laws were being reconsidered and Henry VIII debased the currency.

Concerns about population growth also began to have an effect upon the interest and usury debate. Pressures for expansion softened the critics of usury and indebtedness, especially if the prospect of famines and shortages was the result of stagnant growth. At the same time, there was an Enlightenment suspicion that society had not yet reached the social and intellectual accomplishments achieved in the ancient world. Demography was a hot-button issue of the period. Robert Wallace, a noted Scottish minister, writer, and intellectual forerunner of Thomas Malthus, commented in 1761, "If we compare the ancient and modern state of those countries of which we have the most distinct knowledge . . . several of them were much more populous anciently than they are at present . . . this may give us an idea of the vast numbers of men who might be raised up and maintained by proper care. If I should call them ten times as many as have been actually propagated, I do not conceive I should say anything beyond the truth."[1] Wallace's social ideas were more utopian than those of Malthus, but the desired outcome was clear. Societies needed to grow and the earth had the room for that growth, but as Malthus noted, population would grow geometrically, eventually outstripping food supply and resources. Growth required investment, exploration, and assuming risk, and these activities required lending on a larger scale than ever before. Without the proper combination of factors, a Malthusian catastrophe was certain. What Albert Einstein later called the miracle of compound interest would make a significant contribution to averting the catastrophe, although its evolution was extremely slow.

The concern for demographic matters began well before Malthus and Wallace. The need for certainty about the future, especially after the last English plague abated in 1666, was well recognized by governments and entrepreneurs alike. But the paradox of longer life leading to potential demographic catastrophe loomed and prompted a major intellectual contribution from Edmund Halley, whose seminal work on mortality led to the development of the market for annuities. Sellers of annuities would continue to pay high rates, but now the process would extend to the state on a larger and larger scale to fund wars and exploration. Eventually, the bond markets began to develop.

Annuities became more popular as life expectancy increased and new products were offered to take advantage of the need. Governments offered a range of annuity products to subscribers, a demonstration that the new optimism had established itself financially. Some of the new products on offer were not plain-vanilla annuities, however, but variations that were not universally accepted by any means. They contained a speculative element that made them unacceptable to many.

The best-known variation was a tontine, named after Lorenzo Tonti, an enterprising Neapolitan physician and adventurer who had devised the method with the aim of helping to shore up French finances in the seventeenth century. He made his proposal to Cardinal Mazarin, the chief minister of France, hoping to gain favor with the court of Louis XIV. Mazarin, also an Italian, happened to be a well-known gambler. The tontine, as it became known, was a pool of money contributed by a group of people of various ages, separated into tranches by age group. The pool had an annual return to the youngest group of 4 percent paid by the state while the older groups were paid more according to their average age. As members of each group died, the survivors would split the returns, earning more as a result. When the oldest member finally died, the balance of the pool would revert to the state.

Mazarin favored the idea, but it ultimately was rejected because the finance minister, Jean-Baptiste Colbert, opposed it. Tonti tried other methods of raising money, proposing a lottery system, but again could not win official approval. He died a poor man in 1695, unrecognized for his scheme. But the idea survived him; several tontines were successfully floated in his own lifetime without mentioning him by name. Only the generic name recalled his contribution. Unfortunately, they were not his original concept but variations implemented by others. While the French were not inclined, the Dutch and English became converts and many tontines were issued. But as in the Middle Ages, the specter of war was never far from the discussion. Ironically, most tontines were proposed in order to finance military adventures—not the sort of funding that offered an annuitant reassurance about the reliability of the retirement funds.

Tontines were a financial example of the popularity of the role of chance in society, a recurring theme in the second half of the seventeenth century. Chance was discussed scientifically, politically, and religiously. The Swiss mathematician Jakob Bernoulli wrote on the theory of probability, which would become an indispensable aid in finance and risk management. James Harrington and John Milton wrote about the role of rotating republican governments, which relied on chance to replace those in power with others of similar qualifications on a periodic basis. Many unanticipated events that could not be adequately explained still were attributed to religion, linking chance events with the will of God. Ironically, the discussions of chance also opened the door to speculation. It was not until the scientific discussion of probability defeated the older notions that speculation could be separated from sounder financial planning. Tontine payments were appealing to those who speculated that they would outlive others in their annuity group.

Several Dutch cities adopted tontines and were successful, although they never succeeded originally at the national level. Some were even marketed abroad, especially in Britain.[2] Within a hundred years they would be replaced by state-sponsored annuity plans in both countries that would be more plain vanilla. The name "tontine" lived on, however. Similar financial plans continued to pop up in various places, including the United States before independence, but they officially were frowned on and eventually banned because of their speculative elements. The name also became associated with the early American stock market. The New York stock market got its start when traders gathered at the Tontine Coffee House in New York City when the market was still conducted al fresco on Wall Street. The establishment was financed by selling a tontine and the subscribers were the traders who paid a subscription fee. The property was intended to revert to the last seven surviving members and expired before the Civil War. A coffee house with a similar name also existed in Albany.[3]

The tontines employed nonscientific mortality tables to demonstrate potential payout schedules. They were usually based upon observations of small groups of people or taken from the small-sample birth and death records in parish rolls. This tended to make their returns speculative and somewhat unreliable. State-sponsored annuities introduced later in the seventeenth century needed more scientifically and broadly based actuarial tables in order to be taken more seriously. The first notable contribution to them was made by Edward Halley, who is better known today for discovering the comet that bears his name. Once annuity tables could be integrated with scientific mortality tables, the sale of annuities could proceed on a more firm foundation than in the past.

Halley was an astronomer who became a member of the Royal Society at the age of twenty-two. The son of a wealthy merchant in the City of London, he left Queens College, Oxford before taking his degree but was later awarded one by a grant from the king. At various times, he held jobs as a deputy director at the mint and a royal astronomer. William III put a ship at

Halley's command, which he directed to the South Atlantic and Antarctica in 1700, studying the area and reporting on trade winds, which contributed to a major mathematical study of navigation. After returning to Britain, he was named a professor of geometry at Oxford, which had first denied him a chair in astronomy years before. But it was his work on annuities, based on observations and records from the city of Breslau in Germany, that helped revolutionize annuity calculations and practices. Several German cities had been keeping official birth and death records since the mid-seventeenth century and England had been doing so since 1538. Because of personal connections with Germany, Halley used the Breslau records as the basis for his tables.

His work on mortality would produce substantial benefits, although it would take another one hundred years for it to be appreciated by his own government. Halley successfully demonstrated that longer anticipated life spans required different premium payments from older buyers of annuities than those made by younger buyers. As he said in his famous work on annuities, "For it is plain that the purchaser ought to pay for only such part of the value of the annuity as he has chances that he is living, and this ought to be computed yearly, and the sum of all those yearly values being added together will amount to the value of the annuity for the life of the person proposed." [4] This was a clear rebuttal of the concept of chance used in the tontines, where the payout on an annuity depended upon the good fortune of the survivors to outlive other members of their pool. A later example of Halley's tables can be found in the Appendix.

By contrast, the British government had been collecting the same standard payment from all buyers of annuities, regardless of age, and paying out in a relatively short time, around fourteen years. Under Henry VIII, an annuity was paid in only seven years. Halley's work demonstrated that payouts should occur after longer periods of time and be based on age estimates. [5] Once adopted, this new method would save governments issuing annuities substantial amounts over the past. But they were still issuing what proved to be expensive annuities during Halley's lifetime.

The Glorious Revolution of 1688 weighed heavily on English finances as William of Orange took the crown. The need to raise money became acute and the new government sought innovative ways to raise cash. Taking advantage of the new strides made in estimating life spans, England sold its first annuity to members of the public in 1692, although it was a variation of a tontine. The aim was to sell £1 million to the public in return for what amounted to a generous payout. The proceeds were meant to finance war with France. The interest was to be held for seven years and then paid out at £70,000 to the surviving annuitants. If the total amount was not subscribed, those who did subscribe would receive £14 for each £100 paid in. This was a life annuity, but because it was not totally subscribed another was issued a year later with similar terms. No distinctions were made on the basis of age so younger annuitants stood to benefit well. A mortality table was used to estimate the potential payouts for the next one hundred years using ten thousand annuitants as its basis.

Although the usury conversation had less of a sharp tone than in the past, the new calculations reversed the traditional dialogue by saving the borrowers money. Annuity payouts now would yield less than in the past since they would be paid, on average, over longer periods of time and the premiums paid into them would be adjusted for the age of the potential annuitant. Although the amounts paid for them by older annuitants would rise, the lower yield would mean lower interest, regardless of who paid whom. Science had successfully entered the usury debate by saving annuity sponsors money, although the new practice would take a very long period of time to be accepted.

Ironically, Halley lived to the ripe old age of eighty-six and would have lived even longer, but he ignored his doctor and drank a glass of wine against his orders. He died as a result in 1742. Food poisoning was a relatively rare occurrence at the time, at least for the aristocratic and educated classes. Halley's predecessor, John Graunt, whose *Bills of Mortality* became the standard work on life spans and listed the various causes of death when first published in 1662, calculated the chances of dying from poisoning of any sort to be only 14 in 229,000 (the latter number being the size of his statistical sample). The percentages of which Halley had been so fond and that contributed so much intellectually ultimately caught up with him.[6]

After the Tudor interest rate ceiling was established, it subsequently was lowered. The 10 percent level was reduced to 8 percent in 1624 during the reign of James I, to 6 percent in 1660 at the Restoration by Charles II, and then to 5 percent in 1713 under Queen Anne. But jurists and parliamentarians still made it clear that usury was an issue, despite the lower ceilings. A lord chief justice of the courts in England, recalling Roger Fenton, noted that it was not "toothless" usury, but "biting" usury (the type he attributed to the Jews) that was illegal. Ten percent interest was not condemned but would be tolerated if a man chose to "endanger his conscience."[7]

By most accounts, the churches would have been filled if that were the case. When a statute lowered the official rate to 6 percent at the Restoration,

it was noted that "the Abatement of Interest from Ten in the Hundred in former times hath been found by notable experience beneficial to the advancement of trade and improvement of lands by good husbandry with many
other considerable advantages to this nation."[8] Mercantilism recognized the
benefits of lower interest rates and the door was beginning to open for more
broad-minded views about usury. The process was very gradual, however.

After the Restoration, finances in Britain began to take a more recognizable form. The government began selling long-term notes promising a
payment for a specific number of years. These instruments became the pro-
genitors of the more familiar gilt-edge securities, or U.K. Treasury securities
(called gilts because of their gilt-edged backing). They were first sold during
the Restoration by the Treasury when it was governed by a commission headed
by George Downing. His work in running the commission was responsible
for the British Treasury being separated from the exchequer. The British national debt was becoming larger and the need for more funds greater every
year.

Downing was described by Samuel Pepys as a "perfidious rogue," partly
because he was a roundhead turned royalist at the Restoration. Downing
went to America in 1638 with his family and was a member of the first
graduating class at Harvard College in 1642. He then worked aboard a ship
in the Caribbean before returning to England. He served in Oliver Cromwell's army and Parliament and also represented England as a diplomat in
France and Holland before the Restoration. He is credited with purchasing
New York from the Dutch and building Downing Street in London, adjacent
to one of his properties in the city. His grandson founded Downing College,
Cambridge. Named a baronet by Charles II, he was instrumental in defending England's mercantilist policies while a diplomat and also assisted in
writing and passing the Navigation Act of 1660. He died in 1684, well before
the creation of the Bank of England.

Debtors' Prisons and Bankers

Although brought to popular attention by Charles Dickens in the nineteenth
century, debtors' prisons already were common in England in the seventeenth century. Whether usury was being practiced or not, it was common
for creditors to have customers who could not repay their debts confined,
regardless of the amount owed. The practice was widespread and it snagged
and threatened some well-known debtors in the process.

In 1691, a book appeared decrying the injustices debtors experienced in prison. In his emotional *Cry of the Oppressed*, Moses Pitt cataloged them after spending time in the notorious Fleet Prison in London. They ranged from brutality to rape by jailers, from prisoners feeding on mice for sustenance to being forced to dine with hogs in the same enclosure. Most counties in England and the London boroughs had prisons that housed debtors and the stories were uniformly grim in his account. Pitt's main theme was that debtors were not ordinary criminals but were being treated equally with the rest of the prison population whose crimes were much more serious.

A celebrity debtor possessed the power of the pen and also had much to say about imprisoning bankrupts. Daniel Defoe fell behind in his payments to creditors, owing £17,000, and was pursued by them in 1692, prompting him to comment that there was "no man so much made a fool as a bankrupt . . . [our law] gives a loose to the malice and revenge of the creditor . . . while it leaves the debtor no way to show himself honest."[9] His businesses, including a foray into marine insurance, had failed, leaving him little means with which to settle his debts. He spent several years in Fleet Prison in London and once found it convenient to escape temporarily to Scotland, out of reach of his creditors. His other alternative would have been to seek asylum in a debtors' haven, several of which existed in London and were remnants of the medieval sanctuaries. The best known was the Mint, named after a former government facility for making coins. Those who sought haven were still considered criminals by the law and only full restitution to their creditors could restore their social standing after having been declared a bankrupt. In the interim, the Mint provided protection because the government tolerated it and other unofficial havens. The prisons posed the time-worn paradox in full light: how could a debtor repay his debts if he was unproductively confined?

The problem was never solved. Despite attempts by James Oglethorpe, a member of Parliament, and others, most of the measures passed by Parliament to protect debtors failed miserably in the early eighteenth century. Fifty years later the debtors' prisons remained firmly in place, doing a booming business. Defoe wrote about debtors' problems and even acknowledged that laws to protect bankrupts would be difficult to enforce. The desire to fix the problem was evident, but the political will to enforce legislation did not exist at the time.

Defoe's use of the term "bankrupt" was standard by the seventeenth century. A law passed in 1542 during Henry VIII's reign is acknowledged as the first bankruptcy law in England.[10] It stated that only a "trader" could be declared bankrupt by the chancellor of the exchequer. A trader was defined as someone engaged in commerce who bought and sold things in order to profit. It did not apply to those who traded in intangibles. The idea was not the modern one of protecting a bankrupt from his creditors but rather was the other way around. If a trader reneged on his debts, creditors could have him taken before the chancellor, who could seize his possessions to pay the debts or imprison the debtor until he did so. The law was designed to provide redress to creditors. This explains why bankrupts were treated harshly in Britain despite the presence of what appeared to be bankruptcy laws. Their emphasis was different than it is today.

Subsequent bankruptcy laws were passed during the reigns of Elizabeth I and James I. They expanded on the precepts found in the original and the Elizabethan law distinguished between a bankrupt and an insolvent. Insolvents originally were non-traders who had no prospects of repayment. Over the next two centuries, many methods were devised to protect bankrupts while attempting to placate creditors, but the deck still was usually stacked against the debtor. The law in the eighteenth century allowed creditors and debtors to negotiate a settlement but only if all creditors agreed. One dissenting voice could force a debtor to prison. The original laws also tried to be somewhat humane, declaring that children could not be defined as traders per se, but that did not explain why so many children were found in debtors' prisons over the years.

While debtors suffered, banking got a boost from the continued poor treatment of bankrupts. Remedies against debtors had a positive side in that they also prompted the development of private banking houses. Many merchants realized it often was as profitable to lend money as it was to engage in their everyday businesses. The courts were inclined to side with them against debtors so there was some degree of protection offered. One individual taking advantage of the law became well-known in English banking. In 1692, a Scottish merchant named John Campbell opened a business as a goldsmith and banker on the Strand in London. His shop entrance was located under the sign of three crowns, the banker version of the traditional three golden balls used by pawnbrokers. Campbell took deposits, made loans, and discounted bills as part of his service. He had a powerful patron in the Duke of Argyll and his business was soon performing banking functions for Queen Anne. The firm eventually became known as Coutts and Company and retained strong ties with the crown for three hundred years.

Small bankers proliferated and dotted the English business community, but a large banking institution was lacking. By the end of the seventeenth century, the parlous state of English finances plus a general distrust of government finances had led to pressure to establish a state-chartered bank. Francis Bacon's suspicions about banks would be put to rest when the Bank of England was established in 1694 after heated debate in Parliament. Small merchants like Campbell proved that a comfortable living could be made privately by accepting deposits and making loans and the English government, not always successful at selling annuities to the public, recognized its opportunity. A central institution was necessary to raise larger amounts than smaller bankers could provide. The Dutch established a national bank in 1609 and the English were acutely aware that if they were to overtake them in trade and commerce then they would need more accessible sources of financing. One admirer of Dutch banking was Josiah Child, a successful businessman and member of the East India Company. He remarked that among the many causes of Dutch commercial success was that "their use of banks, which are of so immense advantage to them, that some not without good grounds have estimated the profit of them to the Public to amount to at least one million of pounds sterling per annum."[11] Although an avid exponent of mercantilism, he favored a ceiling on interest rates, claiming that low interest rates were characteristic of wealthy and healthy societies, anticipating Adam Smith by a hundred years.

It would take another "adventurer" to make the idea of a British bank take real form. The Bank of England was officially founded in 1694, following a plan by William Paterson, a Scottish merchant. Paterson recognized that the crown was in constant need of cash and anticipated that it would grant exclusive privileges to anyone who initiated a bank of national scope. He was correct and a bill seeking to establish a bank was presented to the Privy Council and finally approved by Parliament. Political opposition was strong, however. The Jacobites (supporters of James II) argued strongly against the new bank, fearing that it would help solidify the position of William and Mary. Smaller bankers did not want any new competition, realizing they would have to offer higher deposit rates if the new bank were successful. Despite their opposition, the new bank passed Parliament but not without some acrimonious debate.

Paterson served as a director but resigned after one year in office. He later led an expedition to Panama that ended badly and he quietly returned home empty handed. Much as Tonti before him, he never received proper recognition for his role in the founding of the bank; his name was omitted from its list of founding members. Along with Tonti and George Downing, he represented practical views on money and banking that came from commercial experience that many of the opponents of usury and central banking did not possess.

The new bank accepted deposits, made loans, and issued paper money. By its charter, the bank was not subject to the usury laws and regularly paid and charged more interest than other private banks. The monopolistic trading companies such as the East India Company also charged as much as 12 percent for their services but could argue that their business was done mostly overseas. Clearly, institutional interest was above the usury law ceilings. In 1716, Parliament officially allowed the bank to pay interest as it saw fit.[12] The official maximum usury ceiling applied to smaller transactions among ordinary subjects of the realm.

Advocates recognized that using paper money rather than metallic coins would aid immeasurably in credit creation and could easily see the benefits that would accrue to the early subscribers to the bank. The existing coins had dubious metallic content, had been whittled down by citizens in many instances, and were notoriously difficult to quantify for official purposes. Paper money would allow loans to be more uniform and be made in larger quantities. The tenuous financial position of William III made the bank politically expedient. In 1690, it was estimated that the crown's annual revenue amounted to £1.6 million. Two-thirds of that was being spent on a war with France and insurrections in Scotland and Ireland.[13] William needed a war loan, but without a decent credit history his chances were not good.

As a result, the first tontine was raised in 1692, offering to pay annuitants 10 percent beginning in 1700. Unfortunately, the scheme raised only £100,000. But when another tontine increased the payout to 14 percent, almost £900,000 was raised, demonstrating that the public was keenly aware of the variation in the payouts. The continuing need for the war with France brought the government back to the public for money two years later when an early form of government bond was issued for sixteen years at 10 percent interest. Sweeteners had to be added in order to attract investors, but a shortfall still existed so the government finally decided to establish the national bank following Paterson's proposals.

The initial objective of the Bank of England was to raise £1.2 million. Its capital equaled the amount the government needed to raise at the time. A board of the bank was formed, named the governor and directors. The new institution met with much objection from merchants, usurers, and not a few politicians opposing William III. The main objection was that the new bank would monopolize money, drawing all the money in the country to it because of its attractive rate of interest on deposits. It would "crowd out" private investment money, a cry that would be heard for centuries when discussing the effects of government borrowing.

Individual shares were sold in the company up to £10,000. Limits were put on the amount of total investment from any individual investor and the proceeds of the sale were to be lent to the government in return for a payment of 8 percent interest annually. Queen Mary personally subscribed for that amount just before her death in 1694. This was higher than the legal rate at the time, reflecting the risk of the new institution and the willingness to pay more to gather the capital required. A sunset clause of twelve years was built in, requiring the government to renew the charter after that time.[14] Because of the constant need for financing wars, the renewal was almost certain from the beginning.

The beginnings of the Bank of England also gave rise to what became known as stockjobbing, or stock trading. Many of the companies had been organized having shares outstanding, but no market existed for them until the bank came into existence. The potential for its shares to appreciate in value plus the fact that it was the largest institution of its day until the South Sea Company was created made it a favorite of the new stockjobbers, who were responsible for pushing the prices of stock of both the Bank of England and the South Sea Company higher and higher during the bubble. This new occupation was not particularly admired, especially after the bubble burst in 1720, causing widespread pain. Detractors referred to jobbing as "Dutch finance" because the idea was imported from Holland and represented the Bank of England and the new monarchy. The old supporters of James II saw the bank as nothing less than an institution supporting the new king, standing between them and a return to Stuart rule.

Daniel Defoe also leveled serious criticism against stockjobbing and the place where it first occurred—Exchange Alley in London. Among his criticisms against the system of paper money and credit, the most telling reflected his earlier problems with his own creditors. In his view, "bankrupts and beggars have advanced the mystery of stock jobbing, and we can now reckon up a black list of 57 persons who within this ten years past have raised themselves to vast estates . . . by the sharpness, tricking, intriguing, scandalous employment of stock jobbing . . . a mystery too hard to be explained."[15] But his complaints fell on deaf ears; stockjobbing quickly became established and became the cornerstone of the London equities market.

The new bank's capital would be increased by an additional £1 million and the charter would be renewed for a longer period early in the eighteenth century when Britain became involved in the War of Spanish Succession. The war, the most expensive in Europe to date, broke out when King Charles II of Spain died and the throne was contested. The bank again advanced the government a large sum to meet its war expenses. The interest rates it paid, higher than the official rates, attracted many new subscribers. During a financial crisis in 1707, the bank needed additional capital due again to government borrowing requirements. Of the many new subscribers, one man showed himself at the bank and offered to lend it his entire fortune, amounting to £500. When Queen Anne heard of the gesture of confidence, she sent him £100 in return with a promise to pay the entire £500 at a future date.[16]

The bank continued to have its detractors, but its supporters equally were vocal and considered it a good investment. Financing military ventures still was the primary expense and would lead Britain to seek other ways to finance its ever-increasing costs. It would also lead to the first great debt-inspired crisis and have far-reaching repercussions for the changing attitudes toward usury and interest.

The South Sea Bubble

In addition to the Bank of England acting as intermediary between the government and its citizens supplying it with funds, the other main source of revenue (other than taxes) to the crown was revenues earned from exploration and trading. The overseas trading companies added a touch of adventure to the quest for riches, but when combined with debt management the result was less than effective, although still highly adventurous.

By 1710, the Bank of England held a monopoly as a government bank with exclusive rights of issue. It was able to issue paper money up to the amount of its paid-in capital and the law prohibited any other banking institution from doing the same. The rate of interest it offered its subscribers was eventually reduced to 5 percent. But the bank was not universally popular in Britain, necessitating the founding of another institution to provide money for the armed forces in return for an exclusive charter to explore the southern Pacific on behalf of the crown. The concept was recognized as a slight of hand by many but necessary to the state of British public finances.

The South Sea Company was founded in 1711, funded originally by a government loan. For the first six years of its life, it never ventured overseas. Then in 1720, the idea of consolidating all the national debt under one roof was proposed. The South Sea Company proposed to Parliament that it would assume the national debt of approximately £30 million in return for a lump sum payment and annual interest of 5 percent. Not happy at being trumped in such matters, the Bank of England countered with its own proposal but was rejected. Shortly thereafter, the South Sea proposal was accepted and passed by Parliament. The company was funded with shares sold to the public and its price began to rise quickly as a result. In a short period, the share price catapulted from around £125 to over £2,000. A bubble had been inflated, based on the company's assumption of the national debt. Speculators could not buy the stock quickly enough. But the bubble soon burst and prices fell as fast as they had risen. As the shares began to drop in price, many speculators panicked. An English newspaper reported that "a certain Suffolk Knight, who they tell us, upon the first news of the stock falling to eight hundred, has hanged himself, for fear of starving with about eleven thousand pounds capital stock in the South Sea Company, in his own property."[17]

During the height of the bubble mania, the company's logo and name even became fashion accessories. Clothing, carriages, and other household items carried the South Sea name, demonstrating that the bearer was in tune with the recent trend in investment. The enormous increase in the company's stock also gave rise to smaller investment schemes that were so dubious in nature that they could only have been concocted during the giddiness of a bubble. One involved subscribers paying 2 guineas for a 100-guinea certificate in a scheme that was to be revealed to them at a later time. Naturally, the promoter of the scheme absconded by evening of the same day with 2,000 guineas of ill-gotten gains.[18] Another offered investors the opportunity to get in on the ground floor of a scheme to import donkeys from Mexico.

While protecting borrowers from predatory lenders, the lower interest rate ceiling helped fuel interest in the early stock market, where profit as capital gains was not subject to the limitations. Reaping large rewards was becoming publicly fashionable, an idea that was anathema a hundred years before. Seeking higher gains from speculation was no longer solely in the hands of merchants taking risks in their own businesses. Now, it was fashionable and began to support many flamboyant lifestyles. The decadent English gentleman who often went heavily into debt to support an exorbitant lifestyle now had a new way to finance himself while avoiding work.

Within a month of the Suffolk knight's suicide, the South Sea Company's shares were down to £175 and the financial destruction was widespread. All levels of society were affected, from noblemen to simple tradesmen. But most affected were the South Sea Company and, to a lesser extent, the Bank of England. The latter was not directly drawn into the misfortunes of the former, but it did suffer runs on its deposits by subscribers, which it barely managed to withstand. The South Sea Company actually showed a profit after the smoke cleared, but its directors and the chancellor of the exchequer were treated harshly by Parliament, as harshly as usurers had been in the past. The chancellor was imprisoned in the Tower and some of the directors of the company had their wealth confiscated. Many commentators and critics of the institutions blamed the speculation madness for all of England's ills, just as the French had done to John Law, whose land bank scheme caused similar problems, which resulted in the Mississippi Bubble, causing widespread financial ruin. But at the heart of the matter was debt, which had become popular on the national level and was being traded in a surrogate manner by London's stockjobbers. Speculators thought that trading in a government-sponsored enterprise that had been granted a virtual monopoly was a sure thing. It would not be the last time the assumption ended painfully.

Parliament responded to the bubble and the smaller bubbles created by sundry promoters by passing the Bubble Act in 1720. Ironically, the law had been introduced by the South Sea Company in order to control competition in the market, which was becoming crowded with investment schemes in joint stock companies. It required all joint stock companies to obtain a royal charter before they could begin trading and represented one of the first pieces of financial regulation in Britain. The new financial marketplace for share trading was causing problems because the government granted monopolies that no one foresaw.

The Bubble Act attempted to protect the citizenry from bogus annuity schemes as well. The tontines and annuities offered by the government had been subject to wide-ranging fraud on both sides since they were first issued. The pamphleteer Abel Boyer revealed numerous frauds in his monthly "The Political State of Great Britain" beginning in 1718. Annuitants had been guilty of falsifying deaths in order to collect while in other cases the relatives of dead annuitants failed to report the deaths in order to keep on collecting. Tontines became surrounded by a large coterie of interested observers who studied the family histories of members, often placing side bets on the prospects of members surviving or dying. A darker side also suggested that many murders were committed in order to help speed up the actuarial statistics. The lore continued for over two hundred years. In the twentieth century, Agatha Christie's murder mystery *4:50 from Paddington* was based upon murder as a motive in a tontine. Even by 1719, the annuity business in Britain was in very bad shape, with many of the annuities in arrears to their annuitants. When a consolidation of the national debt under the South Sea Company was proposed, annuities were included since they represented a considerable drain on the national revenue.

In order to make reparation to unhappy annuitants, the South Sea Company offered stock to them as reimbursement for missed payments and in lieu of cash payments in arrears. During the bubble, the recipients were happy to receive stock that was rising, but when the bubble burst many annuity schemes burst with it. The result was widespread financial damage. Many of the annuity schemes had offered rates of return that were unsustainable or unrealistic from the outset, ranging from 25 to 50 percent per annum. The serious mortality tables and annuity tables had not yet been fully integrated into the plans and the results were obvious. In previous centuries, charging high interest was equated with beggaring thy neighbor. Now, offering high rates was accomplishing the same. The modern financial scam had been born.

Although the South Sea Company dominated the financial landscape along with the Bank of England prior to 1720, other more positive developments occurred in Britain than would bode well for the future. Many interest rate tables were published in the early eighteenth century. Two life insurance companies were also established, although one was somewhat suspect at the time since it also offered annuities. In 1705, the Amicable Society for Perpetual Assurances was founded. In return for payments, it guaranteed a specific sum upon the deaths of subscribers. Fifty years later, the Equitable Life Assurance Society was established, intended to be broader than the Amicable by offering insurance to those above the age of fifty-five. The Equitable also employed the newer methods of life estimation and was based upon the health of the applicants for policies. Like the Amicable, it also offered annuities. Although life insurance had been offered by governments for centuries, these represented partially funded schemes rather than simply payments made by the state to the survivors of deceased members of the military or government bureaucracy.

The rise of life insurance in Britain also gave rise to a practice that did not always reflect well on those taking out insurance contracts but did provide the link between annuities and life insurance. Private annuities were actually nothing more than borrowing to avoid the usury laws. The most common form of borrowing was when an individual would borrow a sum from another, say £1,000 with a promise to repay £100 per year for life. The lender would assess the age and health of the borrower and decide to lend. If the borrower died soon after taking the money, the lender had no recourse to the principal. But in order to cover himself against the potential loss, he would buy life insurance on the borrower's life. In the beginning, life insurance simply was a device used where lenders, or bettors, laid off the risk of someone dying while the contract between them and their investors was valid.

The tribal concept behind usury raised its head again in a law case in 1751 in Britain. John Spencer (later the Earl of Spencer) found himself in tough financial straits. He was the grandson of the Duchess of Marlborough, who was forty years his senior. He proposed to borrow £5,000 to satisfy his cash needs and repay double the amount upon her death, provided that he survived her. After being turned down by several investors, the proposal was accepted by one Abraham Janssen. When the duchess died, Spencer paid £2,000 of the agreed amount, but he in turn died before paying fully. Janssen then sued his estate for the balance, but the executors resisted, claiming the contract was usurious. The court agreed with Janssen and ordered the amount paid, claiming that the "bargain" (as deals were called) was not a loan. A noteworthy comment on the case was made by Justice J. Burnett, who stated that "the greediness of gain is the only principle on which a stranger can be induced to furnish a stranger."[19] The remark was partly tribal and partly modern, suggesting creditworthiness was at issue.

Despite the proliferation of annuity schemes, not everyone saw them as beneficial. On the contrary, they were often seen as nothing more than disguised borrowing designed to avoid the usury statute. In 1745, Lord Chancellor Hardwicke considered a case of a young man of twenty-two who had been in prison and had spent his last pennies on an annuity. While incarcerated, he paid £1,050 for an annuity, promising to pay £150 a year for life. The annuity could be repurchased by the seller with notice and the young man sued to keep it in force when it was redeemed early. The chancellor ruled that the annuity was nothing but a loan at high interest and ordered restitution to the former prisoner at the legal rate of interest. He commented, "I really believe that ninety nine in one hundred cases of these bargains are nothing but loans put into this shape to avoid the statute of usury."[20]

Tontines and their variations remained extremely popular in Britain during the eighteenth century, offering the possibility of future riches plus a fixed income as long as the sellers remained solvent. Some protection for minors was put into place when Parliament passed the Annuity Act in 1777, which declared that tontines could not be sold to those under twenty-one years of age. In addition to protecting the unsuspecting from potential fraud, the law also inadvertently protected the tontine sellers from early payouts to younger people, similar to the problem Henry VIII had two hundred years before when annuities promised to pay out early, causing severe cash flow problems for the program. The act also required annuities to be declared and registered, a provision that caused the number of private annuities to decline in the years ahead.

Tontines became one of the first examples of financial packaging designed to avoid regulation. Although the courts recognized the potential for fraud and speculation with tontines, it still took many years to recognize their potential to circumvent the usury laws. But at the same time that the British were grappling with interest, the usury laws were being extended through colonization and would be extended to North America in more simple forms.

Exporting Usury Laws

Despite the speculation, bubbles, and frauds, usury had not disappeared from economic discussion by any means. Soon British attitudes toward interest would be exported to the colonies, where they would live on for two hundred years, in many cases sparking more rancorous debate and regulation than they did at home. As they were copied in the colonies, the old tribal prohibitions against usury could be seen again.

British colonies in the New World inherited the mother country's attitudes toward usury and added a new twist. The usury laws were transplanted with some modification. They were incorporated into the new colonies' laws, and later the new state constitutions. This would pave the way for what would become known in the United States as statutory usury laws. The British statutory usury laws had been complemented by common law over the years and both were incorporated in colonial America. They would prove troublesome in the years ahead.

The common law followed English settlers into the thirteen original colonies and more formal usury laws were adopted by colonial legislatures relatively early in most of the colonies. The earliest usury law adopted was by the Massachusetts colonial legislature in 1641. The law read in part, "No man shall be adjudged for a mere forebearance of any debt above eight pound in the hundred, for one year, and not above that rate proportionally, for all sums whatsoever, bills of exchange excepted." This followed the ceiling established under James I. No penalties were mentioned for usurers, however. At least one nineteenth-century writer believed that the usury law was tribal in nature because the Pilgrims were all of like mind and similar backgrounds and actual penalties were omitted from the law, suggesting it was merely a prohibition similar to that of the Hebrews.[21] Exempting bills of exchange was a clear indication that trade was on the minds of the early settlers, indicating the role commerce played in early colonization.

The 8 percent rate remained in force in Massachusetts until 1692, when it was lowered to 6 percent. Other legislatures followed suit. The same year, the Maryland legislature set the maximum rate at 6 percent, allowing for 8 percent for trade-related transactions such as the production of tobacco or shipping. Maryland followed the original Elizabethan statute closely, calling for treble damages if someone was found to be practicing usury at a higher rate. Pennsylvania made 6 percent permanent in 1700, New York in 1717, Connecticut in 1718, and South Carolina in 1719. The first two set the ceiling at 6 percent while South Carolina was higher at 10 percent. New York established a precedent in doing so, however. The original rate of 6 percent was introduced for a five-year period, after which it expired, making it one of the first sunset clauses in American legislative history. It then was raised to 8 percent and was only reduced to the original rate in 1737.

The other colonies followed suit, with 6 percent being the most popular rate used. Georgia, founded by James Oglethorpe, a member of Parliament, in 1733, had the distinction of being the colony settled to provide a haven for debtors from Britain. The concept had been advocated by writers in Britain who enlisted Oglethorpe's help in organizing an expedition, which led to the colony being settled and named after George II. Oglethorpe was ready to oblige, having lost a close friend to smallpox while the friend was incarcerated at Fleet Prison for usury. Georgia's usury statute was passed in 1759, while Virginia (1730), New Jersey (1730), North Carolina (1741), Delaware (1759), and Rhode Island (1759) all passed their own laws at 6 percent. Only New Jersey was higher, at 7 percent.[22] The standard 6 percent rate would prevail until the usury laws began to be effectively dismantled, beginning in the 1980s.

Outside the Americas, Parliament set the rate of interest at 12 percent in India and 6 percent in the West Indies and Ireland during the reign of George III. As with English law, the colonial laws were fairly comprehensive, applying to discounted trade bills and bills of exchange as well. If bills were re-discounted between counterparties, usury ceilings could be violated and most of the American colonies' laws took note of the practice. And maritime contracts usually were exempt from them or had much higher ceilings because of the higher degree of risk associated with shipping. Progress had been made on this latter practice since the Middle Ages, when interest had to be disguised through elaborate maritime contracts.

The distinctions made between different kinds of loans in the colonies was much more simple than it would be two hundred years later and the simple maximum rate could be stated as the official ceiling for most, if not all, loans. Over time, as concepts of property became more complex, the single standard rate would begin to strain under its own weight. When consumer interest became available in the twentieth century on an unsecured basis, the risk profile would change and with it maximum rates of interest. But until then, lending remained a relatively simple affair and usury laws remained the major reference on interest rates for lending, although market rates could, and did, deviate from them substantially. Collateral was almost always required and would be seized if a borrower defaulted.

Despite the widespread use of usury laws in the American colonies, their widespread avoidance also was noteworthy. In most of the colonies, usury was considered a civil offense rather than a criminal one and the penalties were light and almost never enforced. Exceptions and methods to avoid the laws were standard. One method to avoid the laws was the "dry exchange." This was a transaction originating in the Middle Ages where a bill of exchange was drawn by a borrower and then the specifics about the second side of the transaction were purposely omitted so that different rates could be used between the borrower and the lender. The bills, one on each side, where executed simultaneously. The borrower would then compensate the lender at a higher rate than stipulated in the bill, by arrangement. Following this, another common technique was a repurchase transaction where a borrower would sell a lender collateral and then buy it back at a higher price than the usury laws would have stipulated. Both techniques were particularly difficult to detect since they were accomplished by mutual agreement between borrower and lender. The letter of the usury laws was kept but effectively evaded behind the scenes.[23]

But it was not only copying of the mother country's statutes that made usury laws popular in the American colonies. The future proved that they would last longer than the British law, which was repealed in 1854. Their success was assured by the popularity of an unlikely book that became a bestseller in the American colonies and sold almost as many copies there as it did in Britain. Between 1755 and 1765, William Blackstone's *Commentaries on the Laws of England* were published, providing a compendium of the common law lacking until that time on both sides of the Atlantic. Although his comments on usury were not novel or particularly incisive, they formed the basis of American law on the subject for the next two hundred years.

Blackstone was not a noted jurist or advocate when he began writing the *Commentaries*. He was a lawyer who did not have much success practicing and retired to Oxford in 1763 to read and comment on the law. His studies blossomed into four volumes that became the most famous compendium of English law written until that time. In many respects, his achievement was not unlike that of Gratian in canon law centuries before. Blackstone became a member of Parliament, a councilor to the queen, and a judge. Unlike many other noteworthy commentators, his reputation was already made by the time he assumed the bench.

His thoughts on usury dovetailed with mainstream English law and included nothing new. Noting that the Hebrews banned usury and the Scholastics had banned interest of any type entirely, citing the "barrenness" argument of Aristotle, Blackstone stated that "the Mosaical precept was clearly a political, not a moral precept. It only prohibited the Jews from taking interest from their brethren . . . unless money therefore can be borrowed, trade cannot be carried on and if no premium were allowed for the hire of money, few persons would care to lend it; or at least the ease of borrowing would be entirely at an end."[24] The old prohibitions against usury were products of an unenlightened age and ran counter to the idea of progress in business and commerce. This unremarkable comment was standard thinking at the time and formed the basis of American state laws against usury that lasted until the twentieth century.

The method for calculating interest also was imported by the colonists from Britain, as might be expected. Although Simon Stevin's tables had been in use on the Continent since being introduced in 1582, the comprehensive British tables that appeared ninety years later used examples of the present and future value of the pound and its sub-units. Although William Webster's tables were the first published in England, they were not compiled using decimals for future values but rather gave the products of their calculations in pounds, shillings, and pence. They also only covered interest from 5 to 10 percent. Another set of tables, entitled *The Money Monger, or the Usurer's Almanacke*, was published in London in 1626 using 8 percent as its rate after interest had been lowered to that level under James I. Stevin's tables covered the range of rates in one-percent increments from 1 to 20 percent.[25] As a result, another easy-to-use version became more popular and found its way to the colonies on account of its simplicity. The exported British version originally was published as a "reckoner" (table for easy calculations) for schoolboys in the City of London in 1671 by James Hodder, a teacher and headmaster, who entitled his work *Hodder's Decimal Arithmetik*. A later edition of the book was published in Boston in 1719, becoming the first English reckoner published in the American colonies (see the Appendix).

Adam Smith, d'Alembert, and Newton

Moral and theological arguments against usury began to fade in the seventeenth and eighteenth centuries as the common-sense acceptance of usury replaced the indignation felt by many commentators since Thomas Aquinas. The population was growing and with it living standards. Also growing was a keener sense of economic and financial affairs and the role they played in this general sense of well-being despite continued warfare in Europe, notably the Thirty Years' War and continued conflagrations between Britain and France. And with these developments came more ideas that were demographically based.

In France, the usury debate raged as it had done for centuries. Montesquieu added a modern note to the usury debate by commenting that "to lend money without interest, is certainly an action laudable and extremely good; but it is obvious, that it is only a counsel of religion, and not a civil law."[26] The moral overtones were disappearing from the contemporary legal distinctions. Being a nobleman, he reflected the secular view of business rather than the religious one, which was still quite strong despite the growing secularization of society in general. Fond of demographics as part of his political and economic discussions, Montesquieu was also well versed in non-European views of usury, making one of the first European comments about Islamic views. Regarding Islamic practices, he noted that "the laws of Mahomet confound usury with lending upon interest. Usury increases in Mahometan countries, in proportion to the severity of the prohibition. The lender indemnifies himself for the danger he undergoes of suffering the penalty."[27] This was an early exposition of the market view of society, which generally held that prohibitions usually created exactly the sorts of problems they were meant to protect against. Compensatory usury was simply adjusting for credit risk.

Maritime loans also were treated separately by Montesquieu, again demonstrating that they were riskier than other sorts of loans and required higher rates of return to compensate lenders. Daniel Defoe's bankruptcy certainly was evidence of it. Exploration and discovery would not have been possible if medieval merchants and traders adhered to the church's strict laws against usury because it would not have been possible to take on the increased risk of sea voyages without proper compensation. One of the major products of the usury prohibitions was the private partnerships and early forms of stock companies created to circumvent the usury laws.

While attitudes toward usury and lending were changing slowly, the intricacies of compound interest remained something of a mystery. The vast period of time between Fibonacci and Simon Stevin produced little in the way of understanding how interest was calculated, at least to non-bankers. Most of the understanding was based on negative metaphors. Compound interest still was considered "Jewish" interest.

The position of the Catholic Church toward usury did not change during the mercantilist period. Many of the new types of financial contracts had come to the attention of the papacy. Pope Benedict XIV stated in an encyclical in 1745 that usury was interest and vice versa and as such was expressly forbidden by canon law. In *Vix Pervenit* he equated the two, as had been the case since the Council of Nicaea, stating that any loan must be returned in its original amount to the lender. Anything beyond the principal amount was usury. This merely was a reaffirmation of generally accepted doctrine. His encyclical did not have the weight of statutory canon law since it was only circulated to the Italian clergy rather than to the entire church, but nevertheless it was an affirmation of past church teachings.

During the eighteenth century, public finances in Britain became more sophisticated and the government issued more consols, short for consolidated issue. The most famous one, the 3 percent consol, was issued in 1751 and was issued to resemble a perpetual annuity in that it bore no maturity date. Its yield was simple to calculate and it became the best-known British bond for several generations until it was replaced by another consol in the nineteenth century. The perpetual feature was not as onerous as it seemed for the government since the consols bore a call feature, allowing it to call them back if interest rates moved lower.[28]

While most interest rate developments centered on new financial products and annuities, an incisive comment about interest was made by Jean Le Rond d'Alembert, the mathematician, philosopher, and co-author of the *Encyclopedia* with Denis Diderot, which appeared in France between 1751 and 1772. D'Alembert managed to include some astute observations about the subject in the *Encyclopedia*. His observation is better known today because of the use of interest rate tables, which produce a visual proof of the principle even if the reader is not well versed mathematically. The results provided something of a milestone in understanding simple and compound interest and eventually contributed to the technical side of the usury debate. The principle was not well understood beyond mathematical circles at the time.

According to d'Alembert, simple and compound interest can at various points in the life of a loan have different effects on borrower and lender. In periods of less than one year, a borrower being charged compound interest actually pays less than he would if he had been charged simple interest for the loan at the same interest rate. If he pays the loan back early, the amount effectively will be less than if he waits until the end of the year when interest is formally attached to the principal amount. This is because simple interest is calculated by taking the amount due and halving it for six months or dividing by four for a quarter. Compound interest, in contrast, has a higher present value according to the discount tables, which would be used in determining the payback amount.

If a man borrowed £100 for a three-year period (compounded annually) at 6 percent, the amount of interest owed after one year would be £6. After two years it would be £12.36, and after three years it would be £19.10, demonstrating the effect of compound interest. But the point being made is in a loan paid early, after six months. According to interest rate tables, like those of Simon Stevin, if the loan were paid back in the first six months (if the contract allows it), then the tables, which are discount tables based on a compound future value, suggest that the amount of actual interest paid would be £2.92 (using decimal notation, based upon a present value of £0.9708). Simple interest, in contrast, states that the amount of interest paid would be £3.00. Thus, the compound basis actually would be cheaper in real terms than simple interest. But if taken beyond the first year, the opposite would hold true. The conclusion was straightforward: "the advantage of the debtor ends with the first year and that of the creditor then begins to augment with the number of years."[29]

The example d'Alembert used was usurious because it assumed that the rate of interest multiplied three times over the life of the loan term: "exorbitant usury could never doubtless be allowed of in morality, but the example is chosen to make the calculation easier." Usurious rates were used to amplify the argument, suggesting that normal rates would have produced differences in amounts due or actually paid that may not have impressed readers given the ordinary levels. An anti-monarchical newspaper in Britain that resurrected d'Alembert's discussion of usury lamented that it could not "see much practical use that it can be to the men of business in this country, among whom compound interest is scarcely known."[30]

When the *Encyclopedia* was published, d'Alembert was accused of being an apologist for usury for suggesting that compound interest could actually benefit a borrower. That clearly was not the case in his example. What is more telling is the newspaper's suggestion that not many businessmen in Britain would have understood his example in any event. Reckoners and basic interest tables already were in wide use so it is difficult to imagine that someone had not seen his example in a table and made use of it in the late eighteenth century. It appears that compound interest was still considered more of a mystery than the eighth wonder of the world.

On a general level, begrudging acceptance of usury was the guiding force behind the development of mercantilism. In mercantilist thought, achieving the upper hand in trade with one's neighbors was a national goal. More recently, that has become known as the "beggar-thy-neighbor policy" in international trade. The term owes more to the ancient and medieval concepts of usury than it does to international trade, however. The long forgotten connection between accepting usury as high rates of interest and the later idea that the same process was somehow acceptable in international trade even if that meant beggaring the occasional country and trading partner is striking. Mercantilism relied on high rates of interest, especially in shipping and trading. Without them, as many commentators noted, lending would have shifted to even riskier, and less fruitful, activities that would not have created additional value.

An explicit criticism of mercantilism was found in the writings of the Scottish philosopher David Hume. While not a financial practitioner like his countrymen William Paterson and John Law, Hume's comments on interest were entirely practical and were based upon a quantity theory of money. The mercantilist idea was that the amount of precious metals coming into a country was not as important as the supply of domestic wealth and commodities, measured in monetary terms. When an economy was strong, interest rates remained low. Higher interest rates, in contrast, were the product of a weak economy. "High interest arises from three circumstances: A great demand for borrowing; little riches to supply that demand; and great profits arising from commerce: And these circumstances are a clear proof of the small advance of commerce and industry, not of the scarcity of gold and silver."[31] The opposite was true of low interest rates. Hume saw interest rate levels in a historical context; in early societies inequality prevailed and high lending rates were evident as those with more demanded high interest from those with less. The generalization reflected the experience of the Middle Ages and one thousand years of Roman history.

Hume died in the same year (1776) that Adam Smith's *Wealth of Nations* was published. The book generally is considered the tombstone of the mercantilist era and the beginning of the era of market-driven trade. Taken together, Hume's and Smith's comments on rates of interest provided a comprehensive discussion of the topic and reflected their common views over the role of mercantilism. Smith was a bit more expansive and technical. His comments also were historical, but he followed with a technical discussion. Historically, he explained the phenomenon of inflation in the early sixteenth century, which was caused by the import of precious metals from the New World. The imports were accompanied by a subsequent drop in interest rates in Europe generally, although intuitively the opposite might have been expected. Higher interest would be justified by a quantity theory of money like that of Hume, but Smith discussed it using the old debasement example. The discussion was, however, in keeping with the mercantilist philosophy prevalent when it first occurred. He stated that if "£100 now are worth no more than £50 were then, £5 now can be worth no more than £2, 10 shillings were then [£2.50, with 20 shillings per pound]. By reducing the rate of interest, therefore, from ten to five percent, we give for the use of a capital, which is supposed to be equal to one half of its former value, an interest which is equal to one fourth only of the value of the former interest."[32]

Importing gold was not exclusively a Spanish phenomenon. The English also felt the effects of it. Under Charles II, a large amount of gold was found in Guinea, West Africa and brought back to Britain. Charles had a special coin minted for the occasion—the guinea, a gold coin intended to replace the traditional 20 shillings of silver in 1 pound. In 1717, when Isaac Newton was master of the mint, he discovered that the guinea actually contained one pound eight pence worth of gold (240 pence equaled a pound, 12 pence in a shilling). A royal proclamation followed declaring a guinea to be worth a pound and a shilling when by weight the guinea actually was 4 pence short.[33] This announcement occurred in the same year the national debt of Great Britain was consolidated by the South Sea Company.

Newton also demonstrated the power of compound interest in a book published in 1720 entitled *Universal Arithmetick*. The title certainly was simpler than its contents. Tackling the annuity problem, he posited, "If an annual pension of the [Number of] Pounds a, to be paid in the five next following years, be bought for ready Money c, to find what the Compound Interest of 100 l per annum will amount to?"[34] Unlike many reckoners, he did not solve the problem but simply displayed a polynomial that would address it (the original equation can be found in the Appendix). It is doubtful that his demonstration of compound interest would have affected the practical art of charging interest, but it certainly did show that *anatocismus* was alive, well, and being considered by all of those involved in finance and economic planning.

This small part of his book has a special significance because it is the first extant publication of a calculation solving for the rate of compound interest. Newton seemed to be well aware of Fibonacci's work since he posited a problem similar to that of Fibonacci. Rather than solve the future value, he posited an equation that would actually solve the old medieval riddle by solving the rate of return necessary to achieve a desired future result. And his calculation determining that the guinea was actually short of gold content can also be traced to Fibonacci, who dedicated an entire chapter of *Liber abaci* to the same topic. What appeared to be nothing more than another calculation at the time would have significance far beyond the realm of practical arithmetic of the day.

In addition to addressing the subject of interest, Adam Smith commented on the importance of Thomas Mun's book on mercantilism written 150 years before. "The title of Mun's book, *England's Treasure in Foreign Trade*, became a fundamental maxim in the political economy, not of England only, but of all other commercial countries . . . the inland or home trade . . . was considered as subsidiary only to foreign trade . . . the country could never become either richer or poorer by means of it."[35] Smith and Hume may have disagreed, but mercantilism produced a rise in national wealth that dovetailed nicely with many countries' ambitions on the international stage. Accepting usury was an integral part of it.

Regarding usury, Smith applied a much more modern and commonsensical approach to interest than his predecessors. He stated that the maximum rate of interest needed to be set above the lowest market rate so that lenders continued to lend. "The legal rate, it is to be observed, ought not to be much above the lowest market rate. If the legal rate of interest in Great Britain was fixed so high as eight or ten percent, the greater part of the money which was to be lent, would be lent to prodigals and projectors who alone would be willing to give this high interest."[36] Leaving aside the fact that this sort of lending would be defaulted, it would also siphon funds from useful projects requiring capital infusions. Smith's approach laid the framework for a "collar" of tolerable interest to be charged, a concept that would be modified in the years ahead. The miscreants he referred to, who would pay high rates of interest, were the landed English nobility and gentry, many of whom were already so notoriously idle that they borrowed from moneylenders to finance their current consumption, exposing themselves to what he referred to as the "extortion of usury."

Smith's discussion of capital differentiated long-term investment funds from cash, which he referred to as the "stock," or simply money. This distinction was often missing in the earlier anti-usury tracts. Clearly, capital required interest but at low rates if it were to be productive. Productivity and capital created a societal good so the process had an end in its sights, not merely the accumulation of profit or lending for nonproductive purposes. This can be taken alongside Smith's reference in *The Wealth of Nations* to the "invisible hand." This force, which guided individual self-interest to a societal good, has been interpreted in many different ways over the last two hundred years, usually as a reference to the metaphor of the free market. But its religious overtone is difficult to miss. If the invisible hand was the secular surrogate of divine guidance in human affairs, it could also be interpreted as the force that requires usury to be tolerated but still controlled within limits. Smith was well aware of the rancorous history of usury as an economic and moral doctrine. It could be tolerated if it produced both a commercial sense of well-being and a societal well-being at the same time. Put another way, it was necessary for the successful deployment of capital. One hundred years before, Robert Filmer the royalist made essentially the same case in a less analytical sense. Consensus was forming that interest was integral to investing in capital projects. Exorbitantly high rates were reserved for the risky, fools, and knaves. Reasonable rates were necessary for the investment process.

While the discussion of interest was focused increasingly on business investment, the more sordid side of getting too deeply into debt still persisted, especially among the poorer class in England. Oglethorpe's attempts ultimately were not successful, but the effort was not forgotten, at least on a smaller scale. In 1772, a society called the Thatched Roof Society, dedicated to obtaining the release of small debtors from prison, was founded at a London church by James Neild and William Dodd. By passing the collection plate, they raised money and used it to buy small debtors out of prison by repaying their obligations. They also advertised in newspapers, raising money from the wealthy. The list of contributors grew rapidly. Shortly after raising a small amount, they were able to rescue five debtors from various prisons whose total indebtedness amounted to £2 8s. By the end of their first year, they had secured the release of six hundred adults and twice as many children. The total cost was £800.

The good efforts had an underlying motive. The Reverend Dodd, who had several degrees from Cambridge, also had a flamboyant lifestyle and a penchant for gambling for most of his life. He was known to his contemporaries as the Macaroni Parson because of his love of things foreign. Like many of his wealthier contemporaries, he gambled constantly. When he won a lottery for £ 1,000, he used the proceeds to build a chapel. His own debts paled those of the debtors he tried to help. Ultimately, their problems were small when compared to his.

Most of the debtors were imprisoned for small debts, sometimes as little as 18 shillings. Creditors could have a debtor imprisoned by simply demanding it at court. Debtors' wives and children often accompanied them into jail. However, the exact opposite occurred in a similar scenario at the other end of the social scale. In 1793, Frederick, the Prince of Wales, a profligate spender, ran up debts well in excess of his annual allowance. He was pursued by his creditors, whose options did not include imprisoning him, which was not possible by law, but they could seek payment from the king or Parliament. By 1795, his debts had amounted to over £800,000; they were eventually paid, but not before bringing scorn and derision on the monarchy. The Reverend Dodd, however, was less lucky. He met an ignominious end in 1777 when he was convicted of forgery. He signed his name to a document to illegally collect £4,200 in order to settle some debts. His case was taken up by Samuel Johnson, who gathered a petition with over twenty-three thousand signatures supporting Dodd but to no avail. He was publicly hanged since forgery was a capital offense. His successors carried on the humanitarian effort in his absence.

Indebtedness was a serious issue in the later eighteenth century and the stereotypic portrayals of Jews at the center of moneylending continued as they had for centuries. In 1777, Sheridan's *School for Scandal* made its debut on the London stage; it centered on a landed family with some members in dire need of a loan. "Moses" was the friendly Jewish moneylender in the play along with another character named "Mr. Premium." Both found themselves besieged with requests for money when introduced to the members of the family. Business was brisk.

In the last decade of the eighteenth century, tontines were still popular in Britain and were becoming popular in Ireland as well. The contributions made by Halley and others in the previous century made them more viable financially, but there were still skeptics doubting their value. One English newspaper remarked that "the number of tontines evince that there are some good things arising from them to the managers, who tell the subscribers that it will be very profitable—when they are dead."[37]

The comment was more than simple cynicism. Working-class people especially were addicted to the tontines as a way of speculating and the subscription monies spent were driving many of them to a penniless state. Private lotteries had been popular in Britain but had been outlawed because of fraud and the general public propensity to gamble away a week's wages in the hope of getting rich. The tontines appeared to be a way of ensuring for the future but also remained vehicles for gambling. The reader of one London newspaper wrote to the editor asking for some legal advice. Given that many laboring people subscribed to tontines in the desperate hope of getting rich, did the law banning private lotteries apply to them as well? The response was negative. The paper responded, "Generally, all contracts whatsoever, in which there is something to be given for something received, are good . . . therefore, they cannot be extended by implication or analogy, to any thing but the subject of them; and consequently not to tontines."[38]

Tontines still provided a benefit to their subscribers, although the statistics of life expectancy and mortality behind them were indecipherable to the average speculator, who was happy simply to bet against the life expectancies of others in his tontine pool. The continued interest in the schemes provided proof that the population of Britain still flocked to speculative ventures after the South Sea Bubble debacle and would continue to do so. The challenge to the government was to devise an investment that would provide a decent return to the public while achieving some societal benefit at the same time. But the parlous state of British finances did not make that an easy task.

The Sinking Fund

The debt Britain had accumulated through tontines and government bonds became a subject of intense debate, especially after the American Revolution. In 1780, the government debt stood at approximately £250 million and British influence had declined because of the loss of the American colonies. It was, however, a time when most politicians in the United Kingdom expected a prolonged period of peace. As a result, Parliament was presented with a proposal that would work well in peacetime and even better with a presumed government surplus that a reduction in military spending would bring. What was unusual was that this new plan to reduce the sizable British deficit planned to use compound interest to cure the country's financial problems.

When William Pitt the Younger became prime minister in 1783, he espoused a program designed to reduce the national debt. The policy he pursued was that of adopting a new version of a national sinking fund to retire outstanding bonds and tontines. Britain already had employed a sinking fund since 1719, but it had met with mixed results. The new idea was to set aside a specific amount of money per year, presumably from tax revenues or from selling new tontines, and purchase outstanding government bonds with it.[39] The interest that would not have to be paid on the bonds would be added to a similar sum the next year and so on until the national debt was reduced. The sinking fund intended to employ compound interest to reduce the debt.

The idea was simple but had certain faults. One was Pitt's reasoning about interest rates and the effect of the compounding. In a speech delivered in 1784, he stated, "It was always my idea that a fund at a high rate of interest is better to the country than those at low rates; that a four per cent is preferable to a three per cent, and a five per cent better than a four. The reason is that in all operations of finance we should always have in view a plan of redemption. Gradually to redeem and to extinguish our debt ought ever to be the wise pursuit of government."[40] The basic idea appeared somewhat vague, but his comment about higher interest rates seemed to be a political acknowledgment that higher interest rates were anticipated because of the size of the government debt load.

In short, Pitt believed that retiring old debt with new, higher coupon debt eventually would aid the reverse compounding process since all debt issues should be retired with a plan at the time of the initial borrowing. This was a curious example of advocating borrowing at higher rates than the old debt. The only way this could be justified was when the annual amounts set aside for retirement came from a government surplus and were not borrowed or derived from new taxes. That presumed a state of peace in Britain's foreign affairs; if war broke out again the plan would be complicated and the schedule of retirements broken.

The idea was not his. Pitt borrowed the plan from Richard Price, a clergyman who had written extensively about theology, morals, probability, and annuities. Price was one of the better mathematicians of his day, although his early years did not provide any clues to his later success. He was born in Wales in 1723, the son of a Congregational minister. He became a Dissenter, or nonconformist, early in life and his views precluded him from attending either Oxford or Cambridge. He was educated at a Dissenter academy before becoming a minister. After writing extensively about morals and philosophy, he turned his attention to probability and applied mathematics. He was elected a member of the Royal Society in 1765 for a book written on probability. Later, he began to specialize in annuities and interest problems and wrote extensively about them in several books, each seeking to address problems posed by annuities in the United Kingdom and the life expectancies of insurance policy holders. These interests closely followed those of Edmund Halley. Price was adamant that compound interest could be used successfully to reduce the national debt. Before he died in 1791, he was awarded a doctor of divinity degree by Yale for his writings and influence in the United States. He also was a founding member of the Unitarian Society.

The moral problems that he wrote about in his earlier years led him to believe that *anatocism* could be used for positive effect as well as negative. But the term had almost disappeared from the legal lexicon and compound interest became the standard way of describing interest on interest. The principle remained true to its original meaning, but attitudes toward it had changed. The *New Encyclopedia*, published in 1807, said the following about *anatocism*: "After all, it is difficult to discover, wherein the injustice lies, in taking interest upon interest, any more than in taking it upon the principal. It is allowed on all hands, that the creditor, who lends money, may lift the interest: the day it is due, and lend it out, as a *principal* sum to another person, or to the same person, if he grants a new bill for it, in which case, the interest just drawn bears interest anew." [41]

After compound interest had been railed against for centuries, Price finally had discovered a method to make it useful, at least in theory. The real test of its applicability would be found in its reception by the British fiscal authorities. He wrote about the sinking fund for at least twenty-five years before Pitt adopted it, and wrote numerous works about it and its potential effects on the national debt. Price was widely read on both sides of the Atlantic and the combination of morals, theology, and finance struck a chord in his readers and with the U.K. government, which was always in need of new ideas to deal with the debt issue. He maintained correspondence with Benjamin Franklin, among many notable Americans. He supported American independence, prompting Congress to invite him to the United States to assume control of the national finances, which were in disarray after independence. He declined the offer to remain in Britain.[42] Pitt actively sought his advice before the sinking fund was adopted by Parliament and accepted by George III in 1786 and the plan was adopted by the treasury. It became a modest success in time, although it never succeeded in reducing the national debt by more than about 5 percent, far less than the original estimate. The problem was that Britain did not remain at peace. The Napoleonic Wars began and considerable resources had to be devoted to the war effort. The annual payments necessary to ensure success of the fund were diverted for other purposes. Compound interest required time to reduce the deficit, but the necessary number of payments never materialized properly.

Price extolled the virtues of compound interest through all his writings. To make his point, he wrote that "one penny put out at our Savior's birth to 5 per cent compound interest would, before this time [1785], have increased to a greater sum than would be contained in two hundred millions of earths all solid gold. But if put out to simple interest it would have amounted to no more than seven shillings and sixpence. All governments which alienate funds destined for reimbursements choose to improve money in the last rather than the first of these ways." [43] This was his basic explanation of why governments should use a sinking fund with compound interest. He repeated it many times in different works and the principle always was the same.

Invoking the deity was a dramatic effect. The calculations were correct and the point was made. In his book written about the well-being and future of the United States, he claimed that a sinking fund of £100,000 would have beneficial results for the new country and keep it debt free if followed assiduously. He claimed that the sum, if paid annually for seventeen years, would reduce debt by £30 million. He was correct but failed to specify the sort of compounding necessary to achieve the goal since either annual or semi-annual compounding would produce slightly in excess of the £30 million. Price's calculation was nothing more than an annuity assumption re-tooled for the benefit of the state. That amount, paid for seventeen years without fail, compounded at 5 percent, would produce that sum. If followed correctly, the state would be paying itself an annuity, with beneficial results.

Despite his notoriety and polymath abilities, Price's views were not warmly received by all. Shortly after the American Revolution began, a popular newspaper took him to task for his support of the colonies and the sinking fund, among other topics. The sinking fund, according to the article, raised the scepter of universal bankruptcy and was only another one of Price's principles that had caused distress to the British people. But his support of the colonies was the main problem his writings presented. "On persisting in your former principles and endeavors to sustain the cause of rebellion, are you not at once a rebel to your God, your King, your country?," the newspaper asked, suggesting that he was guilty of treason rather than sound fiscal ideas.[44]

Despite Price's views, his version of the sinking fund was adopted, although Pitt took the credit for it rather than widely publicize Price's contribution. What made Price particularly unpopular in many quarters was his constant reference to what he viewed as the perilous state of British finances. He often referred to the topic when pressing for adoption of his sinking fund over the years. That he was a Dissenter did not help his cause, but his mastery of the annuity calculations was not in doubt. Since John Napier, the Scottish mathematician, had discovered logarithms in 1614, more complex math was available to perform future value calculations and Price was well acquainted with them. Although the sinking fund eventually was abandoned in 1829 and Price somewhat forgotten, his attempt to turn *anatocismus* on its head and use it for the public good was noteworthy, if short-lived.

The Rise of International Bankers

The rise of private bankers in England in the late seventeenth century proved lucrative but was not without credit and counterparty risks. The laws against fraud and deceit were harsh and protected bankers to an extent. One fact remained clear about banking in the period leading to the American Revolution that would remain for centuries: providing banking services to large or institutional customers was preferable to providing them to smaller, less disciplined customers who often used loans merely to survive from one day to the next.

By the mid-eighteenth century, the overseas businesses and colonies of the major trading nations required bankers who were diversified and influential. The South Seas Company was not particularly successful at exploration and trading and had stumbled badly after consolidating the national debt. The international role once occupied by the Templars and the Medici banks in Europe had never been filled adequately. England and Europe needed bankers who could reach across borders as successfully as their explorers did. A trans-European, and later a transatlantic, credit institution was needed to channel funds from the wealthy nations to the less developed.

That role would be filled by two banking houses founded in the latter eighteenth century. Both achieved the distinction of being called the "house," the highest unofficial honor given to a private banking firm. Each house was dominated by the founding family members and achieved considerable power in domestic and international affairs for well over two hundred years. Both contributed significantly to the subsequent power of Britain and France in the nineteenth century especially. And both played a major role in American economic development well into the nineteenth century.

In both cases, these banking houses were founded by outsiders. Baring Brothers was founded by John and Francis Baring in 1763, originally as a merchant business specializing in textiles and commodities. Their father was a merchant who immigrated to Britain from Germany. Francis was the more active of the two brothers and directed the firm to diversify. It shifted to the merchant banking business under his guidance in 1776. The rise of the firm was dramatic. Baring made use of close political connections to increase the business. Within a few decades, the partnership served as major banker to the gentry, British businesses, and the crown of England. By the Napoleonic Wars, the bank was considered the "sixth great power" in Europe along with the major European governments. It would later help arrange the Louisiana Purchase and became a major conduit for British funds to be invested in the United States, often through local agents.

Local bankers in the United States with ties to the bank acted as its investment agents, and substantial funds were invested, many in infrastructure, such as the railroads. Baring often acted as an intermediary for the British crown, which also had funds invested in the United States. In the late eighteenth century and the early nineteenth, many Americans feared the influence of Baring because it was assumed that the bank represented the interests of George III, whose mental state was in question at the time of American Independence. The British remained major suppliers of capital to the United States until the 1890s, when the bank suffered major losses on investments in South America.

Francis Baring died in 1810 and eventually was succeeded at the firm by his son Francis. After becoming a member of Parliament, the second Francis often spoke publicly in favor of repealing the usury laws in Britain. Aligned with many notable opponents of usury in the early nineteenth century, including David Ricardo, his voice would add considerable weight for repeal. He spoke against usury in the Commons when still in his twenties. He told the house that the usury laws were "injurious to those for whose benefit they were intended."[45] Later, as repeal drew closer in 1854, he again repeated his objections to them. The Industrial Revolution provided the circumstances that finally caused repeal in the United Kingdom. The founding of the House of Baring coincided almost exactly with the industrialization of Britain in the late eighteenth century and the early nineteenth.

The same was true of the greatest banking house of the era, the House of Rothschild. Founded by Meyer Amschel Rothschild in 1764, the bank was originally a dealer in coins and gold based in the Frankfurt ghetto. It quickly developed from its humble origins and spread to other German and European cities, similar to the spread of the Medici banks three hundred years before. N. M. Rothschild and Sons, the English branch of the European bank, was founded in 1798 by Nathan Mayer Rothschild, who had been sent to Britain to deal in cotton for family interests. It was the English branch that became the conduit for much of the European money that was to find its way to North America. The bank performed what today are called merchant banking operations and one of them was to act as agent for many Continental investors who wanted to invest in the United States. After the War of 1812, the bank competed with Baring in directing investments to the United States, mostly in state and city government bonds. It also helped funnel significant funds to the U.S. Treasury during the Civil War. Baring, on the other hand, helped supply the federal government with financing for war materiels during the conflict.[46] Rothschild never opened an American branch but officially did business through an agent, August Belmont, who was sent to the United States to represent the bank's interest shortly before the panic of 1837 in New York. He subsequently founded August Belmont and Company, an investment and merchant banking firm that continued to represent the Rothschild interests in the United States until late in the nineteenth century.

Bentham on Usury

Despite the advances made in attacking usury as a biblical and moral prohibition that was out of touch with late mercantilism and the early stages of the Industrial Revolution, it still was a powerful force in the law and public opinion. But its intellectual hold was eroding as many commentators attacked its foundations as mistaken or simply wrong. In the late eighteenth century and the early nineteenth, the debate was becoming as binary as it had been three centuries before despite the fact that charging interest was completely part of the business fabric of most countries in the early throes of industrialization.

In 1796, a case was heard in an English court reminiscent of John Shakespeare and many medieval cases before him. A plaintiff filed an action against a defendant in a case in which the defendant had been incarcerated in King's Bench Prison for not paying a debt. This sort of action relied on the testimony of an informant, similar to the medieval cases in which the informants were compensated for information producing a conviction. In this particular case, the informant was not party to the lending transaction and apparently had no pecuniary interest in it other than to relate events as he remembered them. He heard the information in the prison, related by the defendant.

A merchant named Smith sued a borrower named Bromer for not paying a debt of £30,000 lent to him. The two were relatives. Bromer could not pay, claiming that the rates being charged were usurious and drove him to penury. He was a bankrupt. The plaintiff produced the witness, who alleged to have heard Bromer claim in jail that he had no way of extricating himself from his current position unless he claimed that the rates he was being charged were usurious. Other witnesses were produced claiming that Bromer was a bad character and not worthy of trust, recalling tales of bad conduct, seduction, and lying that would have made a playwright smile.

The case was sent to a jury, which decided in minutes that Bromer indeed was guilty. But of the £30,000 that the plaintiff claimed was owed, only a fraction was due to be repaid since the balance had been charged at usurious rates and the traditional treble damages penalty therefore reduced the outstanding balance to £8,700.[47] The usury law applied although the relationship between the plaintiff and the defendant and the testimony about the defendant's character influenced the jury in its decision.

That same element of practicality produced one of the more memorable anti-usury tracts of the period. At the end of the eighteenth century, a purely utilitarian series of essays was written by Jeremy Bentham. Born into a wealthy Tory family, he was educated at Oxford and later admitted to the bar, although he never practiced law. His training enabled him to become one of the leading legal thinkers of his day, although his writing style was hardly dry legalize. His orientation was purely pragmatic and he held precedents in little esteem. In keeping with this, he denied the theory of natural rights and instead advocated a utilitarian philosophy, which judged the efficacy of things by the amount of good they could produce for the greatest number of people.

His *Defence of Usury* was a series of essays first published in 1787 when he resided briefly in Russia. His father sent them to his British publisher.

They would become the most often-quoted reference to the uselessness of the usury laws in the debate that would develop in Britain before the repeal in 1854. In that debate, one either agreed with Bentham or disagreed. Those who did not suffered withering criticism. One of those was the celebrated British legal commentator and jurist William Blackstone. But he was not alone. Aristotle and the Plantagenets also suffered the same fate.

Bentham's argument differed from most of his contemporaries because he had little use for precedents and even less respect for the past opponents of usury. At the heart of these arguments was his overall rejection of natural law theory. His interpretation of the past regarding usury laws had little room for moral overtones. Concerning the emergence of Jews as money-lenders in Plantagenet England and the accompanying usury Christians believed emerged with their appearance, he conceded that the objections to the quest for money had been "pretty well overruled; but still this Jewish way of getting it was too odious to be endured . . . indeed the easier method and a method pretty much in vogue was to let the Jews get the money any how they could and then squeeze it out of them as it was wanted." [48] Edward I's methods had become legendary.

The barrenness of money according to Aristotle was the one concept that came under the most withering scrutiny. Bentham recognized the influence it later had on many medieval Scholastic philosophers but was unsparing. "In process of time, as questions of all sorts came under discussion," he wrote, "and this, not the least interesting, among the rest, the anti-Jewish side of it found no inopportune support in a passage of Aristotle: that celebrated heathen, who, in all matters wherein heathenism did not destroy his competence, had established a despotic empire over the Christian world." Part of this despotism led to the dominance of the idea that money was barren. Bentham thought this peculiar, because as he said, Aristotle should have known about money because "that great philosopher, with all his industry and all his penetration, notwithstanding the great number of the pieces of money that had passed through his hands (more perhaps than ever passed through the hands of philosopher before or since) . . . had never been able to discover, in any one piece of money, any organs for generating any other such piece. Emboldened by so strong a body of negative proof, he ventured at last to usher into the world, the results of his observations, in the form of a universal proposition that all money is in its nature barren." [49] Clearly, Bentham believed that the father of the scientific method used fuzzier thinking when discussing money and the legacy was unmistakable for the next two thousand years.

Bentham also criticized Blackstone's comments on usury but attempted to do so in a comical manner that did not quite hit its mark.[50] What he was able to achieve was showing the inefficacy and poor application of the usury laws that reflected the growing dissatisfaction with them before the Napoleonic Wars. His comments were not the most analytical nor were they even the most trenchant of the period, but they caught the popular imagination unlike many of the others. Usury was easily circumvented by imaginative businessmen and only entered public debate when indignation was expressed over commercial affairs by politicians or disgruntled borrowers. But the debate was alive and well. Both Bentham and Blackstone became the most widely read commentators on usury (among other topics) of their generation and their legacies would be well established in the nineteenth century.

Panic and Inflation

Economic conditions in Britain during the second half of the eighteenth century also contributed to increased speculation and social unrest. By the beginning of the nineteenth century, the Bank of England had to make a £3 million loan to the U.K. government so that it could meet its expenses. The major domestic problem was rising prices. The court records were full of cases where merchants had been prosecuted for what today would be called price gouging. At the time it was known as "forestalling." One particular case involved a Mr. Rusby, a trader who bought 360 bushels of oats at 41 shillings each and sold part of them on the same day at 44 shillings each. The jury quickly found him guilty. The justice, Lord Kenyon, remarked to the jury, "You have conferred by your verdict almost the greatest benefit on your country that was ever conferred by a jury."[51]

The remark was not quite the hyperbole it seemed. The cost of living had risen sharply in England between 1773 and the end of the century. In an early cost of living table, it was demonstrated that a basket of basic household staples like a load of hay, candles, and a load of coal increased from £8 4d. in 1773 to £45 14d. in 1800. That represented a price rise of 537 percent, or an average of 20 percent per year.[52] The inflation was causing numerous problems. Gold was in short supply, prompting many to melt down guineas for their gold content. The price increases were also causing social unrest and much of the blame was put on the traders and middlemen who were seen to be profiting at the expense of the man in the street. Quite often, commercial practices were blamed for government problems, and a rise in prices was considered one of the most egregious offenses a trader could commit against his fellow citizens when, in fact, government policies such as restrictive tariffs were the main culprits.

The three hundred years between the reign of Henry VIII and the introduction of usury repeal laws in Parliament was a period of stark contrast in the United Kingdom, and was mirrored in the United States. Distinct progress had been made in life expectancy, new financial products were being offered, and a distinct shift had occurred in attitudes toward usury. At the same time, war continued to be the main obstacle to even greater stability and economic growth, as it had been under the Tudors as well. Capitalism had emerged in the form of mercantilism and the Industrial Revolution had begun in Britain. Alexander Hamilton wrote about the efficacy of introducing manufacturing into the American agrarian economy, using Britain as his guide, and many politicians and businessmen were advocating finally abolishing the usury laws. Richard Price had demonstrated that compound interest could be useful as well as destructive. The real question confronting the nineteenth century was whether anyone took notice of his message.

Chapter 4

The Great Experiment

> The initiators of the modern credit system take as their point of departure not an anathema against interest-bearing capital in general, but on the contrary, its explicit recognition.
> —Karl Marx, 1867

A s society grew larger and entered the industrial age, the demand for loans and property increased. Usury prohibitions were under pressure in Britain and the United States because they were seen by many as standing in the way of progress. As experience in the eighteenth century proved, credit banking made loans easier to obtain. But the moral stigma surrounding usury and indebtedness lingered. Consumption loans still provided fodder for those who wanted to keep the usury prohibitions. Business loans provided the argument for greater laxity. The last remaining question was if the prohibitions would still hold sway if usury ceilings were abolished.

After almost four millennia of prohibitions and condemnations, the abolishment of usury ceilings was an experiment that became an inexorable force in the face of rapid social and economic developments. Before Waterloo, the Napoleonic Codes had been introduced in France. One of them purposely ignored the French usury laws, giving a clear signal that strictures on lending at interest were to be relaxed. That experiment was watched with great interest by the English. This put them in the uncomfortable position of looking to the French for indications of what might happen in their own country if interest rate levels were free to find their "natural" level.

What became a great experiment on both sides of the Atlantic was a much trickier issue than it seemed. If the British and Americans rescinded their usury laws, both societies would face uncertainty on a large scale. What would happen to interest rates for consumption and business loans?

The answer was clearer for the latter since business loans operated outside the usury laws to a great extent, as they had for years, but the effect on personal consumption loans was murky. Perhaps they would also find a natural level and not be punitive on borrowers. It was universally agreed among the majority of lawmakers that change was coming. The only question was exactly when.

Compound interest was discussed more in the nineteenth century than in the past, due to the lingering influence of Richard Price. The practice was challenged frequently in court in the United States and Britain for most of the century. Generally, the courts on both sides of the Atlantic ruled that the practice was acceptable as long as borrowers were aware of it, but it could never be applied by lenders willy-nilly. *Anatocismus* was recognized for what it had always been, another method to avoid the usury laws and compensate lenders at the expense of borrowers. Even after the usury laws had been repealed in Britain and some American states, the issue continued because borrowers recognized that the math of compound interest could do more harm than simple usury itself.

Market developments also put pressure on lawmakers. Since the advent of stockjobbing in the late seventeenth century, speculation had created even thornier problems for the usury laws since many speculators borrowed to finance their securities positions. Since the founding of the Bank of England, England had grown accustomed to trading in intangible assets. The appetite for speculation was dampened but not extinguished by the South Sea Bubble. Stockjobbing increased and with it a growing number of speculators who, like lenders before them, learned that speculating could certainly be better than working for a living. In America, that sort of speculation involved land to a larger extent than it did in Britain.

The Americans also acquired a taste for securities trading and suffered two panics in their rudimentary markets before 1800. Like the English, they watched many of their well-known public figures get ensnared in speculative deals and come to a bad end, suffering loss of reputation as well as fortune. This complicated an already thorny situation even further, as did the new trend of trading securities rather than tangible goods. Was the idea of excessive interest dying or did it still apply to the complexities of modern life in the early nineteenth century? Those hoping for its demise would find a little of each as the decades wore on.

During the eighteenth century, the concept of leverage made its appearance on the financial stage. Once stockjobbers, adventurers, and serious businessmen recognized its potential to create profits, the die was cast. The appearance of the many private bankers in London made more money available for lending despite the usury laws. The availability of paper money through the Bank of England made the process easier still. All factors contributed to lubricating the credit machine. Individuals would continue to borrow for subsistence, but entrepreneurs borrowed for capital investment and speculation on a larger and larger scale. Debt still was at the heart of the financial system and charging dearly for it still persisted.

The penalties for defaulting on loans remained harsh, although new attempts would be made at introducing or reforming the bankruptcy laws to relieve debtors. The practicality of imprisoning defaulted borrowers was being questioned with renewed vigor, especially since their ranks included some well-known Americans who proved to be spectacular insolvents. If trusted public servants used their knowledge of the financial system to speculate with large amounts of borrowed money, then did human nature enter the usury debate, militating for a continuance of the laws rather than their repeal?

By the end of the Napoleonic era, the concept of creditworthiness still remained much as it had for the previous three hundred years. Reputation and social standing still were the main factors determining whether someone got a loan, regardless of whether it was a personal loan or business loan. Credit-rating agencies and debt-reporting agencies did not exist yet, so the time-hallowed tradition of "my word is my bond" was the socially binding unwritten contract between borrower and lender. John Pierpont Morgan later in the nineteenth century considered a client's character of primary importance when deciding whether to lend to him or not, reflecting the generally accepted principle of the era. A borrower's word was the promise to repay or to act fairly in dealings with lenders. Collateral certainly was involved as it had been for centuries, but the matter of getting a loan in the first place depended upon reputation. Defaulted borrowers faced ostracism and a lack of access to society that were unthinkable to most businessmen. Paying a debt was the foremost financial priority, so naturally the usury laws retained much gravity even when clearly usurious rates were being charged to risky borrowers.

American Bankruptcy

Immediately after independence from the United Kingdom, the New York coffee houses became even busier than usual as business and speculative activity in New York increased. The Tontine Coffee House especially was busy as the traders and stockjobbers who plied their trade outdoors on Wall Street and Broad Street behaved much as their English counterparts on Exchange Alley had done during the South Sea Bubble. Speculation was in the air and it would not end well.

The first stock market panic occurred shortly after independence. William Duer was a well-known figure in New York, having served in various government capacities and as a member of the Continental Congress. Originally from Britain, he settled in New York in 1773 and never returned. Of his many jobs in government, he was secretary to the Board of Treasury, a position that gave him an inside view of American finances. By 1787, he was speculating in land deals and borrowing large amounts of money to speculate in the early securities that were traded on the curbside market along Wall Street. Within five years, the market was poised for collapse.

Duer became overextended in his borrowings and became bankrupt. He was prosecuted by his creditors and sent to the New Gaol in New York, which housed some other famous bankrupts of the day. Congress had deliberated over several bankruptcy bills that had been submitted each year since it first sat but never passed one. Reformers attempted to influence the debtors' prison practice much as British reformers had been doing since the days of Defoe and Oglethorpe. One lawyer who also was imprisoned in the New Gaol for unpaid debts became outspoken against the system. William Keteltas campaigned against imprisoning debtors and published a series of pamphlets from jail entitled the *Forlorn Hope* beginning in 1800.[1] But the effort was too late to help Duer. He spent a total of seven years in prison, with a short reprieve when Alexander Hamilton personally intervened on his behalf. But he never emerged again, dying in 1799 while incarcerated.

Duer's insolvency in 1792 caused widespread financial ruin in New York when he failed on his promissory notes. It also caused the stockjobbers to organize themselves under the Buttonwood Agreement, the first formal organization of the market that would eventually become the New York Stock Exchange. And the experience also prompted Congress to pass the first bankruptcy law in 1800, a year after Duer's death.

Despite repeated efforts, Congress never passed any of the bankruptcy bills presented to it, until the death of William Duer, the second most notorious debtor of his day. Being declared a bankrupt would not have been advantageous to the entrepreneurs and speculators who were numerous in the years following independence. Thus, the possibility of escaping such a legal designation was almost always preferable to being subjected to it, which would not enable them to engage in similar activities in the future.

Bankruptcy was at the center of the debate between Federalists and Jeffersonians during the early years of the republic and any law emerging from Congress was slow to develop as a result. Federalists and Alexander Hamilton claimed that a bankruptcy law was necessary in order to discharge an insolvent from his debts so that business could be renewed and progress achieved. This was a vision based on manufacturing and the credit creation process. Jeffersonians, in contrast, saw the United States primarily as an agrarian economy. Any federal bankruptcy law would shift power to Washington from the states and Jeffersonians feared this would jeopardize their livelihoods. The arguments were similar to those found in Britain at the same time; such arguments succeeded in keeping the usury laws on the books for decades after Bentham had attacked them so successfully, if the opinion of other major writers and pamphleteers was an indication of the public mood.

The case of Robert Morris was the most discussed and most notorious example of the turn-of-the-century debate that continued about a formal federal bankruptcy law. Many states had passed their own bankruptcy laws as they had usury laws, but the movement that began after independence for a federal bankruptcy law gained considerable momentum after Duer. The major bankruptcies of the period all involved borrowing large sums for speculation that collapsed before any profits could be realized. The rate of interest charged on the loans was not the primary issue, only the principal amounts.

Until the latter 1790s, Robert Morris was not the person who would have been associated with high leverage and financial impropriety. He demonstrated a fondness for risk taking as a merchant and became reputedly the richest man in America prior to 1800. Morris was born in Liverpool, and in 1747, when he was thirteen, he immigrated to America with his father. He was apprenticed to Charles Willing, a merchant in Philadelphia, and the firm later became Willing, Morris and Co. after the apprentice was admitted as a partner. Morris specialized in shipping and land, soon becoming very wealthy. He served as a member of the Pennsylvania delegation to the Continental Congress, served in the Pennsylvania Assembly, and signed the Declaration of Independence. His public service was slightly clouded by charges that his firm misdirected public funds on occasion, especially when it provided shipping services to the government. But his financial acumen made him famous and when the new government fell on hard times in 1781 he was named the superintendent of finance. He advanced the young government some of his personal funds on occasion, helping to temper allegations against him for financial sloppiness. In 1784, when he left the job, the federal treasury actually had a small surplus and his reputation as one of the bright lights of American independence had been established.

His resume continued to grow after independence. A member of the Constitutional Convention, he was elected senator from Pennsylvania after the Constitution was signed. He founded the Bank of North America, located in Pennsylvania, contributing $250,000 of his own funds, after having failed to persuade Congress to establish a national bank modeled after the Bank of England. He eventually retired from the Senate in 1795 and immersed himself in land speculation with several partners. They bought thousands of plots around Washington, DC hoping to profit when the capital city was built. He also acquired several million acres of land in western New York and parts of the South. The property was to be used as collateral for more loans, but the bottom soon dropped out. Although he owned vast tracts of land, Morris became insolvent because he had no cash to pay his creditors. Initially, his indebtedness to banks totaled several hundred thousand dollars.

Unable to pay his debts, Morris retired to his home, where he was soon arrested and sent to the Prune Street Prison in Philadelphia in 1798. He remained there until he was discharged in 1801, when his indebtedness was estimated to be over $3 million. During his incarceration, he assiduously tried to avoid being declared a bankrupt, although his finances were so tangled that to do otherwise would have been impossible. He had around one hundred creditors, most of whom had long since abandoned the battle of receiving any payments from him. He was involuntarily declared a bankrupt and finally released in late 1801. Under the bankruptcy law, he was discharged from his debts and his creditors no longer had any claim against him.[2] He died in 1806.

The Bankruptcy Act that helped set him free was passed in 1800. Like English bankruptcy law, the federal act stated that bankruptcy was involuntary and had to be petitioned by a creditor against a debtor owing $1,000 or more. It did not protect insolvents but was intended to protect creditors from businessmen who openly sought to defraud or conceal assets from them in order to avoid payment. The act had great similarities with English bankruptcy law, although the two differed in application in many other respects.[3]

Developments began to quicken in Britain as debtors' prisons continued to come under attack. The old idea that only traders could be declared bankrupt was still valid. Individuals who were not traders simply remained insolvent and could be imprisoned if their creditors petitioned for it. In the years preceding the repeal of the usury law in the United Kingdom, attitudes began to change, however. Beginning in 1808, anyone already imprisoned for unpaid indebtedness for a year for amounts of twenty pounds or less was to be set free, the assumption being that the time served offset the small amount involved. Public opinion naturally was set against imprisoning small debtors, but it had taken several centuries to make serious progress in changing the law.

The Repeal of British Usury Laws

Since the publication of Jeremy Bentham's essays on usury, pressure steadily had mounted to repeal the usury law in Britain. Great strides had been made in British finances since the defeat of Napoleon and a general confidence had arisen that the strictures of the past could be removed in favor of market flexibility due to the increase in national wealth created by the Industrial Revolution.

A powerful economic argument against the usury laws came from the banker and businessman Henry Thornton in 1802. Coming from a business background like many of his peers, Thornton went to work for his father in the banking business while still in his teens. After becoming a partner in a well-known merchant bank, he stood for Parliament and became an influential member of many parliamentary committees. He was also a noted writer on economics, becoming one of the most influential proponents of the quantity theory of money in the nineteenth century. Like many businessmen, he did not favor the usury laws because they were not in line with market rates of interest. His interpretation of them was somewhat different from his contemporaries, however. Problems arose when the usury laws prescribed a rate of interest that was too low in relation to market rates. He wrote, "The borrowers, in consequence of that artificial state of things which is produced by the law against usury, obtain their loans too cheap. That which they obtain too cheap they demand in too great quantity."[4] Adam Smith's concern about the usury ceiling and its relationship to the market could be found in Thornton's work as well, indicating that usury was finally being interpreted in economic terms rather than in moral terms.

Repeal bills frequently were introduced into Parliament after 1815, although overall progress was slow. Arthur Onslow, a member of Parliament, introduced several bills seeking repeal but was not successful with getting any of them passed. In 1816, when Onslow proposed one of several bills, the chancellor of the exchequer reminded him that the nation's finances after Waterloo were too fragile to upset the present system in favor of the unknown.[5] Sentiment against the usury laws was growing, but fear of the unknown made progress slow while a debate developed about the nature of society without them.

Those in favor of eliminating the usury laws persisted. Onslow continued to introduce bills for repeal and was often joined by many well-known colleagues. One was David Ricardo, the stockbroker and lender turned economist. Born into a Jewish family of Portuguese origin, Ricardo became a stockbroker in London like his father before him. He earned a considerable fortune as a broker and was one of the few Britons who bet against a French victory at Waterloo by buying British government bonds, which were selling at a sharp discount before the battle. While still employed as a broker, he read Smith's *Wealth of Nations* in 1799 at the age of twenty-seven and quickly became enamored of economics. He began writing essays, displaying a sharp mind despite his lack of university education, much like Thornton, who never attended university either.

Ricardo soon became opposed to many government policies because of what he considered were their ill-conceived economic foundations. One policy he opposed was the Corn Laws, protectionist tariffs that limited imports of wheat into the United Kingdom. In his *Essay on the Influence of a Low Price of Corn on the Profits of Stock* (1815), he described the law of diminishing marginal returns. He also advocated what today is known as the theory of comparative advantage. Both concepts became cornerstones of modern economic theory. Because of his fortune, estimated at £600,000, he was able to retire from finance in 1814 at the age of forty-two. Five years later, he entered Parliament as a member for Portarlington, in Ireland.

In 1821, two years before his death, Ricardo argued against the existing usury laws along with Arthur Onslow. His opposition was natural given his advocacy of free trade and market forces. After Onslow succeeded in introducing his latest bill, Ricardo argued that repealing the usury laws would not raise interest rates to new heights, as many of the landed gentry sitting in Parliament had argued. The competition between borrowers and lenders would eventually bring rates to a sustainable level, although some inconveniences may occur from time to time. During the war with France, interest rates had risen to 15 percent despite the usury laws, which only stood in the way of market forces.[6] The argument was persuasive but the bill did not pass.

Shortly before Ricardo's death, Onslow again introduced a repeal bill in Parliament. Again Ricardo argued in its favor. He maintained that money should be treated like other commodities. Buyers and sellers were able to negotiate terms on them and they should be allowed to do the same with money. Furthermore, he argued that the only effect of the usury statutes was to place the lending business in the hands of characters who had no scruples. They were encouraged to evade the law, and made a great profit by so doing.[7] But those in favor of maintaining the usury laws prevailed, as they would for another thirty years. Ricardo died soon after, leaving the debate to others.

In his later years, Ricardo also commented on the sinking fund employed by the Treasury to retire U.K. government bonds. He debated the mechanics of the sinking fund with Francis Place in a series of letters. In 1820, he also contributed an article to the *Encyclopedia Britannica*, published four years after his death, on Britain's funding system for its public debt. He argued that countries should defray expenses rather than incur loans to meet them. The sinking fund finally was abolished in 1829 after more than a hundred years of sporadic operations.

But the repeal of the usury laws was the prime economic question of the period. Part of the argument in favor of eliminating them was that they were ineffective, in many cases being circumvented by financial services companies in increasingly complex transactions involving lending. An irate reader wrote to *The Times* of London, signing his letter as "An Enemy to Usury." In it, he described a program devised by a life insurance company in London that lent money against life policies at rates in excess of 20 percent annually. He said that anyone familiar with business practices "will agree that they never heard of a more gross case of usury, and yet this office is put forward with the names of gentlemen and nobles as directors."[8] Similar cases were reported in the United States as well, indicating that the financial services industry knew how to avoid the usury laws while providing high interest loans at the same time. The usury laws were made nonsensical by financial techniques designed to circumvent them, as had been the case for centuries, but the growth and popularity of newspapers were making this plain for all to see. Communications helped propel the repeal movement forward.

After Ricardo's death, another repeal bill by Onslow was introduced in Parliament. Speaking in favor of keeping the usury laws, one MP spoke in historical terms about their importance. "Now, what was the state of this country before the enactment of the usury laws? We had not a ship of our own; we purchased ships from the Hanse Towns, which had usury laws. Since the usury laws had been in force, we had gone on in every succeeding age, flourishing in wealth, industry, comfort, and every blessing which a nation could possess."[9] Arguments of all sorts continued to surround the issue, but in the end the debate did not succeed in getting the usury laws lifted.

In 1835, Parliament passed a bill that created loan societies, limited purpose banks that would make small loans to individuals. Three years before, Parliament passed the Reform Act, which extended voting rights to property holders based on property holdings. This provided the impetus for many individuals to start borrowing in order to build homes or acquire property. The prospect of voting induced many to acquire property, adding to the popularity of building societies, small banks that took deposits and made mortgages to their members. The combination of events encouraged some male citizens to borrow in order to achieve some political status. The financial services industry responded as did Parliament.

Five years later, the loan act was amended substantially. Loans were to be made ordinarily for amounts of fifteen pounds or less. Particularly significant about the Loan Societies Act in 1840 was the fact that it included a table of installment credit, stipulating how much should be repaid on loans contracted by individuals. Interest payable on the loans was discounted, so the lenders received it up front. The installment plan then laid out how much of the loan principal was to be repaid weekly, depending on options the borrowers could choose. The options included beginning to pay back the loan amount from eleven to sixty-six days from incurring the debt. The amount payable varied as a result; the longer postponements carried a higher interest rate, but the act stated that the interest rate charged should not exceed "in the whole the rate of twelve pounds by the hundred for the full term of one year."[10]

Clearly, the 12 percent rate exceeded the usury ceiling of 5 percent at the time. But the act exempted any registered lender from penalties because of the usury laws. This was one of the first times that statutory usury had been superseded in favor of making potential credit available to the small borrower in addition to being one of the first examples of an early installment plan. But the scheme was far from successful or perfect. The loan societies were not mutual or benevolent societies but run strictly for profit and often their investors lost the money put into them. The 12 percent rate included administrative expenses and other costs that added to the official usury ceiling, but the societies still often were unsuccessful and the fifteen-pound amounts were considered too small to be profitable. As an alternative, the mutual society was suggested as a way of ensuring that depositors were paid properly, ensuring a more steady flow of loanable funds for the future.[11]

On the heels of the creation of loan societies, Parliament passed the Insolvent Debtors Act in 1844. Imprisonment for non-payment of debts less than twenty pounds was abolished and was widely welcomed as a step in the right direction by many in the public but not at the loan societies. Since their business was small loans of less than that amount, their ability to imprison an insolvent was severely limited. The business community in general also complained about the new law, claiming that it provided an opening for unscrupulous borrowers who now realized they could renege on a debt without fear of prison. Imprisonment for debtors was still common despite the wave of public indignation against the practice. Charles Dickens wrote about the prisons and helped perpetuate the images originally brought to light by Moses Pitt and Daniel Defoe. Dickens's father, John, spent time in debtors' prison when Charles was still a boy.

One of the most compelling arguments in Parliament for the repeal came from those MPs who argued that the existing usury laws created tenuous situations in which collateral was pledged at different rates of interest. If a businessman took a loan and pledged a commodity as collateral, the rate of interest charged him could be very high, perhaps 40 percent. But if land were pledged, the rate he could be charged could be no more than 5 percent, in keeping with the law. This argument eventually prevailed, helping to remove the restrictions permanently. But it also demonstrated the difference between real property and what were considered the tools of a trader's profession: one was considered sacrosanct while the other was acknowledged to be fraught with business risk. The distinction would carry on well after the usury laws were repealed.

Finally, in 1854 after decades of debate the usury laws were repealed in Britain, ending the three-hundred-year history of statutory prohibitions. Ten years before, bills of exchange had been freed from the interest rate ceiling. The law stated that "the several acts and parts of acts made in the Parliaments of England and Scotland, Great Britain, and Ireland . . . and all existing laws against usury, shall be repealed."[12] The enrollment of annuities with the government also was repealed by the legislation. Pawnbrokers, however, were exempt, being subject to their own set of regulations, which were not affected.

More legislation in Britain did away with the distinction between trader and non-trader in bankruptcy proceedings. The Debtors Act of 1869 and the

Bankruptcy Act of the same year finally did away with imprisonment for bad debts unless debtors defaulted on a court judgment. The power of creditors to have debtors imprisoned became a relic of the past and insolvents who were not guilty of fraud could apply for personal bankruptcy. The new attitude toward debt and debtors finally led to changes in English law that had been in use since the fifteenth century. But none of these developments meant that credit would be cheaper in the future since those in a position to lend saw themselves at a decided disadvantage without recourse to imprisonment. Lending money was considered more hazardous than in the past.

Even after the abolition of the British usury laws, the term still arose in legal proceedings. Although no usury laws existed, in 1870 *The Times* noted in reference to a court case that "mankind will always have a prejudice against 60 percent." In the case of *Miller v. Cook*, the plaintiff, a young man in his twenties, sued Cook, a lender, for charging him more than 60 percent on a relatively small loan of £500. The court held for him, leaving Cook unhappy to say the least. The interest rate was lowered to 5 percent, as it would have been before the usury laws had been repealed sixteen years before. The vice-chancellor remarked upon conclusion of the case that "it is not every bargain which necessity may induce one man to offer which another man is at liberty to accept."[13]

The States and the Church

The American experience with usury laws prior to the British repeal was mixed. Some states had repealed their laws as an experiment, only to reinstate them afterward. Most advocates of keeping the laws in place pointed to the fact that every developed nation had usury laws, as did all the states in the union, and had been able to protect their economies and citizens at the same time. A common complaint was that those advocating repeal of the laws were also those who would benefit most, namely financial institutions and the wealthy, who stood to earn even more interest on loans outstanding than they had before.

In 1819, *The Times* of London reported that a member of the New Hampshire legislature had commented, "The influence of Mr. Bentham's writings has been extensively felt in the United States. His work on usury has passed through several editions in this country; and its principles begin to be pretty generally adopted by men of enlarged views and liberal minds amongst us."[14] The writer cited an example where the Mississippi legislature passed a law that did not restrict the rate of interest made between two consenting parties when a loan was made by contract. It would only restrict the rate when no contract was present. The American tendency would be to maintain usury laws for handshake agreements while allowing parties using contracts much more latitude.

The battle raged in Britain and the United States for several decades following Waterloo. The Americans clearly were looking to the English for some guidance on the matter. The *New-York Daily Times* ran a series of articles and letters before and after the English repeal concerning the usury laws in New York. One advocate of repeal was a banker who signed himself only as "Bentham." He carried on a continual discussion with other readers of the newspaper about the inefficacy of New York's usury laws and called for repeal on practical grounds, much like his namesake. The arguments for lifting state laws were greatest in rural states and those most involved in financial services.

Not all the usury arguments from Europe had an impact on the Americans, however. The curious case of Jeremiah O'Callaghan is one example. A Catholic priest in County Cork, Ireland, O'Callaghan went to administer the last rites to a parishioner in 1819 and started a controversy lasting for years. He would not administer the rites until the dying man confessed to being a usurer and admitted it to his congregation. When he did, O'Callaghan administered the sacrament. The entire issue revolved around the man lending seeds to farmers and then charging them about 30 percent more when they repaid the loans. The amounts lent usually amounted to less than one pound. When his superior in the parish heard of the incident, the priest was suspended from his duties, entering clerical limbo. He tried for the next decade to prove his point, but the church in Rome was in the process of adopting the idea that interest was justified and would hear nothing of, or from, him.

Without a parish, O'Callaghan traveled to the United States and finally found a post when the bishop of Boston assigned him to northern Vermont, a rural area where he could not do much damage. He subsequently published a polemical book on usury, administered to his flock, and added periodic updates to the book. The irony was that his arrival and book publication coincided with the Catholic Church's softening of its attitudes on usury in 1830.

Rome finally changed its stance on usury that year. Little had been said on the subject since the encyclical of Benedict XIV in 1745. Throughout the mercantilist era, the church steadfastly had refused to alter its position, but several decades into the Industrial Revolution it was apparent that the position was irreconcilable with modern business. Finally, in 1830 the Congregation of the Holy Office under Pope Pius VIII recognized interest and suggested that those who charged it would not be disturbed by the church. Less than a hundred years later, the clergy would be allowed to invest in interest-bearing accounts and securities without incurring the wrath of the church hierarchy. The change came about quietly but was a significant departure from previous doctrine. Almost two thousand years of canon law slowly faded from view.

Some critics saw the church softening its views on usury as tantamount to ignoring the plight of the poor in general. James Connery, an Irish supporter of usury laws and a reformer, saw the maintenance of the usury laws as a means of uplifting the state of landless Irish peasants. He approached the topic with a zeal not comparably seen in Britain since the seventeenth century. In his book, *The Reformer*, he maintained that providing low-cost consumption loans to the poor would lead to a general rehabilitation of the population. That would lead in turn to better public habits and a general societal improvement across the board. He noted the case of "two notorious drunkards on application for loans, [who] were informed that their claims were not admissible as long as they were guilty of acts of intemperance. They pledged themselves to give up the practice . . . and have ever since continued to be sober and industrious."[15]

All the states, except California, had usury laws in place before the Civil War, usually in the 6 percent range. This followed the Dutch example. The Netherlands never adopted a national usury law, leaving the matter to its individual provinces. As a result, critics always argued that the Dutch never had an effective national usury law. The same could be said of the Americans for similar reasons. But the states did impose penalties on exceeding the usury ceiling that varied considerably. Penalties for usury usually included forfeiture of the debt and/or interest. Tennessee was only one of two states that included imprisonment as a penalty. New York held usury to be a misdemeanor with a maximum fine of $1,000 and a possible prison sentence. These penalties were harsher than those found (if any) during the colonial period and were more commercial and less tribally based. They were rarely enforced, however. The growing population and increase in national wealth made the older prohibitions, such as the early Massachusetts law, seem Deuteronomic and out of touch with a growing economy.

The experiment with rolling back the laws was more than a blind adherence to the idea that the laws were simply outdated. It had everything to do with an attempt to attract investment capital, especially from abroad since the United States during the nineteenth century was a net capital importer and depended upon foreign investment. In 1852, Ohio experimented with abolishing its low usury ceilings, setting 10 percent as the maximum rate of interest. The hope was to attract foreign capital. A local newspaper commented, "Indeed some of the brokers and legislators seemed to think that this would be the El Dorado where all golden streams would center."[16] But local politics and a reputation for being untrustworthy dissuaded foreign and East Coast investors from investing in the local economy.

A similar situation occurred in Wisconsin. It repealed its usury laws in 1849. The motive and impetus for the repeal came mainly from farmers. As in other frontier and agricultural states, land was cheap but money for lending was restricted. In consequence, a movement developed to repeal the usury laws so that mortgages would be more plentiful.[17] But the experiment was not successful. Senator I. P. Walker of Wisconsin wrote, "The argument in favor of this policy was that competition in the loan of money, the rate of interest being unrestricted, would produce a great influx of capital to the state. It certainly has produced an influx of *money*, but not of *capital*."[18] Lenders were happy with the high rates that often reached 50 percent but would not place capital in local projects yielding less. They were willing to fund consumption but not long-term investments. Lenders were being accused of the old usurer's trick. High returns meant high lending risks and the lenders were only fueling the old cycle of high-interest consumption loans because they could not get an adequate return on longer-term capital investments.

Other states concentrated on the small borrower and consumption loans. In 1852, the Louisiana legislature abolished its usury laws, exempting homes worth $1,000 or less, plus $250 worth of furniture, from seizure should the owners become insolvent. The state senate, however, rejected the vote shortly before adjourning for the year.

A former member of Congress and judge from Indiana drew attention to another trick employed by usurers that drew strong reaction from supporters of the laws. Noting that in his time on the bench he had witnessed many foreclosures and widespread ruin among debtors without the protection of a usury ceiling, he stated, "It is worthy of remark that the usurer rarely brought suit for his money until the accumulating interest had swelled the debt to an amount approximating closely the value of the debtor's estate, or until notified to do so by the surety, or endorser of the debtor."[19] This remark was close to the original spirit of *anatocismus*, but the term was no longer effectively in use.[20] Compound interest certainly aided the process and by implication lenders would not move on a debtor until the collateral could be seized in full or the estate sold to pay off the inflated debt.

Compound interest was a subject of interest on both sides of the Atlantic before the American Civil War, but debates were confined usually to the courts. Both British and American courts ruled that any borrower subject to compounding had to be aware of its presence and it could be used in legal settlements if the parties agreed. There was little mention of the frequency of compounding, but semi-annual interest usually was implied. As in centuries past, the courts recognized that compounding was another method of avoiding usury ceilings where they existed, but since the ceilings themselves were coming under sharp criticism proscribing compound interest made little practical sense. The abhorrence of adding unpaid interest in particular to the principal amount to be paid back had not abated since the time of Cicero, but compounding was as ingrained in the economic system as interest itself so attacking it in general would have been a futile exercise.

Despite widespread complaints about relaxing the usury laws, the American interpretation of their effects coincided with opinions rendered in the past, showing that, if nothing else, Americans were familiar with the usury literature preceding them. A notable example is found in some comments made about usury by an R.W. Wright of Wisconsin in 1851 in a reply to a query by one of the major commentators of the period on usury, John Whipple. Concerning the abolition of usury laws, Wright noted that "this experiment was tried in England in the sixteenth century, and for nineteen years the interest on money had no legal limit. In the reign of Elizabeth, usury laws were restored. Lord Burleigh remarked that the repeal of the statute against usury had not been attended with the hoped for effect; but the high price for money on usury had more and more abounded, to the undoing of many persons and to the hurt of the realm."[21] Wright agreed with Montesquieu, who made the same remark about the effects of the usury ban in the Islamic world. If it is proscribed, it will migrate to the underground economy at higher rates to compensate for the higher risks involved.

In New York, the attempt at repealing the usury laws evoked a debate that appeared incongruous to those not familiar with American politics and the financial system at the time. Arguments for and against repeal revolved around the intrinsic nature of money, a discussion that appeared to have been raised and answered two hundred years before in England. But the discussion in New York had to do with the gold and silver coins circulated by Washington versus the bank notes created by banks in the individual states prior to the Civil War. Since the entire matter of money and its value was political, was not the decision to limit the price for borrowing it political as well? States rights also entered the argument. States determined which banks could create credit through the issuance of notes and they should also be able to abolish the usury laws as well. This argument resonated strongly after the charter of the Second Bank of the United States was not renewed by Congress under pressure from Andrew Jackson in 1836.

The Chamber of Commerce in New York proposed that the usury laws be lifted in 1854 and was fully supported by the banks. The proposal was widely discussed in the press and in the business community and was a central issue of the day. One commentator wrote to the *New-York Daily Times*, "The main question then is, is this money the product of law—is it something which owes its existence to the action of the Government—is it constituted for public purposes and therefore properly the subject of legal regulation, both in the manner of its creation and the price at which the public may be availed of it for the public purpose for which it is intended?"[22] If the answer was in the affirmative, then the usury restrictions should remain in place.

Myron Clark, the governor of New York, was in favor of keeping the laws. In 1855, he stated, "The power of money, chained as it is by the usury laws, is strong enough," adding that, "If the poor must occasionally submit to the lacerations of the 'icy fangs' of unfeeling Shylocks, let it be as seldom as possible, and let some fair Portia be at hand to weigh the flesh, if any be found daring enough to cut it." His remedy for rates charged above the usury ceiling had a simple appeal: "The buyer of lottery tickets is fined as well as the vendor, and let the same law be applied to money-buyers as to money-lenders at illegal rates."[23] While the governor argued for keeping the laws, a group of merchants and businessmen wrote an open letter to the state assembly asking only for a change in the penalty for usury, asking it to repeal the imprisonment penalty while keeping the fines intact.

The argument over repeal in the United States after 1854 was aided considerably by John Whipple of Rhode Island, who framed a powerful argument against it. Born in 1784, three years before Jeremy Bentham's book on the usury laws was published, Whipple was a lawyer in Providence and a member of the Rhode Island assembly. He wrote a strong and powerful rebuttal to Bentham, defending the usury laws against the free-trade thinkers of the period. His booklet, *Stringent Usury Laws: The Best Defense against Hard Times,* was first published in 1836 and reprinted in 1855 as the debate over repeal in many states grew more intense. It attracted many rebuttals but helped win the day for the disparate group favoring status quo for the usury laws.

Whipple tackled Bentham's argument by employing the utilitarian's own technique. He sardonically commented that Bentham lacked experience on the matter. "Mr. Bentham was a theorist in the largest sense of the term, and ought not to be severely censured for believing all the world wrong in this particular instance, inasmuch as he believed they were wrong in almost all others." Attacking the arguments of the abolitionists, he stated, "If the free-trade writers are correct, that an absence of all usury laws does tend to lower the rates of interest . . . but the fact that the lenders themselves are so anxious for a free-trade system . . . would not go far to show that they thought so; for why should they wish the rates reduced?"[24]

The repeal movement before the Civil War eventually failed and New York kept its usury laws while other states reinstated them. But the battle was hardly finished. Recognizing that the usury laws were permanent, opponents argued for a less than uniform application of them in New York. Citing New Jersey as an example, they argued that each county should have its own usury ceilings. The agricultural counties, mostly upstate, could retain the 7 percent ceiling while Wall Street and New York City could have their own higher ceilings to reflect the nature of the risky securities business. This was essentially the same argument that was occasionally made in Britain prior to 1854. Advocates of abolition tried to employ the same arguments that they thought had been used successfully in London to eliminate the interest rate ceilings.

Despite the similarities in the state usury laws, cross-border application of them proved a trickier issue. In a court case brought in New York, a lender was sued for a loan originally made in Minnesota bearing an interest rate of 26 percent, by contract. The New York court ruled in 1862 that although the rate was high, it had no jurisdiction over a contract signed in another state.[25] The principle seemed congruent with the times, although it would be lost for decades and surface again over a hundred years later.

That particular case was the exact opposite of one that was heard twenty years before, also in New York. In *American Dry Dock Company v. The American Life Insurance and Trust Company* (1846), Dry Dock, a bank, applied to the life insurance company for a loan. The company complied and made a loan, directing the loan to a London bank, charging Dry Dock interest in the process. Dry Dock wanted to restore its financial health and resume specie payments in the wake of the panic of 1837, which damaged its financial condition. The Chancery Court in New York ruled that the case was within its jurisdiction and that the interest charged amounted to usury. It overturned the contract, which called for more than 7 percent interest because a discount of 4 percent was taken at the time the loan was made. It was the sort of decision Robert Morris would have wished for forty years before. Ironically, the vice-president of the insurance company and defendant in the case who stood to make a tidy profit from the transaction was John Duer, a son of William Duer. He was also the author of a book on marine insurance, published just before the loan was overturned, that became a standard text on the topic in the United States for many years. In the introduction to his text, Duer described insurance in general and marine insurance in particular as part of the law of nations. "In this sense, which is borrowed from the Roman jurists," he wrote, "the law of nations is strictly synonymous with the moral law, or as some modern writers have chosen to term it, the law of nature."[26]

Always in the vanguard of the fight against usury laws, New York bankers also constantly argued for repeal in order to attract foreign investment. Wall Street and the United States needed and depended upon foreign capital and removing the usury ceilings would signal an openness to attract funds, although the usury ceilings had minimal effect on market rates. But the laws remained in place and bankers then argued that the usury laws put the onus on the local state banks to respond to potential foreign inflows of capital individually, which could lead to mismanagement, the sort of problem that contributed to the panic of 1837, which hit Wall Street and New York City particularly hard.

The argument was not based entirely on principle. Lending money for margin transactions had become big business on Wall Street and higher rates for the loans would bring hefty fees to the lenders. Depositors' funds could be lent to the call money market, earning the banks hefty spreads. The absence of interest rate ceilings could prove to be a valuable marketing ploy to attract domestic and foreign depositors. Liquidity or its absence was a common factor in many nineteenth-century panics and restrictive usury laws did not help, according to the banks.

One other less visible motive was also behind the movement to lift the usury laws. Float management had risen to something of an art form before the Civil War because of the diverse and fragmentary nature of the United States. Communications depended upon the mails and the time lags involved attracted those who realized that there was a profit to be made in the periods that bank transactions took to clear, especially between different parts of the country. Federalism and states' rights became beneficial to bankers who capitalized on sectional differences and the inability of the U.S. Treasury to make its influence felt outside Washington, DC without their aid.

Congress established a national usury law in 1864 when it passed the National Bank Act. Because of jurisdictional problems, it fell slightly short of a comprehensive standard, however. The act created the category of national bank, an institution registered with the comptroller of the currency, also established at the same time. National banks were set apart from state-chartered banks for regulatory purposes. The national banks were not permitted to violate the state usury ceilings in the states in which they resided. If no ceilings existed, then the act established 7 percent as the maximum rate of interest they could charge. Any punitive damages against the national banks required them to forfeit any interest collected on usurious loans.[27]

Many banks avoided registering with the comptroller since being designated as a national bank was voluntary. This meant that the states remained the arbiters of their own usury laws except in cases where there were collisions of jurisdiction with those states that had no usury laws at all. More importantly, the 7 percent ceiling became entrenched as the maximum mortgage rate on real estate. Charging more would be a clear violation of the usury laws since the collateral was real property. This standard would remain in place for more than one hundred years before being seriously challenged successfully.

The increasing demand for credit in the nineteenth century plus the confusing bank note situation put strains on banks to provide credit analysis for their customers as well as develop expertise in counterfeit detection. The financial turmoil of the late 1830s and the early 1840s created many bankruptcies among small businesses and the chaos required standard procedures to be implemented in the future in order to protect lenders. As a result, the first credit-rating agency was established in 1841 by Lewis Tappan in New York City. The Mercantile Agency was the first to provide the sort of information lenders themselves had had to acquire in the past; it did so by acting as a contractual, impartial agent for credit information. Focusing mainly on credit reporting, the agency collected information on businesses for potential lenders, using a network of lawyers and others who provided financial and personal information on the business owners. Revenue was earned by charging subscribers a fee.

The business was based in and around New York City until the agency began adding a national network of correspondents who provided information on businesses from other parts of the country. The success of the agency prompted competition and the Bradstreet Agency was founded eight years later by John Bradstreet. The major difference between them initially was that Bradstreet assigned ratings to companies and published them in what became known as the *Reference Book*. Bradstreet was succeeded at the firm by Robert Dun and the firm became known as Dun and Bradstreet. The book became a standard in business practice and its activities expanded exponentially after the Civil War to the point where it had produced ratings on over 1.25 million businesses by 1900.

Other credit-rating agencies appeared in the nineteenth century and they all began assigning ratings to businesses based on an alphanumeric code of some sort that enabled potential lenders, and later investors, to judge the creditworthiness of a company. Publishing the results became standard practice and provided greater transparency into the financial results of companies. Lenders and investors began to look at the ratings as predictors of corporate and business default. The process was no longer an ad hoc procedure but now was subject to standardized analysis and methods that put the many disparate firms operating in the economy on equal footing. This was especially important because many of these firms were private and the ratings were the only glimpse that lenders may have gotten into their financial accounts. But the ratings were all corporate or business related; the idea of credit ratings for individuals did not exist.

Civil War Debt

During the nineteenth century, debt in the form of bonds became the predominant investment in the United States, as it had in Britain a century before. Despite the publicity the stock market received, the amount of bonds outstanding greatly exceeded the value of equities in existence. As a result, life insurance funding and capital investment were given a substantial boost, allowing for personal security and infrastructure investment that became necessary as the United States grew in size and importance. Uncertain repayment schedules gave way to firmer financial planning and investment.

The success of many British government bond offerings since Waterloo wetted investor appetite for bonds in the United Kingdom as well. Many of them were consols or "perpetuals," the latter bearing no redemption date, an acknowledgment that the debt was permanent. American bonds were less adventurous and more plain vanilla, having a specific redemption date and coupon attached. They were issued by the federal government as well as by the states and municipalities. Many were sold to foreign investors, notably those from Europe. Debt was becoming respectable, although the religious and moral overtones against it continued.

In 1853 the secretary of the Treasury estimated that around 60 percent of the bonds issued by Boston and Jersey City and 25 percent of those issued by New York City were held by foreigners. These amounts exceeded foreign ownership of equity, although some institutions, notably banks, were popular among foreigners. About 10 percent of the equity of the Bank of New York was in foreign hands as well as that of some of the larger life insurance companies.[28] Corporate bonds were still relatively scarce, but railroad bonds would become a favorite of European investors after the Civil War. But it was the war that made bond investing more popular.

Controversy continued to surround indebtedness and usury in the early decades of the American republic. Since the War of 1812 and the continuing debate about the role of the Bank of the United States, the idea of bankers making profits from underwriting bond issues or helping the U.S. Treasury structure debt offerings mostly was negative. Borrowing money and paying interest was standard practice, but paying bankers for their role in the process was frowned upon. Yet practicality dominated. The Civil War proved to be the true watershed for the acceptance of debt. The enormous amount of bonds issued by Washington to fight the war attracted many savers and investors who displayed both their patriotism and financial acumen by investing in issues that paid the maximum allowed by the usury laws. The successful management of the large issues demonstrated confidence in the Treasury's ability to manage the burgeoning national debt without some of the acrimony that surrounded previous war financings.

The role of bankers in the debt process still was viewed with some suspicion. One banker's role in financing the war with Mexico helped underscore the ambivalent attitude toward government debt and the role of private individuals aiding the process. In the 1820s, one of the first securities firms in the United States, S. and M. Allen and Co., was founded; it dealt in lottery tickets and securities. Enoch Clark had joined the Philadelphia office of S. and M. Allen while still in his teens. Several years later, he was sent to open a branch office in Providence, Rhode Island. When the company failed during the panic of 1837, Clark returned to Philadelphia and established his own firm with the aid of a brother-in-law, Edward Dodge. The firm would bear Clark's name for the next one hundred years.

In addition to trading stocks, bonds, commercial bills, and commodities, one of the more lucrative aspects of Clark, Dodge's business was dealing in bank notes and trading gold bullion. Trading in bank notes in particular was a valuable service to clients because of the vast variety of paper money that existed in the United States. Recognizing the values of different sorts of notes was a specialty of the new firm; it was a skill that Clark had learned while working for the Allens, and it combined credit analysis, forgery detection, and common business sense. It was also very profitable. Most private banks of good reputation combined money and note dealing with a gold-trading business. Banking houses that had their notes used as currency needed to maintain a supply of gold that would back their notes.

Business soon prospered and Clark, Dodge began expanding in other cities, especially since the second Bank of the United States was no longer a force in American finance when its sunset clause was allowed to expire. Within two years, the company had branches in St. Louis, New Orleans, New York, Boston, Springfield, Illinois, and Burlington, Iowa. The firm was so successful in the Midwest that its own drafts issued by the branch became one of the major currencies in the region. One cloud on the horizon was the American annexation of Texas. Fears were growing that a war with Mexico was imminent. When war did break out, Clark, Dodge and Co. would be in the forefront of the war financing. Financiers had made reputations before by helping the United States raise capital during the 1790s and again during the War of 1812. The war with Mexico would help solidify the reputation of Clark, Dodge and earn it substantial profit through what would become one of the best-kept banking secrets.

The war lasted less than two years but still required financing for the Treasury from the private sector. Corcoran and Riggs, a well-known Washington, DC banking house, provided the financing along with Clark, Dodge. The government raised over $60 million in bonds, offered to the public at 6 percent interest, the prevailing usury ceiling in most states. But selling for a commission was not the only motive. The firms made more money "floating" funds between their branches than they did by actually selling the bonds for a commission. The undertaking earned them criticism in some quarters for taking advantage of a hard-pressed Treasury.

Enoch Clark realized that a branch network had its advantages, especially when handling and clearing funds. Floating funds between the branches earned the firm much-needed cash but was not a simple operation. The law required the Treasury to deposit the proceeds of the bonds sold at specified sub-offices of the Treasury at various locations around the country. The sub-treasuries were created after the demise of the second Bank of the United States so that not all of the Treasury's cash would be in one place. Clark's St. Louis office took the deposit for the Mexican campaign and mailed it to its New York office, collecting interest on the amount while the slow mails took weeks to deliver the draft. Then the funds were delivered back to St. Louis, where Clark, Dodge acted as the Treasury's sub-branch.

After the transaction finally was complete, the firm had more than doubled the amount it had made from selling the original Treasury bonds, having engaged in what would later be known as "floating" funds to its own advantage. All of this was perfectly legal because of the limited ability of the U.S. Treasury. Jay Cooke, a young employee who played a prominent role in the operation, wrote in his memoirs, "Our firm had a branch office in St. Louis and we proceeded to sell exchange on Philadelphia and New York at a handsome premium, say two and a half or three per cent . . . the mails were sometimes from ten to fifteen days in transit and in addition to the advantage of interest, we had a large profit in the premiums on exchange over and above the profit we made on the loan."[29]

The career of Jay Cooke is perhaps the finest example of banking and patriotism produced in the nineteenth century despite some strong criticism. Cooke was born August 10, 1821 in Sandusky, Ohio. He joined Clark, Dodge in 1839. Within a year, he had already made his mark as a valued employee, being referred to as the "counterfeit clerk." Like Clark before him, he had become expert in detecting bogus bank notes and his keen eye made him invaluable to Clark, Dodge almost from the outset. This was two years before the first credit-rating agency was founded.

When South Carolina seceded from the Union, Cooke rapidly decided to form his own firm and return to what he knew best, raising bond issues for government bodies. He founded Jay Cooke and Co. when he was only thirty-nine. Although Cooke had worked for Clark, Dodge and his firm became well-known on Wall Street, Cooke remained a Philadelphia banker for his entire career. His flair for financing and his strong patriotic bent made him a natural to raise money when it was becoming more and more difficult to find. The war scared away many of the traditional foreign investors and Cooke realized that the funds would have to be raised mainly from domestic investors.

Opportunity arose when Pennsylvania needed funds at the outset of the war. It had been one of a handful of states that had defaulted on its debt in the municipal bond crisis that roiled the markets when the second Bank of the United States failed, causing the panic of 1837. In the interim, its reputation had not improved. One British writer sarcastically wrote before the Civil War, "We all know the Americans can fight. Nobody doubts their courage. I see now in my mind's eye a whole army of the plains of Pennsylvania in battle array, immense corps of insolvent light infantry, regiments of heavy horse debtors, battalions of repudiators, brigades of bankrupts with *Vivre sans payer ou mourir* on their banners."[30] Clearly, money for the Union war effort would not be coming from Britain. Many bankers and politicians in London considered the Americans little more than swindlers and deadbeats.

Pennsylvania commissioned Cooke to raise a bond of $3 million, not an easy task for a state already in debt by $40 million. Pennsylvania needed the money to defend its southern border against attack. It named Drexel and Co., a well-established Philadelphia banking house, and Cooke as agents for the issue. He organized a massive selling effort. The bond was oversubscribed and rated a great success. Salmon Chase was secretary of the Treasury in the Lincoln administration, charged with raising money for the national war effort. Cooke traveled to Washington, hoping to become involved in the financing effort. His brother introduced him to Chase, and Cooke seized the opportunity to meet the secretary. In 1861, he participated in a small part of a Treasury issue that was not going well and succeeded in selling it. The way was now paved for further participation, but it was certainly not automatic. Cooke took it upon himself to gather subscriptions for Treasury bonds and then hand them to Salmon Chase, who could not help but take notice of the Philadelphia banker's dexterity in raising subscriptions so easily.

Chase was duly impressed with Cooke's ability to sell public debt and enlisted him to participate in future offerings that grew larger and larger as the war dragged on. Chase offered Cooke a job in the Treasury as an undersecretary but he refused it. Cooke clearly thought that the best way to serve his country was by selling as many bonds as possible, not by becoming a bureaucrat. He continued to gather subscriptions. The Treasury's tenuous position and Cooke's rising importance were evident in the aftermath of the first Battle of Bull Run. Sounds of the battle could easily be heard in Washington itself, and the city was stunned by the unexpected news that the Union army had been routed and was in disarray. Fearing that Confederates would overrun the city in the near future, Cooke became even more intent on raising as much money as the government needed to defeat the rebels.

Under the circumstances, Chase needed to raise an enormous bond issue. The Union's finances were in a state of disarray and required consolidation. Complicating matters, specie payments had been suspended at the beginning of the war and investors were not keen on government debt as a result, preferring money backed by hard assets rather than a government pledge. The logistics of raising a large issue and the issue price were daunting problems. But Chase proceeded, attempting to raise $500 million by selling bonds known as the 5-20s. The bonds actually paid 6 percent interest and matured in twenty years but were callable after five years. They abided by the general level of state usury laws, mandating a ceiling of 6 percent. Chase attempted to sell them in 1862 at par but the issue was far from successful. Because he refused to sell them at a discount, realizing that it would raise the effective interest rate, he called upon Cooke who had such good success with the Pennsylvania issue and other previous Treasury offerings.

Cooke began selling the bonds at Chase's request in the autumn of 1862. Bankers and merchants were not supplying the necessary funds so other, smaller investors needed to be enticed to buy the issue. The bond was the largest of its type in American history and required a comprehensive selling effort if it was to be successful. Cooke immersed himself in the distribution endeavor in the same way he had in the past. His contribution helped secure a successful outcome of the war for Washington.

Cooke enlisted agents from most of the major Northern cities and states. While many of the large bankers were absent from his distribution group, there was no shortage of small-town bankers, insurance salesmen, and real estate dealers. He enlisted agents from all business ranks and at their peak they numbered more than twenty-five hundred. Having opened a Washington office at the beginning of the war, he coordinated the sales throughout the country via the telegraph. This made Jay Cooke and Co. the first "wire house," a firm that sold securities throughout the country using the telegraph wires to confirm purchases and sales. It allowed the sales to be coordinated from a central point rather than continue haphazard as in the past.

The Philadelphia Press described Cooke as having "succeeded in popularizing the great five-twenty loan, and now finds the people so anxious to convert their currency into bonds that it is only with difficulty he can meet the sudden and increasing demand."[31] But by his own count, he did not make an inordinate profit selling the 5-20s. He eventually sold the issue for a total commission of around $200,000. That amount did not compensate him for the risks he faced, but the exposure he gained made him the best-known merchant banker in the country.

But not everyone considered Cooke the unselfish savior of the Union. He was being compensated for selling the 5-20s at a rate of about a 1 percent commission, less than in the past but still enough to make an enormous profit given the size of the total issue. The bonds were being sold at about $2 million per day in the beginning, totaling over $500 million by the time the sale was complete, suggesting a commission of $3.5 million before costs were subtracted. Cooke himself claimed he made only $200,000 net, but the numbers were suspect. In 1863, the New York *World* took him to task in no uncertain language when it stated, "If, however, Jay Cooke and Company receive from the government one-half of one per centum on all the notes funded, we can readily see a powerful motive for that house to procure as large a sum to be converted into bonds as possible." The newspaper did not do the math for its readers, but the numbers were indeed large. Eventually, one half of 1 percent of $500 million would have netted Cooke $2.5 million. Regardless of the costs, the public outcry could be expected to be shrill. But the *World* also noted, "Our people seem to delight in being cheated. The serenity with which they swallow the false statements of the success of our arms . . . [and] the repudiations and cunning contrivances of the Treasury Department leave little doubt that the luxury of being humbugged is only equaled by that of being imprisoned without law, wasted by war, and impoverished by taxes."[32]

Similar attacks on Cooke came from the Senate, where his detractors claimed that he made millions at the Treasury's expense. Salmon Chase, being a man of high conscience, was uncomfortable with some of the attacks. After reassuring himself that Cooke was acting mostly in the national interest, Chase stepped in to defend his agent and the books were closed on the 5-20s. Cooke was a national hero and had amassed a small fortune as a result. Cynics would later say that the day the war ended he began a grandiose project to build the palatial home of his dreams that would cost over $1 million. But the financings were not yet finished and more bond issues were on the way.

Allegations arose concerning Cooke's conduct, reminiscent of the criticism leveled at Robert Morris decades before. For his part, Chase was criticized for employing such a small Philadelphia banker as an agent for the Treasury. Cooke's success was much envied and he had many detractors. Both the House of Representatives and the Senate studied Cooke's relations with the Treasury, looking for potential fraud or graft. What they found instead was that Cooke had assumed enormous risks for little real compensation and the inquiries promptly ended. Apparently, Cooke was every inch the patriot and bull that he appeared and Congress thought it unwise to pursue him.

Despite Cooke's clean bill of health, Chase did not employ him in the next sale of Treasury offerings. As a result, the very next issue went poorly. Realizing his mistake, Chase invited Cooke back to sell what became known as the 7-30s. These were three-year notes paying 7.3 percent interest. The extra percent was possible because the bonds were offered in New York, where the usury law permitted 7 percent interest rather than 6. Chase offered Cooke better commission terms than those he had received on the 5-20s. However, Chase protected himself and the Treasury by insisting that no notes would be delivered until payment had been received and that he could terminate Cooke's contract as Treasury agent at any time during the offering. This latter stipulation was required in order to avoid any float management by Cooke on the issue, which would have allowed him to reap gains similar to those realized by Enoch Clark on the Mexican War issues. After reading Chase's terms, Cooke remarked, "Some passages of this letter are more fit for the instructions to a fool or a dishonest agent than one deserving confidence & tried & trusted heretofore to millions."[33] He did, however, begin to organize for the sale of the notes in January 1865.

Cooke's technique for selling the 7-30s was much the same as those for the original issue. Around the country he opened what were called "Working Men's Savings Banks," which were actually evening sales offices at which working people could buy bonds after hours. The bonds could be bought in denominations as small as $50. Agents were even instructed to sell bonds to soldiers on days when they received their pay. No potential marketing target escaped Cooke's attentions and no investor was too small. This additional marketing strategy made the 7-30s even more widely distributed than the 5-20s.

The war ended in April 1865 but money was still needed, more desperately than during the war itself. Cooke managed to sell over $500 million of the issue, which finally totaled over $800 million, making it the largest bond issue in American history. During the sale, some of the agents took to discounting the bonds to customers in order to sell them more easily, a practice that infuriated Salmon Chase and Jay Cooke. Cooke asked for, and received, permission to organize a stabilization fund whereby he would buy up those buys being offered at a discount in order to keep their offering price steady.

Cooke also supported the bond sales with his own theory of the national debt. Answering those critics who contended that the debt burden was too large for the U.S. Treasury to service, a pamphlet published under his auspices argued just the opposite. Circulated in 1865, the pamphlet, entitled *How Our National Debt May Be a National Blessing*, argued that making the debt permanent was the best answer to increasing the national wealth. Using the British as an example, it argued that as long as the interest was paid, the principal itself added to the national wealth because it was a treasure. Paying it off was not practical. "The retention of the principal of the debt, and the payment of the interest only, would avoid the wrong of calling on this generation to discharge an obligation contracted in the interest of the nation for all time. There is no entirely just way of discharging a National Debt, except by apportioning the interest from generation to generation, in perpetuity."[34] Pressing the point even further, the pamphlet suggested that the bonds were the perfect widows and orphans investment, another indirect reference to British obligations of the past.

Despite Cooke's popularity, his ideas about the national debt were not that persuasive. One Ohio newspaper stated, "Evidently the memory of Ben Franklin has been lost in Philadelphia. We are no longer to thrive by industry; we are to thrive by running into debt."[35] Part of the criticism stemmed from Cooke's argument that the national debt should not be paid in full by national subscription. He sold bonds in that manner but did not want the debt redeemed in a similar manner. Critics realized there was little profit in that idea.

The marketing of this enormous amount of bonds proved to be the undoing of the Confederate cause. They also became the indirect undoing of Jay Cooke himself. Dealing with such vast amounts of money, often committing for large amounts in very short periods of time, gave Cooke the impression that business would always be successful and fast. Once the war ended, however, such huge sums no longer would be the norm and life would begin to return to normal. But at the time, the outstanding amounts of the 7-30s and the 5-20s were so large that Cooke was able to say that he was the first financier to raise over $1 billion, a measure relatively new to the finance lexicon.

After the war was finished, Cooke and his partners had time to tally the profits they made during the war. But they would not last long. Emboldened by his success, Cooke became a railroad financier and lost everything with the collapse of the Northern Pacific Railroad in 1873. The panic of 1873 was a direct result and his bank and several others were forced to close their doors. He faded from the public view, but his legacy was not forgotten. Cooke had done more than any other individual to popularize bond investing and argue for a permanent national debt. Clearly, his arguments were self-serving, but that did not hurt his image even after the railroad failure. The name Jay became the most popular name given to newborn male babies for decades to come. His selling methods would be adopted again during the two world wars in the twentieth century.

Repeal, of Sorts

After the war, the movement against the usury laws began again. One state considering repeal was Massachusetts. A new law was proposed that would reduce the rate to the 6 percent official rate for damages if excessive interest could be proved. Otherwise, the ceiling would have been lifted. One of the main arguments in favor of abolishing the official 6 percent rate was that New York's rate was 7 percent and that was providing competition for funds. Investors and businessmen could easily find higher rates of return on Wall Street or in the Boston Stock Exchange, but by allowing the rate to rise one percentage point some money would be attracted and mortgage lending would not dry up. The argument proved successful in the long run.

One supporter of removing the old law was Richard Henry Dana Jr., a lawyer, social activist, author, and member of the Massachusetts legislature. His speech before the legislature in 1867 is one of the best-known defenses of what he termed "natural interest," or market rates of interest, versus the old usury ceilings. Drawing upon a lengthy number of past references, including Aristotle and Bentham, Dana took particular aim at John Whipple in his address. Characterizing him as a man of a previous generation who had taken his ideas from an even earlier generation, Dana said that Whipple "no doubt thought that if Rhode Island would only rest her political system on the Charter of Charles II and her financial system on the Statute of Anne she would indeed be the model commonwealth of America."[36] Unfortunately for the old arguments, progress replaced the old Rhode Island usury laws with a much more lenient one, demonstrating to Dana that usury indeed was outdated. Massachusetts adopted a similar law after the debate in the legislature was finished. Official ceilings were abolished, although the 6 percent rate remained, as it did in Rhode Island, as the official rate of recovery in the event of legal action between borrower and lender. The 6 percent rate stood in Rhode Island unless another rate was contracted between borrower and lender.

After the repeal, the *Financial Chronicle* interviewed the president of the Boston Board of Trade about the effects. When asked whether interest rates rose after the repeal, a common problem in some places, he responded, "I do not think they did and for a long time after the passage of the law the effect was hardly to be noticed. But its ultimate effect has been to substitute 7 percent for 6 percent in mortgages and bank loans."[37] Uniformity with New York was vital since investors and lenders could easily move their loanable funds around with ease. The Board of Trade also made sure its views were heard by other states where the usury laws were again on the legislative agendas, notably Ohio and Connecticut.

Not to be preempted by Massachusetts, New Yorkers again raised the possibility of repeal. In January 1873, about the same time repeal was introduced in the Massachusetts legislature, Governor John Adams Dix of New York said in his annual message that his state should consider repeal, given that several neighboring states had already done so or were in the process. The matter was practical and centered on Wall Street. "It is quite clear that in the City of New York," he said, "that for scruples on the one hand and fears on the other by which conscientious and timid capitalists are restrained from lending at prohibitive rates, the enormous interest paid under the pressure of extraordinary demands for the use of money could not be maintained for a single day."[38]

The idea that usury laws were repealed outright was something of an illusion. Although each state differed in its treatment of usury, generally an interest rate ceiling existed that was applied only when damages were sought between two parties involved in borrowing and lending. Interest rates stipulated by contract in a loan agreement were normally not covered and the usury law applied only to those verbal handshake agreements where no contract was signed. How many of those types of cases were adjudicated is another question, although the suspicion is that they were few and far between. Criminal usury provisions were maintained by the states, although again only the plaintiff would have cause to seek redress from the courts. By the end of the Civil War, it was clear that American usury laws represented a variety of ideas on the subject, ideas that were not necessarily put into practice. Business, for example, had been successfully ignoring the usury laws for decades and continued to do so in the future. Unlike the English and European usury laws of the Middle Ages, Renaissance, and Enlightenment, they were nothing more than civil codes akin to a nuisance statute that was considered long out of date. But their influence still was widely felt.

No lender wanted to be accused of attempting to beggar his neighbor. It was bad for business.

American Tontines

While tontine schemes faded away in Britain well before the usury laws were abolished, they became popular in the United States immediately after the Civil War and flourished. But they were no longer called tontines. They acquired a more technical name, although the concept was the same.

The Civil War made life insurance extremely popular. In 1860, forty-three companies offered life insurance, with a total amount outstanding of approximately $173 million. By 1867, the numbers had increased dramatically, with one hundred companies and $1.168 billion outstanding.[39] Part of the phenomenon also was due to tontines being offered, a new concept in American insurance at the time. The product got its start at an American company with a familiar name. The speculative element of the plans appealed to the nation, which has just undergone the wrenching effects of internecine warfare. As in the English example, the usury laws lurked in the background.

The Equitable Society, located in New York City, began offering tontines in 1868. The president of the company, Henry Hyde, wanted to make his company the preeminent insurer in the country during the upsurge in life insurance popularity, and he saw the tontine as a means of achieving that end. The term tontine was not used, however. The more technically correct name was "deferred dividend policy." By 1870, Equitable had written at least fifteen thousand of them. Policyholders did not receive dividends on their policies. They were held in the pools for a later date, deferred as the originals were two hundred years before.

The feature that attracted the most new policyholders was the suggestion that the tontines paid a much higher than average return to the policyholders over their lives. Hyde's insurance salesmen carried booklets that they referred to when selling policies to customers and these sorts of books of expected investment returns became a standard for insurance salesmen for decades to come. The policies became so popular that other well-established New York insurance companies decided to offer them in order to compete. Although there was an insurance investigation in New York in 1877, Hyde and his tontines escaped unscathed. The complexity of the policies was difficult to understand. The policies continued to be offered well into the next century before finally being declared illegal.

Like their English counterparts 150 years before, the American tontines flourished because of the state usury laws. Although the laws had been liberalized rather than repealed outright, they still provided a ceiling for retail customers and small savers that market rates of interest provided to the wealthier and institutional investors. The deferred dividends were a method of borrowing money from policyholders at no interest, promising a payout at some later, indeterminate date. They cleverly took advantage of present value in favor of the insurance companies in return for a potential high payout for policyholders who remained in good standing. Since small investors did not speculate in the stock market in any meaningful numbers, the tontines became the easiest way to subscribe to a potentially large future payout. Unlike the early British tontines, they could be funded by investing in government bonds, not simply relying on future tax revenues for payouts.

During the period after the Civil War, usury laws became associated with the small investor or individual saver and were almost completely disassociated from Wall Street and the business world. On the retail side, they continued to protect the individual from predatory lending. On the wholesale side, they were liberalized enough in some states to attract larger lenders who could provide liquidity for mortgages and bank loans without fear of litigation from borrowers. The balancing act did not always work successfully and loopholes did exist, as the tontines proved once again. But it was becoming clearer that if an individual gave up a benefit in return for a promise of a larger future benefit, the potential was worth the loss of the insurance dividend.

While developments in the financial services industry proceeded at a fast pace, the usury issue remained alive and well on the theoretical and practical levels, although the battle no longer was about its efficacy or fairness but about its fundamental role in the inegalitarian nature of society. From the radical perspective, usury was no longer a practice to be condemned; it was now contributing to the enslavement of the working class by capitalists. From the economic perspective, usury was society's oldest financial practice. From the more radical socialist perspective, it was a cornerstone of repression.

Marx on Usury

With few exceptions, most criticisms of the usury laws from the Renaissance to the Industrial Revolution were practical in nature. The laws were considered too difficult to enforce, badly administered, or simply out of date. When historical criticism did arise, it was usually very selective in nature. Adam

Smith used the past to describe the present as did other writers, but a sharp, critical edge was not evident. When Karl Marx wrote *Capital*, however, usury finally was put in a historical context that certainly would have quickly resulted in its downfall if the author had been a mainstream writer like Bentham or Ricardo.

Marx considered usury in a broad historical context that began with what he called "pre-capitalist relationships" in society. In his historical, dialectical approach usury played a central role in the subjugation of the peasant class by those who seized control of the economic wealth in society. Subjugating peasants and the military, especially in ancient Rome, eventually led to slavery. The main tool in this subjugation was usury. The cycle was as true for Charlemagne as it was for the Romans. In the simplest sense, "the mere death of his cow may render the small peasant incapable of renewing his reproduction on its former scale. He then falls into the clutches of the usurer, and once in the usurer's power he can never extricate himself."[40] Underlying this assessment was a noticeable pessimism about the ability of the peasant to cope with the future. Once enslaved, he remained so without hope.

The pre-capitalist methods by which usury insidiously worked its magic continued when capitalism emerged, helped in part by collecting interest. Interest-bearing capital was distinguished from usurer's capital. The former was capital required and used in capitalist modes of production while the latter was the older type—interest collected as rents or payments from the underclass to the usurer whose sole interest was to keep the status quo so that those payments continued into the future. As Marx noted, the two types became one and the same, operating side by side. Interest-bearing capital was employed in the capitalist mode of production; usurer's capital in the traditional method of making consumption loans. "Usury as such does not only continue to exist but is even freed, among nations with a developed capitalist production, from the fetters imposed upon it by all previous legislation. Interest bearing capital retains the form of usurer's capital in relation to persons or classes ... where money is borrowed by wealthy spendthrifts for the purpose of squandering or where the producer is a non-capitalist producer such as a small farmer or craftsman."[41] Adam Smith and Francis Bacon would have recognized the allusion very quickly.

Marx's ideas on usury agreed with those of Aristotle to a great extent. The barren argument of Aristotle became theft to Marx, but otherwise the two considered the taking of interest of no moral or practical use. Marx recognized that charging usury was a means by which financial capitalists could accumulate a war chest to be used for further investment and exploitation, something the proletariat would never be able to achieve. The lesson was not lost on many industrialists and financiers of the nineteenth century.

Debt as a Weapon

One of the clearest differences between the nineteenth century and those preceding it was the creative use of debt, especially after the Civil War. On the corporate or wholesale level, debt was no longer feared as it once had been but now was considered just another tool in advancing the prospects for profit. Capitalism based on manufacturing and overseas trading was quickly evolving toward financial capitalism and would evolve toward a stronger dependence on debt than ever before.

The vast difference between individual indebtedness and the wholesale variety of trading in debt clearly could be seen on Wall Street in the nineteenth century. Access to funds in the money market was vital in most of the stock market raids and takeover battles that developed, especially after the Civil War. Control of the credit mechanism was a vital tool in fashioning debt as a weapon.

Margin trading had been established on the stock exchange almost from its very inception and buying securities on credit was a well-established practice. Speculators could buy shares in a company for a small percentage of the actual price, carrying the balance on margin. Lenders were more than happy to provide cash because the interest earned was much higher than what could be earned on more everyday lending. Some midwestern states had discovered that attracting New York lenders and investors could be doubly difficult because of the difficulty in luring funds away from the New York money market.

Money market rates between 1830 and the beginning of the Civil War often exceeded the usury limits in most states and often reached into the range of 5–18 percent, although rates less than 10 percent were most common. The higher rates attracted lenders who advanced loans to stock market speculators. This helped add credence to the claim by opponents of usury laws that artificially low rates were diverting funds into riskier forms of lending. The argument had been heard before, but the potential rewards lured many lenders into the bull and bear raids of the nineteenth century nevertheless. In addition, many of the market operations were conducted by speculators with established reputations for market manipulation, and at the time reputation was paramount in lending.

One of the market operations that proved profitable was lending to bear market operators who would sell a stock short and then borrow to cover (buy) the shares at a later date at a lower price. On the other side of the coin, money was equally lent to bulls who bought on margin, hoping for a stock to rise. But the bear operation was not as visible to the casual observer. The only obstacle to a successful bear raid on a stock or stocks was the availability of cash to borrow to cover the short sale. If cash were not available then the shorts could not be covered, leaving the market in confusion.

In London, *The Times* published an account of one operation as a warning to U.K. investors to stay clear of the New York stock market. It stated that "last week the grand jury of New York County indicted sundry Wall Street brokers and money lenders for a violation of the usury laws by lending money at higher rates of interest than the legal 7 percent. The money lenders were arrested and bailed to answer at Court and every one supposed that the New York grand jury had suddenly been endowed with miraculous virtue." But virtue was not on display. The arrests were part of a complaint made by the bulls that the bears were borrowing at high rates of interest to cover their positions, thereby covering themselves properly but expensively. As the newspaper concluded, "The grand jury is thus an instrument less of the law than the Wall Street speculator and the movement could not have been said to be very effective." [42]

Despite the presence of the usury laws, Wall Street took little notice since the laws only stood in the way of making money. The long-time Wall Street veteran Henry Clews noted as early as 1888 that "the simple reason that such laws will not work in practice is that where there is a will there is generally a way to avoid them . . . the ways of getting around these are numerous, and there is practically no limit to the rate of interest that can be exacted except the conscience of the lender, which is frequently very elastic." [43]

Bankers who controlled the money market also controlled operations on the stock market to a large extent. If the bull faction could have deprived the bears of margin money, then the short selling would have been aborted or the bears ruined in the process. By withholding funds from the money market, the bulls were able to achieve their ends. Clearly, the process could easily have worked in reverse at other times since call money was essential to the process. The bull and bear raids of the nineteenth century were replete with such stories where borrowed money was at the heart of the market operation. The next century would see more imaginative uses of borrowed money.

High market rates of interest helped siphon money away from small borrowers. The post–Civil War period was not characterized by a surplus of loanable funds available for the small borrower. Those needing a consumption loan of under $50 had sources available to them, but the rates charged commonly were very high. This was the case in both the United States and Britain. Consumption loans still meant money to tide someone over until the next pay day. The modern notion of consumption where individuals fuel an economy by purchasing a variety of goods and services was not yet ingrained in economic theory. Consumption still was equated with subsistence more than with consumerism.

The Rise of the Loan Shark

With the development of a national banking system, the old arguments about usury seemed out of place given that credit was readily available after the Civil War. But the term did not disappear because usury still was being openly practiced as it had been for centuries. The source of the problem was the same: consumption loans were made to individuals for small amounts of money at extortionate rates of interest. Market rates were reserved for companies and governments at reasonable rates and were subject to the normal forces of supply and demand.

As in the ancient world or in medieval Europe, a large segment of the U.S. population did not have the means to pay its expenses from week to week without having to seek the occasional small loan. This was a growing problem during the nineteenth century because of the rapid growth of the cities in both Europe and the United States at the expense of the countryside. As the populace migrated to cities in search of work, the need for cash to cover expenses rose. Rural peasants were being supplanted by the urban working poor, but in economic terms their plight had not changed materially over the years. The peasant who relied on a loan from his landlord now needed a loan from an anonymous lender in a city. Unlike Martin Luther's landlord, who lent his peasant a goose, or Jeremiah O'Callaghan's parishioner, who lent seed to poor farmers, these new urban lenders were apt to be less forgiving or remorseful if the loan fell into arrears. They enforced the terms and conditions of high-interest loans to the letter. The community or tribal affiliations had given way to a more impersonal business of lending.

Part of the lending problem was solved by mutual societies or cooperative societies in both Britain and the United States. These organizations lent deposits of their members to other members in need of funds so there was a strong motive for repaying on time. In a sense, these organizations were the urban equivalent of a tribal clan: they did not prey on their members. They were local in nature so members of the association tended to know each other. The British building society and the American savings and loan association were examples of this type of limited purpose bank. Their main objective was to provide consumption loans and loans for purchasing a home. They were not commercial lenders in that they did not provide loans for capital investment or working capital to business.

There were not enough of them to meet the demand for consumption loans, however. The shortfall was provided by lenders seeking a return on capital by lending either private funds or shareholder capital to the working classes. These private lenders included loan societies and the infamous loan sharks, a peculiarly American term that came into use in the 1880s for lenders operating outside the usury law restrictions in their respective states. Private lenders operated in similar fashion to mutuals and cooperatives, with one major difference. Their main purpose was to beggar their neighbor with high fees and high interest rates. Their profile had not changed materially in a thousand years.

On the face of it, credit was available for consumption loans, but the price was extremely high. Advertisements for moneylenders appeared in all the newspapers, both in Britain and the United States. Repeal of the U.K. usury laws appeared to make credit available, but the small loan business was rife with abuse. Contracts for small loans, to be paid back within three months, often had blank spaces in the typeset that would enable lenders to change the effective rates of interest easily. Shilling could easily be changed to shillings as could pound and pounds. A solicitor wrote to *The Times* complaining of the practice, stating, "If the interest reserved . . . be at the rate of 75 percent per annum it requires no great effort of the imagination to fancy what it may amount up to on renewals at three months."[44] Usury was alive and well and high rates prevailed, despite theories to the contrary that interest rates would find a natural, reasonable level.

Usually loan-sharking is associated with organized crime, but in the nineteenth century it was nothing more than another business that operated in the shadows of legal lending. Business was brisk, especially (but not exclusively) among members of the working class, who often fell prey to the need for an urgent loan. The loan shark was a provider of loans to the poor and those who had fallen on hard times. He was not considered a well-received member of the business community, but he was not a pariah either. Since his function was begrudgingly accepted, he was tolerated. In short, he was a usurer, as he had been for centuries. But in the American case, he was not singled out by religion or ethnicity. The loan shark was an unequal opportunity lender of no particular ethnic group.

Loan-sharking was a serious social problem, but it was not a uniform one. Loan sharks preyed on the working poor and those in desperate financial straits. Many middle-class people had little idea of the problems loan sharks created. One of the founders of a credit union in Detroit stated that "the great majority of people of means have but the faintest idea of the loan shark evil." Many of the founders of the benevolent lenders' societies thought that charging 1 or 2 percent interest per month was preferable to the much higher rates charged by less scrupulous lenders. "But when we went before the [Michigan] legislature," he added, "and asked for one and one half or two percent interest per month we had no little difficulty in convincing the members that this was not usury in its worst form."[45] A previous bill to raise the usury ceiling failed in 1907, but one was finally passed in 1909.

As in previous centuries, stories abounded of loan sharks at work. Most were found at small finance companies openly advertising themselves as lenders. Quite often, they charged potential borrowers fees for assessing loans before agreeing to advance cash. If they did make a loan, it was also accompanied by more fees that would add to the stated interest rate. Loans had to be collateralized, often for more than their value. Installment payments normally were made weekly and one missed payment would prompt seizure of the collateral unless the lender agreed to extended payments, which would add to the interest bill and the borrowers' ability to repay. Effective rates of interest under these circumstances often amounted to over 40 percent.

One particularly lucrative type of loan originating in the nineteenth century was the advance payroll loan, better known today as the payday loan. Under these schemes, a worker needing a loan before he was paid arranged to be paid an advance on wages by a lender before payday, receiving a fraction of his payroll amount. The lender would receive the full payment on the appointed day, usually at the end of the week. The charge for the service was high, around 25 percent was average. Although it was recognized that the rates were usurious by any standard, the lack of alternative sources of payroll advances insured that the lenders would thrive without much interference. Nearly forty years after the usury ceiling was raised in 1909, Fiorello LaGuardia was still complaining about the lenders when he was mayor of New York City, but the loan sharks continued to thrive. The continual source of immigrant labor and the working poor provided demand for the high-interest loans.

Despite the increasing use of debt in the nineteenth century and a grow-ing opposition to usury laws in general, usury on the local level was still considered an indictable offense and was pursued by authorities when com-plaints were made. In 1894, an elderly man living in Harlem complained to the New York City mayor that he had been the victim of a loan shark. The mayor passed the complaint to the district attorney, who in turn handed it to an assistant. The assistant district attorney charged the man with violat-ing the usury law and summoned him to his office. When he appeared, the accused left an envelope with $15 with the assistant, claiming that he wanted to make amends to the elderly man. But the assistant forgot to pass the money on and when the affair came to light, he resigned his job so that he would not shed a poor light on his boss for appearing to take a small bribe. The amount was small, but the charge of usury and the subsequent oversight underlined the newsworthy nature of loan-sharking in New York.

The lack of lending facilities to provide consumption loans in the latter nineteenth century eventually led many not-for-profit groups to enter the lending business in order to relieve low-paid workers. In New York City, the pastor of St. Bartholomew's Church in 1895 devised a scheme to lend to his parishioners after receiving many requests for aid. The plan was to provide loans for $50 or under at reasonable rates of interest. Loans were secured by non–real estate property (chattel mortgages). This was at a time when the average annual wage was $438 per year.[46] Loans were made at 6 percent an-nual interest and installments were paid monthly. Business increased so quickly that over $30,000 was extended to borrowers within the first nine months of operation and $12,000 of that amount was already repaid when the church decided to make the program permanent. "Many of the people who have come to the bureau were in the clutches of the money lenders," the pastor of St. Bart's stated. "It is the common practice of the note-shavers and so-called brokers who lend at usurious rates to charge at the rate of 160 to 200 percent per annum on small loans with a chattel mortgage as security." [47]

As St. Bart's venture into lending grew larger, the interest rates it charged diminished. Originally, it was allowed to charge up to 1.5 percent per month for a secured loan but later reduced the rate to 1 percent. The original 6 per-cent rate was the effective rate borrowers paid, not the stated annual rate since many paid back their loans as quickly as possible. Within a decade of its founding, it was lending an average of $300,000 per year with a default rate of only five-eighths of 1 percent.[48] Despite the success, the demand for small loans still exceeded the supply of cash to be lent by a substantial mar-gin. As with many other benevolent loan associations around the country, it helped force some of the usurious lenders out of business in its home city. Many other examples in other cities displayed the same results.

Chicago had similar problems with loan sharks and payday loans toward the end of the century. Merchants there and in other cities recognized that if their employees were at the mercy of a loan shark they would begin to steal from them in order to make ends meet. The *Des Moines Daily News* stated in an editorial that "the loan shark who lives on blood money is the most nefarious of all the humans." As a result, employers began to band together, pooling money to be made available to workers at reasonable rates of interest. Employers in similar businesses provided the impetus for what became known as credit unions, available to workers in industry groups. The credit unions would expand over the course of the next one hundred years to become a major supplier of consumption loans to their members. The tribal concept was alive and well.

Despite the usury ceilings still in place in most states, lenders were able to avoid the restrictions by designing the loans to avoid any suggestion that they were secured by real estate. Real property was inviolate under the laws so chattel mortgages retained their popularity, as they had for centuries. Usually, borrowers who resorted to loan sharks offered little complaint unless they seriously fell behind and repayments became impossible. Even then it was difficult to tell how many insolvencies occurred because of these lenders or what the impact was upon the national income. It remained an unknown factor.

Despite the attempts to abolish usury laws, the matter of definition remained a thorny problem in both the United States and Britain. Massachusetts and Rhode Island among others claimed to have abolished it while keeping the standard 6 percent rate as the recovery rate in the event of litigation. The courts in Britain also recognized that interest rates became usurious beyond a certain threshold, although the level remained flexible and depended upon the nature of the lawsuit brought against lenders by plaintiff borrowers. The usury debate had not ended in Britain with the repeal in 1854. The term was still an active part of the business vocabulary, although the moral connotations against it were fading somewhat. Several legal cases later in the century acted to constrain the nature of lenders' contracts or the rates at which bargains were struck. While statutory usury ended in some places, references continued to be made in the courts to it, reestablishing a debate about legal usury even though statutory usury was officially at an end.

In Britain, Parliament passed the Money-Lenders Act in 1900 to try to deal with the problem of excessive interest that was being charged on many loans since the repeal of the usury laws. The new law gave the courts the ability to rule on any suit brought by a lender against a borrower and reduce any interest or damages based on interest to the old 5 percent rate. After the law was passed, many cases came before the courts that were deemed to be "harsh and unconscionable" regarding the rates of interest charged to borrowers. In one case that reached the House of Lords, the question of excessive interest arose. In comments, Lord James remarked that "excessive interest of itself is sufficient to render a transaction harsh and unconscionable ... what amounts to excessive interest is to be determined by the tribunal in each case ... when excessive interest is apparently established any facts which tend to show such excess does not prove the contract 'harsh and unconscionable' should be proved in evidence by the lender. The burthen is on him." [49]

But the problem of defining excessive interest remained. The act left that interpretation to the courts to settle and the interpretation could vary from case to case. In one instance, a man needed a loan for which he was charged 75 percent interest per annum by a moneylender. The borrower was of advancing years, a director of a company earning £1,000 per year. He listed assets of a house, furniture, and artwork worth £10,000 and needed a loan to pay his creditors. When the case eventually reached the courts, the judges ruled that the contract was fair and must be paid. Other cases were decided in a similar manner. Borrowers of some means entered these arrangements with their eyes wide open and could not later claim that usury was involved. [50] The interest rate level was not absolute and depended upon the circumstances of the borrower and the treatment given him by the lender.

After the Money-Lenders Act was passed, a judge remarked in a subsequent case that "the intention of the Legislature was to deal with the cases of persons in financial distress coming to money-lenders to borrow money in order to get out of their financial distress ... and not to deal with persons who were in a position to make their own bargain on terms of equality with the money-lender." [51] Market rates prevailed, but if borrowers proved that they were being exploited by lenders then the courts could remedy their problem. After three millennia of usury laws, the oldest principle still prevailed. Usury was defined as taking advantage of a borrower by a lender who was in a superior position to press his advantage by charging excessive interest. But the agreement between borrower and lender still assumed that borrowers entered into the contracts voluntarily.

The bankruptcy laws passed by Congress in 1800, 1841, and 1867 were all quickly repealed, leaving the United States with no effective law until 1898. In that year, Congress again attempted to pass a new bankruptcy law. The American experience with bankruptcy laws was as tortured as the British experience with repeal of the usury laws for decades prior to 1854. After much discussion and debate in the 1890s, a bill finally emerged, which was passed by Congress. The National Bankruptcy Act of 1898 was the first such law in the country to include both individuals and corporations that proved long-lasting. The law provided for both voluntary and involuntary bankruptcy. Its provisions stood for forty years before being substantially revised. According to the act,

> Any person who owes debts, except a corporation, shall be entitled to the benefits of this Act as a voluntary bankrupt. . . . Any natural person, except a wage-earner or a person engaged chiefly in farming or the tillage of the soil, any unincorporated company, and any corporation engaged principally in manufacturing, trading, printing, publishing, or mercantile pursuits, owing debts to the amount of one thousand dollars or over, may be adjudged an involuntary bankrupt upon default of an impartial trial, and shall be subject to the provisions and entitled to the benefits of this Act. Private bankers, but not national banks or banks incorporated under State or Territorial laws, may be adjudged involuntary bankrupts.[52]

The provision about private bankers was included because they stood outside regulation and public accounting because of their private status.

The bankruptcy laws were passed in the nick of time because the next century was to prove a landmark in the history of interest and debt. Although it would take several decades to develop, the debt revolution of the twentieth century would prove a milestone in the usury discussion as that old bête noire of lending, the consumption loan, was poised to lead the way to a new era of prosperity, disguised not as debt but as its more euphemistic cousin—credit.

Chapter 5

The New Debt Revolution

Recent investigations have shown fairly conclusively that in every city of more than 30,000 population there is one usurer to every 5,000 to 10,000 people; in cities where manufactories employing large numbers of workman have congregated these figures are greatly increased.

—*New York Times,* 1911

The new attitude toward debt emerging from the nineteenth century was best found in a book by Thorstein Veblen that was published in 1899. In his *Theory of the Leisure Class,* he described the new class of consumers who had grown rich over the previous decades. "Conspicuous consumption of valuable goods is a means of reputability to the gentleman of leisure," he wrote about the current consumers who provided demand for luxury goods during the Gilded Age. Their goal was to emulate other wealthy individuals in a quest for status and luxury. In previous centuries, the sumptuary laws tried to keep behavior like that to a minimum, without much success. During the Gilded Age, it was clear that behaving like wealthy bankers and industrialists was no longer condemned but encouraged. It was good for the economy.

Despite the repeal of the usury laws in Britain and the experiments with repeal in the United States, high lending rates persisted. Consumption loans mostly were unaffected, as they had been for centuries. While business loans conformed to the realities of the markets, consumption loans with effective interest rates in excess of 100 percent were still common, with the poor and marginal borrowers paying the highest rates. The building societies and friendly societies did make reasonable interest loans available to many, but large portions of the population did not qualify to be their members and paid the price as a result.

Compound interest had long since become common practice, but its potential deleterious effects were not forgotten. In the view of John Maynard Keynes, it had become the preoccupation of society at the expense of societal growth and well-being as a whole. The earlier discoveries of Darwin and the demographic warnings of Malthus had been pushed aside by financial math. If only the benefits of evolution could have been reconciled with a solution to the dire predictions of population growth to produce a true societal state of well-being. But as Keynes saw it, the opposite was occurring. The rates of growth in population and the benefits of science were diverging. Immediately after World War I he wrote, "One geometrical ratio might cancel another, and the nineteenth century was able to forget the fertility of the species in a contemplation of the dizzy virtues of compound interest."[1] Finance was poised to assert its magic over politics and economics.

Prohibitions against compound interest had long since disappeared and the only debate still surrounding it was legal. Most of the discussions about whether and when it should be charged were matters of contract law. A large body of literature developed on both sides of the Atlantic about the role of compound interest calculations in legal contracts, not unlike the discussion of usufruct and usury in Justinian's day. Charging it, especially by legal guardians and the courts, was closely monitored so that borrowers or minors were not exploited by lenders or other intermediaries.

The twentieth century introduced many new twists and derivations to the idea of credit and debt. The sharp increase in population generally put pressure on financial institutions to make credit more readily available. Credit unions, friendly societies, and building societies continued to grow but did not reach the larger part of the population, many of whom relied on "private lenders" for their borrowing needs. Specialized finance companies providing loans with high interest rates and payday lenders continued to flourish and saw an increase in demand for their services. Lending facilities for the working man and average citizen with a small or medium-size bank account were scant and loan-sharking was a far-reaching problem nationally. Money was readily available at 50 percent or more, but much less was available at lower rates. But the harm done to the economy was indeterminate because statistics were not kept on personal credit in the United States and would not be collected until the 1920s.

The period before World War II was characterized by the continuing debate about the appropriate levels of interest charged for consumption, or consumer, loans as they were now called. The argument was remarkably similar to those of the past even though the credit markets had become much more developed than in previous centuries and were capable of raising substantial amounts of long- and short-term capital for companies. The same could not be said for consumer credit, however. The credit mechanism for supplying small loans to working people had definitely improved by the 1920s but still fell far short of the amounts, and low interest rates, needed. The Swedish economist Gustav Cassel described the state of usury best in 1903 when he wrote, "Usury is that surplus price which the lender is able to exact because of the defective organisation of the market, or where the circumstances, particularly the risks, are of such an extraordinary character that no market could possibly exist." Usury did exist because of structural deficiencies in the market for credit. "Thus usury is only one variety of that more general form of robbery which consists in taking advantage of the defects of the organisation of the market," he continued, concluding that

> the main problem is how to secure for every legitimate loan that rate of interest which would have been agreed upon, with due regard to all circumstances, under an ideal organisation of the market. Hence it follows immediately that the chief remedy lies in the *organisation of credit*, with the purpose of *securing to everybody the credit he is worth*. This involves not only the creating of organisations, co-operative or otherwise, to provide loans for the small farmer, the artisan, etc., but also the spread of such elementary business-knowledge as will prevent the borrower from entering upon a contract of which he does not quite realise the bearing, and will enable him in some degree to understand the conditions of the market.[2]

The American credit markets appear to have heard the call for stronger organizations as the banking system began to develop more outlets to provide consumer credit over the next forty years.

After the initial phases of building infrastructure and other capital projects, industrialized nations, and particularly the United States, began to realize the value of consumption in their domestic economies. The market for the increasing number of manufactured goods and services depended upon the population, now called consumers, buying a wide variety of new products so that the prosperity brought by the Industrial Revolution could continue. This was a marked break with the past: societies from the Romans to the Elizabethans had passed sumptuary laws to discourage their people from living above their means or assuming ideas above their station. If

modern industrial society was to prove successful, a more democratic notion would have to replace these older ideas of noblesse oblige. The new
consumer would have to be encouraged, not discouraged.

If consumer markets were to develop and allow the average citizen to
purchase some of the wide array of goods available, society would have to
switch from the pay-as-you-go basis to which it was accustomed to one allowing consumers more latitude in paying for purchases. Traditionally, the
only sort of credit available was extended by merchants to customers on an
individual basis. If a customer could not pay for a purchase on the spot, the
merchant often allowed him to pay in arrears, perhaps a week or two later.
For the most part, consumers paid as they went: if an item could not be paid
for immediately it was unaffordable. The only exception to the rule was buying a home using a mortgage, usually extended by savings and loan institutions for around ten years. Before World War I, few of these facilities were
provided by commercial banks. The big banks, including private banks,
provided mostly business loans, while some underwrote securities and
served wealthy private individuals. The retail banking that did occur was
marketed to the wealthiest 10 percent of the population. It was not until A.
P. Giannini founded the Bank of Italy in California (later renamed the Bank
of America) after the turn of the century, that a commercial bank actively
sought retail business. Once the bank and others like it grew, the consumer
boom found institutional support. Only after World War I did the large
banks begin to serve the average citizen, when it became apparent that consumers were a growing force that could produce profits for lenders.

The permanent U.S. income tax for individuals was introduced for the
first time in 1913, although the rates were very modest for the average working person. Those most affected were those with higher incomes. The first
corporate tax was introduced in 1909 and it would rise during World War I.
From the beginning, interest payments were tax deductible for both corporations and individuals. The latter could deduct interest payments on cars
and homes and would continue to do so until well into the 1980s. But in the
1910s, the taxes were still new and many believed that they stood in the way
of economic progress.

The wealthy classes always had been able to enjoy a high standard of living because they possessed equity, either in terms of real property or intangibles like securities. The working class was not in the same position, many
people living from paycheck to paycheck with little savings or property. The
payday loan was a major source of credit for them despite rates that reached
as high as 120 percent per annum. These obstacles soon were overcome with

the help of modern finance. The average guy on the street wanted to live as well as his wealthier counterparts but did not have the means to do so. The solution would be to develop alternatives to the traditional pay-as-you-go system in use for centuries. This solution proved to be the first phase of the financial revolution of the twentieth century. The result was dramatic. By 1929, consumption accounted for two-thirds of the U.S. gross national product.

Effects of War

In the twentieth century, war provided as good a justification for fixed-income investing as it had in the past. The American experience with Civil War borrowings proved that government bonds were good investments with minimal chance of default risk. When the U.S. Treasury needed funding for World War I, it had little problem selling new bonds.

When the Treasury issued war bonds to finance American involvement in the First World War, memories were evoked of Jay Cooke. Buying war bonds was a popular form of investment and a display of patriotism, although actual American involvement in the war itself was much less popular. Advertising for the war loans was pitched at the small saver and evoked memories of many immigrants' personal flights to the safety of the United States. One of the most popular advertising posters that urged citizens to buy war bonds showed a graphic of Ellis Island in the shadow of the Statue of Liberty. Advertising was certainly needed. Between 1917 and 1919 the Treasury announced five Liberty Loans totaling a staggering $21.5 billion. This was by far the largest financing in American history.

The bonds were issued by the Treasury and sent to the Federal Reserve Bank of New York, which distributed them to banks and brokers for sale to customers. The Treasury itself supervised the sale, avoiding the Wall Street investment banks that often had participated in former sales. Many of the techniques originally employed by Jay Cooke more than fifty years before were used again. Denominations were small, averaging around $100. After a slow start, most of the issues were oversubscribed. The Treasury considered the financings a great success.

All sorts of investors bought the Liberty Bond issues for one simple reason: the bonds were exempt from federal income tax. Tax rates were high in the years immediately following the passing of the tax and demand for the bonds was unusually high. The fact was not lost on the investment community. Millions of individuals subscribed to the loans. Investment bankers estimated that only 350,000 individuals were invested in bonds before the war, but the numbers increased dramatically after 1914.[3] The legion of investors would make a lasting impression. Financial marketing would quickly begin to focus on the individual investor. While his individual holdings were of little consequence, on aggregate the potential market was enormous. As Charles Mitchell, the president of the National City Company, beamed, "The development of [a] large, new army of investors in this country who have never heretofore known what it means to own a coupon bond and who may in the future be developed into savers and bond buyers" was the ultimate reward of the Liberty Loan-selling efforts.[4]

In addition to Treasury bonds, those of municipalities, companies, and foreign governments and companies also existed. Railroad bonds were slowly giving way to those of industrial companies and many municipalities were tapping the market to find money with which to provide for the increasing demand for municipal services. Many foreign governments and companies were also tapping the market for dollars, adding unfamiliar names to the growing list of borrowers. Borrowing countries came from Europe, both east and west, as well as from Latin America.

In 1915, J. P. Morgan and Co. helped arrange the largest single bond financing to date, a massive issue nicknamed the Anglo-French loan of 1915. The proceeds were to be used to help finance those countries' war efforts against Germany. All the major banking houses were invited to participate, and the banks split underwriting fees, unlike the Liberty Loan practice. Morgan performed various financial functions for the U.S. Treasury during the conflict but was most influential in the peace negotiations that followed at the Versailles conference. The Morgan partners reigned supreme over the political banking world. Thomas Lamont, a Morgan partner, became Woodrow Wilson's most trusted adviser during the conference, which began in 1919. The eventual reparations bill put to the Germans, in excess of $35 billion, was strongly influenced by the bankers. Bernard Baruch, Wilson's erstwhile head of the War Industries Board, jealously remarked that there were so many Morgan men at the conference that it clearly was apparent they were running the show.

The dollar amount of the reparations was enormous and its consequences uncertain. John Maynard Keynes argued against them in his *Economic Consequences of the Peace*, which was published in 1919. As a financial representative of the U.K. Treasury at the Versailles conference, he had firsthand knowledge of the negotiations and the reparations imposed on

Germany and argued against them, to no avail. The mood following the war was punitive and harsh conditions were imposed. In his book, he demonstrated the effects of compound interest on the reparations bill to strengthen his point. The payments were to be made over a period of years following the conference and he found the payment schedule especially onerous both for the Germans and the prospects for future peace. The totals were only approximate at the time and his calculations produced a number that was slightly higher than the Allies' own estimates. He wrote:

> On the basis of my estimate of $40,000,000,000 for the total liability . . . [and] assuming interest at 5 percent, this will raise the annual payment to $2,150,000,000 without allowance for amortization. . . . At 5 percent compound interest, a capital sum doubles itself in fifteen years. On the assumption that Germany cannot pay more than $750,000,000 annually until 1936 . . . the $25,000,000,000 on which interest is deferred will have risen to $50,000,000,000, carrying an annual interest charge of $2,500,000,000 . . . at the end of any year in which she pays less than this sum she will owe more than she did at the beginning of it.[5]

Compound interest clearly exacerbated the reparations problem. Germany never fully repaid the debt and hyperinflation and World War II eventually followed. The compound interest applied to the reparations debt underscored Keynes's fears but proved politically expedient and popular in the wake of the war. The German problem proved to be the exact opposite of Richard Price's suggestions in Britain in the late eighteenth century. Now compound interest was being employed to exact reparations, adding a staggering total to the German national debt. The exact opposite of the original suggestions for a sinking fund was now occurring.

Debt in the 1920s

The exuberance of the 1920s was based on a postwar prosperity that raised the standard of living substantially. Credit became much easier to obtain and the range of consumer goods available was greater than at any time in American history. It was this sort of atmosphere that led people to borrow, purchase, and then borrow more. The previous optimism of Robert Wallace succeeded over Malthusian pessimism. Credit was becoming democratized, fitting in neatly with the growth in population and the demand for a better life and increased living standards.

Even before the war, when the boom was only a few years old, there was a feeling of unease about the new consumerism. There was fear that consumers were spending too much and saving little if any money. The fear coincided with concerns about the level of drunkenness and alcoholic consumption, especially among working people, that eventually led to Prohibition. But Prohibition and the ever-present usury laws had one thing in common. During the 1920s, they would be violated repeatedly, to the point where both became almost useless.

During World War I, the "thrift movement" blossomed on several levels and urged Americans to save as much as possible. For its part, the government wanted people to channel their funds into government war bonds. Post office savings banks were established, providing a convenience that many savings banks and credit unions could not match. Woodrow Wilson suggested that each dollar invested in war bonds would mean less competition for the government's fundraising. Saving money became the patriotic duty of everyone and the results were highly successful. All that cash also proved tempting to lenders.

In the United States, the long-standing affinity for consumer credit began in earnest in the 1920s. At the time, the changes in buying power and its implications were clear and a long boom began that only ended with the crash of the stock market in 1929. The standard of living in turn permanently changed lifestyles and future attitudes toward debt. Consumer debt more than doubled in the 1920s. A population of 60 million had about $6.4 billion in consumer debt before the crash of 1929, representing an indebtedness of $106 per person, or about 8 percent of the average annual per capita income.[6] Housing also was in demand and the second mortgage became popular since one no longer accommodated many homeowners' desire to buy more and more consumer goods. Old ideas about the burdens of debt were quickly disappearing in the face of its more positive interpretation from the lenders' point of view—it was now an extension of credit. The implication was positive, not negative as it had been for centuries. The phenomenon prompted the *New York Times* to remark in 1923, "It might be desirable to draw a line between credit and debt but it is difficult to find the dividing point."

By 1925, over five hundred installment credit companies existed. Credit agencies developed that would keep manual tabs on account holders provided by merchants and lenders and take notes on them on a daily basis.

One of the problems these agencies identified was the customer who took his own good time paying back a loan rather than adhering to a payment schedule. This especially was important because repossession of goods in arrears often occurred. Consumer loans required collateral, as they always had.

Despite the fact that many of these new purchases were financed by credit, it still was quite different from the credit that would develop after World War II. Credit facilities were available, but they hardly were universal. A large percentage of the population continued to pay for goods and services when needed and most did not have banking facilities. The credit phenomenon of the 1920s was all the more remarkable because it involved probably only 10 percent of the population. The Twentieth Century Fund estimated in 1930 that nine of ten people one met in the street did not have access to credit. Retail banking statistics demonstrated that the consumption that was occurring was financed to a large degree with borrowed money. Those consumers who banked, if they banked at all, did so at savings and loan associations, credit unions, or savings banks rather than commercial banks. The commercial banks curtailed their newly instituted retail activities once the Depression began.

Most merchant lenders allowed customers to put away money on a regular basis in order to make future purchases. The merchant set the goods aside but would not release them until payment had been received in full. The major difference between those plans and the contemporary ones is that the older ones required consumers to save *before* spending, not after it. Technically, these "lay-away plans" were a method for funding a future purchase, not a means of retiring existing consumer debt. The horse was still pulling the financial cart in this case, not walking behind it as it would later in the century.

While these lay-away plans would remain popular for several more decades, they were eclipsed by the new installment credit. The concept was simple but still somewhat radical at the time. Consumers were required to make a down payment on a purchase and then pay the balance in equal installments. Sears, Roebuck and Co. established its consumer credit operation in 1911, being one of the first established retail stores to do so. Automobiles were the first big ticket items to be bought in this manner. The Maxwell Motor Car Company was the first manufacturer to offer its cars on credit in 1916. It required a payment of 50 percent down, with the balance to be paid in eight equal installments. Most other car companies followed suit. Big ticket items were among the first items for which installment credit was available, although such credit would be offered on all sorts of consumer goods within ten years.

The concept of collateral was still a prerequisite for lending, indirectly if not directly. When a customer wanted a home mortgage, he or she would normally use a building association with which a relationship of savings had been built over a period of time. Ordinarily, the customer had to have a savings account at the small bank in order to apply for a mortgage. Often, the account had to be kept open after a house was purchased, so it was in the bank's best interest to do the math to ensure the customer could afford the mortgage payments. In banking terms, the customer had to have a small compensating balance for the loan. And the mortgage terms were far less generous than after World War II. In the mid-1920s, a standard mortgage had to be repaid in three to five years. The building associations and savings banks offered more generous terms, stretching as far out as eleven years and seven months. Most mortgage financings actually were a blend of primary mortgages and secondary mortgages to produce longer repayment periods, although amortization periods of more than fifteen years were rare. The smaller lenders clearly had the advantage over the larger and did the majority of the residential mortgage business.

The average citizen's second largest cash purchase involved clever financing so that everyone could get behind the wheel of an automobile. Immediately after the war, manufacturers quickly recognized the need for extending credit to customers. In 1919, General Motors created the General Motors Acceptance Corporation (GMAC) to lend money to its dealers and customers. The operation was a success within three years, lending over $227 million for purchases and becoming the largest installment credit company in the process.[7] Ford established its credit subsidiary later in 1928 with the avowed purpose of helping everyone own a Ford at the lowest cost possible. It stated that it was not establishing the company to make a profit but only to provide financing for buyers. Its success was noteworthy. Within two years, it had provided $425 million in financing to 800,000 "time" buyers. At the time, the least expensive car cost slightly less than one year's salary for the average workingman. Wages rose from about $1,100 to $1,500 over the decade.[8]

Installment credit had become so popular by 1926 that many of the leading lenders joined together to form a discount company that would serve as a back-up facility by purchasing their notes at a discount to provide liquidity. The results were clear. By the end of the 1920s, installment credit was becoming the most popular type of credit granted. Of the approximately $6.4 billion credit generated annually, about half was installment credit.[9] The next two most popular sources were "unlicensed lenders" and pawnbrokers, representing $750 million and $600 million annually respectively. These two demonstrated that despite the advances made in consumer lending, society still was relying heavily on sources that had been more popular in the past. Unlicensed lenders represented a wide variety of sources, but the best known was one that had plagued American society for generations.

The War against Loan Sharks

American society was plagued by two serious social problems after World War I—alcoholism and usury. The two were closely related, although alcoholism clearly was considered the more serious, resulting in Prohibition. Prohibiting the manufacture of spirits was the closest American society came to imposing sumptuary laws, although technically the onus was upon the producers, not the consumers.

Loan-sharking became associated with organized crime after the war, providing ready cash for those in need at rates that were truly usurious. One notable example prompted reporting. After the gangster Dutch Shultz was shot in 1933, the *New York Times* remarked that "the ancient racket of usury, refurbished with the strong-arm methods of modern gangsters, was said yesterday to have been an important contributing factor which brought about the shooting." Shultz was a notorious loan shark and New York authorities revealed that his racket charged unwitting borrowers interest of 1,042 percent per year. It was clear that loans of that sort could never be repaid. The late 1920s and the Depression only made the demand for consumption loans greater and those who did not use banks were forced into dire straits.

During the 1920s and 1930s, organized crime captured the headlines. Producing illegal spirits during Prohibition gave way to loan-sharking for mobsters in the later 1930s. The market for a loan shark's services were in demand since the large banks still did not deal with the small saver at the lower end of the income scale, and when a loan was needed many small businessmen and individuals sought the services of a "private" lender. Tough economic times put their services in demand. Loan-sharking was a major social and economic problem in the first several decades of the twentieth century. The high rates charged choked the ability of the unfortunate borrower to make any real economic progress. But there were other methods of exacting high rates on interest where the charge was taken before the loan was made. And not all loan sharks wore dark raincoats and did business in the shadows. Most were unlicensed loan companies preying on the cash-strapped workingman. Their claim was that they were providing credit to a segment of the population that was not served by traditional banking institutions. This argument struck a responsive chord with many in wholesale banking who wanted no part of the retail lending business. Besides making a mockery of existing usury laws, loan-sharking became the center of legislation aimed directly at the laws.

During the 1920s, consumer credit got a boost from two different sources. Because of the loan-sharking problem, a movement began to make small consumer loans more widely available. Usually, this meant individual loans of $300 or less, or about 15 percent of the average salary. Many states attempted to modify their usury ceilings to allow lenders to charge more for these loans under the assumption that higher rates would attract more legitimate lenders, and fewer loan sharks. The idea became very popular, especially after several large lenders decided to enter the small loan market. The Russell Sage Foundation was instrumental in lobbying many state legislatures to liberalize their interest rate ceilings for small loans, and as a result two large commercial banks in addition to the Bank of America entered the market.

The two were New York City institutions—the National City Bank and the Bank of United States. By 1928, both had geared themselves for the small loan business. National City announced its program first. Its president, Charles Mitchell, declared that the bank recognized that small customers, previously ignored by the large banks, needed and would receive assistance. His statement displayed that the bank was not accustomed to dealing with the average working customer, despite the bank's avowed intentions: "Our contacts with people of this class have given us a confidence in the integrity and character of the average individual. While it is not our purpose to encourage any one to borrow except under the stress of circumstances, we have faith that loans so made can and will be paid when incident thereto the spirit of thrift can be kept alive."[10]

The Bank of United States entered the market a few months later but did not remain in business long. It became the largest bank failure in American history in 1930 when it was forced to shut its doors following revelations that its directors were using customer deposits to speculate in its stock. The market crash in 1929 destroyed its price along with the bank. Many of its depositors were new immigrants who lost their savings as a result. New York State eventually stepped in to restore some of its deposits.

In 1922, forty-three of the forty-eight states of the United States had usury laws on their books. They were not all the same, however. Some of them stipulated the maximum rate of interest that lenders could charge borrowers while others were broader, designed to prevent what was known as "moral usury." In this latter case, usury was considered charging high rates of interest to someone who clearly could not afford it, without the benefit of a written loan contract. In other words, lenders were taking advantage of someone in poor economic straits. While those terms sounded fine, they were very difficult to prove, especially moral usury. Ironically, the notion of moral usury sounded much the same as the original beggar-thy-neighbor ideas of antiquity. Unfortunately, it was just as vague.

Generally, many states had statutory rates of around 6 percent to 12 percent, depending on the type of loan. Mortgages were on the lower end of the scale while term consumer loans were on the higher end. The statutory rate was stated in the loan contract. But the legal rate was different. During the twentieth century, a distinction increasingly was made between "civil" usury and "criminal" usury. The terms were more clear than moral usury. And the remedies were different as well, with criminal usury carrying heavier penalties if proved. The statutory side of lending in the states was the maximum rate specified in the constitution, if it still existed, and was easy to monitor since it applied mostly to mortgage rates. The legal rate applied when no specific rate was established in the loan contract, if such a contract actually existed, and it was applied to the rate by which the loan could be discounted if no specific repayment schedule was specified. It also applied to consumer loans and term loans other than mortgages. The types of loans the legal rate applied to were of lesser quality than those with long-term contract rates. Despite the usury laws, it was recognized that loans of lesser quality needed to command a higher rate because lenders would be frightened away from making such loans without risk-premium pricing of some sort. Generally, these rates could be as high as 18 percent by the mid- to late 1920s.

While the statutory rates were fairly easy to monitor, legal rates for consumption loans were more problematic and often created the fuzzy question of "moral" usury. This type of usury was almost impossible to assess since it depended on a borrower claiming successfully that he had been treated unfairly. Such an outcome was feasible when dealing with an institutional lender if it could be shown that the rate that applied to a loan exceeded the legal limit. But when dealing with a private lender or loan shark, it was improbable and probably impossible. The concept certainly applied to lenders like Dutch Schultz, but the snag was that the borrower had to instigate legal proceedings. The strong-arm tactics often employed by criminal loan sharks and extortionate rates of interest forced many employers to form the mutual societies originally so that their employees could borrow money at more reasonable rates, causing less harm to themselves and their employers in the process.

Some of the legal limit laws were passed during or after World War I. In 1915, the comptroller of the currency shocked the financial world by stating that over two hundred nationally chartered banks were charging interest at usurious rates. Usury laws had been on the books for years. Why then was this discussion still raging? Central to the debate in the World War I era was a long-standing political problem that would raise its head time and again over the next century. The National Bank Act passed during the Civil War imposed a national usury ceiling on federally chartered banks that was supposed to apply to state banks by default. The state banks did not follow the lead of the larger federally chartered banks, however. Competition between the two sectors constantly had the two sides at loggerheads about jurisdictions and interest rates that could be charged. The comptroller complained about the banks under his jurisdiction as if he had no real regulatory authority over them. The national banks then set a standard for higher interest rates that state banks could comfortably follow. The age-old tension between usury laws and lending practices was on full display yet again.

In addition to the usury law for national banks, the United States effectively had an unofficial usury law on the books for almost fifty years, beginning during the Depression. When Congress passed the Banking Act of 1933 (the Glass-Steagall Act), it gave the Federal Reserve power to enforce Regulation Q. In order to achieve a level playing field between banks and limit competition among them, the regulation enabled the Fed to set the maximum rate of deposit at its member banks so that they could not outbid each other for depositors' funds. For most of the next forty-seven years, the maximum rate did not exceed 6 percent and was sometimes lower. This limited a bank's major cost of funds and helped establish a lending rate in a specific range about the deposit rate. This type of spread banking was easy to maintain because banks only offered two types of customer accounts—savings and checking. The loan rate usually was several percentage points above the deposit rate for a bank's best customers. Consumer loans naturally would be set higher, but setting lending rates too high would bring questions about the excessively high levels. If the Fed protected the cost of funds on one side it would frown on excessive rates on the other. Regulation Q dovetailed nicely with state usury ceilings to provide a range, although admittedly wide, between deposit and lending rates.

In 1928, the Russell Sage Foundation estimated that commercial banks were charging between 13 and 35 percent for loans, small loan companies up to 42 percent, licensed pawnbrokers up to 60 percent, and the ubiquitous loan sharks up to 480 percent. It had been following the problem since 1912 when it first published results of its surveys about high lending rates.[11] Pawnbrokers found themselves exempt from criticism in the 1920s despite the fact that they charged high effective interest rates. They were seen as a lender of last resort for the workingman who admittedly was overextended in the consumer society. Without them, it would be difficult to introduce the poor and the working poor to capitalism in general.[12] Loan-sharking and the rates charged would increase dramatically after the Depression began, when the nationwide credit crunch made less money available for borrowing. Somehow rates for consumption had drifted near the 20 percent range without much fanfare. The idea of growth in the economy and business generally allowed for higher rates, which were tolerated with a wink and a nod.

Part of the discrepancy can be explained by the language of many state usury laws. They prohibited charging rates above a maximum stated rate as long as the loans were in written contract form. No one could charge another a high rate by written agreement. But when there was no written agreement, the complexion of the issue changed. It was generally accepted that contracts lasted for periods of one year or more, like mortgages, so the stated rate had to adhere to the usury laws. But when a loan was for shorter-term items involving personal purposes or consumer purchases then the rate was dictated by shorter periods, usually months. Then the rate could be stated in monthly terms, almost all of which would be below the annual usury limits. One and a half percent per month, in annual terms, is 18 percent, but the effective annual rate did not have to be stated explicitly until the Truth in Lending Act was passed in 1968. If the borrower paid back the loan in three months, the effective rate would be 4.5 percent or marginally higher if compounding was used. If it became a longer-standing obligation, legal usury limits applied, but it is not clear that the borrower could ask for relief from the courts unless the effective rate became outrageously high.

Another common method of avoiding charges of usury involved what was known as "salary buying," the polite period term for a payday loan. This was simply a method used to lend workers money while avoiding charges of usury. A lender would require a worker to sign over his weekly paycheck and then make a loan to the worker, less a stiff charge. This payday loan skirted the usury laws by claiming that it was not a loan but simply an advance service. Regardless of what it was called, the rates were high. A worker typically received $20 for the right to receive his next $25 paycheck from the loan-sharking company making the loan.

Despite the extortionate rates charged by payday lenders, little progress had been made since the nineteenth century. Mayor Fiorello LaGuardia of New York City was outraged when it was discovered that city workers, whose average paycheck was around $40 per week, regularly paid 10 percent of the amount in each check to get their cash as early as possible. "I have long since adopted the policy of protecting city employees from loan sharks and usurers," he said, to little avail. The situation had proven insoluble since before World War I. In 1911, a study was done of loan-sharking in New York City at the behest of the mayor William Jay Gaynor. The commissioner of accounts, Raymond Fosdick, discovered that one in five city employees required the use of a loan shark from time to time. The mayor considered the situation intolerable and it was only exacerbated by many of the stories that Commissioner Fosdick uncovered during the investigation. One particular story related how a city fireman had lost five children in a five-month period and borrowed $100 for funeral services. He paid a $10 fee and after two years and loan renewals he was $200 in debt with little prospect of paying off the loan. New York State passed a loan-shark law at the time, but the best it could do was require lenders to be registered if they intended to make personal property loans.[13]

Ironically, one of society's oldest lenders acquired some respect in the 1920s even as installment credit became very popular. Pawnbrokers remained one of largest lenders in the country, behind the installment companies and the unlicensed lenders. Their business was not that different from an ordinary lender in that collateral was provided for the loan and the rates charged were regulated in theory if the pawnbroker was licensed by the state in which it operated. Pawnbroking still was very much a local affair. The brokers never consolidated into national companies and remained small merchants, their businesses often being passed down from father to son. Given that the average citizen was becoming stretched to the limit on credit, their facilities were often the only relief for someone needing quick cash. A pawnbroker remarked in 1928 that the average New Yorker probably did not have access to $100 cash in an emergency and often sought his services as a result. Before World War I, only one pawnbroker was reputed to be doing business in France, charging rates of about 8 percent annually. Yet in the United States in the 1920s, their services were actively sought.

The loan-sharking problem brought investigations in many states. Access to consumer credit had made significant strides since the beginning of the century, but the rate of interest charged remained a problem. The Boston merchant Edward A. Filene remarked in 1928 that increased credit facilities such as credit unions were the best remedy against usury: "The usury investigations in New York and other parts of the country are a compelling challenge that we shall banish this social injustice," he stated on a radio broadcast, noting that many established credit unions were so successful that they allowed workers to borrow at rates competitive with those obtained by large corporations.[14]

The New York usury investigation began in 1928, investigating loan-sharking and salary buying. The latter practice was of special interest because it was openly practiced in New York and many legislators were aware that the buying of salary at discount was the main mischief committed by salary buyers, who claimed that the amounts they advanced were not loans but the purchase of a salary at a discount. The state legislature proposed a small loan bill that conformed to the template proposed by the advocates of a national usury law, setting the maximum rate of interest on small, unsecured loans at 2.5 percent per month, in line with the states that had already adopted the idea. Salary buying was to be considered lending and would fall under the bill.

At the same time, the state attorney general convened a series of conferences to discuss the rates of interest being charged for small loans in the state. Rates ranging from 30 to 1,000 percent were discovered, almost all on loans made to working people in need of liquidity. Arresting suspected loan sharks was advocated and several high-profile arrests were made, but the cases were not actively pursued despite all the publicity. Attorney General Alfred Ottinger claimed that $26 million per year was being lost to loan sharks in the state, most of it in New York City. He described the amount, rising every year, as the "annual gouge" and urged the legislature to adopt the small loan law circulating among the states.[15]

Many small lenders responded quickly, packing their bags to move out of the state. New Jersey recognized the danger and quickly called for its own loan-shark investigation before many of the lenders could decamp across the Hudson River. But the New York problem was not one that could be solved easily. The call money market also played a major role in the amount of money available for small borrowers. When the rate for money lent for stock market loans (margin) was low, lenders extended more credit to smaller borrowers than they did when the call money rate was high. Funds would simply shift from one sector to the other, in search of higher returns. Call money was exempt from the New York usury laws because it was not considered a time loan. It competed with time loans and when call money was high, time loans necessarily had to raise their rates in order to compete. The *New York Times* noted that "this compels brokers to bid up for time money to attract those who are willing to run the risk of facing a charge of usury. Foreign money at once disappears as such lenders face the loss of principal as well as interest."[16]

Loans to speculators were also a volatile issue among Progressives in the 1920s, especially those who were labeled Prairie Populists by the Eastern establishment. A great deal of tension arose because margin rates were attracting lenders to make loans to stock market speculators while draining possibly lower rate funds from consumers. The Progressives blamed the Fed for the problem, noting that it did not pay interest on its reserves to member banks. As a result, the banks lent money to the market instead, seeking higher interest income. Overall, interest rates were too high across the board, they argued, with Wall Street enjoying low rates while forcing higher rates for the general population. The argument continued until the Depression, when it became less relevant in the face of other economic problems.

The New York and New Jersey measures did not necessarily help matters, however. A spokesman for the Household Finance Corporation, one of the major lenders to small businesses and individuals, commented, "The New York small loans law fixed the rate at 2 per cent per month with fees and additions, which makes the rate equivalent to 2.5 per cent per month and the law practically inoperative. Only 17 [lending] licensees were doing business in that state last year. The amount of loans outstanding was insignificant when compared to the demand as shown by the enormous amounts advanced at high rates through illegal channels." Across the river, a similar problem occurred: "In New Jersey, the issue became politically involved and last year a 1.75 per cent per month rate went into effect. The result of this was that all but one of the licensed companies practically withdrew from that state."[17] While many technically may have been labeled usurers, the availability of funds for small borrowers was becoming smaller. Only liberalizing the laws substantially would entice reputable lenders into the market with rates that would compensate them for the perceived risks involved.

Indicative of the sentiment against usurers and loan sharks, a London play imported from the West End opened in New York in the summer of 1928. *The Moneylender* received mixed reviews because it attempted to probe the complexities of a Jewish moneylender named Samuel Levi marrying a gentile English woman named Lillian Luttrell, the sort of alliance considered to be a mixed marriage at the time. Ironically, the prospective bride's father founded a lending institution in London, although that fact is kept secret by her family. The marriage never takes place because of religious and financial considerations and each goes their separate way. The original London title of the play was *Love in Pawn*, a not-so-subtle reference to the religion of many pawnbrokers.

In 1928, the legislation called the Uniform Small Loan Law, sponsored by the Russell Sage Foundation and the Household Finance Corporation, which had been founded fifty years earlier, began to be adopted by individual states as a way of making the usury laws more flexible. Congress was unable to rescind the usury law imposed on the national banks, so the legislation began to be introduced in the individual states. Loans of $300 or less were made to individuals for household items and were secured by the items themselves. The small loan law was adopted in twenty-eight states in 1928 and the usury laws were waived to provide for higher interest, under the assumption that all consumer lending rates would eventually drop as a result. Many states were urged to raise the monthly interest a lender could charge from 1.5 percent to 3.5 percent, indicating a rise in annual interest charges from 18 to 42 percent. The generally accepted argument was that the rates were high but needed to be in order to entice legitimate lenders to make consumer loans, especially to the workingman. Loans of 40 percent were preferable to those of 200 percent or more. Not everyone was convinced by the argument that market forces would eventually intervene, however. Taking the more obvious interpretation, the governor of Wisconsin stated flatly that the uniform law encouraged usury. But the horse already was out of the barn. Many states passed their own versions of the law, swayed by the argument that rates would eventually fall when the programs became widespread. As a result, Household Finance decided to expand its retail lending activities in 1928 and went to Wall Street to raise money for expansion. Of all the parties involved, it was the clear winner.

Empires of Debt

The difficulties and logistics of supplying credit to consumers were often difficult, but in the corporate world the exact opposite was true. Debt was the favorite American form of financing throughout the nineteenth century despite the publicity the stock market attracted, especially after the many crashes or panics that occurred with some regularity in the years after 1837. Corporate indebtedness was not feared. On the contrary, corporate bonds were an investor favorite even when the financials of the issuing companies often suggested they should be otherwise.

Acquiring leverage, as increased debt (as opposed to equity) became known, was the favorite tool for acquiring vast industrial empires during the heyday of trust formation in the United States between 1870 and the early 1920s. The old bugaboos about incurring debt and paying interest had given way to acquiring high degrees of leverage in the quest for acquiring market domination. Industries ranging from commodity suppliers and producers to railroads, manufacturers, and public utilities all took on substantial debts in order to consolidate and expand. As many discovered, corporate debt was a two-edged weapon, as was consumer debt. It could help carve out significant market share or it could help dismember the debtor.

The formation of vast public utility holding companies provided a stark reminder of the risk to those advocating heavy leverage as an effective tool of corporate control. During and after World War I, utilities were a growth industry. Their growth rates were based on geographic expansion, especially in the South and the West, while their long-term bond yields were under 6 percent. The consolidation in the industry had formed large empires for the few companies producing electric power on a large scale. Anti-trust regulators were examining these large holding companies to determine whether they violated the Sherman or Clayton Acts. At the heart of most, but not all, utility holding companies was a tightly organized group of bankers providing funds for their expansion. The groups were either tied to J. P. Morgan and Company or not. One that was not was the vast Chicago-based utility run by Samuel Insull.

Insull was the utilities baron of the Midwest, where he controlled Middle West Utilities. He was born in Britain in 1859 and attended private school before beginning to work at the age of fourteen as an office boy in order to help his family. He also worked part-time for the editor of *Vanity Fair* magazine as a stenographer, learning something of politics and current affairs in the process. His second job brought him into contact with the London representatives of Thomas Edison, who happened to be the young Insull's idol. Subsequently, he was invited to the United States to become Edison's private secretary. He emigrated in 1881, arriving in New York to begin a long business career that would take him to the pinnacle of his adopted profession.

Working as Edison's secretary in New York City introduced Insull to the world of finance. Edison's first commercial customer in the city was John Pierpont Morgan, who purchased electricity provided by a power-generating substation operated by Edison on Pearl Street. Power generation was one of the few areas in which Morgan had an inside track as a result of the relationship and he exploited it fully in the years ahead. Insull's job with Edison was secure only as long as the inventor remained at the helm of his electric company. Morgan eventually took over Edison Electric and created the General Electric Company. Insull eventually found himself out of a job as a result and had to seek greener pastures elsewhere. He gravitated to Chicago, where the utilities industry was less concentrated than in New York. In 1892, he became the president of the Chicago Edison Company.

Leaving his position as a vice-president of Edison Electric convinced Insull that Wall Street bankers were anathema. As a result, he swore never again to use a New York investment bank for raising funds and insisted on using Chicago banks at every opportunity. At first, many of the established banks would not deal with him, so he turned instead to a smaller securities dealer that was eager for the business. His main investment banker became Halsey Stuart and Co. of Chicago. The firm's principal, Harold Stuart, shared a common philosophy with Insull. Midwestern utilities should be run and financed by midwesterners. The New York syndicates did not bother with small and medium-size utilities in the Midwest. Disavowing the New York banking elite was a local source both of pride and profit.

Harold Stuart was one of the main cheerleaders of the boom of the 1920s, selling bonds in Chicago at a frantic pace, in much the same way Charles Mitchell and the National City Company had done in New York. Many of those bonds were for the Insull companies. When the Depression set in, many Chicagoans would be highly displeased with Stuart and his firm. Among other marketing tactics, the firm employed a University of Chicago English professor to tout the virtues of bond investments, using a melodic voice to influence listeners. It subsequently was discovered that the advice was actually written by Halsey Stuart and that the professor knew little, if anything, about bond investing.[18]

The growing empire was assembled mainly through two holding companies, the reorganized Commonwealth Edison Company, founded in 1907, and Middle West Utilities Co., Insull's main operating company, founded in 1912. Insull was a firm believer that monopoly concentration was necessary to eliminate ruinous competition. He considered the utilities a "natural monopoly," a business that needed to be concentrated in only a few hands in order to provide efficient service. He was fond of saying that "all the electrical energy for a given area must be produced by one concern." And he certainly practiced what he preached in Chicago and the Midwest. Insull became the main power supplier for a vast stretch of the central United States, patching together his companies using the holding company to acquire other smaller operating companies. He casually remarked to a Harvard professor that he was "personally responsible for one thousand million dollars [$1 billion] of other people's money."

Insull was extremely efficient at his work. His power plants produced electricity at less than half the competition's prices and business expanded rapidly as a result. The holding company that he headed had relatively little common stock in existence. Most of it was closely held by the top directors. The rest of the capital was supplied by borrowing. Thus, a few were able to control vast empires with little investment. Insull bought back shares of the stock on one occasion and distributed it to his employees. That largesse also ensured that the company remained in local hands rather than fall into those of unfriendly predators. When that situation changed, the empire crumbled quickly.

Insull's Middle West, J. P. Morgan's United Corporation, only recently formed in 1928, and the Electric Bond and Share Company, a truly national system spanning over thirty states coast to coast, controlled almost 50 percent of national electric production between them. Insull's companies supplied power to most western states and several Canadian provinces. Alone, they produced about 12 percent of the country's total power. This concentration of power was dubbed the "power trust." A power monopoly was rapidly forming and threatened to be the same sort of monopoly issue railways had been in the previous century. For a brief time, they were more powerful than the railroads had been, but the approaching depression in 1930 would put an end to their short, monopolistic rule.

Being a transplanted Briton earned Insull some celebrity and criticism at the same time. Harold Ickes, one of Franklin Roosevelt's advisers, once referred to Insull as a "great and colorful figure from the American stage . . . even if he was dangerous to our economic well-being and a threat to our American institutions." That was something of a compliment from someone whom Insull once referred to as "an unsuccessful newspaper reporter who married money." But the celebrity and the efficiency of his enterprises attracted attention from the same quarters that he had assiduously avoided for decades.

As a result of his presence, Chicago often was referred to as "Insullopolis." Despite his many contributions to the city, he was still considered something of an outsider because of his nationality. Insull personally led Britain's propaganda efforts in the United States during World War I and later took criticism for it, especially since he was otherwise the head of a large American corporation. During the mid-1920s, the utilities were being widely criticized for influence peddling, dictating their wishes to politicians through campaign contributions. Insull's role as corporate chieftain and foreigner at the same time made him especially vulnerable despite his good works in Chicago.

After having a tight grip on the city for over twenty years, Insull was not accustomed to competition. The capital structure of his empire began to attract the attention of a corporate raider named Cyrus Eaton, who recognized that the relatively small number of shares outstanding provided a tempting takeover target. Suddenly Eaton began acquiring shares in Insull's interests, using his Continental Shares Corp. as the investing vehicle. His main targets were Commonwealth Edison and Middle West Utilities. From the outset, it was clear that outright control of the companies was out of the question, but Eaton devoted considerable resources to the acquisitions.

Insull reacted as expected and began buying shares of the companies himself to fend off Eaton. After spending some of his personal fortune in the battle, he raised extra capital by forming two investment trusts—Insull Utility Investment Inc. (IUI) and the Corporation Securities Company. Both borrowed heavily to fund the purchase. Eaton then responded by raising additional funds through Continental and the battle was joined. Insull raised an additional $300 million and the stocks of his companies soared to unheard of prices. The buying spree continued into 1930. Then Eaton visited Insull personally and offered to withdraw from the battle, for a price. He demanded $400 per share for his holdings, a premium to the current market price. Insull responded by offering $350. Finally, in June 1930 they reached an agreement by which Eaton was paid $350 per share for the 160,000 shares he held in the Insull companies. The amount was $6 million above the market price prevailing at the time. The deal smelled bad and prompted an investigation by the Federal Trade Commission several months after it was completed. The inquiry proved of no consequence, however. After the smoke cleared, the Eaton investment trust made a $19 million profit through its Insull investments, a tidy sum considering that the country was plunging into the Depression.[19]

Insull was momentarily safe, but more problems were only beginning. The pyramid of holding companies he created had become unsustainable and began to wobble badly under the weight of too much debt. In 1930 and 1931, he helped Chicago out of financial difficulties by providing financing from his own resources so that the city would not have to declare bankruptcy. He also embarked on several other capital projects after the stock market crash that were not immediately relevant to his operating companies; they were risky ventures given the declining state of the economy. After the market crash in 1929, equity financing was not possible, so he turned to debt financing to raise the necessary money. Each of his operating companies increased their debts by about 10 percent for a total of slightly less than $200 million in 1930 alone.[20] It was then that the two Insull trusts borrowed the necessary money to fend off Eaton. When local Chicago banks failed to provide the necessary loans, Insull had to raise about 40 percent of the money from New York banks in a last ditch attempt to save his empire. The collateral supporting the loans was stock in his major operating companies. If he failed on the loans, the empire would collapse.

The debt securities were sold by his local investment bank. Insull then added insult to injury by delivering a blast against New York bankers at a speech at the Chicago Stock Exchange in May 1930 in which he condemned the power of New York and called for "a war of financial liberation against Wall Street."[21] His tone was becoming more strident as it became clear that his empire was being squeezed. In a Senate investigation that was begun by Herbert Hoover in 1932, Insull's son, Samuel Jr., was questioned about the nature of the IUI and the Corporation Securities Company. He freely admitted that the purpose of the two investment trusts was to maintain control of the utilities empire. Under questioning from Ferdinand Pecora, the counsel for the committee, he also added, "If the public generally were sympathetic with the operating management there should be, in these investment companies, a large enough block of stock, together with the general public, to offset any other interests that might want to come in and get control."[22] Clearly, the two investment trusts were viewed as shark repellents against Eaton.

After borrowing to support the Eaton purchase, Insull also had to borrow personally to keep his empire afloat. He was so hard pressed that the money he borrowed from Wall Street banks included several million from the National City Bank of New York and the General Electric Company. General Electric was run by Owen Young, a ally of Morgan's. Young subsequently remarked to the Pecora committee, "I should like to say here that I believe Mr. Samuel Insull was very largely the victim of [a] complicated structure which got even beyond his power, competent as he was, to understand it."[23] Insull's supporters would counter that it was just a story concocted by Morgan's interests to show that he was not competent enough to run it properly.

Unlike many investment bankers and securities dealers, Insull adopted the investment trust as a defense against an unwanted takeover, not merely as a vehicle to pyramid and run up stock prices. Unfortunately, the result was the same for all of the investment trusts created in the 1920s: their prices plummeted, leaving investors with millions in losses. The downfall of the Insull empire was the major news story of the early 1930s. It dwarfed even the Pecora hearings into the activities of Wall Street before and after the crash. The vast empire that had taken Insull decades to assemble came crashing down under a heavy load of leverage and pyramiding. The expatriate Briton was accused of violating the public trust, as well as a more specific host of felonies filed in Chicago courts. How his empire came to crumble became less important at the time than the fact that it did crumble. The unraveling of Middle West Utilities caused serious concern in Chicago.

The financing that Insull used to fend off Eaton was the proverbial straw that broke the camel's back. The New York investment bankers took as collateral stock worth about half the value of the loans made to Insull. That alone would not have threatened his empire unless the value of the collateral declined sharply and they asked for more stock as a result. Declining stock prices would mean relinquishing more and more of his certificates to creditors. After the crash of 1929, business on the stock exchanges began to slow considerably. When his companies finally fell into the hands of bankers, Insull fled the country for Greece in the fall of 1932. Herbert Hoover learned that Insull was in transit in Italy and asked the Italian authorities to detain him, to no avail. Insull reached Greece and remained there for a year and a half. During that time, the U.S. government attempted to have him extradited several times but failed. Finally, the new Democratic administration of Franklin Roosevelt pressured the Greek government again and it responded by expelling Insull. He finally decided to return to the United States in 1934. He eventually was exonerated of state and federal charges and attempted a financial comeback later in life. He was the most noteworthy casualty of the debt crisis that emerged after the crash of 1929.

There were many other noteworthy debt problems following 1929 that brought to light issues not anticipated in the great debt explosion of the early twentieth century. In addition to the Insull crisis, another emerged with the appearance of Ivar Kreuger, a Swedish financier. Kreuger was one of Europe's best-known financiers and industrial empire builders. Most of his holdings centered around match and sulphur production and various chemical companies. His best known holdings were the Swedish Match Company and Kreuger and Toll. The former was his core company while the latter was a financing arm that began borrowing money on the New York bond market and then lending the proceeds to foreign governments. One particular bond's proceeds, floated in 1927, was lent to the French government in order to help stabilize the franc. That particular deal earned Kreuger the everlasting antagonism of J. P. Morgan and Company, which was considered the preeminent adviser to governments based in part on its role in the German debt reparations. It was only one of many financings, helping to shore up European finances in the postwar period. They invariably put him in good stead with many European governments that came to rely upon him as their intermediary in the American capital market.

In return for his largesse, many governments granted him monopolies over match production. Swedish Match was the jewel in his crown and helped market his name around the world. Kreuger did not publish financial statements, preferring to rely upon his record with governments to speak for itself. In 1923, he founded the International Match Corporation, which sold $150 million worth of shares in the American market. Two years later, the company and his Polish subsidiary transferred $25 million of the proceeds to his personal account, an amount never to be accounted for again. His American bankers appeared never to have fully understood the nature of his business or were not perceptive enough to realize that he was a swindler. He had adopted that well-known trick of the post–Civil War era of borrowing large amounts of money at high rates of interest and then using the proceeds to pay dividends on the common stock of his companies. When the stocks rose, he sold more, and so on. This form of financing was quite common leading up to the crash of 1929 and no one took much notice of it at the time. No one suspected anything amiss as long as the market continued to rise. But International Match and several of his other companies failed early during the Depression. A borrowing defaulted when it was learned that some of the collateral Kreuger had pledged to the American bond issue had been switched after the sale and replaced with lower-quality collateral that later became worthless. These activities later forced Congress to pass the Trust Indenture Act in 1939, which regulated collateral in order to protect bondholders. It became known as the Kreuger Rule. Kreuger himself committed suicide shortly after the bankruptcy in 1932, when many of his corrupt dealings were exposed.

Bonds for Everyone

Stocks were not the only major casualties of the crash of 1929. Many of the corporate and foreign bonds sold to an unwary public as safe investments turned out to be extremely risky and often worthless, as the Insull and Kreuger bonds had proven. In their great rush to underwrite debt securities, the bond underwriters often overlooked some very basic financial information when bringing new issues to market. Those oversights created as much trouble in the long run as the market crash itself.

Foreign bonds sold to American investors were some of the main casualties of the post-crash period. Most were bought not by large institutions but by small investors, many of whom had previously bought Liberty Bonds. Dwight Morrow, a former J. P. Morgan partner and a senator from New Jersey, analyzed several foreign bond issues in an issue of *Foreign Affairs*. His conclusion was fairly startling: "When we talk about the person who is investing in foreign bonds we are not talking about a great institution in New York or Chicago or Boston. We are talking about thousands of people living in the United States . . . about school teachers and Army officers and country doctors and stenographers and clerks . . . he is a person who has saved something, who has done without something today in order that his children may have something tomorrow."[24]

Fraud and inadequate credit analysis were not limited to corporate bonds such as those sold by Ivar Kreuger's enterprises. Many Latin American government bonds also lost a substantial part of their value. Almost every country in Latin America ran into serious financial difficulties. Peruvian bonds were among the best-known casualties. Rumor had it that aggressive investment bankers at a New York investment banking house bribed the son of the president of Peru to have the bonds issued despite the country's poor financial condition. When the economic downturn began, the bonds naturally dropped in value; they fell from par to only 5 percent of their nominal value. The *New York Times* ran a story illustrating the price history of the bonds following their calamitous fall from grace.

Another debt issue underwritten by the National City Company, a unit of the National City Bank, also caused a great stir after the crash. In 1928, the bank had arranged a $16 million bond issue for the Brazilian state of Minas Gerais. When the issue was arranged, the state already was having a difficult time paying its existing bondholders. But that did not deter National City. The bond was probably the best example of National City not performing what would become known as due diligence. The state was portrayed in glowing terms in its sales literature and sold to clueless investors.

About the same time, in a limp attempt to dissuade investors from putting too much cash into the stock market, Secretary of the Treasury Andrew Mellon stated in 1929 that investors probably should confine themselves to bonds rather than overpriced stocks, giving a boost to the bond market as a whole. National City was only happy to oblige by bringing as many new issues to market as possible. Only about twelve years had passed since the World War I war bond programs had ended and the public's investment appetite for debt had not changed substantially. The real change was seen in the sort of issues that were being purchased. In an attempt to gain more yield than that offered by Treasury bonds, investors assumed more risk by purchasing bonds of dubious borrowers, assuming they had been vetted by the investment bankers. The credit-rating agencies still confined themselves mostly to ratings on companies and individuals for counterparty risk; bond credit ratings were not standard and not sought until after the Securities Act of 1933 was passed.

Fixed income research also produced some noteworthy gains in the 1920s that would become an integral part of investing. The rate of interest received its first serious discussion, free of religion, ethics, or ideology, when the economist Irving Fisher descried the real rate of interest. For centuries, interest had been described in nominal, or absolute, terms without regard for the accompanying inflation rate. Fisher described the real rate as the nominal rate minus the inflation rate; put another way, the nominal rate was the real rate plus inflation. The real rate measured the true growth of money over time by showing its growth in purchasing power, not simply its growth by an unadjusted nominal rate. The idea had a pronounced effect on the fixed income investment community as well as the world of corporate finance. This view changed attitudes substantially. As Fisher described it: "In Germany at the height of inflation [during the Weimer Republic], August to September, 1923, the real rate of interest fell to the absurd level of minus 99.9 per cent, which means that lenders lost all interest and nearly all their capital as well; and then suddenly prices were deflated and the real interest rate jumped to plus 100 per cent."[25] This was a different way of explaining the destructive force of inflation, not simply relying on the astronomical inflation rate that caused prices to double every two hours to demonstrate nominal inflation alone.

Fisher's development was followed by another milestone in fixed income theory. In 1938, Frederick Macaulay published research describing the concept known as bond duration.[26] The term to maturity on a bond was not the best indicator of its interest rate risk. Instead, the idea of duration should be used to show its sensitiveness to changes in interest rates in the market. The sensitiveness was measured in years. Basically, bonds with high coupon rates attached were less sensitive to interest rate changes than bonds with lower coupon rates. In a changing interest rate environment, their change in price would be less in percentage terms than a lower coupon bond. Investors desiring to immunize themselves against interest rate changes should buy bonds with the higher coupon rates, giving some credence to buying issues of riskier borrowers, although that was not the intended effect. This fundamental research paved the way for dozens more applications and variations of fixed income analytical techniques. All too often it also was used to tout the virtues of high coupon debt at the expense of better rated bonds necessarily paying less interest.

Advertising also helped change consumer attitudes toward debt. In the 1930s, Madison Avenue, influenced by motivation research experts, designed advertising programs for banks and other lenders that emphasized credit over debt. This was part of banks' and other lenders' new emphasis on retail lending. One of their early successes was convincing banks to offer overdraft facilities on checking accounts so that consumers could continue to spend even if they did not have the proper balances.[27] The implication was simple yet appealing. By offering credit, a lender trusted the borrowers' ability to repay and was helping the borrowers bank on their future. "Buy now and pay later" slowly was creeping into the American consumer psyche.

Also during the 1930s, one of the most enduring marketing phrases ever devised was coined. The writer James Truslow Adams used the term "American Dream" in magazine articles in the 1930s to describe the idyllic notion that had been lost during the Depression. The American quest to own one's own home, have a car in the driveway, and to be better off financially than one's parents had been tarnished by the Depression. The term had not been used before, but during the Depression it gained quick circulation and popularity. It soon became a widely used and oft-quoted allusion to the idea that all Americans aspired to be part of the rapidly emerging middle class. With high unemployment and diminished sources of consumer credit, the notion had been put in abeyance. When the economy rebounded and the term reemerged after World War II, acquiring consumer debt would become synonymous with achieving the dream and would trigger the second round of the debt revolution.

War and Boom, Again

The greatest economic expansion yet witnessed in the United States began after World War II. Circumstances similar to those in 1921 appeared, giving support to a revival of consumer credit. Once again, pent-up consumer demand was directed at consumer goods and many initially were paid for with maturing Treasury bonds. The result was much the same. All areas of the economy spurted ahead. Consumer finance companies were poised for the greatest gains yet recorded. A victorious America would celebrate the end of the war by spending its way to prosperity, setting a precedent for the future.

Because of the disastrous performance of many bonds in the 1920s and 1930s, investors of all sorts again flocked to Treasury bonds during World War II. The massive borrowings necessary for the war were organized by Henry Morgenthau, Franklin Roosevelt's secretary of the Treasury. Like during World War I, publicity campaigns were organized to sell bonds to as many savers and investors as possible. A total of approximately $200 billion was raised in what was the most successful wartime sales campaign yet launched. Because of the antagonism between the Roosevelt administration and Wall Street, which dated back to 1933, Morgenthau successfully avoided using Wall Street banks and brokers to underwrite and distribute the bonds, choosing instead to employ direct sales campaigns reminiscent of Jay Cooke's efforts during the Civil War. Brokers and banks had to settle for pennies distributing bonds rather than a percentage of the amount raised, as they were accustomed to receiving from the private sector.

Old problems did not disappear but did recede from view temporarily. The usury laws still proved to be the underlying obstacle to consumer credit. They would have to be avoided if finance was to provide the demand element necessary for the economy to grow. Lenders were reluctant to make small loans conforming to the usury laws, forcing many consumers into the hands of the ubiquitous loan sharks. Loan-sharking still prevailed, but consumers became more prosperous as the expanded postwar middle class emerged. While the usury laws loomed in the background, credit became easier to obtain because of an expansion of lenders. Many were forced to enter the market for consumer loans for fear of being left behind if they did not. The usury laws themselves were as relatively easy to circumvent as they had been in the past. Most charges of loan-sharking were made against organized crime, through bookmakers and collection agents. Easier credit eventually forced the traditional loan sharks underground before they would appear in a more legitimate form.

Banking became a leaner, more concentrated business in the 1950s than it was in the 1920s. Before and after the crash of 1929, hundreds of banks failed because of their exposure to the real estate market and the collapsing stock market. Being undiversified, they fell quickly under the weight of bad loans and the market in late 1929. Law prevented banks from crossing state lines and banking remained a local or regional affair. The same law prohibiting banks from crossing state lines (the McFadden Act of 1927) opened a bruising battle between state-chartered banks and nationally chartered ones that would persist intermittently until the next century. And it would also indirectly cause great confusion in interpreting existing usury laws. The only uniform usury law nationwide was still the one created by the National Bank Act in 1864. Ironically, it applied to those nationally chartered banks that did less retail business than their state-chartered counterparts: Corporate lenders had nothing to fear from the state usury laws since they did not apply to corporate loans usually in excess of $250,000.

The 1950s became the decade of home building, automobile production, general manufacturing, and the expansion of American business abroad. All areas required massive amounts of credit. Home building reached new records; in 1954 one million new residential units were built in the United States for the first time, double the number produced annually during the 1920s. Suburban developments like Levittown on Long Island made homes affordable and many were purchased by returning servicemen using veterans' mortgages. These subsidized loans were supported by the Veterans Administration (VA) as a form of compensation for soldiers who served in the war. After the war, the VA authorized the Federal National Mortgage Association (Fannie Mae) to purchase the mortgages, insuring the expansion of the program. This became the underpinning of the housing boom.

The boom was reflected in the consumer credit numbers for the ten years following the war. From 1946 through 1956, installment credit continued to explode, from $8.3 billion to $45.2 billion, an increase of over 400 percent. In the same period non-installment credit jumped from $4.2 to $11.1 billion, demonstrating that many Americans were buying consumer durables. As in the 1920s, they required time to pay them off, although quick repayment of borrowed money still was popular. Notes outstanding from the car-financing companies increased an astounding 1,500 percent, from $981 million to $15.4 billion. That was reflected in the explosive demand for autos, with better highways, suburban shopping malls, and cheap gasoline contributing to the phenomenon.[28]

Financial services expanded considerably in the postwar period, with demands for insurance and retirement plans increasing substantially, although tontines were long gone. Individuals began buying more life insurance and annuities. Installment credit was as popular as ever, although a challenge to the way people paid off their loans was developing slowly. During the 1940s, a new marketing concept initially designed for convenience was introduced. No one at the time could have imagined the revolution it would cause in spending habits because the idea was simple. In 1946, Brooklyn banker John Biggins introduced a plan called Charg-It, which had the distinction of being the first credit card. Used by local merchants, the card holders had to be customers of his bank. Broader in scope, the Diners' Club was formed in 1950. Originally, the cards were distributed to only a few dozen people in New York City so that they could pay for meals at restaurants that accepted them. Within a short time, the number of people using them had increased to over twenty thousand. Several years later, American Express entered the field by offering its own card. The terms required customers to pay the balance in full when billed. In credit terms, they were simple payment facilities. The balance had to be paid in full before credit was extended again. In this respect, the cards were similar to corporate paydown loan facilities but on a much smaller scale.

The first bank credit card was offered by the Franklin National Bank in New York in 1951. It too was a pay-on-demand card like its predecessors. Then a significant new wrinkle was added when the Bank of America announced its own card, the BankAmericard in 1958 (renamed Visa in 1976), allowing customers to pay their balances over time while being charged interest on the unpaid balance. The higher levels of interest allowed on consumer loans in many states as a result of the Uniform Small Loan Act allowed lenders to charge relatively high rates for these facilities, often at levels approaching 18 percent. At the time, cards were issued to those in higher-income brackets as a convenience and were viewed as prestigious, a marketing idea that many card companies fostered for decades. In its first year, BankAmericard signed up 60,000 cardholders and 300 retailers. Within a year, the numbers had increased to 2 million cardholders and 25,000 retailers.[29]

Revolving and installment credit raised many problems almost from the time they were first offered, although the card companies marketed their services as a convenience to middle-class households with wage earners under forty-five years of age. The highest default rates in the late 1960s and early 1970s were among those whom the cards were meant to serve, middle-class householders earning on average between $10,000 and $15,000 at the time. Among those using installment credit, the average was higher per household: 17 percent of after-tax income.[30] Over the following decades, those sorts of numbers were repeated time and again, indicating an average

American middle income household that was heavily in debt. Similar warnings would be sounded over the next forty years before the debt crisis of 2007–2008.

Intellectual Seeds of the Revolution

For centuries, the discussion about usury and indebtedness centered on consumption loans and the level of interest charged to a borrower. As long as lenders remained inflexible, especially for consumption loans, interest rates remained high on those loans and therefore were roundly condemned as usury. But the usury discussion usually faded on the corporate level because assuming interest rate charges was considered one of the basic risks of doing business. Discussions in that regard revolved around the level of indebtedness in relation to a firm's equity, or its leverage. Debt/equity ratios and the amount of debt to assets were more important than the amount of interest paid. Then the basic concept came under theoretical and empirical scrutiny.

Companies already were abandoning the older caveats about debt in favor of higher degrees of leverage when an article appeared in an academic journal that supported the notion that debt itself was neither good nor bad. It was only how it was employed that mattered. The authors, Franco Modigliani and Merton Miller, demonstrated that levels of indebtedness were not as important as the bottom line of a company. As long as the debt could be supported and profits enhanced, the financial structure of the firm was not as important as the fact that it was profitable.

The article, along with several that followed, became known as the MM theory. In their paper, Miller and Modigliani showed that a firm's value is determined by its investment decisions as well as by its financing decisions.[31] In theory, as long as a firm's profits exceeded its cost of capital, its capital structure was not important. Debt could increase as long as it was accompanied by a rise in profits. The new idea was highly appealing, especially since shareholder interest in stocks and the market in general was at an all-time high in the late 1950s and the early 1960s, when the idea began to circulate that profits could be enhanced by additional debt and not be endangered if the debt was employed properly. The idea found quick acceptance in academic circles and spread quickly to future generations of financial managers and chief financial officers.

Thirty years later when Modigliani was awarded the Nobel Prize in Economics, the Swedish Academy summarized his work with Miller: "Until the latter part of the 1950s, no viable theory of corporate financing of investment, debt, taxes, and so forth had been developed. It was not till Modigliani and Miller presented their theorems that more stringent theorizing began to appear in this field." Almost thirty years after the articles were written, it was clear that a significant contribution had been made to corporate America. Debt was no longer something to be feared. The next stage in the evolution was to extend that idea to consumers.

The MM theory became widely disseminated through graduate schools of business, which were becoming more respected and popular at the time. Within thirty years, the ideas had become firmly embedded in several generations of financial managers. Moving far from its original accounting base, finance now was a complicated discipline. The older version of finance relied on hallowed notions and untested theories such as simple portfolio diversification. Most MBA programs taught the MM theory with heavy doses of math and it was spread among their graduates. The ideas helped fuel the growth trend of the entire period and appealed politically to Republican administrations that were naturally friendly to the growth of big business. The idea became affiliated with the Chicago school of economics at the University of Chicago, which was in the foreground of growth-oriented research. After three decades, Miller was able to proclaim proudly, "At the theoretical level, we have won the day."

Modigliani and Miller were not alone in the finance revolution. Other members of the Chicago school doing research in finance included Harry Markowitz, whose theory of portfolio selection and diversification became a cornerstone of investment theory and won its author a Nobel Prize in 1990. His theory built on the older investment principle of diversity. The old idea of not putting all one's eggs in the same basket would now be refined and given empirical support. The multi-stock portfolio, taking the place of the one-stock portfolio, demonstrated that investors should build disparate holdings of stocks within their own comfort levels of risk and return.

According to Markowitz, traditional portfolios were a selection of stocks chosen for their investment qualities. His basic idea was that investors essentially were risk averse and that portfolios composed of many stocks rather than just one would protect them over time. Using mathematics to demonstrate his theory, he proposed that investors select their portfolios based on risk-reward characteristics of the group rather than compiling portfolios of individual securities assembled because they had individual attractive risk-reward characteristics.[32]

One of the limitations in the theory was exactly how to measure risk. In 1964, William Sharpe developed another well-known and widely disseminated idea called the capital assets pricing model (CAPM). His work earned him a share of the same Nobel won by Markowitz and Miller. Proceeding from Markowitz, Sharpe broke risk into two components—systematic risk and specific risk. Systematic risk is the risk of holding the "market portfolio." As the market moves, all assets are affected. All assets therefore have systematic risk. Specific risk, in contrast, is risk unique to an individual asset. In equity investing, this is also known as company-specific risk. It represents the risk on an asset, which can be diversified. Market risk cannot.[33]

According to the CAPM, the marketplace risk cannot be avoided and should be chosen carefully. Specific risk can be diversified. When an investor holds a carefully selected market portfolio, each individual asset in the portfolio carries specific risk, but through proper diversification the net exposure becomes the systematic risk of the portfolio. Systematic risk itself can be measured by a beta coefficient, a measure of an individual stock's relation to the market. Although this basically was a theory of equity risk, extending it to debt was an easy transformation. Investors normally accustomed to holding highly rated bonds could, and should, extend their holdings to issues previously thought to be too risky in default terms because the enhanced return would raise their marginal rate of return.

The growing use of debt was also reflected in another more practical theory, published in 1968. Edward Altman developed his Z ratio, a predictor of bankruptcy risk. Using a multivariate formula, he demonstrated how a company's probability of bankruptcy could be predicted about two years before it occurred by plugging its financials into his weighted formula. The resulting Z score would give investors an indication of the company's solvency prospects, an important contribution given the increasing use of debt financing. Over time, the Z scores proved to be correct in about 75 percent of applications.[34]

The ideas presented by Markowitz and Sharpe, like those of Modigliani and Miller, were refined many times after the publication of the original articles by the authors as well as their colleagues and former students. The seed had been planted of assets being treated in portfolio terms rather than as individual assets, chosen for portfolio qualities rather than individual ones. Within thirty years of the MM theories and those of Markowitz and Sharpe, the idea of debt had subtly shifted to that of credit. The negative connotations of being in debt shifted to the more positive connotations of having credit. Although the idea had been around since World War I, it now had become a standard part of financial theory and practice. This was in no small part due to the idea that debtors were part of a credit company's portfolio of investments. Credit card loans would be sold to third party investors who treated them as investments; they were not the original lenders of years past. Those investments can be managed as long as the return they provide is greater than the credit company's cost of capital. In most cases, that spread is always in the company's favor so the application of the MM theory is appropriate. According to the ideas of Markowitz and Sharpe, the credit portfolio should be constructed broadly since only diversification can offset the risk of a single asset, meaning that its pool of creditors should be well diversified. If it is not constructed following portfolio guidelines, some consumers will not receive credit and the portfolio's yield will be lower than if it were diversified. In theory, that would hurt both consumers and creditors and would justify granting more debt, not less.

The combination of the MM theory plus Markowitz's emphasis on diverse portfolios provided the intellectual basis for the debt revolution. Sharpe's notion of the CAPM also demonstrated that the more volatile the stock market, the better it would be to issue debt since the cost of debt is traditionally lower than the cost of using equity, in part because of the tax deductible nature of interest. While not the intent of the theories, they all nevertheless gave implicit support to the idea of treating a company as an investor in the market, not simply as a producer. Even pure producers like manufacturers could diversify somewhat and behave like investors rather than classic providers. General Motors and Ford had already showed that they had made a success of producing autos and financing them at the same time by developing credit subsidiaries.

The Credit Card Explosion

The first credit cards were a step in the transition to a cashless society. They would take their place alongside installment loans as a bridge between older forms of payment for purchases and the newer types, allowing consumers much greater latitude in determining how much they paid and when. But their true revolutionary nature in the annals of credit was that they were unsecured loans. The ultimate recourse of the lender was to seek payment from the borrowers' general assets if the borrower failed to pay. The repo agents were not required in this case.

Credit cards also offered banks latitude that was rarely discussed publicly. Since the revolving credit card was the first American experiment with adjustable interest rates of any sort, its success was ensured. To date, it is the only bank instrument having the flexibility to adjust lending rates if market conditions warrant it. And when that flexibility was recognized, the growth of revolving credit cards became exponential. The banks wisely marketed the cards as a convenience to the consumer. Credit would continue to be made available even if interest rates rose. This was an argument that no regulator would oppose, at least in public, but it was feared in private. No one wanted to be seen interfering with the engine that drove 67 percent of the GNP. The term "consumption loan" had completely disappeared from the finance lexicon, replaced by "consumerism." But in the new credit environment, a defaulted credit card loan carried potentially much more individual risk than the older collateralized consumption loans. Failing to pay a credit card loan could lead to a court judgment affecting a consumer's home or other assets. The irony created by credit cards was that traditional secured loans now were reserved for the poor, as they had been for centuries. Those with the potentially riskier form of unsecured credit were considered middle income earners or higher. The credit card companies turned centuries of lending on its head, marketing the changes to the new generations of consumers as convenient, safe, and a privilege.

Before interest on a revolving basis through credit cards became widespread, Congress intervened to pass the Truth in Lending Act in 1968, part of the larger Consumer Protection Act (Title I). For the first time, consumers had the right to be informed about the nature of charges they would pay when incurring loans. The power to enforce truth in lending was delegated to the Fed through Regulation Z. It required lenders to describe fully to customers applying for consumer credit the nature of the credit facility and the finance charges involved on an effective annual basis. The key part of the act was the term "consumer credit." It only applied to installment loans and revolving credit granted to individuals for "household purposes." It did not apply to corporate credit agreements or those involving mortgages.

The new law had been several decades in the making and was given impetus when unusually high effective rates of interest were shown against ostensibly low nominal rates quoted by many lenders. This included time loans and installment loans, although the presence of the new credit cards only made the matter more urgent. The bill was sponsored in the Senate by William Proxmire, a Democrat of Wisconsin, who said that "the central aim of the bill is to permit consumers to shop as carefully for credit as they shop for merchandise."[35]

The Truth in Lending Act was the only federal law ever passed dealing with consumer interest rates. In a sense, it was the closest Congress ever came to passing a national usury law since the National Bank Act of 1864. The original bill actually contained a clause limiting consumer interest to 18 percent (in line with the older usury limits of the 1920s), but that never made it to the final vote. Passed during a period when "let the buyer beware" was the dominant consumer mantra, it recognized that the patchwork of state usury laws could not be superseded by federal law and simply required lenders to state their terms clearly and fairly. The maximum rate of interest charged was a decision left to the states, but at least the consumer could make the decision among lenders offering credit. But it was a full disclosure law only; if a lender charged too much it was assumed that consumers would avoid it in favor of others with lower rates.

As a result of the law, lenders were required to notify borrowers by letter of the rates they were charged, in both nominal and effective terms. The early notifications revealed high rates, eliciting widespread criticism, especially when rates as high as 36 percent were disclosed. The revelations prompted one newspaper in California to declare, " 'Truth in lending' helps because it translates devious mathematics into simple English. But knowing that one is being legally 'taken' does not reduce the unconscionable interest rates and 'service' and 'finance' fees being charged the American consumer."[36] Despite the revelations and the indignation they aroused, the same issue would be found with credit cards for the next forty years. Hidden interest charges like fees became embedded in consumer credit.

Ten years later, Congress added the Fair Debt Collection Practices Act to the law of 1968. This new law sought to protect borrowers from debt collectors, who had become increasingly aggressive in collecting debts since revolving credit had been introduced. The law gave consumers the ability to report aggressive practices such as calling debtors in the middle of the night or trying to collect debts from third parties such as the debtors' employers. Unlike Truth in Lending, this law was administered by the Federal Trade Commission rather than the Federal Reserve and quickly became engrained in what became known as the consumer bill of rights.

Many lawsuits against lenders were filed in the states, charging violation of their usury laws. Most of the suits were filed against credit card lenders, which were charging a routine 1.5 percent per month, or 18 percent per year, by the early 1970s. Cases were brought against revolving credit lenders in

Minnesota, South Dakota, Connecticut, Indiana, and Wisconsin, all alleging violations of the local usury laws. When revolving credit became common, beginning in the early 1970s, the interest rate charged to unpaid balances was about 1.5 percent. The annualized rate of 18 percent per year was below most (but not all) state usury ceilings for consumer loans and also was lower than the rates charged in the 1920s during that consumer boom. And since the amount was tax deductible, individuals could build up interest charges and still get some relief on their tax forms. Many early explanations of cards included the tax deductibility as proof that the real cost was less than the stated rate.

For the first fifteen years of their existence, credit cards fared well and consumers embraced them. Only when interest rates rose to historic American high levels did problems with the usury laws resurface. In 1980 and 1981, rates began to climb into double digits as a result of Paul Volcker's restrictive monetary policy at the Fed. The yield curve became negatively sloped, with short-term rates yielding more than long-term rates. Commercial paper rates soon were above 15–16 percent, higher than New York's usury ceiling by 4 percent. This did not affect money market borrowing but put pressure on credit card companies, in particular New York credit card operations since the maximum lending rates in the state were low when compared to market rates. Citicorp had its credit card operations on Long Island and was faced with a dilemma. The bank's margins were being squeezed and Jimmy Carter's special credit controls, imposed in the late winter of 1980 for six months prior to the presidential election in November 1980, exacerbated the situation.

The controls were the Carter administration's answer to high market interest rates and the lack of control over some forms of credit creation. The Fed of Paul Volcker had little choice but to accommodate them, although it was in the midst of its own battle with inflation. The administration imposed higher bank reserve requirements and also imposed reserve requirements against credit card lenders if they exceeded certain limits. This was done to prevent shoppers from using their cards by clamping down on the card companies. The control worked for a short period of time before being dismantled. From the late winter of 1980 until a year later, revolving credit declined and remained flat before resuming an upward course. This was the first time a decline of that sort had been seen since revolving debt was introduced in 1968.

The usury laws in the states were suspended temporarily by the Depository Institutions Deregulation and Monetary Control Act (DIDMCA) of

1980, in which Congress helped deregulate Regulation Q, allowing banks to offer market rates of interest on savings deposits rather than adhere to the Fed's limits under the power it had since 1933. The usury laws were suspended so that they would not conflict with the new broad deregulation. Many states elected to re-impose them, however, in keeping with their long-standing traditions. The final deregulation of deposit rates and other banking limitations on interest finally was effected by the Depository Institutions Act, passed by Congress in 1982 during the early years of the Reagan administration.

The temporary suspension of the usury laws prompted many banks to push for higher mortgage rates. High interest rates in general caused a slow-down in the residential mortgage market. The banks claimed that if the suspension of the usury laws were made permanent then more mortgage money would be made available. In New York City, Citibank announced that it would make up to $1 billion of residential mortgage loans available to home-owners if the interest rate cap were removed. Other local lenders followed suit. "As long as we are allowed to charge a market rate of interest," a bank spokesman said, "Citibank's money is there."[37]

Before Truth in Lending was passed in 1968, credit card companies had been searching for ways to charge higher rates of interest on balances without appearing to do so overtly. Past experience demonstrated that adding fees to credit card balances could be justified by claiming that costs of handling and administration were rising and that by adding fees now the card companies were protecting consumers from even more odious costs in the future. Additionally, if card balances could be extended, the companies would ensure themselves of more revenue in the future. Customers who paid their balances promptly every month actually cut a card company's profits since no interest was earned on the balance due. If the length of the payment process could be extended, all the better for the bottom line. With these two objectives in mind, the annual fee and the minimum balance were born.

The annual fee simply was a $15 or $20 charge added to a customer's balance. The net effect was to raise the effective rate of interest charged, especially when balance and credit lines were smaller than they are today. A card charging a customer 18 percent interest on a $1,000 line could add 1.5 percent to that rate by charging a $15 annual fee, effectively raising the rate to 19.5 percent. If that rate exceeded a usury ceiling before 1980, the company could always claim it was not interest, just a one-time charge. And it had the extra advantage of being a present value charge. The card company did not have to wait months to collect it.

The minimum payment solved the problem of relatively short life spans for some credit card balances. Rather than treat card balances as installment loans to be paid back after three years, the minimum was devised as a way to keep customer credit in good standing while requiring less of a payment than a three-year payback required. Because the minimum was just that, the balance would be outstanding longer, and the effective interest rate higher. All of this was perfectly legal since the minimum was designed to "help" customers from becoming overburdened with monthly payments. The fact that it kept the customer in debt for longer periods of time meant little to the card companies as long as the balances remained in good standing. So by adopting the minimum payment policy, creditors insured that customers would at some time choose that option, extending the time for repayment, and raising the effective interest rate, all in one fell swoop.

Despite adding the extra charges, the combination of interest rates and usury ceilings forced Citi, Chase, and the other large banks with significant retail business to plot a new strategy for dealing with the situation. For over a decade, Citi had been aggressively moving into retail banking. Consumers were enjoying the benefits briefly since the maximum rate charged in New York for consumer loans was 18 percent for the first $500 borrowed and then 12 percent for higher amounts. At the time, Citi's prime rate for business customers was above 17 percent. Consumers were paying lower than market rates. The usury laws were creating an arbitrage situation whereby consumers could borrow against their cards and, if their credit lines were large enough, take the proceeds and buy Treasury bills yielding about 4–5 percent more. This was one of the unforeseen problems that plastic money and revolving credit had created.

Because of the high interest rate environment, Citi claimed it lost $100 million on its credit card operations despite the temporary relaxing of the usury laws by DIDMCA. As a result, it imposed a $15 fee on its card users and increased the interest rate on them to 19.8 percent. In addition, the bank required that all customers with outstanding balances pay 1/36 of what was owed on balances above $720. That would require a $20 payment. Previously, a customer could have remained in good standing with a minimum payment of $5. This reversal of the minimum payment practice underscored the problem Citibank thought it had.

Fees and other miscellaneous charges could not entirely make up for lost revenue, however. The credit card movement was given a substantial boost in 1978 when the U.S. Supreme Court heard a case involving a suit over usury charges. A Nebraska bank, registered with the comptroller of the currency as a national association, was charging interest to its customers in Minnesota in excess of that state's usury ceiling. A Minnesota bank sued, since it could not do the same under Minnesota law. The Marquette National Bank of Minneapolis claimed that the First of Omaha Service Corporation, a BankAmericard provider, should be enjoined from charging the higher rate. But the Supreme Court disagreed, stating that the National Bank Act of 1864 only required banks designated as "national" to comply with the usury laws (if any) in their home states, not where a customer used the card.[38] While subject to Nebraska's usury law, the provider was not subject to Minnesota's. The decision reaffirmed the New York case of the nineteenth century, which stated the same principle on a state level.

As a result of the case, Citi began seeking a new venue for its credit card operations. New York was aware of the problem and sought ways to allow Citi to keep its card operations on Long Island. Over two thousand jobs were at stake. Governor Hugh Carey's office acknowledged the problem, stating, "[We are] always concerned if we have an inoperative set of laws." But the outlook in the state legislature was bleak. Members of the assembly admitted that they were sympathetic to the bank but not sanguine about the prospects of removing the usury law. Although the action sounded as if it were running counter to Citi's claims of wanting to get rid of the usury laws, the New York legislature did rescind the rate limits on consumer loans. Technically, part of the civil usury ceiling had been lifted, but the criminal usury ceiling remained, at 25 percent. Citi objected to the criminal law remaining because it was possible that interest rates could rise even further, setting off a string of criminal lawsuits.

Although the civil portion of the law was removed fairly quickly, Citi had already made its plans to move and did not change them. As a result, Citi, Chase Manhattan (both national associations), and others went shopping for new real estate in more friendly states. The banks' past experience proved useful since credit card operations were not a core banking activity; the finance and credit card subsidiaries could be located anywhere in the domestic United States that they were welcome. Banks soon discovered that several states were willing to extend their hospitality even if it meant giving the impression that they were catering to Eastern money interests.

Citibank found a reception in one of the least likely places. South Dakota had usury ceilings but was willing to repeal them in return for the bank's investment in the state. The bank saw the opportunity. In quick fashion, the state legislature removed all trappings of the law. At a legislative session in 1980, the state adopted new banking laws, allowing out-of-state bank holding companies to acquire a local banking charter. Citi agreed to base its operations in Sioux Falls late in 1980. The workforce was competent, corporate and personal income taxes did not exist, and the cost of labor was inexpensive when compared to urban states.

South Dakota was not alone in attracting bank-processing facilities. Closer to home, Chase Manhattan and others also were successful in persuading Delaware to abolish its usury laws. This was a less surprising development since the tiny state always had been in the forefront of seeking business from large corporations. It was already known for its bankruptcy courts and liberal incorporation procedures. In 1980, Chase began lobbying for the state to abolish its usury laws but met with a cool reception until several of the state's senior business people were approached. A year later, the legislature passed its own version of a bank liberalization law, allowing out-of-state banks to open operations on the condition that they did not engage in retail banking, in order to protect the local banks. In return, a very low state tax rate was imposed that actually decreased to only 2.7 percent when the card subsidiaries earned more than $30 million.

Other consumer finance businesses seized the opportunity. Chase was joined by other banks and brokerage firms seeking an operations base for their credit cards. Several retail store chains joined by opening credit operations. It seemed that abolishing usury laws could be profitable. Some smaller banks followed Citi and Chase in requesting a rollback of usury laws in their own states. Twin City Savings and Loan, based in Minnesota, requested that the state rescind its usury laws so that it could offer card services in the state. Part of its argument was that it would then not have to charge the $25 fee it leveled against cardholders in the state as compensation for operating under the usury law. Citicorp's argument resonated well.

In Massachusetts, the case was slightly different. Two of the state's larger banks adopted the time proven strategy of threatening to move their card operations out-of-state to avoid the state's 18 percent interest ceiling. Both government and community leaders protested and threatened a boycott. However, the banks acquiesced and lowered their rates as a sign of good faith. The problem for the state banks was simple. Citicorp and others not based in Massachusetts were actively soliciting their cards in the state and were charging customers 19.8 percent interest, effectively using their out-of-state subsidiaries to circumvent the local usury laws. The state banks wanted to do the same, but the official usury ceiling governing them was lower. When Massachusetts did revise its usury law in 1985, it used a flexible market-based formula. It calculated the usury ceiling as twice the ninety-one-day T-bill rate, which at the time was 8 percent.

Many of the state usury laws fell because of loopholes in the various laws. Searching for the loopholes became a cottage industry for those seeking to overturn what they considered outdated legislation. John Reed, the chairman of Citibank and the successor to Walter Wriston, remarked that exploiting loopholes made him somewhat uneasy, but, he said, "We live in a world of legal loopholes." He also suggested that regulators many times encouraged financial institutions to exploit loopholes when they found them.[39] The trend of financial institutions leading, and being encouraged by, regulators agreeing with them on instituting change was becoming established in the United States and would accelerate in the years ahead.

The consumer credit boom received aid from many quarters. A change in the bankruptcy law certainly was one of them. Just as the consumer lenders were gearing up to produce even more unsecured credit, Congress gave the debt revolution a significant boost by passing more liberal bankruptcy laws than had been seen before. In the past, bankruptcy was declared in order to protect lenders from default by borrowers. The effect of the new law was to protect borrowers until they could restore their credit after a default. The results would be widespread and significant.

Congress overhauled the bankruptcy code in 1978 in a sweeping change designed to make the existing code more flexible. The previous law, the Chandler Act, which was revised in 1938, was considered too cumbersome and unwieldy. One of its noteworthy parts was the addition of Chapter 11, a filing that would allow companies to be reorganized under the auspices of a court under certain circumstances, and not simply dissolved to satisfy creditors. In part, it was meant to streamline the bankruptcy process. Cases took too long to get before the courts and then took too long to be resolved. Whoever claimed bankruptcy before getting to court certainly was bankrupt by the time the case was resolved. But the new law had its opponents furious.

Advocates of the bankruptcy code adopted in 1978 called it imperfect but a good start on the road to reforming problems in the system. Critics thought otherwise. The new law provided corporations and individuals with similar sorts of remedies. Two types of bankruptcy could be filed. Corporations could file for Chapters 7 and 11. Individuals could file for Chapters 7 and 13. In either case, the outcome could be similar.

Under Chapter 7, a company or individual could liquidate assets to satisfy creditors, with any uncovered debts being discharged by the courts.

That would enable a fresh start. Under Chapters 11 or 13, assets would be frozen and protection granted from creditors while a reorganization plan was worked out under the court's auspices. That usually required paying debts over a specified number of years and then being officially discharged from the debt. These latter two chapters were the parts that rubbed critics the wrong way.

Prior to 1978, bankruptcy filings had been rising constantly, choking the courts. By allowing reorganization, the courts were given the discretion to allow time for potentially viable businesses or individuals to get their houses in order while keeping their assets intact. What was to prevent anyone from simply filing Chapter 13 in order to dodge debts that he or she did not want to pay, asked the critics. The law was too liberal and allowed individuals to ignore debt whenever it suited them. The backdrop to the opposition was the ease at which credit could be obtained in the United States. A bankrupt could be back in business in little time, without fear of a penalty.

Of all the causes of bankruptcy, the one that was most common was having too much debt. For the consumer, this clearly meant too much consumer debt. In 1986 alone, over four hundred thousand cases of personal bankruptcy were filed, more than twice the number a decade earlier.[40] Critics pointed to the increase as a direct result of the flexible new law. The combination provided powerful ammunition for those who thought that consumers were much too profligate in their spending, unwilling to face the consequences of debt.

The shifting attitudes toward indebtedness certainly contributed to this bankruptcy trend. After an economic recovery began in 1983, consumer debt as a percentage of household disposable income began to rise. Credit card debt also showed a strong increase, aiding in the recovery. The logic used by the credit card companies seemed foolproof. If write-offs could be contained as small percentages of the total credit card debt outstanding, the business could grow even more. Then a new element was introduced, which at first appeared to turn the entire unsecured credit process on its head. In order to enhance yields, the card companies offered limited credit to those in riskier categories, such as college students or those in low-income groups. Initially, it appeared that the new bankruptcy law and easy credit had not significantly added to the card companies' default rate.[41] If that were the case, then even more credit could be extended to marginal groups, at higher rates of annual interest.

This trend illustrated that the portfolio concept as applied to consumer loans was leading to a democratization of credit. But the expansion of so many forms of credit needed innovative financing techniques if the growth was to continue. During the 1980s, a major goal of banks was to keep their balance sheets as clear as possible. Although a bull market began to develop in the stock market in 1983, it was far from clear at the time that it would last and the banks' need for capital continued. The banks were intent on creating fewer loans and finding new ways to make money. More innovation was needed from the banks' perspective. The business was booming to the point where all of the consumer loans began to clog their balance sheets.

Salable Loans

As the portfolio concept for debt instruments became accepted, it became clear that investors were interested in bond borrowings that were collateralized by loans. There was a tradition of this type of borrowing on Wall Street, but it still was relatively new. When the concept was applied to consumer loans, the consumer debt revolution reached maturity. Under this new arrangement, borrowers and lenders would no longer know each other as they had for centuries. Loans soon would be "pooled."

This new wrinkle was taken from the government-sponsored enterprises (GSEs). The Government National Mortgage Association, or Ginnie Mae, the residential housing assistance agency that was (and is) owned by the Treasury, was mandated to intermediate in favor of urban housing for those in lower-income brackets. The Federal National Mortgage Association, or Fannie Mae, intervened on behalf of its own borrower-assisted programs and continued buying approved mortgages of the Federal Housing Administration, the Veterans Administration, and other programs designed to help specific target groups within society. The Federal Home Loan Mortgage Corporation (Freddie Mac) was the mortgage arm of the Federal Home Loan Bank Board, the national regulator of the federally chartered thrifts.

Since the early 1970s, these three mortgage-assistance agencies had been securitizing residential mortgages successfully, but no private enterprise had attempted it. The mortgage-assistance agencies were founded to help finance residential housing and all three of the agencies were at one time owned by the government before two of them subsequently were privatized. Their intervention in the market for mortgages had become so extensive that they needed to be removed from government ownership because their balance sheets had become too large. If they had remained as government entities, the direct government debt would have increased several times. If they were privatized and also adopted securitization, the mortgage debt they purchased from mortgage originators would be the collateral of bond investors, not the assets of the agencies.

When a GSE securitized a mortgage, there was an assumption that the agency was a better credit risk than the collateral. If the pool of mortgages failed, the agency would step in and make up the shortfall. This was known as "covering" the liability if necessary, making the bonds "covered" bonds. And there was the implicit assumption that if the agency failed, then the Treasury would support it. The formula and the guarantee assumption worked well for the first fifteen years that the agencies securitized debt. Securitization took the mortgages off the books of the lenders and transferred them to pools supporting bonds.[42] Banks saw the success of the agencies in the market for residential mortgages as an opportunity to extend the securitization idea beyond mortgages.

The development of the mortgage assistance agencies drew some striking parallels with the establishment of the South Seas Company almost three hundred years before. These companies on both sides of the Atlantic were designed to relieve their respective governments of burdensome debt by developing borrowing capacities of their own, operating as parallel financing entities to government, with their own separate financial statements that were considered independent. Essentially, they were mercantilist companies operating at markedly different historical periods. They also had the same unfortunate results at the end of their relatively short corporate histories.[43]

The commercial banks viewed securitization as a tool that could help them in difficult financial situations as well. They were not in an enviable position. In many cases, their balance sheets had been weakened in the high interest rate environment of the early 1980s. Some of their loans were of better quality than their overall balance sheets. In this situation, opportunity presented itself. If the banks could securitize their better-quality loans, investors would buy bonds backed by them when they otherwise might have rejected the direct bank debt itself. In the process, however, the banks would separate themselves initially from some of their better-quality assets, another new phenomenon in the debt revolution of the twentieth century.

While the mortgage agencies securitized long-term debt based on thirty-year mortgages, the banks began securitizing shorter assets such as credit card receivables and car loans. Securitization can be applied to any pool of financial assets that investors are willing to accept as collateral. Asset-backed securities (ABSs) use only financial assets as collateral, such as the lease on an airplane or locomotive or mortgages on property, not the real property asset. In other words, portfolio investors were not interested in the property itself but only the income stream that its loans produced.

The banks would remove the assets from their loan portfolios, sometimes over-collateralize the amount nominally pledged and get insurance for a portion of the pool of mortgages from one of the bond insurers, and then sell the bond or commercial paper based on the strength of the collateral. Investors bought the debt obligations based on the quality of the underlying collateral, not the banks' credit ratings. The process began in the 1980s in what became known as "asset securitization." The first credit card ABSs appeared in 1987. On paper, the new ABSs were the perfect answer to banks' need to clear loans off their books. How investors would react and how the new bonds would perform in the market were unknowns in the equation. One of the reasons for caution came from bank investors themselves. Clearly, banks were adding to their liquidity and clearing the balance sheets to engage in even more business. But at what cost? An underwriter summed it up succinctly: "We may be disenfranchising existing shareholders by selling off the best assets and leaving them with what is left." Unfortunately, twenty years later when the crisis occurred in the subprime mortgage market, shareholders were disenfranchised along with a legion of unhappy bond investors.

For the first twenty years, credit card ABSs stood on the credit of the pool of assets pledged to back the bond. Technically, the bank or finance company wanting to securitize would create a special purpose vehicle, or trust in this case, which would issue the bonds and pledge the receivables as collateral. Since the assets were now off the balance sheet of the original lender, the trust was considered "bankruptcy remote," meaning that even if the bank or finance company went bankrupt the bonds would survive standing alone and be paid by the trust.

Securitization transformed the credit card market like no other single innovation since the cards were first introduced. In 1989, about 11 percent of all securitized consumer debt was revolving. By year end 2009, the percentage had risen to 43 percent of the total.[44] Lenders were no longer traditional lenders in the old standard banking sense. They now were nothing more than agents creating debt to be packaged and cleared off the books. These packagers of debt, operating alongside the traditional banks, became known as members of the shadow banking system, which was not as transparent as the regulated banks themselves. Once traditional banks entered the shadow business, the financial system underwent a change, rapidly moving away from prudential regulation in favor of high-velocity credit creation.

When securitization became popular among banks, it was billed as a win-win situation. The banks benefited, Wall Street underwriters benefited, and consumers benefited. The banks were free to create new credit card debt after clearing the older loans off their books. Investment bankers had a new source of underwriting and packaging fees, and consumers got easier credit. Clearly, there had to be some downside to the process, however. At the mechanical level the proposition proved true, but at a slightly higher level the process was fraught with risk to the banking system. But since consumers were benefiting by receiving easy credit, the risks mainly were ignored.

The securitization process had put credit card companies in the credit creation process and that process was outside the Federal Reserve's regulatory scope since any finance company with access to a cheap source of funds could enter the credit card business. Non-banks were now fully engaged in credit creation, which was also taking place at the wholesale level of banking, where non-banks were competing with the banks when making short-term business loans. Their source was commercial paper, not deposits. The business was not as profitable as credit cards but was much cheaper to administer. Banking had gradually gained new members to its ranks that were outside the regulators' orbit. The shadow banking system was constructed on a mountain of debt securities.

The net effect of securitization was to make banks more lax when extending credit to customers. If the receivables remained on the books of the credit card subsidiary, write-offs would have eventually put a brake on the card business by forcing banks to reassess their policies toward unsecured loans. However, the ability of banks to place them in a pool with other receivables meant that their portfolio characteristics were more important than their credit quality. A pool of $100 million of card receivables may have contained $10 million of card balances extended to students or to the working poor, not the most reliable payers. The risk was worth taking because the yield on that marginal portion of the pool would be higher, helping to raise the overall yield.

The combination of the older provisions of the National Bank Act, Regulations Q and Z, and the state usury laws all combined to contain interest charged on fixed rate home mortgages because long-term debt was covered by a long-term contract. Other loans similarly constructed were also protected, but newer financial instruments, notably credit cards, were constructed to appear less like term loans and more like lender services provided for a fee or a stated rate of interest that, when combined with fees, raised the effective rate of interest to a point where the usury laws could be easily violated. This was all a part of the rapidly changing financial landscape of the 1960s and 1970s, especially when theory and practice converged to produce the most significant debt revolution since the 1690s when the Bank of England was created. But even in this new environment, consumer debt still was separated from mortgage debt. The home was subject to low legal rates of interest even if the furnishings and other trappings of the consumer society were significantly more expensive to finance. Within a few decades, the equation would change substantially.

Chapter 6

Something Old, Something New

A little debt makes a debtor, a great one an enemy.
—Arab proverb

In 1970, a new edition of the King James Bible appeared, the first since the original English translation appeared in 1611. The New English Bible was a collaboration by noted biblical scholars and incorporated the most advanced knowledge available. It also modernized the text by using contemporary language. But its treatment of one Old Testament passage concerning usury was more than a reiteration of the original. The new interpretation was significant.

The new translation of the passage in Leviticus (25:36) concerning usury reflected the advances made in understanding the concept since the early seventeenth century as well as some that were already known at the time but not included in the original version. The passage in King James originally was translated as, "Take thou no usury of him, or increase: but fear thy God; that thy brother may live with thee." In the new version, it appeared as, "You shall not charge him interest on a loan, either by deducting it in advance from the capital sum, or by adding it on repayment due for food supplied on credit." The other traditional passages mentioning usury (Deuteronomy 23:19, 20 and Psalms 15:5) were not changed materially.

Clearly, the new version embellished the original idea of usury with the addition of discounting and add-on interest at the end of the loan term. *Anatocismus* had raised its head again, but the original translation of the biblical admonition did not mention compound or discounted interest in any form. What the new version of the Bible did illustrate was that the original, simple concept of usury still was being confused with later applications, underlining the intellectual conundrum that had carried on for centuries. As it turned out, the publication date of the new Bible was fortuitous for more than one reason. Cicero's old admonition against compound interest still rang true in the twentieth century. Soon it would become a major economic issue again but with so many modern twists that it virtually was overlooked in favor of modern economic arguments.

One of the most profound influences on the financial markets occurred in 1971. In the late summer, the fixed parities of currencies against the U.S. dollar and gold collapsed when Richard Nixon suspended the convertibility of the dollar into gold as prescribed by the Bretton Woods conference twenty-five years before. Within a year, the major currencies began to float against each other on the foreign exchange markets, adding a new dimension of volatility to the financial markets generally. The original Bretton Woods treaty was signed by most industrialized nations in order to prevent the unilateral devaluations of the 1930s that added to the severity of the Great Depression. Without the parity system, which gave each major currency a tightly defined value against the dollar, individual countries were free to pursue trade policies that soon would be described as beggar-thy-neighbor policies, evoking policies of the mercantilist era.

The collapse of Bretton Woods effectively devalued the dollar and many oil-exporting countries experienced a loss of international purchasing power as a result. Following the Yom Kippur War in 1973 between Israel and Egypt, the Middle East oil producers raised the price of a barrel from $5.50 to $11.00. Part of this price rise could be attributed to the loss of purchasing power the oil producers experienced as a result of the devaluation. The new price helped them as well as producers in other parts of the world. The oil and commodities producers became the nouveau riche of the world's trading nations, experiencing increased cash flows and new prosperity. Many of them were developing nations unaccustomed to a sudden turn in fortune.

Those among them who were borrowers were also unaccustomed to borrowing from banks and having access to the credit markets. Since World War II, most funds supplied to the developing countries came as foreign aid from wealthier governments or as loans from international organizations, usually on favorable terms. Defaults had not been well publicized, prompting many bankers to boldly claim that sovereign entities could not default in reality. Walter Wriston, the chairman of Citibank, remarked on more than one occasion that "countries don't go out of business." Bankers realized that a sovereign default would be rare because if a country could not pay its obligations and did default, it would lose its lifeline to the credit markets. It could also have its overseas assets seized by its creditors, which was unlikely but legally possible. While the claim seemed brash, it provided the basis for a lending explosion unparalleled in the twentieth century.

In addition to denying a debtor nation its lines of credit in the future, lenders could take other steps to indemnify themselves against a sovereign default, but they were cumbersome and almost never used. The most notable was seizing a country's assets held abroad, notably in ports, where assets such as ships or exports were waiting to be off-loaded. Seizing assets in that fashion was politically inflammable and used mostly as a threat to defaulted borrowers.

The influx of cash into many developing countries spawned domestic spending on infrastructure and domestic needs. The increase in their current account balances made some less reliant on the World Bank or other regional development banks and led them to the doors of commercial bankers, which were eager to lend to sovereign entities with an increased source of revenue. The external markets became their major source of medium-term funds. The currencies available for borrowing were confined to the major trading currencies but were concentrated mostly in U.S. dollars. A major lending market developed among the banks that provided the bulk of money to Third World entities. This market also was a new phenomenon, dating only from the late 1960s at the earliest.

The Present Value Game

Since the development of modern banking, traditional lenders have behaved in standard fashion. Bankers have accepted deposits at a rate of interest and then lent the money to borrowers at a higher rate, the difference between the two being known as the spread. The creditworthiness of the borrowers determined the size of the spread; riskier borrowers paid more than better-quality ones. Riskier borrowers meant more profit to banks than better-quality ones, but prudence suggested that higher-quality borrowers were preferred. Bankers also applied portfolio concepts to their loans, using the diversification model that has been in use since World War II.

Since domestic U.S. banking remained largely a local state affair until the 1990s, bankers created a portfolio by mixing loans from different sectors of the economy and geographical regions. Business loans were complemented by retail loans (credit cards, personal loans), mortgage loans, and in some cases sovereign loans to other countries. The latter were the only loans that crossed boundaries since they were made from a bank's foreign branch rather than from its home office. This meant that a bank could make or participate in a loan made to a foreign country but could not conduct retail or small business banking across state lines. Credit card loans were one means of avoiding the state banking strictures and in the 1970s the sovereign loans were added to the mix. But the genuine alchemy concerned how the interest rate spread produced profits.

American banks had been known since the nineteenth century as commercial banks. They made mostly short-term loans to businesses at small spreads over their cost of funds. The profits were not spectacular, but the risk in this business model was low. It also enabled the banks to realize the profit in relatively short periods. A six-month loan repaid its principal and interest within that six-month period. When bankers wandered into the retail business beginning in the 1920s, loans became longer and profits had to wait to be booked each year for the life of the loan. In terms that English bankers of the seventeenth and eighteenth centuries would easily understand, a five-year loan made to a customer would book its annual revenue and profit five times in sequential years. In short, bankers who became involved in anything but traditional commercial lending became exposed to time risk and to possible opportunity losses if interest rates moved higher over the course of the loan, assuming that it originally was made at a fixed rate.

In the 1970s, this model of banking came under pressure. Rising interest rates and volatile foreign exchange rates created a more combustible business environment for financial services companies, putting more pressure on current profits and deemphasizing longer term fixed rate loans as an industry standard. As a result, banks began considering alternatives to the traditional loan that had the promise of being more profitable. Initially, they turned to two alternative products—syndicated loans and fee banking. Syndicated loans behaved more like an investment banking product while fee banking, an investment banking concept, helped book profits in the present rather than wait for future revenues to be received.

One of the reasons that investment banking activities were more profitable than commercial banking was that the former realized present value over future cash flow streams. Investment bankers charged a fee for their work without owning the securities or loans they underwrote. The fees could be sizable given the short period in which their capital was at risk. If an investment banker underwrote a five-year loan for $100 million, charging a 2 percent fee, then the $2 million would be realized in the present accounting period. Investors bought the securities and bore the risk of interest and principal repayment. In contrast, if a commercial banker underwrote a

$100 million loan, it would profit in the spread over the cost of funds. If the spread was 2.75 percent, then it would earn $2.75 million per year for five years. But in present value (discount) terms, the results were not as clear.[1] While the stream of revenues was certainly greater than the investment banking fee, the risks to the lender were clear. If interest rates rose, the fixed rate loan suffered an opportunity loss. There was also the default risk of the borrower itself. Investment bankers could underwrite five loans like this in a year and suffer none of those associated risks. Naturally, commercial bankers began to look at the investment banking model with envy.

That envy, plus the desire of most money center banks (largest banks in major cities) to engage in investment banking in the United States, led many of them to establish overseas activities with an eye to bringing them home once domestic regulations were lifted. Although prohibited from engaging in investment banking activities for corporations by the Glass-Steagall Act of 1933, many banks were performing some of these functions for corporations through the syndicated loan market and their underwriting activities in the Eurobond market. While not confronted with usury laws directly in these activities, the banks envisioned a day when variable rate lending would be standard in the U.S. retail market. Lending in the market for syndicated loans based on the London Interbank Offered Rate (LIBOR), discussed below, was considered good practice for the day when the domestic American market would become more flexible.

Putting the Model to Work

In the latter twentieth century, usury still was an issue for banks and retail lenders. The machinations of Citibank to avoid the New York usury laws by moving its credit card operations to South Dakota were ample testimony that even the largest lenders felt uncomfortable and vulnerable in locales that took the usury laws seriously. Both South Dakota and Delaware owed their recent prosperity to the more stringent usury laws in other states, demonstrating that employment and local investment trumped what was considered to be a fuzzy, outdated notion. Credit card lending employed compounding interest on outstanding balances in an increasingly bewildering fashion. But the greatest profits made by banks between 1970 and the early 1980s were not generated by loans using compound interest formulas. Instead, the loans employed what appeared to be a simple interest formula that coincided with rapidly rising interest rates to produce a bonanza for banks while helping to push many of their borrowers to the edge of insolvency. The classic beggar-thy-neighbor stratagem appeared again, although the banks involved claimed that it was just another case of lending gone bad in unusual circumstances.

The lending explosion that began in the 1970s occurred in the offshore market for what became known as Eurodollars. These were U.S. dollars deposited in banks, foreign and American, located outside the territorial United States. The deposits were outside the jurisdiction of American banking regulators. The market grew slowly but within ten years became a substantial lending force in its own right. The origins of the market were political. In the late 1960s, the Russian government had a dollar balance it wanted to deposit, but it wanted to avoid American banks because of the Cold War. A French bank agreed to accept the deposit, leading to what became known as the first Eurodollar deposit. In order to make the deposit profitable, it needed to make a dollar loan with it. Soon, what became known as the Eurodollar sector was born.

Since the U.S. dollar was the major reserve currency in the period after World War II, the success of the market was ensured. Banks rushed to begin accepting dollar deposits regardless of their own native currencies as long as domestic banking authorities agreed to allow them to do the business as external to their normal domestic functions. The American banks trying to avoid the complexities of the usury ceilings were joined by a host of other foreign banks united in their effort to appeal to dollar borrowing and lending on a global scale. Their customers were purely institutional, coming from the corporate and governmental ranks. They were joined by a host of international and supranational institutions all cashing in or trying to offset the effects of the international oil crisis that began in the early 1970s.

The new lending formula was based upon the rates quoted in London by the major international banks. A series of short-term deposit and lending rates referred to as the London Interbank Bid Rate (LIBID) and the London Interbank Offered Rate (LIBOR) were quoted by the banks as the basic rates for borrowing and lending. Institutional depositors received the bid rate while institutional borrowers got the offered rate plus a spread reflecting their credit risk—the smaller the spread, the smaller the perceived risk and vice versa. The rates were based purely on the supply and demand for dollars on a daily basis.[2]

The advantage to the banks was that this interest rate structure, also known simply as Eurodollar rates, was not subject to any domestic American regulations. This structure necessarily fell outside the usury laws and, more importantly, Federal Reserve regulations because the banks were not domiciled domestically. Neither were they subject to local domestic laws in the countries in which they were quoted because they were not denominated in local currency. Until the 1970s, most U.S. bank loans had been made at a spread over the prime rate. While not a fixed rate, the prime was somewhat phlegmatic compared with LIBOR since any changes made to it, and the loans based upon it, were announced by banks based upon changes in money market rates. But LIBOR was more flexible and did not require official announcements about a change. While domestic retail loans still were governed by usury laws, international loans made on this basis were free of constraint, but even in that case the usury laws could prove troublesome, especially if a domestic rate like prime was used to price them. The popularity of the new LIBOR formula for lending became clear quickly. It soon supplanted the less flexible prime rate as the standard U.S. dollar lending rate. In 1971, one senior New York banker remarked that "the convention of the prime rate has outlived its usefulness."[3]

In order to use LIBOR as the benchmark, banks initially had to make loans from an overseas branch, mainly London. Borrowers came from all quarters of corporate and governmental life, including American corporations. Usury laws applied only to laws made within a state; the national usury law, not often mentioned, applied to banks officially designated as national organizations and then only applied to mortgage rates. This latter group included many of the largest banks in the country. Predictably, that same group became some of the largest Eurodollar lenders. Operating offshore allowed the banks complete freedom from even the remnants of the usury laws, especially if a charge of criminal usury ever was pursued successfully by an aggrieved borrower. Offshore deposit-taking and lending simply was a successful attempt to move banking operations into the unregulated sector and the results would be less than successful for most of the banks involved.

More importantly, LIBOR-based borrowing and lending was the original source of adjustable, or floating, interest rates attached to loans. A loan made at 1 percent above LIBOR for six months meant that the rate was adjusted every six months to 1 percent above the prevailing LIBOR rate. If interest rates changed, the loan rate would also change, reflecting changes in money market rates. Banks were fond of this method of adjustment because it meant that their cost of funds (the bid rate) was always below the offered rate while the spread they charged borrowers was above the offered rate. Money could be made regardless of the level of interest rates. The same could not be said in locales that adhered to usury ceilings. This would take on increased importance when adjustable rate mortgages were introduced.

These bank loans were designed with features resembling bonds. The amounts were large, so in many cases lenders did not want to hold the entire amount on their books. As a result, the loans were syndicated as bond issues were; the original lender divided the loan into pieces, inviting other banks to take portions on their books. Some of the loans carried fees, paid up-front, of as much as 2 percent of the amount borrowed. For a loan of $100 million for five years, the lending banks could split $2 million in fees at the time the loan officially was disbursed. This was similar to the way bond deals compensated underwriters. The incentives were obvious, although no secondary market existed for the loans. They had to be kept on the books of the lenders.

The amounts borrowed usually were not secured, especially if the borrower was a sovereign entity or owned by one. Bankers eagerly made as many loans as they could because of the claim that sovereign defaults did not occur frequently in the international bond markets. The same could be said of this new market because of its relatively young age. After the initial round of oil price shocks, business was brisk.

Many non-oil-producing nations in the developing world began to run trade deficits as the price of oil rose while those of their major exports often did not, at least immediately. Not all the oil producers were members of the cartel of oil producers, the Organization of the Petroleum Exporting Countries (OPEC). Countries such as Mexico produced and exported increasing amounts of oil during the 1970s but still were outside OPEC and considered less-developed countries (LDCs) by most Western bankers. As a result, the alignment of LDCs ran from oil producers to commodity exporters. At the very opposite end of the spectrum were developing countries with no substantial commodity business of any sort such as Poland, Yugoslavia, and North Korea.

The lending phenomenon that followed became euphemistically known as balance of payments lending, supplying funds to countries in deficit. The source of the funds was the deposits made by the oil producers in London and other Euromarket banking centers. The major banks became the intermediaries in the process. The lending boom came at a propitious time for the American banks in particular. New developments in the credit markets put pressure on their traditional business. The development of the commercial paper market in particular during the late 1960s and the early 1970s drew many prime corporate clients directly into the money market, bypassing the banks in the process. The credit card business was not well developed and the banks were on a quest to find new profit centers. The offshore lending business fit the bill nicely because it had enormous potential, lent money to sovereign borrowers for the most part, and was free of domestic regulation.

The 1970s produced a lending boom on a scale never seen before. Many LDC borrowers were put in a precarious position of having to borrow to defend their exchange rates in the face of balance of payments deficits that would have potentially volatile consequences if not financed in the medium term. Oil was the key leading price indicator in this fragile equation. Higher oil prices would mean higher commodity prices as well, but prices did not move in tandem. Commodity prices followed oil, but the time between their movements was crucial to many countries' financial situations. A rise in the price of oil followed by a slow rise in commodity prices meant that many LDCs were already in bad shape by the time they realized increased commodity revenues. On the other end of the spectrum, a drop in commodity prices followed eventually by a drop in the price of oil would produce the same results. The same leading-lagging phenomenon was seen in the relationship between the price of oil and short-term interest rates. Oil and commodity prices were the primary cause of a rise in interest rates. When that inflationary cycle ended, the real question would be whether they would lead interest rates lower.

During the 1970s, the borrowing explosion was a universal affair. The amount borrowed by industrialized countries in the syndicated loan market rose from $4.25 billion in 1970 to $17.2 billion in 1977. The non-OPEC LDCs borrowed $446 million in 1970, rising to $20.85 billion in 1977, while OPEC borrowings rose from $146 million to $7.4 billion in the same period. Borrowings by the Soviet Union and its satellites rose from $38 million to $3.4 billion. A similar explosion was found in the international bond markets, where borrowings by all entities increased by over 800 percent.[4] But clearly it was the LDC increase of forty-five times the 1970 borrowing that led the way and provided the most profits for the banks since their syndicated borrowing provided the highest margins over LIBOR and the fattest fees. The banks found their new source of revenue, but it soon turned into their largest single source of losses in the twentieth century.

The Crisis Begins

The banks used the overseas markets to their advantage for a brief period, roughly 1970–1982. The lack of regulation in the Euromarkets and their desire to expand beyond the traditional commercial banking model led to an exuberance in lending that worried regulators and politicians because of the change in the international financial system since the collapse of Bretton Woods. Previously disconnected markets now seemed to be connected in ways not thought practical before.

What appeared to be excessive borrowing by the LDCs worried many policymakers. In 1977 Arthur Burns, the chairman of the Federal Reserve Board, criticized commercial banks for assuming excessive risks in their Third World lending, noting that "under the circumstances, many countries will be forced to borrow heavily, and lending institutions may well be tempted to extend credit more generously than is prudent . . . commercial and investment bankers need to monitor their foreign lending with great care, and bank examiners need to be alert to excessive concentrations of loans in individual countries."[5]

High energy prices and interest rates took their toll on two banks in the early 1980s. Both were connected through their lending to oil and gas exploration companies operating mostly in the United States. The increase in the price of commodities increased the popularity of many small oil and gas explorers, although many of their assets were unproven reserves to which they held the rights. One of the lenders was the Penn Square Bank, a medium-size regional bank located in Oklahoma. The other was the Continental Illinois National Bank and Trust, the seventh largest bank in the United States, located in Chicago. The failure of the former upset the financial markets, but the collapse of the latter brought into question the stability of the entire banking system.

Penn Square failed in 1982 because of poor quality loans made to exploration companies and others in the oil and gas business. It sold many participations in them to other banks, including Continental, and when they failed the FDIC had to step in and support Penn Square's depositors. The failure cast unfavorable light on Continental, which suffered financially and in terms of reputation because of the losses. Continental was mostly a wholesale bank; it did less retail business with the public than many of its counterparts. As a result, it was able to offer high-rate loans to corporate customers as well as high deposit rates, although it still took many risky positions in its loan book. When the prime rate was at 20 percent, it offered favorable fixed rate loans to corporate customers at 16 percent, amazing many competitors who would not assume similar risky positions.[6] But it was a fall in oil prices in the summer of 1981 that hurt the bank most because of its exposure to the oil and gas industry. The government in Mexico would suffer a similar fate.

Within a year, Continental began to rely heavily on Eurodollar deposits for its funding, a particularly risky strategy since LIBOR was especially volatile. Additionally, many of its institutional customers were keenly aware of the bank's problems and credit rating. When rumors began to circulate about its ability to continue in business, many of the institutional depositors demanded their cash rather than roll over their maturing deposits as would have been expected. The bank then faced a liquidity crisis, which amounted to a run on its deposits. It had to be rescued by the Treasury and became the best example to date of the concept of "too big to fail." The repercussions for the economy were deemed too great to allow it to fail outright.

This worst-case scenario for the LDCs began to develop in 1980 as oil prices and American interest rates began to rise. The price of crude oil jumped from $25.00 per barrel in 1979 to $37.00 in 1980 and remained high at $36.00 in 1981. In 1982, the price dropped to $32.00 per barrel and declined again in 1983 to $29.00. The decline provided some relief for importers but little consolation for producers. During the same period, six-month Eurodollar rates rose from 14.28 percent in 1979 (year end) to 17.82 percent in 1980. They dropped to 14 percent in 1981, and declined to 9.72 percent in 1982. They remained steady at 10.26 percent in 1983 (year end).[7] The two series of data moved in similar fashion, although the spot price of oil led interest rates higher and subsequently lower. But the percentage changes in oil prices were significantly higher than those changes in LIBID and LIBOR. While oil prices rose approximately 50 percent between 1979 and 1980, interest rates rose only 25 percent, allowing oil-producing borrowers an easy way to pay their interest. Between 1980 and 1981, oil slid about 3 percent while interest rates slid 21 percent. But between 1981 and 1982, oil dropped 9 percent while interest rates held steady. This last lagging indicator between the two spelled economic trouble for the two banks and the LDCs.

The problem for syndicated borrowers was that the base interest rate alone did not fully indicate their economic plight. Their spread over LIBOR added as much as 150 to 175 basis points (1.5 to 1.75 percent) to their costs of borrowing. At the height of the spike in Eurodollar interest rates in July and August 1981, this meant that any loan re-fixing would amount to more than a 20 percent annual rate of interest. That high rate was more than most borrowers could bear, oil producers included.

In 1981, Poland provided a prelude of future problems when it could no longer pay the interest on its external debt and had to undergo a restructuring. In the preceding years, bankers had made the no-default assumption about Poland and some other communist states. David Rockefeller committed loans by Chase Manhattan Bank to Poland, by stating, "In terms of straight credit risk, the presumption is that there is greater continuity of government in certain Socialist states than in non-Socialist states." Rockefeller also noted that bankers were becoming worried about Poland in the late 1970s but were "still eager to lend to these Socialist states."[8] This may have been part of a greater strategy of moving Poland closer to a market economy, but the stability part of the calculation proved wrong, as did the financial calculation.

A year later, high interest rates finally took their toll. The LDC crisis began in August 1982, when the Mexican minister of finance informed American officials and the International Monetary Fund (IMF) that the country would be unable to meet its August interest obligation to service $80 billion in debt. Other countries were in a similar situation. By October 1983, twenty-seven countries owing $239 billion had rescheduled their debts to banks or were in the process of doing so. Sixteen of the borrower nations were from Latin America, and the four largest—Mexico, Brazil, Venezuela, and Argentina—owed various commercial banks $176 billion, or approximately 74 percent of the total LDC debt outstanding. Of that amount, roughly $37 billion was owed to the eight largest U.S. banks and constituted approximately 147 percent of their capital and reserves at the time.[9] As a result, several of the world's largest banks, including several leading American banks, including Continental Illinois, faced the possibility of major loan defaults, capital impairment, and eventually failure.

The restructurings that many countries negotiated with their bank lenders were not necessarily in their long-term interests. Mexico and Brazil were the two largest borrowers among the LDCs with total debt outstanding of approximately $200 billion in 1982. They all received similar treatment from the banks, which refused to acknowledge that the lending may have been imprudent in the first place. The borrowers were pressured by the United States and other major countries belonging to the Organisation for Economic Co-operation and Development (OECD) to take more loans from the banks in order to pay their interest due. By doing so, many incurred debt at unsustainable levels in comparison to their economies. At the time, this solution was referred to as a "band-aid" because it was acknowledged that the solution was nothing more than temporary. Many LDCs believed that they had not been properly informed about the risks involved in syndicated loan lending but saw the handwriting on the wall. Others did not accept their debt problems complacently. Many countries refused to accept the terms and conditions that would be placed upon them and proposed their own remedies instead.

President Alan Garcia of Peru proposed that Peru limit its debt payments to 10 percent of the country's exports. His proposal was radical because it actually attempted to link the ability to pay off debts with actual revenue, something many bankers had overlooked. Diplomatic language was also extremely important. Garcia remarked in 1985, "We want to pay because we are honest, and though we are mindful of the injustices of that debt, we assume our responsibility as a people that stands by recognizing its own mistakes."[10]

The banking community was not pleased with Peru's stand. Recognizing the displeasure, the Peruvian government repatriated about $700 million of the country's reserves and assets held abroad in the event creditors attempted to seize them or tie them up in lengthy legal proceedings. Over the next few years, the banks responded by lowering the overall amount of credit available to Peru. Nevertheless, Peru's response was unusual and the bankers' assumption that not many others would follow Peru proved correct. The lure of access to the credit markets proved too strong to jeopardize.

Crucial to the debt problem was the role of the IMF. The international agency played a pivotal role in negotiating conditions for the banks to extend new loans. The banks and their home governments insisted on a role for the IMF so that the borrowing countries would apply appropriate austere economic measures in order to preserve their domestic resources. Among the various conditions the IMF imposed on delinquent borrowers were wage controls, price liberalization, currency devaluation, and allowing local interest rates to rise to "natural" market levels.[11]

These sorts of conditions were known as IMF "conditionality" and the combination applied dictated whether the conditions were high, medium, or low. In most cases, conditions were set high. While the results in a macro sense pleased the IMF and bankers, the domestic repercussions were wide and sometimes violent. Wage controls and liberalized prices often meant that already poor and marginal workers lost what little purchasing power they possessed, often taking to the streets to protest. The IMF became the disciplinary power imposed on sovereign governments from the outside, a situation that many LDCs likened to the gunboat diplomacy of the early twentieth century. The crisis caused many LDC borrowers, especially those in Latin America, to align their interests further away from the United States. President Osvaldo Hurtado of Ecuador stated in 1983 that "what is at stake is the social and political peace of the nations [involved] and the stability of the democratic system."[12]

By implication, the threat was not perceived as one to the LDCs alone. Approximately $700 billion of previously outstanding LDC debt was in jeopardy in the early 1980s and posed an imminent threat to banks and the industrialized societies as well. Paul Volcker, the chairman of the Fed, remarked, "Failure to manage and diffuse these strains could deliver a serious blow to the recovery of the United States and the world economy."[13] The difficult part of managing the problem was that he and other regulators had to ensure that the debtors continued to negotiate with the banks so that none of them defaulted; if one did default, the banks' reaction could possibly inspire others to do the same in the hope of receiving a sympathetic deal to wind down their indebtedness.

The greatest international debt crisis of the twentieth century did not appear to occur because of compound interest. The LIBOR-based formula upon which most syndicated loans were made was based on simple interest. If the pricing formula suggested a 10 percent annual rate of interest for a six-month period, then the effective rate was 5 percent for the period until the next re-set. The interest was calculated on the amount originally lent, and the principal and last interest payment were due at maturity. This naturally had the practical effect of being a rate higher than the nominal rate(s) suggested since no amortization payments were required in the interim; put another way, there was no declining balance that would have reduced the amount of interest paid. But for medium-term loans of three to five years, interim payments of principal were not practical.

Charging simple interest at market rates of interest demonstrated that compounding was not necessary because of the absence of any sort of interest rate ceiling. Rates were on the rise throughout the 1970s and reached their peak in the early 1980s. More subtle tricks such as charging interest more frequently than once per month, a favorite technique of the credit card companies was eschewed in favor of a net margin on large amounts borrowed.[14] These large, mostly sovereign loans were considered ideal by bankers, who were able to charge high margins over the LIBOR benchmark while running what they believed to be relatively little risk because the borrowers were sovereign entities that were thought to be unlikely to default Those margins did not help the LDCs meet their debt payments. They represented another set of fees that the bankers could book as profits immediately and sometimes amounted to as much as 2 percent of the amount lent. In addition, other fees and expenses were included, all paid by the borrowers. At one Mexican loan signing, the country's finance minister complained that the banks even charged for the gold pens used to sign the documents as well as the expensive cigars provided by the bankers to celebrate after the ink had dried.

While the interest was simple, the loan principal amounts were increasing in the early 1980s and the LDC borrowers faced the same sort of problem about which Cicero had complained two thousand years before. Despite the advances made in understanding interest, *alterum tantum* again had been achieved by lenders; interest charges led to a doubling of debt outstanding. In this case, it was not simply high interest rates but a desire to lend in order to book revenue in the near future and avoid a messy series of defaults. The result was the same. Between 1980 and 1986, the total amount of Latin American debt outstanding doubled; the new loans added to those existing to produce unserviceable debts for the borrowers.[15] The new principal amounts outstanding became the problem in the latter part of the 1980s. Even more radical measures would be needed to remedy the situation.

The impact of the debt arrears and increased loans could be seen in the financial performance of the eight major money center banks in the United States. All of them suffered credit rating declines between 1982 and 1988, sometimes by three or more categories until some were trading only slightly above junk bond grade. Their financial ratios, regulatory capital, and reserves were all seriously depleted. Ordinarily, this situation would have caused an immediate response from bank regulators, but the reaction in the 1980s was purposely slow. The catchword for it became "regulatory forbearance." This regulatory forbearance was granted to the large banks for their present problems as well as their past-due LDC loans. According to one regulator, this forbearance was necessary because seven or eight of the ten largest banks in the United States might have been deemed insolvent, a situation that would have precipitated an economic and political crisis.[16] Continental Illinois was portrayed as an anomaly, although in reality the same fate could have hit any of the U.S. banks during that period.

The LDC debt occupied most of the public attention in the 1980s, but debt in general was increasing significantly on all balance sheets. The moribund stock market of the early 1980s pushed new equity financing into the background as debt continued its popularity with borrowers and investors. The new levels of accumulated debt even worried some Wall Street analysts who made their livings analyzing the credit markets in general. Noting that all types of debt in the United States had grown from $2.4 trillion in 1974 to $7.2 trillion in 1984, Henry Kaufman, a Wall Street analyst, citing the dangers of the burgeoning traditional debt, acknowledged that much more debt was disguised and not counted because of swaps, options, and other debt derivatives. The unprecedented debt levels also posed additional problems not traditionally discussed on Wall Street and among the banks. Private debt among U.S. households especially was troublesome, given the role of consumption in the American economy. "We will have to subordinate many vested interests for the sake of preserving the integrity of credit," Kaufman noted, adding that "[it is] an absolute essential for the preservation of a democratic economic society."[17]

The growth in debt outstanding during the period 1977 to 1986 underscored the point. The annual rate of growth in debt grew in all sectors of the economy at double digit rates. In the household sector, the growth in home mortgages and credit card debt increased as did municipal government borrowing. Federal government borrowing increased because of a growing budget deficit. But the growth in the borrowing in the financial sector in particular was notable. It recorded the highest rates of annual percentage growth, from 18.9 percent in 1977 to 26.2 percent in 1986. The United States had become increasingly reliant on debt financing over the years since World War II. Until 1986, when the Tax Reform Act abolished it, the interest deduction for personal (consumer) interest remained in place, as it had been since World War I. But after 1987, the growth rate in consumer debt began to slow, coinciding with the recession in the early 1990s. Although it recovered in the mid-1990s, the domestic financial sector continued to lead the way in debt issuance as the new century approached.[18]

The Mexican Defeasance

The high interest rate environment that followed the new Federal Reserve policy after 1979 caused considerable problems in the fixed income markets. Inflation rose to historic American heights and both long-term and short-term interest rates also rose to unprecedented levels. With both inflation and rates in the low- to mid-teens, financial planning became difficult, especially for pension funds and insurance companies, both of which found achieving future financial obligations difficult because of the uncertainty in the markets. In the midst of difficult market conditions, investment banks devised a new financial product that would substantially alter the fixed income markets and provide a solution for future financial crises.

The innovation was the first example of what would become known as financial engineering, later called structured finance. Bond dealers recognized that many institutional investors continued to need cash flow from their bond investments but were less sanguine about bond values in the face of rising interest rates. The rise would diminish the value of the bond principal.

As a result, several dealers experimented with stripping the coupons from a bond's principal, creating what became known as a zero coupon bond. The new instrument was actually nothing more than a series of annuity payments on the one hand and a lump-sum payment to be made at a future date on the other. The zero coupon bond, priced at a discount from par value, could be sold to investors needing a distinct lump sum at a future date. The coupons, or annuity payments, could be sold to investors needing periodic interest payments only. The payments were also priced at a discount. If recombined, the two sides would again equal the price of the ordinary bond without being officially stripped.

The new instruments became extremely popular with investors. Soon, the U.S. Treasury allowed official stripping of its own obligations, recognizing that the innovation helped market traditional bonds in difficult market conditions.[19] The technique became the most significant use of debt instruments since Richard Price suggested his sinking fund in Britain two hundred years before. But the beneficiaries in this case were investors rather than the U.S. Treasury. Financial planning received a major boost from the technique because investors now could calculate the present and future value of their investments with certainty, a calculation that no other financial instrument provided. The same certainty would help solve the Third World debt crisis, which had been created in part by the same market conditions.

The plight of the banks rather than that of the LDCs was the critical factor in finding a solution to the crisis. The loan losses and threat of impending losses put in jeopardy many of the balance sheets of the international money center banks. Their capital ratios fell sharply due to their large exposure. Bank of America alone had an oversized exposure to Mexico that threatened its viability even before its other troubled loans were considered. While Mexico again was on the verge of an outright default in 1986, even Mexicans questioned whether its plight or that of the Bank of America and other U.S. lenders was most important. A compromise was needed so that the banks' losses would be limited while the LDC debt was rescheduled. That meant extending the loans for longer periods of time to reduce annual amortization while reducing interest rates on the loans at the same time. This was not an easy solution, however, because the bond markets only lent to investment grade quality borrowers, not LDCs on the brink of outright default.

Part of the solution to Mexico's problem came in the form of what became known as Brady bonds, first issued for Mexico in 1988. Named after Nicholas Brady, the secretary of the Treasury, these bonds helped restructure Mexico's debt using the zero coupon bonds devised only a few years before. The formula included revised repayment schedules and interest rates as well as a haircut (discount) forced on the banks, requiring them to acknowledge their losses. The existing debt was exchanged for new bonds of Mexico, and later other indebted countries. The new bonds were nicknamed "Aztec" bonds. They were meant to be interest-paying assets to replace the loans most often in arrears. In order to participate in the program, the banks were required to forgive 30 percent of a country's debt, receiving bonds in return. The difference between the bonds and the old loans was that the bonds were collateralized by U.S. Treasury zero coupon bonds. This was done to reassure lenders that the principal amount would be available at maturity. In essence, the 30 percent forgiveness allowed the country involved to use the money to purchase the zeros at a deep discount, then pledging or "defeasing" them against the face value of the new bonds for redemption in the future.

The technique used to collateralize the principal of the new Mexican bonds appeared to be an example of the new financial engineering. Legally, it was called a "defeasance." But the technique was hardly new; the term had been in use for several hundred years in English law and recently had been used successfully in the American municipal bond market. Its technical definition was that it was a pre-refunding of an outstanding bond or debt. Others understood it as a marketing technique to make a collateralized debt obligation look more appealing than if it stood on its own.

Both views proved correct. In the U.S. market for municipal bonds, many small issues were described as "refunding issues." This meant that the borrower was obliged to buy a certain amount of U.S. Treasury bonds to set aside against the borrowing so that the principal and/or interest would be paid in a timely fashion in the future. Borrowers that were relatively unknown to the bond market needed to adopt the technique, along with those that may have had credit problems in the past. The set aside or defeasance would ordinarily earn the issue a high credit rating as a result, regardless of the borrower's rating without it. This was the same effect that the Mexican defeasance had on international investors. The escrowed collateral allowed Mexico to borrow at interest rates much lower than would have been the case if it had been on its own without the intercession of the U.S. Treasury.

The irony in the situation was that defeasance was as old as the bond markets but had not been used in years. The term had become somewhat obsolete in finance until revived for the Brady bonds and even then was not used in public discussion. The concept could be traced back to the Tudors. In the statutes of Henry VIII, defeasance was mentioned along with the usury laws. Two hundred years later, it was described in a leading compendium of legal terms: "Defeasance, (from the Fr. *Defaire*, to defeat) Signifies a Condition relating to a Deed, which being performed, the Deed is defeated, and render'd void, as if it never had been made. The Difference between a common Condition and a Defeasance is, that the Condition is annexed to, or inserted in the Deed; and a Defeasance is a Deed by itself, concluded and agreed on between the Parties, and having Relation to another Deed."[20] A new debt problem apparently had been solved by an older legal practice.

In other words, a defeasance stood separate from the debt it was meant to retire. In current use, a defeasance was (and is) part of off-balance-sheet financing. If a debt security was defeased, it was not recorded on the borrower's balance sheet as a liability. The same generalization was made about the mortgage-backed securities issued by Fannie Mae, Freddie Mac, and Ginnie Mae. Their securitized obligations were also off the balance sheet since the mortgages securing them were assets of the bondholders, although that sort of collateral was not as secure as U.S. Treasury obligations. The same also was true of many of the derivatives that would be developed in the wake of the Third World debt crisis. While technically different, these instruments all had the common characteristic of being difficult to detect on financial statements. In the case of defeasances, they were virtually impossible.

Setting aside high-quality debt obligations as collateral to retire issues of lesser quality invoked memories of Ivar Kreuger in the 1920s. In that case, the collateral supposedly backing his bonds was switched and when it collapsed the original bonds had no support. In the case of the LDC issues supported in this manner, the Brady bonds proved successful and helped resolve the crisis, although it took about fifteen years to do so completely. That other new debt market technique—securitization—also started strongly and was hailed as the other debt innovation that had transformed the market. Once acclaimed as the newest and most clever twist devised in the debt markets, it would fall into serious disrepute twenty years later in the credit market crisis following 2007.

After Mexico employed Brady bonds, more than a dozen other countries also issued them, including Argentina, Bulgaria, Brazil, Nigeria, the Philippines, and Venezuela. Part of the deal for issuing these bonds was the agreement of the debtor countries to abide by debt restructuring efforts led by the IMF and the World Bank. The conditionality of the IMF again prevailed in many places and many of the debtor countries were not happy with the strictures imposed on them but had little choice but to acquiesce in order to alleviate their previous debt burden. But defeasance did not solve all of the

LDC debt problems. By the late 1980s, much LDC debt was priced at a sharp discount from par. These prices were calculated in a new market for distressed debt developed by the banks that were anxious to get the troublesome loans off their books. As a result, many loans were selling for less than 50 percent of the original loan value. The market was brisk, with many being bought at those discounts, which the banks had to write off as losses. The market was useful for the lenders, but the real question centered on exactly who the buyers of this distressed debt were.

The nature of the investors was politically charged and often criticized in the LDCs. Many corporations bought the debt and exchanged it for equity in local businesses within the LDCs, with the host country's blessing in most cases. The host country retired its debt, encouraged direct foreign investment in its economy, and hopefully witnessed an increase in employment as a result. Economically, the new market produced some tangible benefits while helping to ameliorate the debt problem to an extent. But critics were not content with the new distressed debt market because they saw it as another way of selling out to foreign business interests, many of which had helped exploit the local populations in the first place.

The New Look of Debt

During the early 1980s, significant developments occurred in the debt markets in addition to zero coupon bonds and securitization. Even before the LDC crisis began, several of them began to attract attention because of the high rates of interest found in the money and bond markets. The crises of the 1980s only made them more popular among banks and investors.

The LDC debt crisis provided the incentive to develop debt derivatives and other types of off-balance-sheet instruments. As a result of a decade of crisis, the Bank for International Settlements (BIS) in Basle, acting as the international regulatory agency for the developed countries' commercial banks, mandated that the banks maintain higher capital standards, setting their capital requirement at 8 percent.[21] Many of the banks were deficient at the time, some with a cushion of only 3 percent. This move forced many banks to raise additional capital for their balance sheets either by selling new equity or, in some cases, by reducing assets. Securitization fitted this latter technique perfectly by pledging loans against bond borrowings, clearing them off the lenders' balance sheets and with them the need for regulatory capital. When banks could not reduce the amount of loans (assets) on their books, they were inclined to find new types of business not requiring them to make loans.

By developing various types of swap contracts and trading them actively, banks were able to generate revenue without putting loans on the books. A swap arrangement was classified as a contingent (off-balance-sheet) liability and relegated to a footnote under shareholders' equity. So if a client swapped interest rate payments or currencies with a bank, the nominal amount swapped became a contingent liability for both parties until the arrangement ended. As a result, the bank enjoyed the income and fees produced by swaps without having to maintain the 8 percent capital requirement necessary for loans. In the beginning, this seemed like just another bank product, but as swaps became more popular they helped change the nature of traditional commercial banking institutions. Within twenty years, commercial banks were behaving more like investment banks or hedge funds than traditional lenders, freely swapping with corporate clients and assuming risks relatively new for banking institutions as a result.

Bankers argued that these new arrangements were not risky but were hedging instruments, designed to help institutional clients manage their various exposures. But in many cases, the banks assumed the risks the clients were attempting to mitigate. As a result, banks became exposed to whatever sort of risks the swap arrangements were meant to offset and that list grew considerably as swaps became more popular and numerous. Prior to the 1980s, banks were exposed to interest rate risk, currency risk, counterparty risk, and the credit risk of their clients. By the latter 1990s, the number of risks had doubled and included credit risk of non-clients, stock market risk, commodities risk, and event risk.[22] Banks were no longer banks: they were fast becoming quasi-insurance companies willing to partially underwrite any sort of known financial risk for a price.

This prospect appeared disturbing, even to some Wall Street analysts and regulators. Many realized that swaps were a disguised form of extending credit to companies or other institutional clients and that banking standards for lending should apply. E. Gerald Corrigan, the president of the Federal Reserve Bank of New York, remarked in 1985 that swaps gave him "a tinge of uneasiness" because of their complexity and potential for abuse. Another Fed official commented that "anytime a market grows this rapidly without being tested under adverse conditions and without attention to systematically monitoring and assessing the practices that develop, there is an element of concern."[23]

The new swaps market appeared to be exactly the sort of product banks needed in the post-LDC crisis. Loans were not the only major source of revenue for them; by agreeing to be counterparty to a swap arrangement they derived revenue without having to book a loan, keeping space available on their balance sheets while earning revenue in the current quarter. And the service they provided appeared to be more prudent than lending to LDCs. Swaps were designed as hedging instruments, so banks claimed they helped their clients avoid interest rate or currency risk. The risks they assumed by doing so could be laid off with other banks or clients in turn.

In the early years of the swaps market, most transactions were limited either to currency or interest rate swaps. In the latter, an institutional client and a bank agreed to exchange cash flows on a notional amount of money on a periodic basis. Usually, one interest rate was fixed while the other floated, based on LIBOR. Over a three-year period as an example, the fixed payer paid a constant amount to the other party while the floating rate payer paid an amount re-fixed every three or six months, as dictated by the swap contract. Differences between the payments were netted between them. The notional amount the payments were based upon never entered the picture unless a default occurred by one or both parties. The party at the most risk in this arrangement, called a plain vanilla swap, was the one paying the floating amount. If interest rates rose, the payments would increase. In contrast, if the swap were a carefully constructed hedge, the risk would be minimal.

The swaps market developed during the same period that the LDC crisis appeared. Interest rates proved volatile in the United States and the United Kingdom during the mid-1980s and swapping became popular very quickly. But as in all markets designed for hedging purposes, speculation also existed. If a market debacle were to surface, it would be because of speculation, by its nature the antithesis of hedging.

The first publicized swaps scandal appeared in 1987 when an auditor discovered an inordinate number of swaps contracts on the books of the London Borough of Hammersmith and Fulham. The municipality had a budget at the time of £85 million. Its swaps totaled about £110 million. Within two years, the outstanding amount exploded to over £6 billion.[24] Clearly, the borough was not hedging its operating budget. It was discovered that Hammersmith was mostly a payer of floating rates based on sterling LIBOR and had suffered losses when interest rates in the United Kingdom rose in the latter 1980s. More revealing was the fact that it also had acted as an intermediary between the banks and other boroughs (or local councils) that had less credit standing and reputation in the markets. In addition to speculating on interest rates for its own books, it also fronted for the others with the banks. Some of the other local councils were notoriously left-wing and would not have been welcome clients of the banks, several of which were American.

The auditor sued the borough and the case wound its way through the courts. The lower court rulings dismayed the banks because the courts decided that the swaps were not hedges, only speculation, and ruled them invalid in 1989. The case was appealed to the House of Lords, which upheld the lower courts' ruling in 1991. The court declared finally that swaps were beyond the scope of the council (*ultra vires*) and were null and void. The losses caused by the swaps were laid at the door of the banks, which had to absorb them. The losses of the four major banks involved ranged from an estimated $7 million to about $50 million, amounts the banks considered insignificant. But the case had far-ranging implications because almost eighty other local councils were involved in the market and the losses would be magnified as a result.

The Lords' ruling was not applauded among the American banks involved because in the United States it was assumed that customers take losses for their own trading mistakes, not the intermediaries or the financial services firms that provide them with services. This difference became abundantly clear in the second major swaps scandal, which occurred in the United States a few years later.

At the time the Hammersmith problem was first discovered, an estimated $1 trillion worth of notional swaps were in existence. Despite the bad publicity, the complexity of swaps kept them out of public scrutiny. Their esoteric nature allowed them to proliferate among the faithful at the banks and corporations that wanted to use them for hedging. Within a decade, the $1 trillion would increase one hundred times over and within twenty years, the amount would quadruple again. As far as the banks were concerned, swaps did not represent debt and they did not consider them part of corporate liabilities. But the sheer number outstanding suggested that even in the best-case scenario, the promise to pay that they represented could not be treated so lightly.

Oranges and Lemons

Hammersmith was not the only municipality involved in the swap market. Many American municipalities also used the market to enhance their cash flows, mainly by engaging in fixed for floating interest rate swaps. The larger municipalities also allowed smaller ones to participate in their portfolios through swap pools. The smaller entities could buy a small portion of the pool and assume the risk of its performance while the larger ones earned fees for offering the service. Several large derivatives pools existed. One of the largest was operated by the municipal government of Orange County, California. Its name was the Orange County Investment Pool (OCIP).

By the late 1980s, it had become apparent that companies and municipalities of all sorts were using derivatives and many were clearly losing on the deals. The time bomb that many had anticipated finally exploded in the United States when Orange County announced that it had experienced enormous losses on a huge derivatives portfolio it had accumulated over several years. Almost immediately, reverberations were felt throughout the country.

By any standard, the county had a formidable economy. It generated an annual gross domestic product of $74 billion in 1993, larger than the economies of Portugal, Israel, or Singapore. Standing alone, it was the thirtieth largest economic entity in the world.[25] The county overwhelmingly was a Republican district. In 1978, the California legislature passed Proposition 13. This was widely seen at the time as part of a nationwide revolt against higher taxes, in this case higher property taxes. Since the law limited property tax increases, revenue shortfall had to be made up in some other way and investment pools like the OCIP originally fit the bill, proving successful initially. That fact was repeated many times in the press since the support for the OCIP stemmed from the local distrust of strong government combined with a paradoxically strong demand for high-quality municipal services.

Orange County was also managing money for other smaller entities around the country, so the losses were not confined to California alone. Other municipal entities entrusted part of their investment funds to it, impressed by the gains it had reported over the previous few years. But local taxpayers were not prepared for the sorts of losses Orange County claimed. It had borrowed over $1 billion in the municipal bond market as part of its normal funding requirements. The swap fund was separate but equal since payments were required if the swaps moved against the county. Interest payments on the bonds became doubtful almost immediately as the swap portfolio lost.

The derivatives fund totaled about $8 billion. Losses were estimated at around $1.5 billion. Problems arose immediately because even experts called in by the county and its court-appointed monitors found the portfolio difficult to understand. Parts of it had been invested in derivatives tied to foreign interest rates rather than U.S. rates, a position that would be difficult to explain in hedging terms. In the early 1990s, the county began an aggressive series of investments with money the county borrowed through municipal bond offerings. It purchased millions of government agency bonds of five years to maturity. In one particular deal, its investment banker distributed a new issue for Sallie Mae, the student loan guarantee agency, for $600 million. Orange County bought the entire issue from the bankers at a slight premium to par. On the day the issue was announced, one financial services company calculated the market price to be four full points lower than the county paid. The bankers pocketed several million dollars on the trade.[26] Newfound cash flow from the swap market was making the municipality oblivious to market prices.

The investment strategy was not finished; it was only beginning. The county then borrowed money against the bonds on margin and used the proceeds to assemble the derivatives portfolio. By doing so, it was able to triple the outstanding amount of investments under its control. The strategy was clever because investing in derivatives alone would have been prohibited, but by parlaying them with the bonds the idea appeared to be on a sound footing. Unfortunately, the technique was not investment quality, only a bet. The county effectively tripled its exposure to changes in the interest rate.

The derivatives portion of the portfolio (in notional terms), when added to the bonds, gave it an enormous value, estimated at $20 billion. There were many other investors in the pool. In fact, its own investment amounted to only about 37 percent of the portfolio. Other investors included school districts, transportation authorities, sanitation districts, and water districts from around the country. Over two hundred local entities participated. Superficially, this seemed to diversify the ownership base adequately. The problem was that the fund was the only investment made by many of the smaller entities. Any loss had the potential to leave them in serious straits.

The portfolio was closely tied to an interest rate formula that was based on LIBOR. This was the standard method of pricing floating rate notes and bonds. The LIBOR rate was used as a reference rate and the periodic interest rate was set at a specific percentage above it, as found on syndicated loans. Because LIBOR fluctuated, paying interest based upon this formula could be risky to the borrower since interest is re-set normally twice a year for the life of the loan. Orange County was subject to fluctuating short-term interest rates, but its exposure was more complicated. The county took it one step further by arranging for exposure to what are known as "negative floaters."

Most of the OCIP portfolio was based on the formula of 15 or 10 LIBOR. Ten LIBOR meant that an exposure was 10 percent minus the Eurodollar rate. Fifteen LIBOR usually meant that the exposure was 15 percent minus twice the Eurodollar rate. In either case, the formula was designed to expose an investor to the opposite of what normally was expected when short-term interest rates rose. Regardless of which formula was used, a rise in Eurodollar rates would mean a lower rate of interest paid out and vice versa.

When interest rates were low, the yield on the OCIP portfolio was high, sometimes reaching 8 percent when the market rates were only around 4–5 percent. But the entire situation changed when the Fed raised interest rates in 1994, acting against market expectations. Much of the portfolio at the time was based upon receiving payments using the negative LIBOR formula, so incoming payments started to decline rather than rise. The rise in short-term interest rates beginning in the winter of 1994 cut into the return on the portfolio and spelled eventual doom for Orange County's previously high returns. Prior to its bankruptcy announcement, the return had fallen. If it had been receiving traditional floating LIBOR, its return would have risen, as expected.

The condition of the OCIP was not widely known, but those who did understand it were dismayed by its exposure to rising interest rates. The county treasurer's opponent in the municipal election in 1994 remarked that the pool was "a major bull market bet in the middle of a bear market . . . the incumbent has structured the portfolio . . . on the premise that interest rates would continue to decline."[27] That may have been something of an overstatement since his knowledge of the complicated exposure was sketchy at best. But politics in California had created a situation that made extraordinary returns for unsophisticated, financially limited municipalities a godsend.

Modern Alchemy

The development of debt derivatives turned the traditional notion of debt and indebtedness on its head. A fundamental characteristic of debt had always been that a debtor admitted his liability and was not free to take on more debt without acknowledging any debts preceding it. In short, a debt had to be acknowledged; to fail to do so was fundamentally misleading. Debt derivatives, in contrast, exposed contracted parties to pay interest but fell short of requiring the payments to be acknowledged as immediately pending, in short, to be real debt. A new form of debt was now a contingent liability, depending on a variety of factors that could, or could not, occur during the life of the derivatives contract.

Debt derivatives contracts had the net effect of diverting attention away from the levels of interest paid on a contract and focused solely on the net cash flows between the two parties in the swap arrangement. The complex nature of a swap contract completely obfuscated the relationship between debtor, creditor, and the nature of the obligation itself. Now, a payer could become a payee if interest rate conditions changed during the life of a swap contract. The situation could change again during the next time period and would continue indeterminately until the contract ended. The certainty and urgency of debt had become nothing more than a probability that many risk managers thought they could anticipate.

Even before the swap market became highly developed, both Hammersmith and Orange County provided proof of the difficult problems swaps presented: the same as that posed by any debt too large for a borrower to pay. Swaps had been invented as a hedging tool, but the well-publicized failures demonstrated that many were being used for speculation. The positive net cash flows they presented initially to some swap parties were too tempting to ignore. Defenders of the market argued that any hedging market needs speculators to provide it with liquidity. No market can survive intact if only hedgers are present. At the same time, liquidity problems and misuse of the market were inevitable if the risks were not understood. What the swap market did accomplish was to remove the principal or notional amounts of the swaps from the debt discussion. Debt moved into the background in favor of net cash flows.

While the LDC crisis was unfolding, the benefits of floating LIBOR had become clear to bankers. The rates were already essential to the swap market and soon the bankers' dream of using the interbank rates domestically would prove reality. The increasing use of floating interest rates was also witnessed in the U.S. market for residential mortgages about the same time that the debt crisis began. Beginning in 1980 when the Depository Institutions Deregulation and Monetary Control Act (DIDMCA) was passed, variable rate mortgages made their appearance for the first time. They were the clearest example yet of a domestic attempt to circumvent usury laws by allowing mortgage rates to change with interest rates. The new innovation effectively spelled the end of usury laws on mortgages.

The act had a timetable to abolish Regulation Q's interest rate ceilings that applied to banks. It planned to phase them out over a six-year period. But a subsequent law, the Depository Institutions Act, also known as the

Garn–St Germain Act, passed two years later, effectively allowed banks and thrifts to offer competitive rates of deposit interest, accelerating the phase-out period. State usury ceilings on mortgages also were abolished as well as any state ceilings on interest that could be paid at banks and other institutions. But there was an exception. These new usury provisions were set to expire in 1983 unless states reinstated their laws before then. As a result, the abolition of the many state usury laws was only temporary. The law was written to allow the system to become deregulated, but ultimately the states' concerns about maximum rates of interest still were paramount.

The DIDMCA was passed because of historically high real rates of interest in the United States and the negative effects they were having on the financial system. The act was one of the most complicated banking laws ever passed by Congress, but one clear point emerged in its wake. The path was now unobstructed for adjustable rates of interest on mortgages after 1983. But the yield curve would have to be positively sloped because no one would borrow at an adjustable rate based on money market rates if the adjustable rate was higher than the long-term rate. And the adjustable mortgage rate could not violate a state usury ceiling if one still existed in some locales. The answer to these potential problems was simple: caps (maximum rates) were written into adjustable mortgages to provide some potential relief for mortgagees. If market rates on adjustables suggested a new rate higher than the cap, the mortgage holder was obliged to pay no more than the cap rate. Those sorts of caps made many LDC finance ministers quite unhappy. If only they had had them on LIBOR-based term loans that were incurred in the past. Caps on sovereign debt had been discussed for years by the Fed, the IMF, and the World Bank, and were mostly opposed by bankers. Perhaps the debt crisis could have been avoided if any of the talks had proved successful went the LDC argument.

Within a few years, adjustable rate mortgages (ARMs) would become extremely popular among homeowners because they offered an alternative to very high fixed rate mortgages, some approaching 15 percent. Although the early ARMs were set at around 12 percent, like all mortgages they offered the possibility of being refinanced later at lower rates. Once the mortgage-assistance agencies Fannie Mae and Freddie Mac began buying them, the market opened and ARMs accounted for 50 percent of all mortgages originated in the 1980s, especially when interest rates were still high. Once introduced, ARMs helped save the mortgage and housing industries from even more severe losses. The high interest rates of the late 1970s and the early 1980s created the first crisis in the savings and loan industry in

1981, which saw a large number of those limited purpose banks either fail or be absorbed by larger banking institutions.

Adjustable rate mortgages also brought about a shift in risk from banks to homeowners. If short-term interest rates rose, then mortgage payments increased. The increase in interest was passed to homeowners. If rates passed through the cap, the risk shifted back to the bank. Below the floor at the opposite end, the risk was back on the homeowner, who could be paying a rate higher than the market rate. The difference between the floor and the cap was known as a collar and could be managed by a bank more easily than being saddled with a mortgage that may have been lower than the prevailing market rate, as in the time before securitization and adjustable lending rates.

The popularity of ARMs also helped spell the death knell for many state usury laws. Traditionally, the laws had been written to protect property owners from high interest rates, but the language and terms of adjustables defeated those protections. In times of high short-term interest rates, the adjustables would easily violate most states' older usury ceilings, even with caps attached. Many states dismantled their usury laws in the 1980s as a result but did so in piecemeal fashion, as had always been the case. But in most cases, ARMs were not considered to be in violation of those laws that remained because they re-set their rates of interest every year. Lenders therefore argued that they were technically not in violation of usury laws because of the possibility rates could fall in the future. The homeowner was not locked into a high rate and therefore usury was not an issue.

Despite that argument, adjustables purposely were created to shift the risk of rising interest rates from lenders to homeowners. This violated the spirit of the original usury laws, although critics contended that they were out-of-date with modern finance. But the re-setting periods, and collars under which they operated, suggest that the original design of the ARMs was meant to circumvent the usury laws on a broad scale. In their absence, many homeowners were left without protection from floating interest rates and the damage they could cause.

In Britain, mortgage rates based upon an adjustable formula had been offered since World War II and were based upon the British banks' base rate, which was similar to the prime in the United States. In that case, the adjustables were not tied directly to a market rate but to a declared rate, so lenders were not obliged to mark them to extremely high market rates. But U.K. rates in theory could exceed American rates on comparable mortgages because they lacked a specific market cap. In the examples from the United Kingdom and the United States, however, interest rates had never moved high enough in recent memory, until the early 1980s, to make loans based on these two similar bank rates controversial.

Fallen Angels, Junk, and Heavy Leverage

Bond markets in the United States and the other developed countries were reserved for creditworthy borrowers with investment grade ratings from one of the ratings agencies. Companies falling below the standard usually found financing either through equity or bank loans. This confirmed the traditional practice of lending only to highly rated borrowers while either ignoring the lesser rated or charging them higher rates through the banks, which traditionally lent only for the short- or medium-term. Financial success was the key to companies receiving funds at lower rates. Lending at risk to lesser rated companies was not a traditional strategy for most investors.

At the same time, there was a group of companies, once investment grade, whose fortunes had slipped and were downgraded as a result. Many times institutional investors were obliged to sell these sorts of bonds because they fell outside the realm of investment grade.[28] Falling prices and higher yields made it difficult for them to obtain new credit. Some speculative investors began to trade these bonds in the secondary market, hoping for the same sort of potential price rise that long-since defaulted Cuban bonds had built into their prices and yields. In this case, the odds were better and the market attracted investors to what became euphemistically known as "fallen angels," bonds that had fallen from grace. The credit markets recognized the predicament into which these companies had fallen.

The debt revolution had helped soften attitudes toward indebtedness since World War II. Despite the advances in theory and practice, the idea of a separate primary market for less-than-investment-grade debt did not emerge until the 1970s. The fallen angel market remained a secondary market that added new members during economic slowdowns as revenues for former quality borrowers slowed, lowering their ability to service their existing debt and their credit ratings as a result. The true revolution would come when the secondary market was complemented by a true primary market for these lower-rated issues.

In order for that to happen, any market for new issue fallen angels required institutional help. Because of its unorthodox nature, the secondary market for fallen angels was confined mostly to second-tier investment banks on Wall Street. The major, well-established banks confined themselves to the traditional areas of investment banking, namely underwriting corporate securities and mergers and acquisitions deals. A new market required a bank willing to commit to an unproven concept. As it turned out, an odd marriage of an established firm and a relatively recent addition to Wall Street proved the combination that gave birth to the high-yield, or junk bond, market. The firm, combining Drexel, Firestone and Company and Burnham and Company in 1971 to form Drexel Burnham, proved to be the combination that gave birth to the most radical innovation in the bond markets in over a hundred years.

The major impetus behind Drexel Burnham's entry into what became known as the junk bond market was a recent business school graduate, Michael Milken. The firm was desperate to make its merger work and Milken's ideas about distressed debt held potential. A more established, old-line firm would not have accepted ideas as readily as the firm did in the 1970s. Then in 1977 Lehman Brothers brought four high-yield issues to market for well-known but troubled companies. The junk bond market was born, but Lehman exited the market as quickly as it had entered, leaving the path clear for Drexel and Milken.

The first junk bond issue that Drexel underwrote was for Texas International, a small oil and gas company in need of fresh financing. Because the company was not familiar to investors Milken designed the issue with interest payments that would quickly attract their attention. The bonds bore a coupon of 11.5 percent, several hundred basis points higher than a quality bond, and the original issue amount was for $30 million.[29] The issue was syndicated to sixty other firms with Drexel retaining $7.5 million for its own underwriting portion. The firm earned almost $1 million in fees for the deal and Milken would keep 35 percent of that for himself. Building on its success, Drexel did six more deals in 1977 with underwriting fees between 3 and 4 percent of the amounts issued. There was little competition from the more established firms on Wall Street after Lehman withdrew.

Demand for junk bonds was stronger than anyone could have imagined in the late 1970s and continued well into the 1980s. The established banks took notice, but the upstart Drexel Burnham had become the market's most recognizable name. Milken also helped develop the market by introducing a mutual fund based primarily on high-yield bonds that helped defuse investor risk by being diversified. The fund offered yields far in excess of what could be achieved on investment grade obligations. Milken literally was able to corner the market by originating, selling, trading, and creating funds in junk bonds, reaping enormous profits for Drexel.

Success led Drexel Burnham into more traditional businesses on Wall Street. But the firm still had an outsider reputation and that attracted outsider clients that were overlooked by the larger investment banks. One of Milken's close associates put the firm's philosophy bluntly when he said that Drexel Burnham's avowed goal was to search out and finance the robber barons of tomorrow. Drexel and Company, because of its original ties with J. P. Morgan seventy-five years before, had helped finance the industrialists of the past, who were often called robber barons. The trick would be to remain at a distance if any of them fell by the wayside, casting shadows over Drexel in the process. Ultimately, Drexel failed in this respect.

By the early 1980s, Drexel was listing gambling casinos, oil and gas companies, and other cyclical companies as its prime clients. The high-yield market attracted many of those that could not find a traditional investment bank for their financings. With the equities markets in the doldrums in the early 1980s, debt had taken increased importance in corporate financing generally and Drexel's emergence was fortuitous. New issues of bonds became the preferred way of financing companies. As a merger and acquisitions boom developed after the stock market's rebound in 1983, junk bond financing continued and became the centerpiece of the trend, especially for doing heavily indebted deals on behalf of the corporate raiders who developed a new method of debt financing called the leveraged buyout.

Within several years of its inception, the junk bond explosion had become the hottest market that Wall Street had experienced in years. In 1983, the market for new junk issues jumped almost 50 percent over the entire existing number of issues outstanding and totaled an estimated $40 billion in par value. Two large deals came to market: one for MGM/UA Entertainment and the other for MCI Communications, which was in the last stages of its battle with AT&T for the right to offer long distance telephone services, breaking the phone company's monopoly. Neither was a highly rated company and both quickly gravitated to Drexel Burnham. Drexel underwrote both issues successfully, adding to its reputation as a new Wall Street powerhouse. Large dollar amount deals were a relatively new phenomenon and the ones that were completed successfully until then had all been done for highly rated companies by established investment banks. Drexel's ratings in the underwriting league tables reflected its newly acquired influence. In 1983 it was ranked as Wall Street's sixth highest underwriter with profits of $150 million. Four years earlier it had earned only $6 million.

In 1982, Congress passed the Depository Institutions Act, or the Garn–St Germain Act, which allowed savings institutions (thrifts) to purchase corporate bonds in order to enhance their return on assets.[30] The law gave Drexel and Milken an enormous boost. Without it, it is doubtful the market for junk would have developed to the next stage in the mid-1980s. Since the Glass-Steagall Act was passed in 1933, no banking institution had been allowed to purchase corporate securities. This new legislation was something of a milestone in banking history. At the time, most observers concluded that it would help the thrift industry regain its feet after several years of losses after 1981, due mostly to rising interest rates and Regulation Q's restrictions on depository institutions. President Reagan announced the signing of the new law with Treasury Secretary Donald Regan at his side, proclaiming it a significant piece of deregulatory legislation that would change the industry. Ironically, within five years it almost destroyed the industry it was designed to save.

The Garn–St Germain Act became the single most important political factor in the growth of the junk bond market. Thrift institutions were able to allocate some of their assets to corporate bonds and Milken quickly moved in to acquaint them with the virtues of high-yield securities. While the yield on investment grade bonds was high, the yield on junk was too tempting because it exceeded quality bonds and even the return on home mortgages—the thrifts' usual asset. What was not immediately apparent was that these bonds were akin to common stock in one important respect. Due to their fragile credit ratings, any slowdown in economic activity would hit them quite hard, making them the first potential victims of an economic downturn.

The mergers and acquisitions increased dramatically in the 1980s. They also created a phenomenon not seen in decades on Wall Street. Many of Drexel Burnham's clients needed money to participate in the boom. Normally, investment bankers provided the capital to finance mergers. But Drexel did not have access to the sort of capital necessary to finance a corporate raider in the 1980s. It lacked a blue chip roster of corporate clients and a pool of capital. But in order to cash in on the merger trend, it simply announced that it had $1 billion to commit to the merger trend. The side of the merger business it would enter with its clients was through the hostile takeover bid. Rather than announcing a target company and then displaying enough cash to buy it fully or partially, the new takeover strategy involved announcing interest in the company first and then attempting to find the necessary cash to finance it after the announcement. Often, the potential buyer had a stake in the company to begin with and the announcement would force up the price of the stock. The potential bidder did not actually want the company but only wanted to sell his holding back to it at a higher price, a process called "greenmail." The arbitrageur Ivan Boesky described it somewhat blandly when he said, "Occasionally, management will buy out a hostile shareholder group even if there is no other bidder. When done at a premium, this is known as greenmail."[31]

Many of Milken's clients entered the arena because of Drexel's commitment to financing their needs even if it was only feigning to have the necessary funds. Most of the famous, or infamous, corporate raiders of the decade were represented by Drexel. In the beginning, Drexel's audacity was nothing short of startling. The nonexistent pool of money that the firm claimed it raised to handle mergers was nicknamed the "Air Fund." One Drexel executive recalled, "We would announce to the world that we had raised one billion dollars for hostile takeovers. There would be no money in this fund—it was just a threat. The Air Fund stood for our not having a client with deep pockets who could be in a takeover. It was a substitute for that client we didn't have."[32]

The stock market's dramatic fall in October 1987, demonstrating once again that a link of excessive debt and equity was inimical to the markets, was the event that brought severe pressure on the economy and the junk bond market. The growing problems of many of the junk bond issuers that followed dried up the secondary junk market at a time when many thrift institutions desperately wanted to sell their holdings. By late 1988, the thrift crisis was emerging as many of the thrifts lost capital as a result of declining junk bonds and real estate loans. As the crisis deepened, many began to blame Milken and Drexel Burnham, noting that they had developed the market in the first place. Events became more complicated when several of Milken's associates and colleagues were indicted for insider trading, using their knowledge of impending merger deals to profit personally. Besides being blamed for the travails of the thrift institutions, the insider trading connections cast Drexel in a very bad light. Once events had been put in motion, it would only be a matter of time before legal charges were filed against Milken. A massive two-hundred-page indictment against him was filed in September 1988, charging insider trading and fraud by the Securities and Exchange Commission (SEC).

At first, Milken refused to settle the charges, claiming he would be vindicated in the end. But the case was too comprehensive. In addition to charges of securities violations, charges were also threatened against him and Drexel under anti-racketeering laws, treating a Wall Street firm in the same way in which organized crime was for influencing organizations engaged in interstate commerce. Separate indictments also were brought against Drexel itself. Rather than face prosecution, the firm settled by agreeing to pay a $650 million fine, the largest ever paid. Unfortunately, the money came from the firm's capital, effectively ending its existence. Milken was charged with over one hundred counts of violating racketeering laws and was sentenced to ten years in prison and fined almost $1 billion. Part of the settlement was based upon the money he earned at Drexel in the 1980s. Between 1983 and 1987, he reportedly earned $1.1 billion from Drexel, earning $550 million in 1987 alone. He served three years of his sentence. After all the publicity concerning the charges and the eventual sentencing, Milken was sentenced for his role in the junk bond market and the savings and loan crisis as much as he was for the actual conspiracy and fraud charges.

Despite the charges eventually brought against Milken and Drexel Burnham, the junk bond concept showed that the speculative elements of what were once known as fallen angels could be channeled into a new market for debt. But it was not the only leveraged instrument or technique used in the 1980s. The takeover of Beatrice Foods, a major food company, began a trend that accomplished some of the most notable deals in merger history. The deal was orchestrated by Kohlberg Kravis Roberts (KKR), a specialized buyout firm that frequently used high degrees of leverage to buy companies and return them to the private sector. The three principals in the firm were among the first to take part in the conglomerate acquisition trend beginning almost twenty years before. They used Drexel Burnham as their investment banker in the Beatrice takeover. Beatrice was a large, diversified company that had extensive interests in areas other than food. It also possessed a management team that KKR sought to replace. The strategy was based on the notion that the company would have more potential value broken up than it did in its current form. Pursuing the strategy, KKR bid $50 per share for Beatrice in 1985 but reconsidered when Drexel informed it that the price was too high and that investors in junk bonds would balk. The price was eventually lowered to $40. When the deal went through, the cost to KKR was $5.6 billion. The firm acquired the company and Drexel Burnham did well with the underwriting fees for the deal.

The buyout firm then went on a spending spree and acquired many well-known brands. By the time it made its bid for RJR Nabisco, the most publicized takeover of the post–World War II period, it had already acquired Beatrice, along with some well-known nationwide retailers. But the largest takeover of the decade, and in history, was certainly the RJR Nabisco takeover, which was engineered in 1988 and completed in 1990. The two companies were originally merged in order to help RJR diversify away from selling tobacco. KKR spotted the company as one with potential for eventual re-structuring. The purchase price paid by RJR was $23 billion, a record. The financing was so large that a host of Wall Street firms and banks were employed in the massive financing. Drexel Burnham was working on the deal when its legal problems were first announced.

Many junk bonds also were used in management buyouts, where a company's managers leveraged themselves to buy the outstanding stock. The Kohlberg Kravis Roberts takeover of RJR Nabisco actually was a buyout, specifically a leveraged buyout. All the borrowed money was used to buy the stock and take the company private. The debt/equity ratios of buyout targets were close to 100 percent debt. Many conglomerates constructed during the 1960s and 1970s began to shed some of their acquisitions and the companies were bought by their management teams. Borrowed money became the tool used to take a company private. Funds were supplied by banks and the junk bond market. The amounts borrowed were so large that actually repaying the debt was not feasible, or affordable. And the restructuring that needed to occur after the deals were completed needed to bring in enough cash to repay the debt and interest when superfluous assets were sold.

Once a buyout was complete, controls imposed upon the managers and workers of the newly acquired company could be stringent. Goals had to be met for the strategy to work in the longer run so that the company could be made more efficient and leaner. The chief executive of one acquired firm commented that his new owners at KKR did not take prisoners if predetermined goals were not met. He related their attitude as, "If you miss the targets, we don't want to know about the dollar, or the weather, or the economy . . . there are negatives if we don't meet those targets."[33] But despite the aggressiveness of the firm, it was dependent upon easy credit flowing from the banks. Without it, most of the leveraged deals would never be completed. The junk bond market by itself could not supply all the necessary funds. The 1980s witnessed such a boom in buyouts that the Federal Reserve began taking notice of the dangers to the banks in general. In 1989, it required banks lending to buyout firms to report their net positions to shareholders once per quarter. Several years before, it had already taken criticism for monetizing the buyout trend by making credit easily available.

The enormous amounts borrowed demonstrated once again that debt was no longer feared by borrowers if debt were employed in what was considered a viable corporate strategy of purchasing and restructuring. The ultimate goal was to sell the private company again to investors, hoping for a profit in the end. The leveraged buyout trend was still in its infancy, but time proved that the earlier deals were more profitable than later ones. Companies that had acquired substantial assets before the severe inflation occurring in the early 1980s were better targets for a buyout than those acquiring assets later, at higher prices. Cheaper assets on balance sheets could be sold for a greater profit when new buyers were found for these old assets, at higher prices after inflation. The strategy had mixed results with RJR Nabisco and other deals in the later 1980s and 1990s.

The leveraged buyout trend was a test of the Modigliani-Miller theory in its most practical form. The idea that leverage did not matter as long as a company produced profits certainly was put to the acid test with a buyout the size of RJR Nabisco. While it displayed the tenacity of the principals involved in the deal, it also displayed the confidence that participating investors had in accumulating debt on such an enormous scale. As long as the goal or profitability could be met and it could be managed properly, the risks of insolvency were ignored. Asset reshuffling was becoming the norm in corporate America and the leveraged buyout business contributed to the trend. The same could not be said for many of the LDCs suffering during the same time period, however. Unlike their corporate brethren, LDCs had nothing but their commodity-based revenues to service their debt. When they declined, the sovereign version of bankruptcy was only a short step away.

Sovereign Defaults

Although bankers claimed that sovereign defaults were extremely rare in international banking, several notable examples occurred both before and after the LDC crisis. In fact, sovereign defaults could be traced back to the 1890s when a South American debt crisis helped bring the Baring Brothers to the brink of insolvency. But in the modern era, only Cuba and a handful of other marginal borrowers such as Yemen, Nicaragua, and Iran were considered "exotics" because of their default records.

After Fidel Castro overthrew the existing government of Cuba in 1959, the new government repudiated all the country's external debt. Castro also expropriated American enterprises in the country, valued at the time at around $1 billion. The debt has not yet been repaid, although Cuba has borrowed again, mostly from enterprises or countries eager to do business with it. But the original bonds are still outstanding. Over the years, they have traded sporadically in a unique sector of the bond market reserved for exotic debt. Although many of the bonds have already matured, they still have a value when traded, even if infrequently. Their putative value is greater than zero, a position that traditional investors find difficult to understand. But the lesson learned from Cuban debt is that speculative forces create a value where none is normally expected. This premise gave these bonds a minimal value and also opened the door for a new market for less-than-investment grade debt in the United States a few decades later.

The price of distressed debt was not worthless because of investors attracted to this sort of debt obligation. The bond prices displayed an elasticity that created a heavily discounted price when none would have been expected at all. The gambit was, and is, mostly political. If Cuba ever returned to the market-oriented sector again, went the argument, it would be required to pay off its repudiated debt before being allowed to borrow again. Its patron, Russia, had repudiated the debts of Tsarist Russia in 1918 but had to make a token payment in the late 1980s when it reentered the international debt markets.[34] In such cases, holders of the debt have a chance to make a windfall gain by surrendering bonds bought for pennies in the hope of receiving some significant portion of par when a settlement is reached. As a result, seemingly worthless debt displays price elasticity that is based upon an anticipation of future events.

The worst sovereign debt crisis since the 1980s occurred in 1998 when Russia officially defaulted on its external debt. This default had more widespread repercussions than many other international defaults because Russian debt obligations were held by a growing number of hedge funds, a relatively new type of trader and investor in the international debt markets. Given Russia's status on the international stage, the default was not anticipated, as those of many exotics and Latin American nations had been in the past.

The events leading to the default began several years earlier as the Russians attempted to cope with the remaining debt of the old Soviet Union. Then in 1997, an economic calamity struck the Pacific Rim countries, which had been experiencing an economic boom and an influx of foreign capital as a result. The result was the "Asian contagion," a crisis that undermined the region's economies and reputation for years to come. Many of the portfolio investments that had been quick to find attractive returns quickly exited, leaving the local markets and economies in disarray.

After the fall of Soviet communism, the Russians experienced high inflation and interest rates. In 1995, inflation approached 250 percent and short-term interest rates were over 100 percent. Wages in the country were falling and over 60 percent of workers' salaries were not being paid on time.[35] Stories abounded of rising domestic prices as the ruble weakened on the foreign exchange markets; the price of a hamburger at a fast-food restaurant in Moscow exceeded a month's average salary. At the time, the price of oil, a major Russian source of foreign exchange, was in the mid-$20 range per barrel but weakened in 1998, precipitating a ruble crisis. Finally, in August 1998 the ruble was devalued, payments to foreign creditors of domestic banks suspended, and payments on foreign external debt suspended. The IMF stepped in with assistance totaling $23 billion to support the restructuring effort.

The Russian default also was remembered for a particular incident that overshadowed the actual event itself, at least in the United States. After the default on external debt, a financial crisis in the United States was precipitated when a hedge fund, Long-Term Capital Management, collapsed and required assistance from its bankers, orchestrated by the Federal Reserve. The incident cast light on a traditionally shadowy area of the financial markets—bond arbitrage—and displayed financial connections previously ignored or thought unimportant.

Long-Term Capital Management was highly leveraged, using large amounts of borrowed money to trade and arbitrage bonds. In this particular case, the arbitrage was between U.S. Treasury securities and their Russian counterparts. The difference in yields between the two sectors was considered too wide and the arbitrage was intended to take advantage of it, assuming it would close to a narrower gap. The assumption again was made that sovereign defaults did not occur and that the cross-market arbitrage was not as risky as it appeared from the outside. But when the Russian default occurred, the prices of the bonds collapsed and investors rushed to buy U.S. Treasuries as a safe haven investment. The hedge fund was long (held) Russian bonds at the time and short (sold) Treasuries, the opposite position from that which would have profited from the trade. As a result, both positions lost and the hedge funds' capital immediately was in peril.

Adding insult to injury was the ostensible investment theory the hedge fund employed. It claimed that its positions were relatively safe because it purportedly employed risk management techniques designed by two Nobel Prize winners, Myron Scholes and Robert Merton, who were both principals with the hedge fund. Scholes was one of the originators of the Black-Scholes options model, developed at the same time Bretton Woods collapsed. Since that time, the original equity options model had been extended to other financial instruments as well. Merton was well known for his empirical work on the efficient markets hypothesis, the predominant theory concerning how stock markets operate in a world where there is no asymmetry of information.

A group of banks, primarily lenders to Long-Term Capital, was organized by the Fed to provide funds in order to stabilize the hedge fund so that it would not have to default on its loans to the same banks. Although the hedge fund survived after the rescue in a greatly diminished form, the esoteric world of bond arbitrage had been made public, although briefly. The collapse served to cast further shadows over the assumption that sovereign states do not default since Russia, unlike the LDCs in the 1980s, did not follow the procedures established during the prior crisis but simply risked its reputation in the international credit markets in a gambit that it would be welcomed back eventually.

Although Russia in 1918 established something of a precedent that a regime change often signaled default on debt obligations, the default in 2001 by Argentina on its external obligations had a longer history. Despite the claims made by bankers during the 1970s and 1980s, many sovereign states had defaulted on their debts since the nineteenth century, especially those in Latin America.[36] Some, like Argentina, regularly defaulted during the downturn of most major economic cycles and were no strangers to debt renegotiations. But since the international markets for trans-border lending based on Eurodollars was relatively new, history began with it as far as most lenders were concerned. According to this, in the new international arena, sovereign states would not be so foolish as to default. The exotics were small countries with little to lose by adopting radical ideologies and repudiating their debt.

During the LDC crisis, Argentina among others used Brady bonds to restructure its debts.[37] In 1991, it adopted a currency board, a policy that linked its currency directly to the U.S. dollar. The new arrangement produced some stability and prosperity, but the Asian contagion and its effects in Latin America, forcing a Brazilian devaluation among other notable events, created a new currency crisis because the Argentine public sector was heavily indebted. By the end of the decade, the spread over U.S. Treasuries that Argentina had to pay on its dollar-denominated debt became extremely wide. By 2001, it amounted to almost 1,000 basis points (10 percent). While the country had always faced high spreads, that was a record and directly contributed to the events that unfolded later that year.

From the beginning of its 1990 currency and debt crisis, Argentina suffered under a high interest rate regime, both domestically and internationally. Domestic pesos reflected the country's monetary policies while dollar LIBOR charged on its loans reflected its spotty credit history and economic problems. The high interest rates caused social problems that did little to help the country economically. One of the country's leading industrialists complained that high peso interest rates were creating a situation where "there are entire provinces where people live without working... countries can't function that way," he remarked, asking, "How many civilized countries are there where it is possible to make fortunes doing absolutely nothing?"[38] He was referring to the high interest earned on simple bank deposits that many people were able to live on without working or creating value.

There was a paradox in the U.S. dollar interest rates paid by Argentina when compared to those paid by much poorer countries. Because Argentina, along with Brazil and Mexico, were considered middle income countries by international lenders and the IMF, they paid higher than average market rates for their debt. Poorer countries often were able to borrow for the long term from programs at the World Bank or other regional development banks at subsidized rates, taking into account their low levels of national income and lack of infrastructure. In a sense, the poor countries paid less than the wealthier countries, a fact not lost on those dependent upon international banking loans. What the poorer countries did not have was a constant source of capital from banks, however.

In 2001, the peso was under extreme pressure, with many Argentines converting their domestic currency holdings to U.S. dollars. The collapsing peso also impoverished many and unemployment soared. Pressure on the banking sector led the government to declare a banking holiday in December in order to prevent a collapse of the banks. On Christmas Eve, the country defaulted on its debt because it no longer had the resources to service it. The defaulted amount was approximately equivalent to $82 billion, making it the largest Latin American sovereign default on record. Argentina wisely did not default on its obligations to international institutions such as the World Bank because those lenders were too valuable to it at the end of the day.

The devaluation of the peso and the suspension of interest payments helped the Argentine economy recover over the next several years. Finally in 2005, the government of Nestor Kirchner made an offer to exchange new bonds for the old. Investors lost approximately 75 percent of their original principal through the exchange since the new bonds amounted to only 25 percent of the old. The terms were made as a "take it or leave it" deal and accepted by a large majority of the existing bondholders. Some commentators remarked that the resolution of the default in 2005 did not punish the country for its behavior and that its default and recovery occurred without much international incident.

While sovereign near-defaults were not new to international finance, the speed with which they were recurring and the threats of future defaults began to change attitudes toward debt in general. The restructurings as a result of the LDC debt crisis of the 1980s managed to keep the international banks from collapsing and preserved the credit lines of most of the countries involved, although they came with a cost. During the period that the Brady bonds were outstanding, many countries that used them experienced little economic growth, using their revenues to service their restructured debt instead. That arrangement suited the banks but was not well received in Latin America especially, where many leaders privately agreed with Fidel Castro that the deck was stacked against them regardless of their economic circumstances.

The idea of filing for international bankruptcy became popular in the 1990s in recognition of the political problem and the LDC problem in general. Why not allow countries the same protections from creditors that both personal and business borrowers received in the United States when they filed for bankruptcy protection? The idea was novel, but it was thought that it would allow an orderly sorting out of a country's economic affairs. In many restructurings, creditors were not in agreement on how best to settle debts, with some accepting less while others held out for full restitution. The resulting negotiations could be prolonged and unsatisfactory. Jeffrey Sachs, who helped advise Russia among others after its default, maintained that "the free-for-all—letting the market do it—doesn't work."[39] But consensus on how to implement an authority to sort out debt problems internationally did not appeal to many lenders, who feared that any structured system would be abused worse than the old ad hoc system that had been used for decades.

The debt revolution of the twentieth century proved that attitudes toward indebtedness were changing. Constantly increasing amounts of debt and the willingness of many debtors to threaten default began to make the idea of heavy indebtedness passé. The moral stigma attached to being a bankrupt had long since disappeared. Debt now was nothing more than just another financial option when all others failed. This was the American view, but it was not shared by all.

Chapter 7

Islam, Interest, and Microlending

Microfinance is an idea whose time has come.
—Kofi Annan, 2003

Developments in finance were centered mostly in New York and London after World War II. New financial theories, products, and practices developed at a torrid pace, beginning in the 1950s, and by the 2000s most of the developed world had adopted them in one form or other. But in the developing world, and in the Islamic world in particular, not much had changed for centuries. Banking was relatively primitive by Western standards and religious prohibitions held great sway over financial practices, much as they had in the West centuries before.

By the late 1970s, usury prohibitions still were a problem in the United States but could be avoided by regulatory arbitrage. If a jurisdiction prohibited high interest rates, lenders could simply find others in which to base their lending activities. Attitudes toward usury varied. In some locales it was taken seriously while in others it was nothing more than an outdated nuisance law that needed repeal. And new financial products were making usury laws a paper tiger, long since having lost their teeth in the face of complicated financial innovation.

In more traditional societies, the opposite was true. Usury laws were taken very seriously. In many Islamic societies, religious law—*sharia*—was taken literally. Usury was prohibited by the Koran and many sacred texts in the Muslim world, and time had not changed attitudes toward it. Ironically, as in the West, banks charged interest but when disputes arose between borrowers and lenders, religious courts normally held for borrowers. As in the West eight hundred years before, the debate over usury took on an academic, almost casuistical tone. As discussions about *riba* (interest) and different forms of financial products offered in Islamic countries became more sophisticated, it became clear that Islamic thought about usury owed much to the practices of pre-Islamic Arabs, Aristotle, Justinian, and the Scholastics. Many of the ancient and medieval ideas about usury were preserved in the Islamic tradition, making them difficult to understand in the modern world. Prohibitions against interest were based upon a notion of social equity. Business practices had to benefit the parties involved and risk had to be shared equally. Any hint of *riba* was put to the religious acid test and invariably found failing. The Koran and the sacred texts simply did not allow interest, presenting an enormous problem to modern Islamic bankers. Modern Islamic finance attempted to accommodate both sides of the issue, although not all agreed on its success.

The Islamic ban on *riba* did not mean that charging and paying interest was not practiced in most of the Muslim world. But the tension between religious doctrine and banking practice created a moral rift that persisted for centuries. The lack of economic development in many parts of the Islamic and Arab worlds in particular has been attributed to this tension. The logical outcome of many arguments about *riba* was that anyone who practiced it was acting in a manner banned by scripture. Therefore, economic development was antithetical to the word of God. As long as that attitude prevailed, capital investment and fixed return on investment operated under a cloud dominated by the spirit of Aristotle rather than Adam Smith.

Financial modernity finally invaded the Islamic world in the early 1970s. The economic turmoil of the 1970s and 1980s created a new economic balance of power. Many of the oil producers found themselves in the position of having immeasurable wealth flowing into their economies while possessing banking systems unable to cope with the vast inflow of funds. At the same time, many of the non-oil-producing LDCs in the Islamic world and elsewhere still were mired in poverty, unable to participate in the new gold rush caused by higher oil prices. Initially, the two worlds used the Western banking system as an intermediary of funds between rich and poor. But the results were clearly unsatisfactory as volatile interest rates impoverished many LDCS during the 1980s.

The same economic phenomena that caused widespread misery among the LDCs and their bankers in Europe and the United States also caused severe tensions between business practices and religious law. Practically, many businessmen had to deal with international banks in their daily business affairs while turning a blind eye toward usury if they held Islamic religious beliefs. Oil revenues created tensions in many of these traditional societies. As many Islamic societies developed economically, compliance with *sharia* in finance became accepted as an integral part of broader nationalist movements that were attempting to distance themselves from Western politics and finance.

The greatest challenge to the Islamic prohibition against interest occurred after the price of OPEC oil began to rise in the early 1970s. Many of the foreign exchange reserves of the central banks of OPEC members were invested in dollar-denominated international bonds, clearly creating a moral dilemma for the investors that otherwise professed to be true to Islam. The same was true for businessmen from OPEC countries who faced a religious dilemma by investing profits for the future. Buying bonds was relatively safe but frowned upon, so other alternatives presented themselves that increased counterparty, event, or credit risk. Interest rate risk technically was not part of the equation. Profit itself was not prohibited by Islamic law; trading for a reasonable gain had been part of the barter and (later) money traditions since antiquity. But usury again had taken center stage after centuries. Until the nineteenth century under the Ottoman Empire, Western style banking was unknown in Arab countries, and when the Ottomans began borrowing from foreign banks the experience was new. But after the oil price shocks in the 1970s, new Arab and Islamic banking institutions were being founded. As in the West centuries before, money was demanding a rate of return and interest was the safest and most predictable form. A clear tension was being created between religion and business that needed to be resolved.

There was an element of politics and revenge in the rise in the price of oil. Under IMF guidelines, any country wishing to devalue its currency in order to redress a trade imbalance was required to apply to the agency in order to arrange an orderly change in its currency alignment in consultation with major trading partners. When the United States unilaterally devalued the dollar, causing the breakdown of the Bretton Woods system, it effectively devalued the purchasing power of many foreigners whose main revenues were in dollars by around 20 percent. The devaluation was unilateral, ignoring the IMF in the process. As a result many holders of dollar assets were shocked by the devaluation, which was dubbed the "Nixon shock."[1] A subsequent markup of oil prices naturally followed. The oil producers seemed intent on recovering their lost revenues by pushing up the price. When they did, the results caused a major change in direction for Islamic finance.

Almost thirty years later, that shock was followed by another that would have a profound effect on Islamic financial institutions and markets. After the terrorist attacks on September 11, 2001, a large amount of funds held in the United States and Europe by depositors and investors in Islamic countries began to be repatriated. A general fear arose that future transfers of cash and investment would be blocked as authorities sought to block money transfers that they construed could possibly be used as funding to terrorists. Many of these funds returned to their countries of origin, benefiting the growing Islamic financial sector. As a result of prior growth plus the influx of new funds, the Islamic markets began to grow in size and importance. New international agencies were established to span the Islamic world with the aim of fostering *sharia*-based investments as well as market liberalization policies and tax neutrality policies designed to stimulate cross-border investments and encourage foreign investors. Islamic markets grew rapidly as a result, although they had to abide by basic religious principles, giving them their unique characteristics.

The Traditional Islamic View of Usury

Many Islamic countries experienced strong nationalist movements in the wake of the increased revenues in the 1970s and bankers recognized both the need for compliance with religious law and the profit opportunities that the massive influx of funds created. Fusing the Islamic and Western banking traditions resurrected many debates that had been heard centuries before in Europe about usury and interest. Structured finance helped resolve the problem of fusing the traditional and the modern in the same manner it had aided American housing finance twenty-five years before.

Of all the prohibitions against undesirable activities in the Koran, usury is mentioned the most. Interest, or *riba*, is considered usury and no distinction is made between them. The terms are interchangeable and the prohibition is immutable. Unlike the Christian tradition, there was no confusion with compound interest. The term was understood and compound interest itself was common among Arabs in particular before the advent of Islam. The practice was *alterum tantum* in its classic form. The Koran forbade it in very specific terms: "O ye who believe. Devour not usury, doubling and quadrupling (the sum lent). Observe your duty to Allah, that ye may be successful."[2] Similar to the medieval Christian tradition, no exceptions or modifications were made to the precepts of religious law, and none were allowed to exist alongside it.

Two examples demonstrate the contrasting attitudes of the two traditions. When Bernard of Clairvaux first saw Notre Dame in Paris being built, he exclaimed, "Wealth is drawn up by ropes of wealth . . . thus money bringeth money." The archbishop of Paris used donations from usurers to help complete the construction of the cathedral. In contrast, when the holiest shrine in Saudi Arabia, the Ka'bah, was being refurbished even before the introduction of Islam in the seventh century, a stipulation was made that no income from usury was to be accepted as a donation, stating that only "clean wealth" was to be used. Income from usury was considered polluted and undesirable by Arabs of the pre-Islamic period, who were often referred to as pagan Arabs.[3] After the establishment of Islam, usury was prohibited completely.

The usury prohibitions in Islam and Christianity were similar until the Middle Ages, when the Christian tradition, although deploring usury, began to make allowances for it. The same could not be said of Islam, at least in theory. Consumption loans were tolerated but had to be made free of interest. The reasons were similar to those in Christianity: charging interest on a consumption loan was inequitable because the borrower probably would never be able to pay the interest and thus would be at the mercy of the lender. Not charging interest made the parties to a loan closer in terms of fairness. Interest, in contrast, gave the lender the upper hand, which he would exploit inevitably.

After the oil crisis of the 1970s discussions ensued, both condemning interest and devising clever ways to pay bank depositors a fixed rate of return. This paradoxical situation marked the beginning of an Islamic movement to develop alternative methods of finance to those used in the West. Once indigenous banks became established in the 1970s, most practiced traditional Western-style banking, including paying interest on deposits and charging it on loans. Only a small percentage of banking was done with *sharia* compliance in mind. Part of this paradox was due to the lack of financial expertise necessary to structure and market Islamic banking products. Paying traditional interest was much easier than designing deposits that were based on profit rather than *riba*. Loan revenue usually supplies the funds necessary to pay deposit interest, so any change from one side of the equation would require a change in the other. When banking was still in its infancy in many parts of the Islamic world, that sort of change was not possible until modern finance lent it a helping hand.

Not all Islamic sources considered paying a fixed rate of return on bank deposits to be strictly forbidden. Over the last 150 years, many Islamic scholars and jurists have issued *fatwas* (pronouncements) on the topic, both approving and disapproving fixed bank returns on deposits. Some have claimed that such fixed rates were simply *riba* while others have claimed that paying a fixed rate (never called interest) is a form of partnership, or profit sharing (*mudarabah*) arrangement in which counterparty risk is present, validating the transaction. Pronouncements from Islamic courts and jurists in Pakistan especially condemned any practice that smacked of *riba*. But in 2002, the situation changed in favor of allowing a fixed return based upon a *fatwa* issued by Al-Azhar Islamic Research Institute in Egypt. Because of the high academic and religious standing of the institution, its *fatwa* began to convince some doubters that paying a fixed return on deposits was in compliance with Islamic law.

This particular *fatwa* was issued in response to a letter sent to Muhammad Sayyid, the rector of Al-Azhar, by the chairman of the Arab Banking Corporation. In the letter, the chairman described a simple deposit transaction, asking for Sayyid's opinion: "Customers of the International Arab Banking Corporation forward their funds and savings to the bank to use and invest them in its permissible dealings, in exchange for profit distributions that are predetermined, and the distribution times are likewise agreed upon with the customer. We respectfully ask you for the legal status of this dealing."[4] The controversial part of this request was the word "predetermined." Profits agreed between parties before a transaction occurred often were equated with *riba*.

Sayyid agreed with the bank. "This dealing, in this form, is permissible," he stated, "without any doubt of impermissibility. This follows from the fact that no canonical text in the Koran or the prophetic Sunna forbids this type of transaction within which profits or returns are pre-specified, as long as the transaction is concluded with mutual consent."[5] This opinion has been repeated and cited many times, conveying the impression that a highly respected *fatwa* condoned payment of interest. But the opinion followed established practice. Those who thought it was just a backdoor to accepting *riba* continued to criticize the ruling while others saw it as another step in developing more sophisticated Islamic banking practices.

More specifically, there are two types of *riba*—surplus *riba* and credit *riba*. Both are sales transactions. Surplus *riba* is a sale with an increase in the capital assets involved in a transaction above legal standards in an exchange of like kinds. Credit *riba* is a preference for immediate payment over postponement, a sale of one kind for another or for a different kind with an excess in volume against a delay of payment.[6] The term "sale" implies a profit of some sort but the distinction is clear. The relationship between interest and profit is a fine but distinct one in Islamic thought. Why prohibit one while encouraging the other? Bankers for centuries considered interest their profit for lending money. That simple distinction became the source of much debate in Islamic religious thought, much as it had in Europe in the Middle Ages. In Islamic thought, *riba* was prohibited because it involved reward without any sort of commensurate risk by the lender. Trading relationships between two parties did fulfill the standard of commensurate risk, as did partnership arrangements.

This idea of mutuality provides the underlying basis for the development of Islamic financial products, many of which are patterned after Western products but still retain their unique nature. As many of these new products developed, other mechanical and theoretical problems appeared, challenging the notion that Islamic products were indeed unique or asking whether they were simply a variation of more familiar financial services sold elsewhere. The mechanics of many of these products often replicated established Western financial instruments but remained true to their ethical principles, but not without some controversy nevertheless.

Islamic Financial Products

In the Middle Ages, partnership arrangements for oceanic shipping helped develop the first types of property and casualty insurance contracts, avoiding allegations of usury in the process. Life insurance developed several centuries later, after tontines were introduced. Islamic finance also wrestled with life insurance as understood in Europe and the United States and concluded in most instances that it was nothing more than a disguised form of *riba* and therefore prohibited. Along with a prohibition against bonds, this became one of the factors retarding the passing of wealth from one generation to the next while at the same time leaving a serious gap in Islamic risk management.

Also central to the banning of insurance was the concept of *gharar*—uncertainty or risk. Risk that was not shared was nothing more than outright speculation, prohibited by *sharia*. The theory behind the banning of *riba* and *gharar* is explained most succinctly as the prohibition against unbundled credit and unbundled risk.[7] Interest is not structured to be shared by both parties to a credit transaction and the risk involved equally is open-ended, intended to benefit one party only. The same sort of prohibition originally was extended to other financial products such as futures contracts, considered a form of *gharar*. Any financial practice that involved a zero-sum game was considered gambling.

The argument against life insurance held that insurance contracts were a form of gambling since they paid out much more than was paid in through premiums. Since gambling was (in theory) a prohibited activity, life insurance in particular could not be condoned. The idea of betting against someone's life was also frowned upon as being contrary to the spirit of Islam. Furthermore, traditional insurance companies relied on bonds for a large proportion of their investment returns so compliance with *sharia* was not possible unless an Islamic product was devised that would pay a return to the insurers free of *riba*. As with other Islamic financial products, many *fatwas* were issued on both sides of the issue.

The central idea behind Islamic insurance is the concept of *takaful*, or mutual guarantee. This concept was practiced in the pre-Islamic Arab world and is generally assumed to be the Islamic equivalent of insurance, but there are differences. Adopting the idea of a partnership, a mutual guarantee company providing insurance would involve the policyholders acting in partnership with the company itself, sharing gains and losses.[8] This is akin to a mutual insurance company in the United States or Britain, but the idea of both equity ownership and sharing in profit or loss prevails in the Islamic model. In the traditional Western insurance model, premiums paid by policyholders are invested by the insurance company, the profits to be distributed to shareholders. In Islamic terms, this is an inequity between the two sides; in a *takaful* arrangement the policyholders are also shareholders and any potential profits are shared by the policyholders, technically the owners of the insurance funds. This was based upon an ancient liability concept among pre-Islamic Arabs that pooled funds to pay for damages demanded by heirs of those who had been killed by members of the tribe. The concept spread later to other types of activity, including maritime adventures, to compensate anyone who suffered a loss at sea. In this latter respect, it shared a heritage with Western maritime insurance, which was recognized early as necessary for overseas exploration and trade.

Attitudes began to change about insurance, and life insurance in particular, after Islamic banking began to develop. Insurance began to be viewed as a risk management technique that aided business and was not simply a bet against life, death, or bad fortune. But the spirit of *takaful* had to be followed. Investment gains or losses in the insurance fund were shared by policyholders and a fixed return was not guaranteed in order to avoid *riba*. Once the mechanics had been settled, life and health policies could be offered. In all cases, the principles of joint indemnity and common, shared responsibility had to be followed.

Other Islamic investments also are designed to ensure that *riba* is not involved and does not enter through the back door. For those banks that adhere to *sharia*, deposits and other traditional banking instruments that ordinarily bear interest are designed like mutual funds or unit trusts, giving the customer a return on the deposit that is structured as profit in the underlying investments. This may be more risky than a traditional interest-bearing deposit account because the fund manager must find suitable investments for the deposits and they may not include *riba* either. Further, in keeping with *sharia*, fund investments are not permitted in what are considered unsuitable investments; in addition to not receiving interest, investments in companies that engage in gambling or fostering unacceptable social activities or products are prohibited. Those prohibited activities include investing in banks that carry on traditional interest activities. When Saudi investors made sizable investments in American banks in the 1990s and 2000s during times of financial crisis, their investments were structured as preferred stocks rather than bonds. Preferreds were a form of fixed income investment but paid dividends rather than interest, avoiding *riba*.

Unsuitable investments would include investing in companies that are engaged in interest-charging activities, producing alcohol or pork products, gambling, or any of what Wall Street or the City of London would refer to as the "sin" industries. But even when determining the suitability of a stock for investment, *riba* still is considered. In addition to its basic business activities, a company's balance sheet is analyzed to determine if it derives a portion of its profit from interest. Banks and financial services companies naturally are excluded, but non-financial companies also come under scrutiny. Most standard analytic tools for screening include comparing a company's accounts receivables to its market capitalization or total assets. In general, a ratio of over 49 percent (receivables to market capitalization) means that the revenues are being derived at least in part by credit granted to others and therefore precludes it from compliance. If compared to total assets, the ratio should be no higher than 70 percent.[9]

The drop in oil prices reduced revenues in the OPEC and non-OPEC oil producers after 1983. Saudi Arabia experienced a 75 percent drop in revenues between 1980 and 1985. That had an adverse effect on many domestic Saudi companies, although imports remained strong as the country continued to spend despite the declining revenues. The Saudi banking sector was especially hard hit as many individuals and companies reneged on their debts. Some were banks with part foreign ownership, charging interest to borrowers. The decline had consequences that were not anticipated by bankers. When borrowers and lenders found themselves in court to settle debts, the Islamic courts usually financially found in favor of the borrower, even if the bank won the case. Borrowers had the accrued interest deducted from the amount owed, in compliance with *sharia*. As a result, bankers grew more reluctant to make loans. "The courts are basically on the side of the Saudi borrower," one banker commented.[10]

Investment guidelines and practices are monitored by Islamic clerics and jurists who form committees to ensure that the new financial products are comply with *sharia*. The committees also help engineer and market the new products, acting as expert consultants to the investment bankers who do the actual design and packaging. But as the market for Islamic products exploded in the 2000s, criticisms arose that the products were watered down substantially or simply were not compliant. Sheikh Muhammad Taqi Usmani, of the Accounting and Auditing Organization for Islamic Financial Institutions, a regulatory institution that sets standards for the global industry, said that 85 percent of *sukuk* (Islamic certificates of investment, mistakenly called bonds) were not compliant with *sharia*, despite claims to the contrary. As the BBC news noted, "Usmani is the granddaddy of modern-day Islamic finance, so having him make this statement is synonymous with Adam Smith saying that free-markets are inefficient."[11]

Much of the problem complicating compliance was the sheer number of Islamic products issued versus the number of competent *sharia* scholars available to rule on their soundness. Because of the extra due diligence banks, mainly in London, had to do to ensure compliance, complaints arose about the extra costs involved in issuing *sukuk* rather than other forms of traditional financing. One expert in Islamic finance stated simply that "the main beneficiaries are lawyers, multi-national banks, and self-styled religious scholars retained as consultants to certify the Islamicity of re-engineered financial products."[12] A news agency dubbed the experts, "Million Dollar Scholars" because of the fees the top Islamic scholars were reported to earn as a result of their consulting activities. Furthermore, each structured product required a *fatwa* to be issued and critics maintained that issuing so many undermined the value of the *fatwa* in general.

The prohibition against *riba* made certain financial products that were well known outside the Muslim world impossible to implement and that in turn impeded economic development in many Islamic countries since the traditional source of funds, namely private lending or interest-free lending, was limited. In the late 1990s, Islamic banking principles began to be developed in Europe to serve the growing Muslim communities there. An Arab bank began offering *sharia*-compliant mortgages in Britain in 1997. The Islamic term for this type of product is a *murabaha* mortgage. Islamic financial products retain their Arabic names rather than translate into English. This term means a cost plus mark-up transaction. The structure of the mortgage avoided interest in favor of profit. A seller wanting to sell his home to a potential buyer sold it to the bank instead and the bank then sold it at the higher price to the buyer. The buyer paid the increased amount in installments that carefully avoided interest, with the financier booking the difference in prices as profit. In order to avoid excessive paperwork, the buyer of the property is considered to act as the financier's agent in the transaction, technically buying and selling the property to himself.[13]

The *murabaha* concept currently is the major underlying theme of many *sharia*-compliant products. Its use is so widespread that one commentator referred to it as the "*murabaha* syndrome."[14] The structure predominantly used for financing is a debt instrument, while strict compliance with the religious precepts would suggest that an equity partnership investment (*musharakah*) should be used instead to demonstrate joint indemnity and the sharing of any gains or losses. This has long-term implications for the capital structure of entities that rely heavily on *murabaha* financing. Indebtedness increases on balance sheets, often replacing equity, providing a contradiction for those professing to be true to Islamic financial principles. Debt should, at least in theory, be subordinate to equity but often dominates Islamic financing.

By the early 2000s, the market for *sharia*-based financial services was estimated at around $200 billion. Despite the rapid growth of the sector, Islamic banking still was not the norm in most Islamic countries. Islamic banks increased their share of bank deposits in the Muslim world over the two decades since they were founded, but the numbers grew gradually rather than dramatically. Kuwait, Jordan, and Saudi Arabia were among the oldest and largest of the Islamic banking centers, beginning *sharia*-compliant deposits in 1977, 1978, and 1988 respectively. But growth was modest. Jordan began with 7 percent of its deposits falling under Islamic guidelines and the percentages remained the same in 2000. Kuwait declined from 18 percent to 15.5 percent during the same general time period, while Saudi Arabia increased from 11 percent to 13 percent. Sudan, despite the absence of oil revenues, had the highest percentage in the late 1990s at close to 30 percent.[15] In Malaysia, with the largest Muslim population, *sharia*-compliant deposits remained negligible, although the debate surrounding Islamic products continued unabated. Despite *fatwas* against interest, the debate extended well into the 2000s. A local Malaysian newspaper reported in 2010, "Despite the *Sharia* ban on usury, Islamic financial products are routinely priced using conventional rates such as London Interbank Offered Rates (LIBOR) in the absence of a *Sharia* compliant benchmark."[16] The absence of a suitable benchmark retarded the growth of Islamic banking, especially among more than a generation of Islamic businesses that had grown accustomed to British and American banking styles and services.

Of all the new Islamic financial products, the Islamic certificate of investment, or *sakk*, is the most paradoxical on the surface. *Sukuk* (plural) are generally referred to as bonds outside the Islamic world, although that term is problematic. By its very nature, a bond is a debt instrument with periodic interest payments attached. A *sakk* is the same except that the payments are structured as profit rather than as *riba*. This is accomplished by incorporating established Western financial vehicles and fitting them to be compliant with *sharia*. The shell structure for this is the special purpose vehicle (SPV), the same instrument used in securitization on Wall Street and the City of London. In this case, it also holds segregated assets for investors. Many of the early *sukuk* paid their revenues from a series of bundled leases, known as *ijara*, that were fitted into *sukuk* structures.

Technically, the SPV buys a pool of revenue-producing assets and then passes the income stream produced to the bondholders in lieu of interest payments. When the bond matures, the SPV administrator will conclude the transaction by selling the assets, returning the principal to the bondholders. The packaging process resembles in part an asset-backed security (ABS) in the American bond market. It also resembles the packaging for revenue bonds in the municipal bond market, based upon specific municipal revenues to repay principal and interest. As with revenue bonds, the borrowing process is more complicated and the quality of the bond riskier than if it were a simple general obligation (*pari passu*) obligation. Critics argued that the final product was nothing more than a sheepish bond disguised in wolf's clothing to satisfy *sharia*. But the packaging and marketing proved successful. The number of *sukuk* began to increase dramatically.

The use of Islamic bonds also revived the old issue of usufruct and its role in the long history of usury and interest. Unlike the debate that usufruct sparked in Roman and early Christian thought, usufruct fitted neatly into Islamic finance because of the profit element. *Sukuk* can be issued for the usufruct of an asset under certain conditions. The *ijara* is an example. If a lessee of an asset legally is able to sublease the asset with consent from the lessor, then the lessee can legally issue a *sukuk* passing the revenues to bondholders, considered the owners of the usufruct itself (an investment *sukuk*). This is different from a *murabaha sukuk*, which collects funds to purchase the asset itself, which can be sold. In either case, the ownership of assets is clear and complies with the religious law. The original definition of a usufruct in Justinian's *Institutes* prevailed. An investor could benefit from the fruits of an investment, although he may not have been the owner of the revenue-producing assets.

Islamic financial products proved cyclical, increasing and decreasing with the price of crude oil. The investment banking deals were done mostly in London or in the Middle Eastern financial centers. In 2004, $7 billion in *sukuk* were issued; in 2006, $27 billion due to the increase in the price of oil. In 2010, the new issue amount rose again to $51 billion.[17] Throughout the late 1990s and 2000s, the number of issuers steadily increased. Borrowers ranged from companies to sovereign states to Islamic international finance agencies such as the Islamic Development Bank, which was founded in 1975 to promote Islamic finance and Islamic capital markets. Many non-Islamic borrowers also took advantage of the market as a source of funds, with borrowers ranging from a German *land* (state) to Japanese and Chinese borrowers to a British luxury car manufacturer.

The issue for the German state of Saxony Anhalt was an example of a usufruct or *ijara sukuk*. Sold to investors in 2004, the *sukuk* were denominated in euros and were technically an obligation of a specially designed Dutch trust. The trust paid a lump sum as rent for a long-term lease on a property owned by Saxony's Ministry of Finance. This meant that the holders of the bonds owned the usufruct of the properties for the life of the bond. Similar usufructs were used for housing projects in the Saudi cities of Mecca and Medina in order to maintain ownership of the land in official government hands.[18]

Issuing *sukuk* by non-Islamic borrowers was not without controversy, however. In 2007, Great Britain announced plans to issue a *sukuk* in order to cement its reputation as the major financial center for Islamic finance. It would have been the first Western nation with plans to do so. The borrowing was to be structured as an *ijara sukuk* with specific government assets leased to an SPV used to generate revenue to be paid to *sukuk* holders. When the term of the *sukuk* was finished, the government would buy back the asset to pay off the debt. But the idea encountered difficulty from many who saw it as bowing to the wealth of Arab investors or selling out national interests to foreigners. One London newspaper described it as leading to "the ownership of Government buildings and other assets currently belonging to British taxpayers being switched to wealthy Middle Eastern businessmen and banks."[19] The controversial financing eventually was postponed indefinitely.

The Dubai Default

Some of the intrinsic riskiness of *sukuk* first surfaced during the post-2007 financial crisis. The property boom and subsequent collapse caused the severe economic downturn in the United States and Britain and had a parallel in the Arab world as well. The high price of property in the United Arab Emirates and particularly Dubai was created by heavy borrowing and property speculation that collapsed under its own weight, creating the first major threat of default in Islamic finance.

During the 2000s, Dubai engaged in extensive property development that was intended to transform the emirate into a tourist resort since the country had no oil revenues. Luxury residences were built as well as a series of artificial islands off its coastline. In order to finance the projects, the emirate embarked on an ambitious borrowing program amounting to over $50 billion in a package of bank loans and *sukuk*. But the worldwide drop in property prices following the credit market crisis beginning in 2007 reached the Persian Gulf and property values began to fall precipitously. In November 2009, the government of Dubai announced that it intended to restructure part of the approximately $26 billion debt of Dubai World, the largest state-owned conglomerate in the emirate. One of the companies in the conglomerate was a property subsidiary, Nakheel. Another, Dubai Ports Authority, was the operator of more than two dozen ports around the world. A key element of the restructuring proposal was the request by Dubai World to delay the maturity repayment on a $3.5 billion *ijara sukuk* with Nakheel that was due for redemption in late 2009.

Nakheel, as the property arm of Dubai World, issued three *sukuk*. In an *ijara sakk*, Nakheel leased property located at the Dubai Waterfront development to an SPV issuer, which then leased it back to a Nakheel entity. The rental payments paid by the Nakheel entity were used by the SPV to make payments to the *sukuk* holders. This structure was utilized to allow the *sukuk* holders to hold the beneficial ownership interest in the *sukuk* assets. Creditors stand to benefit if a *sakk* is declared the same as a conventional bond, whereas issuers stand to benefit if it is defined as an instrument that is compliant with *shariah*, subject to profit sharing. The Nakheel *sukuk* had a fixed return of 6.35 percent per annum. When they were issued in 2006, the land was valued at $4.25 billion. When property prices fell by 50 percent or more, the value of the assets also collapsed, causing the default. Despite the intricacy of the instrument, the event demonstrated the reliance on the underlying revenues and the risk of default as a result.

Dubai World asked the courts for a standstill agreement on its debts as it attempted to sort out its problems and propose a restructuring. That portion of the debt load represented by *sukuk* presented many problems the courts had to confront. One credit analyst commented, "The whole presentation of the structure is one where investors are meant to receive a share of the profits and not interest on debts—two very different obligations. It could be argued that, because an issuer is not generating profits, it should not have to pay *sukuk* investors." But most bankers took the opposite position, arguing that standard bond market procedures should apply. One stated, "This is a credit issue, not an Islamic issue. A *sukuk* is a bond and issuers need to pay back the money they borrowed."[20]

A sister state to Dubai agreed. Before the *sukuk* could default, the government in Abu Dhabi provided the funds to make the final redemption payments on time. The other debts were not covered, indicating that the *sukuk* took precedence in the debt structure. Part of the problem for investors, and ultimately the two governments, was that the obligations appeared to be government-guaranteed as part of the Dubai World conglomerate. They were not direct obligations, but a default would have dampened the enthusiasm for further financings had not a payment been made.

Legal issues also made matters confusing. Although structured to be compliant with *sharia*, the obligations originally were issued under English law as were many other Gulf debt obligations. By intervening, Abu Dhabi prevented the *sukuk* from being ruled upon by a religious court, which could have further confused the issue by potentially bringing two legal systems into conflict. Part of the problem centered on the nature of the assets in SPVs. The assets pledged to *sukuk* SPVs did not mean that the obligations were secured. They were only meant to provide compliance with religious law. As an Islamic banker said during the Dubai crisis, "Even with asset backing behind it, or a true sale or whatever in the framework, those assets are there to facilitate a financial transaction of the issuers. They are not there to provide security to the investors."[21]

The Dubai obligations were not the first *sukuk* to verge on default. In the late 1990s, after the "Asian contagion" crisis, several Malaysian borrowers defaulted, but the Dubai World obligations were the most noteworthy problems to date. The incident also underscored some intrinsic problems with these types of obligations that only began to appear after the credit market crisis in 2007. Because of the need to structure bonds to be *sharia* compliant, investment bankers and borrowers went to great lengths to find suitable assets to structure as usufructs. This meant that the obligations were only as strong as the underlying asset pool supporting them, giving them a resemblance to mortgage-related securities in the United States. When the credit crisis developed, it became clear that mortgage-related securities, especially those private label issues packaged by banks, were the first to default because of the questionable nature of the underlying subprime mortgages. The Naheel *sukuk* were very similar because the underlying mortgages were inflated during the Dubai property boom. But because of the structure of the *sukuk*, financial assets were not involved, only tangible assets as prescribed by *sharia*. By their nature, *sukuk* securitize only tangible assets whereas American mortgage-related bonds securitize the mortgages, not the real property they represent. Many involved in Islamic finance pointed out that subprime obligations were not found in Islamic financings.

One of the major attractions of *sharia*-compliant investments for investors was the claim that they were ethical investments, offered as an alternative to Muslims and others who wanted to avoid traditional Western finance and debt investments. But by using SPVs and pooling together bundles of assets to pay a return, the packagers of *sukuk* created obligations that closely resembled asset-backed bonds that had been routinely created in the United States and Britain since the 1980s. The structural and technical differences between ABSs and *sukuk* still were obvious, but the net result could be the same in times of financial crisis. Because of the need to base returns on something other than interest, other credit and counterparty problems were created.

The rapid development of Islamic banking and finance demonstrated that intermediation of funds between borrowers and lenders could be accomplished by using Islamic principles rather than relying upon Western techniques. Not all investors in *sukuk* were Muslim and many institutional investors outside Asia and the Middle East appreciated the sharia-compliant nature of the investments because they conformed with the growing trend in Europe and the United States for ethical investments. Because of this factor,

London became the center for Islamic finance outside the Middle East, using well-known techniques of structured finance to fashion compliant investment instruments.

Microlending

Applying Islamic principles to bond financings was a natural consequence of the events of the 1970s, paralleling developments in Western structured finance. While some critics maintained that these structured deals were nothing more than interest payments in disguise, there was one other area of Islamic finance where no controversy over religious principles existed. The development of lending to the poor, better known as microlending, quickly became an acknowledged synthesis of extremely basic banking and religious principles in a sector that banks traditionally neglected.

In traditional, Western banking, basic lending principles had been standard since the nineteenth century. Highly rated borrowers received loans at low rates of interest while lesser-rated ones did so at higher rates in order to compensate the lender for the increased default risk incurred. Beyond a certain threshold, potential borrowers were excluded from the process because default risk was considered too great. Those potential borrowers falling into this category automatically were assumed to be seeking loans for consumption purposes, as they had for centuries. More importantly, those in this category also were precluded from borrowing for productive purposes. It was difficult, if not impossible, for the poor to start a business or engage in entrepreneurial activities because of their lowly status.

The advanced state of finance on Wall Street and the City of London had expanded its boundaries slightly since World War II to allow new marginal sectors to develop, but they were hardly revolutionary in scope. The high-yield (junk bond) market allowed non-investment-grade borrowers access to the bond market. Lesser-known sectors such as the market for forfeit paper allowed lowly rated borrowers access to short-term trade paper where no options had existed before. Both were institutional markets where the borrowers were established business entities with track records. Any true revolution would have to come in an area previously untouched by finance, extending credit to those with no credit records and little prospect—in short, the poor.

The long, controversial history of debt had one underlying theme that emerged during the Enlightenment in Europe. Credit facilities were available for productive (non-consumption) loans when lenders believed there was a good chance that the borrower would be successful in his venture and be able to repay the loan. As societies grew larger, opportunities for profitable lending became more abundant and capitalism emerged. Once it did, financial ingenuity and innovation played a large role in making finance one of the developed world's largest industries.

The same was not true in the developing world, however. The wizardry of finance was unknown in most of the world outside the West and in parts of Asia. This was a startling fact; in the twenty-first century banking and formal lending procedures still were unavailable to half the world's population. Finance had been late in arriving in the Muslim world, but the dramatic growth experienced after 1972 demonstrated that Western financial techniques could be fused with Islamic principles to foster a new market for those who had been traditionally "underbanked." At the same time, the gap between rich and poor was growing larger. While advanced countries could benefit from financial innovation, poor countries could not because their people were still pressed to scrape a living by any means possible. In 2010, the per capita income in the United States was approximately \$46,000 while it was \$41,000 in the United Kingdom. In Kenya it was \$760 and in Bangladesh it was \$600.[22] It may be argued that many developing countries with low incomes do not require sophisticated banking services, but they also lack adequate credit facilities because banking on the retail level is considered unprofitable and risky. Their situation is similar to that in Europe after the fall of Rome, when production and trade plummeted and credit facilities disappeared. Without credit facilities at reasonable rates of interest, progress was stalled until the moral and economic climate changed.

Arguably, the European situation changed when the *montes* were allowed to do credit business in northern Italy in the late Middle Ages. By recognizing that loans offered at low rates of interest could provide some incentive to the poor who became the *montes'* best customers, the Catholic Church provided some rudimentary economic stimulus to the population while still maintaining the ban on usury. The problem was that those loans often were consumption loans and the lending business was pawnbroking. Business activity and eventual capital formation were slow to develop because lending was not based upon an entrepreneurial idea that could provide a profit but simply on providing adequate collateral to the lender.

The realization that there was a potential market for lending in the developing world began to materialize in the post-OPEC oil boom. In this case, the idea was implemented not by banks or other traditional lenders but by a former university lecturer who had seen the worst poverty in his own country. Muhammad Yunus, the founder of the Grameen Bank in Bangladesh, said in 2001, "Today, if you look at financial systems around the globe, more than half the population of the world—out of six billion people, more than three billion—do not qualify to take out a loan from a bank. This is a shame." By that date, his bank had already been lending extensively to the poor in Asia and Africa. The moral and economic questions this activity posed were simple and historical at the same time. Was there a market for such microlending and if so, was it anything more than lending for consumption?

Yunus founded the Grameen Bank in 1976 as a not-for-profit institution dedicated to making loans to the poor and destitute. The idea was an oxymoron in traditional finance. These were loans providing small amounts of working capital in order to spark an entrepreneurial spirit in the borrowers. The amounts, ranging from as little as $50 to around $500 were for relatively short periods of time. But the loans adhered to Islamic principles rather than those of traditional finance. The Grameen Bank became the model for microlending in the developing world, extending through Asia to Africa, the Caribbean, and eventually to the United States. Its philosophy was unique, unheard of in traditional banking circles. "Grameen Bank starts with the belief that credit should be accepted as a human right, and builds a system where one who does not possess anything gets the highest priority in getting a loan. Grameen methodology is not based on assessing the material possession of a person, it is based on the potential of a person. Grameen believes that all human beings, including the poorest, are endowed with endless potential."[23] The poor borrowers also hold equity in the bank.

Yunus related an experience that prompted him to seek an alternative to help the poor avoid usurious moneylenders in his native Bangladesh. After meeting a local woman who sold bamboo stools, he discovered the role of the usurer in impeding economic enterprise. She had to borrow from a moneylender to buy the raw materials needed. Even after successfully selling her products, she only made about two cents a day in profit on twenty-two cents of proceeds, which was not enough to free her from the moneylender the next day when the process was repeated. When Yunus collected data on the borrowers from the woman's town, he discovered that forty-two people owed the equivalent of a total of $27 to the local usurers.[24] He gave them the money to free them from the moneylenders. The experience prompted him to think of lending directly to the poor, avoiding banks in the process. The affair was reminiscent of eighteenth-century London and the humane attempts to repay debts in order to free borrowers and their families from debtors' prisons.

Most of Grameen Bank's customers were women and they remained its major customers as it expanded around the developing world. The emphasis was not a political stance by the bank as much as an anthropological assumption about the role of women in many developing economies. They were seen as more forthright than men about their financial positions in life and their desire to improve their own lot. There was also an assumption, proved correct, that they were more likely to repay the loans on time and not default. Severely repressed in many of their own societies, they became the natural customers for the bank, which was actively searching for the poorest in society to become its customers. The bank described itself by stating, "Conventional banks are owned by the rich, generally men. Grameen Bank is owned by poor women."

The bank began lending in 1976 through other banks and started its own independent operations in 1983. In 1976, it disbursed the equivalent of $73 million in loans. By 2009, the annual amount had increased to $8.72 billion, being dispersed through more than 2,500 branches and more than 81,000 villages in the developing world. But the year-end amount outstanding in 2009 was only $792 million, indicating that most of the loans remained short-term and were being paid back promptly. The bank also held $650 million in deposits at year end 2009. Besides making productive loans, the bank also embarked on a house-building program that began with 317 houses built in 1984 to more than 680,000 in 2009. The number of female customers also increased from 56 percent in 1984 to 97 percent in 2009, representing 8.35 million borrowers.[25]

The default rate on loans was about 3.5 percent in 2009. The relatively low rate was achieved by requiring borrowers to attend weekly meetings with others and making payments in person to the lending officer, who continually traveled around the country. The mutual concept was also evident since it made the borrowers of the bank its owners, providing them with a continuing interest in repaying their debts on time. Most importantly, the ethical guidelines of the bank prohibited lending officers from making more than one loan to a borrower until the first loan was repaid.

For those who did not repay on time, the penalty was less severe than it would be in traditional banking. The Koranic ban on *alterum tantum* could be clearly seen in the bank's statement concerning unpaid debts: "In conventional banks charging interest does not stop unless specific exception is made to a particular defaulted loan. Interest charged on a loan can be multiple of the principal, depending on the length of the loan period. In Grameen Bank, under no circumstances total interest on a loan can exceed the amount of the loan, no matter how long the loan remains un-repaid. No interest is charged after the interest amount equals the principal."[26]

This Islamic practice was based upon a business model that comes as close to a statement of natural law that has ever been found in banking, traditional or otherwise. Equally, debts did not pass to heirs if the borrower died since they were covered by a life insurance policy good for the life of the loan, a response to debtors' prisons and passing unpayable debts to families. Unfortunately, the insurance idea evoked some unsavory practices in other institutions practicing microlending.

For his efforts, Yunus and his bank shared the Nobel Peace Prize in 2006, both being cited "for their efforts to create economic and social development from below." The Nobel committee later admitted that it had subjected Grameen and Yunus to close scrutiny before awarding the prize, confirmation that the bank and its principles were intact and succeeding as advertised. By the time the award was presented, microlending had been introduced by hundreds of other lenders in poor countries, not all of whom were intent on helping the poor out of poverty. Even more curious was its introduction into the United States, which is not normally associated with the extremely poor and destitute. When it reached developed countries, it began to change its nature to conform with more sophisticated banking systems.

Microlending for Profit

Despite the objectives and success of the not-for-profit microlending model, other microlenders clearly were constructed for profit and became widespread in the developing world. Success bred similar and copycat programs throughout Asia and Latin America. It appeared that the old cycle found in the United States when credit unions and friendly societies were founded was being repeated. The principled lenders were being followed by those attracted by the prospects of charging high interest rates.

On the surface, the for-profit lending was constructed similar to Grameen's program, with group meetings, weekly payments on loans, and insurance for the borrowers, all common traits. Loan officers traveled around their assigned districts meeting with borrowers on a weekly basis, collecting payments. In sophisticated banking markets, this ultimately meant an added cost, which would be borne by borrowers. The idea was appealing. Investors viewed microlending as a combination of altruism plus the ability to charge high rates of interest. It was not an easy combination.

Microlending in general did not have a long history before lending abuses began to appear. Lending to the poor in India became one of the first nationwide crises caused by abuses commonly seen for centuries. The profit motive was blamed for the problems not ordinarily witnessed in the not-for-profit sector. When private investors took notice of microlending in the mid-2000s, the need for a high required rate of return quickly infected lending procedures. In 2010, a large lender went public on the Mumbai stock exchange, raising the equivalent of over $350 million. Since the average loan was around $200, a vast number of loans could be created from sums that were considered very small by traditional banking standards.

The same trend had been developing for the previous several years. Many of the major international development banks entered microlending, extending loans in those countries in which they were operating already. They operated on a not-for-profit basis but already had competition from the private lenders. Hedge funds had already been attracted in limited numbers in the United States and Europe and microlenders were awash with loanable funds. India provided an excellent market because of the vast number of poor. The state of Andhra Pradesh in particular attracted around 75 percent of the lenders since it was in one of the poorest sections of the country. Lenders treated the vast number of poor as potential clients for their services and logically the poorest states were the most attractive target markets. The growth registered by the microlenders was impressive by any banking standard. In 2006, microlenders had 80 branches in India; by 2009, there were over 1,350. Among them, the listed company SKS Finance grew 90 percent per year during the same short time period.[27] Citibank, attracted by the rates of return, also entered the market in 2005.

Lenders routinely charged as much as 30 percent for the loans, which were structured not as Islamic instruments but simply as traditional interest-bearing loans. "Most people find it very hard that this interest rate does any good to poor people who are recipients," the president of a microlending trade in India group remarked.[28] The lending procedures of many of the microlenders included making loans to women who already had outstanding loans to other microlenders without regard for the ability to repay. This created a situation in which many women who had only about $200 in annual income were in debt for five or six times that amount, with no prospect of ever repaying the loans. Stories abounded of many suicides occurring among borrowers who were insured by lenders. Often, it was suggested to them by lenders as a way out of their difficulties. The idea that lenders would shame a woman into suicide so that they could collect the life insurance prompted the legislature of Andhar Pradesh to pass legislation to regulate the microlenders. When it did, there were complaints that any regulation would hinder the ability of the poor to advance economically; similar arguments were made in the United States in the 1920s when the usury ceilings were being increased.

Regarding microlending in India, Yunus commented, "One reason for this problem [in India] is some of these microfinance programs have taken a wrong turn. They see microcredit as a money-making opportunity to make profit for themselves. That has shaken the trust of people who believed in its mission."[29] But the for-profit lenders abounded since most potential borrowers did not understand the mechanics of microlending. And the phenomenon was not confined to the developing world. By the end of the 2000s, approximately 250 microlenders were doing business in the United States, including the Grameen Bank America, with several locations in New York and one in Omaha, Nebraska. The sizes of the loans made in the United States were larger than those in the developing world but helped to underscore a banking fact usually overlooked by American bankers: a segment of the population had little or no banking facilities available to them.

This phenomenon was underscored by a report made in 2009 by the Federal Deposit Insurance Corporation (FDIC). In it, the agency reported that an estimated 7.7 percent, or 9 million, of U.S. households were "unbanked." In addition, an estimated 17.9 percent, or 21 million households, were "underbanked," representing about 43 million people. In total, approximately 25.6 percent, or 60 million adults, fell into both categories, approximately 20 percent of the population.[30] The numbers appeared high, especially to those who thought of the United States as the most sophisticated banking market in the world. But the numbers coincided with the early success of microlending and the statistics proved complementary. Microlending was aimed at those overlooked by traditional lenders. Apparently, those falling into that category in the United States were much higher than previously thought.

The households classified as underbanked used alternate financial services, including payday loans, pawn shops, check-cashing services, and refund anticipation loans. Of these services, 81 percent used money orders rather than checks, 16 percent used payday lenders and pawn shops, and 30 percent used check-cashing services. Most often, the users of these services were in the lower quartile of the national income bracket and came from minority or immigrant groups. Many were single women with families.[31] As the past experiences of many microlenders demonstrated, women proved to be the largest group of borrowers of small business loans and they also formed an important segment of the unbanked and underbanked in the United States.

The FDIC's study did not mention the rates of interest charged by the alternative banking services. Payday loans in particular had been attacked for decades as usurious even by the more liberal standards of the post–World War II era but managed to survive regulation in most states. The payday loan was the favorite service of the underbanked population, with some 11.4 percent of them using the service during the course of a year. Among the unbanked, pawn shops were the most popular, with 14.3 percent using pawnbrokers' services at least once per year.[32] For the unbanked, payday lending was not a viable option, suggesting that pawnbroking remained the lender of last resort for the poor, as it had for centuries.

During the 2000s, following the financial deregulation of 1999, the increase in securitization and structured finance helped a shadow banking system develop alongside the more traditional commercial banking system. That system faded after the credit market crisis, but the microlending phenomenon appeared to buck the trend, showing resilience that the institutional market did not demonstrate. Microlending appeared to prosper in a poor financial environment since the demand for small amounts of credit did not diminish. The traditional market for credit, affected by a credit crunch, saw many small business customers of banks desperate for credit due to the banks' unwillingness to lend to risky borrowers in times of distress. The microcredit market appeared unfazed since its customers' needs were more elementary than many other more traditional business owners and the amounts borrowed were not substantial enough to frighten potential lenders.

Although microlending rates in the United States were high by other commercial banking standards (with the possible exception of credit card loans) they were substantially lower than the rates charged by pawnbrokers and payday lenders. This alone provided an attraction for those desiring working capital to start a small business enterprise since the loan rates were low by those lenders' standards. After the credit market crisis began in late 2007, they also proved lower than credit card rates. Credit cards often were a source of capital for those developing small businesses and when card companies began raising their interest rates as the crisis progressed, many small businesses were hurt and forced to close.

Microlending in the United States quickly became known as microbusiness lending—technically loans of less than $100,000 made by financial institutions to small businesses. Although many lenders made these loans, they were favorite products of credit unions and thrift institutions. When compared with the explosion of microlending in Asia, the increase in them was modest. Microbusiness loans totaled $170.5 billion in mid-2008, an increase of 6.8 percent, or $10.8 billion, compared with an increase of 9.4 percent in the period ending mid-2007. Increases in volume were also attributed to continued efforts to promote small business credit cards by credit card issuers.[33]

The popularity of the alternative lenders underscored the need for their services, at least according to their supporters. They claimed that lowering the effective rates alternative lenders charged would force many of them out of business because they could not be compensated for the risks of lending, leaving a large gap in services to the underbanked and unbanked portions of the population. The large number of payday customers often was used by the lenders and their supporters as an example of how vital their services were to the group since without them there would have been no credit available at all to the working poor. But most payday lenders did not admit making loans; they did not technically consider their services to be loans for fear of violating usury laws in the states that still retained them. This argument still carried substantial weight one hundred years after payday loans first were offered to the working poor. The other side of the argument was seldom mentioned. The high rates charged made it less likely that the poor would be able to improve their lot and join the majority of people who banked at traditional financial institutions. It was for that reason that microlending was able to gain a small foothold in American banking, but consumption loans still dominated the landscape.

Microlenders in the United States typically lent from $500 to $30,000 to borrowers, with terms ranging from six months to about five years. Rates charged ranged from single digits to about 15 percent, although collecting data about lending rates was spotty. Many of the loans were made during the credit crisis after 2007 and not all were made to those in lower-income groups. Many loans were made to the unemployed who decided to try new entrepreneurial ventures but were excluded from borrowing from banks because of the lack of credit available to small businesses generally. In addition to private lenders, the U.S. Small Business Administration (SBA) also intermediated microlending facilities by providing funds to select lenders that then made loans to borrowers.

Microlending in the United States differed from the original model on several counts and statistics underlined them. Many of the six hundred microlenders in the country were listed as not-for-profit, although many of the larger ones attached to banks clearly were for-profit institutions. The short experience with microlending demonstrated that default rates were higher in the United States than in developing countries, loans certainly were larger, and less than 1 percent of those people identified as micro-entrepreneurs were actual customers of microlenders. Microlenders in the United States also abandoned the weekly personal meeting between banker and customer that had proved successful in the developing world.[34] Traveling loan officers only added another expense to the costs of doing business that most institutional microlenders wanted to avoid.

The idea of microlending in advanced industrial societies underlined the problem many potential borrowers encountered accessing credit. The need for entrepreneurial credit by those with poor or inadequate credit histories initially helped spread the idea of microlending and demonstrated to banks that a market existed for small business loans. But many practices associated with the original microlenders would not travel well. The hands-on approach that Grameen Bank and others practiced was too cumbersome and costly for American lenders more accustomed to high-speed transactions and an arms-length distance from their customers. The original model helped the movement become highly successful with poor individuals seeking loans but was less successful with other institutional lenders that sought profit first and development of the borrower second, if at all.

There were also fundamental differences between original microlending and its subsequent variations. In the original model, the past was a guide. The amount borrowed had to be realistic when compared to the return that could be earned on the use of the funds. Borrowing to pay other debts was discouraged but hard to enforce because of poor record keeping in many developing countries. Passing debt to the next generation was discouraged by life insurance designed to retire debt at the death of the original borrower. The long history of debtors' prisons and debt passed to succeeding generations suggested to the developers of microlending that such practices needed to be avoided in order to help poor countries modernize economically and become more productive.

In the Western model of banking, the past meant little and present value prevailed. As a result, microlending and its institutional counterpart, Islamic finance, were both reactions to Western finance. Throughout its three thousand years in Europe and its shorter time in the United States, banking has had a long and often tortured history that has not managed to answer many of the basic questions posed by lending and interest rates. Readily available credit in developed societies led to a marked increase in the standard of living but had also produced some remarkable boom and bust cycles that often pushed back the course of previous economic progress. Microlenders and the architects of Islamic finance sought to circumvent these problems with an ethically based lending system designed to share enterprise risk while being transparent to religious principles. In the West, the battle with ethics had been won by finance two hundred years before as the economic growth needed to serve a growing population trumped ethical and moral precepts surrounding lending practices.

Chapter 8

The Consumer Debt Revolution

Solvency should be a simple financial concept: if your assets are worth more than your liabilities, you are solvent; if not you are in danger of bankruptcy.
—Financial Crisis Inquiry Commission, 2011

The erosion of state usury laws in the United States reflected the new attitude that had been developing toward debt since the 1970s. Debt was no longer feared. The term had been replaced in consumer culture by the term credit; how much credit lenders extended to borrowers was a reflection of the borrowers' status in life, not a potentially damaging tool that could alter the borrowers' lifestyles and future prospects. Debt was being accumulated at a fast rate, suggesting that consumers either were borrowing with a high degree of certainty about their future earnings prospects or were being sold a financial product with which they were not familiar.

Decades of finance theory and political ideology combined to relegate worries about the absolute levels of interest rates to the back burners. Real rates of interest were more important than absolute levels. Portfolio theory assumed that poorly rated debt could enhance the yield on a fixed income portfolio, justifying its issuance in the first place. Securitization had made credit generation easy, especially for institutions outside traditional banking known collectively as the shadow banking system. And bankruptcy had become somewhat predictable. Models could predict a corporate bankruptcy with a fairly high degree of confidence. Debt was no longer the bête noire in the financial jungle; now it was just another financial tool.

During the latter twentieth century and the early twenty-first, rates of interest charged for loans became less of an issue than in the past. Credit was so widely available in the United States that there was a credit line for everyone, at a price. Those charged high rates through readily accessible credit lines such as subprime credit cards, payday loans, and pawnbroker loans were assumed to realize why they were being charged usurious rates. Unlike the microlending trend in the developing world, high rates were not considered damaging but simply the cost of business for those whose credit ratings were sub-standard. Like the other assumptions about debt in general, this was valid for corporate finance but less so for personal finance where uncertainty was much more common and potentially volatile.

The old beggar-thy-neighbor idea was well understood in the developing world but mainly ignored in the United States. Marketing notions such as the American Dream and "unlocking the equity" in a home led to an unprecedented explosion in borrowing on the consumer, governmental, and corporate levels. Borrowing in anticipation of future income became the norm and was approached with great abandon. Since first used in the 1920s, discounting anticipated future revenues and had been the norm in the corporate world; it was becoming increasingly popular with consumers as well. The problem was obvious, however. Anticipating a high future growth rate in earnings may have been feasible for many companies but unrealistically high rates used by individuals could be much too optimistic. Most companies were required to keep their debt to equity and interest cover ratios in sensible proportion to maintain decent credit ratings. The same would not be said for consumers who viewed easy credit as a rite of passage. That assumption was aided immeasurably by politics.

The debt bubble beginning in the 1990s affected Britain as well as the United States. Traditionally, Britons and Americans had differing views on indebtedness, based in no small measure on the differences in per capita income and property values. Britain also came to the credit game later than the United States, only embracing credit card use and higher levels of mortgage leverage during the 1980s. Data showed that the average Briton was borrowing 3.5 times his or her salary to mortgage a home; not far from the average American level of mortgage indebtedness after 2001.[1] This liberal attitude has common roots extending back almost thirty years. But the problem was that it replaced the older multiple of 2.5 times, meaning that Britons and Americans added another year's income to their mortgage indebtedness.

During the post–World War II years, the average British family had a higher household savings ratio and a lower household debt ratio than the average American family. Until the mid-1980s, prosperity there in the American sense was a bit more elusive. Consumer credit was not as easy to obtain, mortgages were granted on the traditional 20 percent down basis, and spending was hardly a national pastime. The factor that changed attitudes in Britain and reinforced them in the United States was the Thatcher revolution of the early and mid-1980s. This marked shift in political ideology was responsible for the benign approach adopted by policymakers on both sides of the Atlantic. The result was increased consumption, borrowing, and speculation not seen since the 1920s.

Margaret Thatcher described her economic and social philosophy in simple terms, stating that it called for "a man's right to work as he will, to spend what he earns, to have property, to have the state as a servant, and not as a master; these are the British inheritance." These goals were consistent with similar American ideals advocated by Ronald Reagan and helped the two leaders form a philosophical bond. Thatcher reacted to the labor and economic strife besetting Britain in the late 1970s and early 1980s while Reagan and his supporters were dedicated to rolling back many of the New Deal reforms they maintained created a government intrusion into economic and personal affairs. While Thatcher responded to economic troubles that Conservatives thought were created by years of Labour governments pandering to trade unions, Reagan responded to ideological differences with previous Democratic administrations that Republicans believed had caused the problems leading to high interest rates and stagflation. In the end, both theories were very similar.

The president was advised by Milton Friedman, a member of the President's Economic Policy Advisory Board, a group of experts from outside government who were appointed in 1981. An advocate of free market economics, Friedman was well known as an advocate of market self-regulation and individual initiative in place of strong central government. The philosophy dovetailed with the contributions made by other free market economists and finance experts, many of whom contributed intellectually to the debt revolution. By the mid-1980s, the table already was set for a celebration of hands-off economic policies contributing to historic stock and bond market rallies that would help set the course of social and economic policy for the next twenty-five years. Free markets were in; regulated ones were out.

Since the Middle Ages, most of the bad press that interest received was attributable to consumption or consumer loans. Business loans were often exempt from usury laws and were rarely discussed prior to the nineteenth century. So when usury laws were imposed in the colonial period and heatedly debated in the nineteenth century, a natural tension arose. Were these limits meant for personal or business loans? Should the same standard be used for both? These natural yet troublesome questions became more pressing as businesses grew larger and became incorporated. They mostly went unanswered because the governments of many locales did not consider them important or only paid lip service to consumer interest rates.

The relationship between indebtedness and the asset markets, especially in the United States, had been inextricably intertwined since the nineteenth century but received little attention. When equities markets fell, their relationship with debt was overlooked in favor of more obvious reasons such as the erosion of corporate earnings or market bubbles that could no longer be sustained. But as every panic in the markets had demonstrated since the days of William Duer, indebtedness lurked in the background. Debt instruments were considered more conservative among investors than equities, so when the more conservative began to fail the speculative would not be far behind.

The years leading to the financial crisis of 2007 and beyond were relatively free of regulation when compared to prior decades. The developments in finance theory dovetailed well with the free market ideology of the post-Reagan years, establishing the groundwork for a significant bull market in equities and a strong bond market. But as previous markets demonstrated, the cheap cost of funds provided by low-yielding bonds prompted many borrowers to add to their indebtedness. The increase in leverage on governmental, corporate, and consumer levels endangered balance sheets, but interest rates remained historically low, masking the perils of leverage.

The separation of commercial and investment banking in the United States since the Glass-Steagall Act had provided relative peace in the financial markets. Banking crises like Continental Illinois and Penn Square did occur but were contained so that no contagion spread. The crisis involving developing countries in the 1980s showed distinct weaknesses in the regulation of banks, but the large lenders managed to survive intact. Of more immediate concern were the methods they were developing to act more like investment banks than commercial banks, crossing the Glass-Steagall line in search of more lucrative non-banking businesses. At the time, this trend was not seen as a danger but rather as an indication of how clever banks adapted to changing market conditions. In this respect, they had considerable assistance from regulatory authorities.

The separation of investment banking from commercial banking began to erode after Alan Greenspan became chairman of the Federal Reserve in 1987. Over the next decade, commercial banks were allowed to purchase investment banks based upon a formula that kept the bank holding company's revenue from investment banking from exceeding a certain percentage of total revenues. Smaller securities houses were absorbed by the bank holding companies and Glass-Steagall came under increasing pressure. While technically separate from the banking operations in a holding company, the securities side of the business began to contribute a larger and larger proportion of the total profits. Advocates wanted to dismantle Glass-Steagall, but the law remained resilient, as it had over the previous decades. But by the mid-1990s, it was obvious that the wall of separation it had created was mostly gone. Those in favor of deregulation wanted to replace it entirely, allowing banks to become more universal in nature. Overlooked in the heat of the moment was that this was the sort of situation that had existed in the 1920s, before the crash occurred.

Glass-Steagall was tested when a proposed merger between Travelers Insurance and Citibank was suggested in 1997. The proposal was approved by the Fed (as banking regulator) under Greenspan, and insurance, securities, and commercial banking operations were brought together under one roof for the first time since the early 1930s. Even in the years between the two world wars, insurance was not part of the equation because of a movement in the 1900s in the states to keep it separate from banking. That effectively kept investment bankers at a distance from the portfolios of life insurance companies, the major buyers of corporate bonds. But in the new deregulatory era, total separation was not considered necessary if profits could be enhanced by combining operations and risks could be managed successfully.

The merger partners were given two years by the Fed to make their combined operations successful. By the end of 1999, Congress obliged by making the new world of banking official by passing the Financial Services Modernization Act. A new financial holding company was recognized in it, supplanting the older bank holding company. The new holding company could own any sort of financial services company, sweeping aside the older restrictions. The new enlarged bank could now engage in traditional commercial banking, securities underwriting and trading, insurance, and proprietary trading under one roof. The new bank also now was subject to more than one potential regulator, depending upon its mix of activities.

The risks apparent in the new environment were the same as the old, but now they were combined under the same roof. Banking institutions were faced with the vagaries of the equities markets in addition to their own traditional lending problems. Derivatives added another layer of risk since many of them were based on credit, fixed income, equities, and commodities. Twenty years before, during the Third World debt crisis, banks were required to limit their exposure to any particular country to avoid a repetition of loose lending policies that severely hurt their balance sheets. Now, the risk of overexposure had reappeared and could take many forms, not simply credit risk through loans.

In the 1990s, the concept of risk also was discussed more than in the past. The new, revamped banks faced more risks than ever before, but the assumption that their internal risk managers could manage them properly became increasingly popular. The notion became so widespread that many banking and market participants believed that catastrophic risk to the financial system itself was very small. In statistical terms, this was referred to as a fat tail, or kurtosis, an aberration to a normal probability distribution of risk. Falling outside normal distributions, a fat tail, or more popularly a black swan event, is assumed impossible to predict, although the general assumption is that one will occur eventually in some form or other. In the era after World War II, before the official deregulation of the financial system, black swan events had occurred infrequently, but they began to appear with more frequency after the stock market collapse in 1987. That market collapse was one example while the collapse of Continental Illinois several years earlier was another. The problems encountered by Long-Term Capital Management, a well-known hedge fund, as well as the Enron and WorldCom scandals of the early 2000s occurred after deregulation and demonstrated the increasing frequency of events thought to occur rarely. By the time the credit market crisis of 2007 began, more black swan events had occurred in the period after 1980 than had occurred since the Great Depression up until that year.

The most significant of the financial crises was the Third World debt crisis of the 1980s. As a result of the weakened bank balance sheets in the United States and Europe, the Bank for International Settlements (BIS) imposed more strict capital requirements, known as Basel 1. These requirements sought to calculate a bank's capital as a percentage of its loan portfolio, set at 8 percent. Equity and senior debt were the main elements of primary capital. Over the next fifteen years, many banks lobbied to use a different, risk-adjusted approach to calculating capital, called value at risk, or VAR. This adjustment set capital requirements as a percentage of the average risk a bank experienced in the markets over a period of time. The banks reported their own exposures to regulators, which then monitored the positions. The banks claimed, and most regulators agreed, that this method was more equitable in setting capital levels than the older Basel 1 approach. This regime became known as Basel 2.

The effect of Basel 2 was to lower capital levels at many banks to half of Basel 1 or less. The banks employed risk management techniques to convince regulators that under normal circumstances (normal distribution) the likelihood of a black swan event occurring in the market was very small indeed, around 1 percent. As a result, less capital was needed. Myron Scholes, the developer of the well-known and widely used Black-Scholes options model and a Nobel Prize winner in economics, described a hypothetical situation using it: "VAR might be computed to be $100 million for a two week period with 99 percent probability. Loosely put, there is about a one percent chance that a loss greater than $100 million would be sustained in the next two weeks."[2]

Assuming the probability to be correct, banks could then hold less capital. A black swan event was not likely in the new deregulated financial environment after 1999, according to theory. But an institutional factor not experienced before in American banking would cloud the issue and the 1 percent assumption. With so many different types of banking and financial services under one roof, the percentage chances of a black swan event could increase. Events in the mortgage market were no longer isolated; they could affect and be affected by events in the derivatives markets and debt markets because of swaps and securitization. There may have been a 1 percent chance in any one market, but when market lines became blurry did the chances increase? If they did, what would become of the usury debate, which had been quiet if not dormant for the past twenty years? These questions were not answered immediately in the early 2000s, so they were assumed to be only marginally relevant.

Float Management

One of the main criticisms aimed at usury prohibitions is that if they were still important regulators would have acknowledged that by reenacting them. But the real problem with nominal interest rates set for consumers is that they have been overshadowed by the management of money supply by the Federal Reserve, such management being considered more important than the absolute level of interest rates. The oversight allowed those rates to rise to what were once considered usurious levels.

Over the centuries, usury debates were often centered on political or moral arguments. The early quantity theories of money appearing in the eighteenth century began to challenge the idea that limits needed to be set on interest rates, arguing instead that the amount of money in circulation dictated interest rates rather than moral notions of what was just. When usury ceilings began to be challenged in the nineteenth and twentieth centuries, more technical discussions of economic efficiency, access to capital, and free market theory all helped to push usury debates to the back burners. Part of the debate became practical. Financial institutions were making too much money designated as interest income for anyone to seriously suggest that an interest rate debate would be of much use. When central bankers and other regulators decided to stimulate or contract credit, they increasingly had come to rely on the amount of money in circulation rather than the rates at which it could be borrowed. If they took care of the supply side, the demand side would fall into place. Interest rate levels took a back seat to the supply of credit and overall economic conditions. Nominal rates were not as important as real rates of interest, even when credit card lenders charged more than 25 percent real rates for the use of their cards.

Part of this argument was purely market oriented. Regulators worried about rates in the money market, not what financial institutions charged retail customers for their services. As long as rates were advertised properly, customers decided what was in their own best interests. Access to credit and a consumer lifestyle had its costs and they had nothing to do with regulators attempting to impose arbitrary rates of maximum interest. Efficiency in the markets trumped other considerations unless there was a blatant case of criminal usury involved. Even the term "loan shark" was receding from use as *anatocismus* and *alterum tantum* had done years before. Banks and financial service companies were earning revenues that were masked from view by using information sciences and computers to obfuscate effective rates of interest, techniques almost unknown to those outside the financial services industry.

One of these areas was "float," a generic term mostly known to bankers. The practice had been known for centuries and had been used successfully in dry exchange contracts, during the Mexican War, and more recently in settling international financial transactions. Float is the difference between the time when a check is written and when it settles. Usually, float benefits the payer, at the expense of the payee. The American Express Company successfully used float in the late nineteenth century when it developed travelers' checks and became a model for many financial services companies as a result. If used in a well-managed fashion, the float balance could be placed in the money market, earning interest, until the draft was presented for payment and cleared. By the latter twentieth century, even though the payment and clearing had been refined so that float was shortened, float could still be profitable. When the clearing of a payment was delayed, it was still possible to earn interest on the float even if the lag was only a day or two.

On a higher level, "fed float" was a topic for policymakers at the Federal Reserve and other central banks. Fed float is the effect that the float balance has on the money supply because it is displayed on the balance sheets of both banking institutions until the check clears. This sort of double counting obscures the amount of money in circulation and makes it difficult to implement monetary policy. Reducing float became a policy goal and was implemented in several stages.

Managing float in the modern era reflected the traditional tension between indebtedness and payment of debts. If a renter knew that his monthly rent was payable on the first of the month and that day happened to fall on a Saturday, he could arrange to have the payment arrive on that day without having the proper funds in his checking account. The check would not be deposited to the landlord's bank until Monday at the earliest and would probably take two days (at least) to clear. That meant that funds would not have to be deposited in the checking account until Wednesday, indicating a float on the payer's behalf of five days. In competitive terms, the renter wanted to extend the float while the landlord sought to shorten it as much as possible.

The ability to manage this process depended upon the structure of the banking system. If the payer's bank and that of the landlord were the same, the clearing time fell to zero. If both banks were members of the Federal Reserve, the process took a couple of days. If one bank was a Fed member while the other was a state-chartered bank, the process took longer. Float management became an art, especially on Wall Street. When many retail customers of securities firms requested cash from their accounts, they often discovered that the checks were drawn on small banks located far from the East Coast, usually in the Midwest or West (using "transportation float"). The purposeful mismatching of clearing was designed to keep the funds in the float of the securities firms for as long as possible.

While well known to corporate treasurers, float used by individuals paying bills raised the old question of whether it allowed debtors to delay repayment of a debt even if for only a short period. An illegal form was known as "kiting," where checks were written by a party who knew sufficient funds were not available but who wrote the check in any event, covering it with another temporary transaction somewhere else. Simply, the check was being held up by nothing but air.

The Federal Reserve took several measures over the years to keep float under control so that it would not negatively affect the money supply.[3] Of all the measures affecting the amount of float outstanding, electronic banking and payments have had the greatest effect, reducing the number of checks cleared annually at the Fed. When introduced, direct deposit and online banking helped reduce float, but one traditional area of high-interest banking remains unaffected. Payday loans still rely on traditional checks changing hands, another example of how financial services for the marginal earners in a population still carry high interest rates, disguised as fees. Two hundred and thirty years before, David Hume thought that high interest rates were the product of inequality in society while Adam Smith believed that low interest rates were the product of a healthy economy. The unbanked and the underbanked were proving the premise still true in general terms.

In order to reduce float, Congress passed the Check Clearing Act for the Twenty First Century in 2003. In previous years, float had increased when interest rates were high as potential floaters, both individuals and institutions, attempted to take advantage of the opportunity gains to be made by extending check clearing. The act followed recent trends in banking, however, since the number of checks used by the public was declining rapidly as the use of credit cards and online banking increased. The payments mechanism increasingly was evolving into private hands, with less being cleared by the Fed and more being accomplished by the private sector.

But economic philosophy alone would not explain the debt phenomenon in the 1990s and 2000s. The debt crisis of the twenty-first century occurred after lenders concocted a mix of real estate loans and consumer loans, crossing the line between the two types of loan that traditionally had been kept separate. The problems that ensued provided the last chapter in the continuous debate about interest and usury that had raged since antiquity. In many ways, the combination brought the debate full circle. After three thousand years, the old premises about indebtedness still proved true. Tradition trumped modern finance, proving that debt was debt, no matter how it was packaged or marketed to sound more like a privilege than a burden.

The Mortgage Explosion

The best example of this axiom could be found in a traditional debt product and what appeared to be only a minor derivation of it. On the surface, the products embodying the two types of debt appeared simple, but they displayed the nuances of the new economic climate. The new loan products included home equity loans and home equity lines of credit (HELOCs). The two, combined with increases in credit card debt, set off a wave of unprecedented consumerism. By 2004–2005, the percentage of the gross domestic product driven by consumption had risen to over 78 percent, demonstrating that much of that money was being used for consumer spending in addition to paying off outstanding credit card balances. According to a Federal Reserve paper co-authored by Alan Greenspan, from 1996 to 2006 home equity of almost $800 billion was used to pay off consumer debt, including credit cards, installment credit, and other loans along with financing home improvements and paying for education expenses. It was not possible to tell how much of the total was used to pay down credit card debt alone, but credit card debt as a percentage of overall debt outstanding declined to slightly under 3 percent of the total U.S. debt bill of $30.5 trillion in late 2006.[4] This is the point where conspicuous consumption can be seen turning into cannibal consumption—using home equity to pay off unsecured credit card debt.[5] In short, using real property equity to pay for consumption.

Consumers were using the rising equity in their homes, fueled by the rising housing market, to "cash out the equity" in their homes, a favorite phrase of mortgage bankers. But the actual percentage of equity in their homes was not rising as a result of these refinancings; it was falling, replaced by more debt. That strategy worked tolerably well as long as prices in the housing market rose. But most home equity loans are made on an adjustable basis, so if interest rates rose or if the property market stopped rising, the strategy had the potential to backfire. When the subprime crisis began, prices fell sharply, eroding the increased equity against which many homeowners had borrowed.

Home equity loans were similar to the second mortgages that had been used in the United States since the 1920s. Originally, second mortgages were used to augment the traditional residential mortgage, which was still relatively short in years to maturity. The original second mortgage was only used for extraordinary expenses and clearly tied to the home as collateral. The HELOC was no different. But instead of being used to pay extraordinary expenses on a one-time basis, HELOCs could be tapped frequently for small amounts or large as the homeowner experienced a need for cash. Each time the line was used, the equity in the home diminished. The frequency was almost assured because most of the HELOCS came with a credit card or check-writing facility attached.

The results of these seemingly simple credit facilities were far-reaching. Real estate loans became mixed with consumption loans, which were unsecured debt. The irony was that high-interest unsecured debt was being refinanced at much lower rates, but the savings in actual interest charges masked a more serious problem. Increasing debt and decreasing equity meant that the home itself was at risk if the homeowner defaulted on the mortgage. A direct link had been established between consumption and real property loans. The trade-off was between optimism and actual interest costs: the homeowner believed that the mortgage could be maintained in good standing while incurring extra debt to pay off high consumption-rate charges.

This phenomenon marked the first time that consumer credit products crossed the line with real property investments. The individual now had access to the equity side of his own personal balance sheet and was able to use it as a source of cash. The equilibrium could only be maintained if property values increased or held steady. A drop would imperil the balance sheets of many homeowners and change the dynamics of savings and investment.

Home ownership grew steadily in the latter twentieth century and the early part of the twenty-first. In 1900, about 47 percent of Americans owned their homes. By 1950, 55 percent did so; in 2000 around 67 percent did so.[6] After 2000, tax advantages led many to purchase new homes, especially since the exemption from capital gains tax allowed many homeowners to buy with a view to a quick sale. This set off a round of real estate speculation not seen since the 1920s. It was aided immeasurably by the tax code. The income tax deduction had been kept intact on home mortgage interest and that included the interest deduction on home equity loans. When all factors were considered, the home was considered the best investment an individual could have made in the post–World War II period. Despite the constant comparisons between real estate and stocks over the same period, most individuals did not have accounts with brokers and only dabbled in the markets at best. Housing proved to be their major, and often only, investment. Home prices had proven inviolate over the decades: they represented an investment that offered housing, tax breaks, and the potential for capital appreciation.

Real estate lending traditionally was based upon sound banking practices. Potential homeowners were required to deposit a 20 percent down payment on a home with the mortgage amounting to around 2.5 times their annual earnings. This process was encouraged by the GSEs, which set their own standards for the types of mortgages they would buy from lenders. For the majority of potential homeowners, these standards and the rates applied to them became known as the conventional, conforming mortgage—a fifteen- or thirty-year debt with fixed income payments. Another option was the adjustable rate mortgage (ARM), which contained caps and floors that limited the maximum and minimum rates of interest. The standards imposed meant that many potential homeowners who did not meet the standards were extremely limited in their financing options.

After the recession of 1990–1991, the mortgage market made up for lost ground. Over $1 trillion worth of mortgages were issued in 1993. The number fell to around $750 billion in 1994, and to around $500 billion in 1995.[7] By the mid-1990s, some banks were offering twenty different types of mortgages where they had offered only three a decade before. In addition to fifteen- and thirty-year conventional mortgages, there were adjustables, balloons, and hybrids. Negative amortization loans were often attached to the balloons so that after perhaps five years at a low, sweetener rate the mortgage would require refinancing or payment in full. Any interest accrued during the grace period was added to the outstanding amount when it was refinanced, increasing the homeowners' debt burden.

Other than fixed rate mortgages, the most troublesome feature with which homeowners had to contend still was the adjustable rate. The variable mortgages sounded relatively simple by the late 1990s but concealed many features that could prove troublesome. The benchmark rates upon which the periodic adjustments were based were dazzling. Over that twenty-year period, mortgage holders had loans adjusted to varying maturities of LIBOR, Treasury bill rates, commercial paper, and formulas based on the prime rate. Maximum rates and minimum rates created a band of risk that consumers could appreciate. If a mortgage were capped at 8 percent and carried a minimum rate of 4 percent, then homeowners knew the range of their risk and could estimate the dollar value of the payments.[8] Lenders continued to adhere to relatively tight standards as they had in the past, requiring down payments in excess of 10 percent and income verification. The standards imposed by the mortgage assistance agencies and the lenders provided some stability to the housing market that would be sorely lacking in the years ahead. When those standards were relaxed in the late 1990s, adjustables with exotic features attached again became a problem. The pool of potential borrowers increased due to political pressures.

In 1990, a trend began when several Boston-area banks began offering mortgages to low-income families earning less than $25,000 per household, bowing to pressure from community activist groups that were demanding better access to housing credit for lower-income groups. The mortgages were made both on fixed and adjustable rate bases. Part of the pressure came from complaints heard over the years about a mortgage-lending activity known as "red lining." This was practiced in poor minority neighborhoods when banks regularly red lined out whole districts, declaring them off limits for mortgage lending because of their racial composition or low-income status. But by bowing to the pressure, lenders also opened a new avenue for higher profits since these mortgages clearly required a higher rate of interest than traditional ones.

Politically, banks had been under federal pressure to provide more effective banking services to families with low and moderate incomes in their communities. The Community Reinvestment Act (CRA) that was passed in 1977 required federal banking regulators to assess a bank's performance in serving its community on a periodic basis. This led to the Riegle Community Development and Regulatory Improvement Act, which was passed in 1994. Between the two, they pressured lenders to do as much as possible to encourage minority home ownership and required banks to report their results to federal regulators. As long as the lenders received high scores from their respective regulator, few questions were asked about the actual quality of the home loans being made. These two laws paved the way to the subprime mortgage loan crisis in 2007.

Securitization took an unexpected turn after 2001 when the two mortgage agencies—Fannie Mae or Freddie Mac—began purchasing and securitizing subprime mortgages. Throughout the previous thirty years, both agencies had followed a relatively conservative model when purchasing mortgages for securitization. But political pressures became more intense after the Gramm-Leach-Bliley deregulation bill was passed late in 1999. Both agencies came under pressure from Congress and lobby groups, notably the mortgage industry, to provide low and moderate income mortgages. The decision to do so proved catastrophic for the industry and the markets.

The mortgage boom also was aided immeasurably by the tax code. The Taxpayer Relief Act of 1998 increased the exempt amount of capital gain made when a home was sold to $250,000 for a single taxpayer and to $500,000 for a married couple. These were the largest tax exempt amounts ever granted for the sale of primary residences and stipulated only that the home had to have been used as a primary residence for two of the previous five years. The changes from the older law proved to be a tax benefit to many individuals who had held their homes for long periods of time before selling.

It also proved an irresistible lure for those who thought they could quickly sell their homes for a profit after two years' time.[9]

Once these factors were in place, a mortgage boom began that only ended when the credit market crisis of 2007 began. The combination of tax incentives, lax lending standards, and a buoyant stock market combined to produce the greatest escalation in real estate prices ever seen in the United States. Mortgage loans increased exponentially after 2000 as homeowners bought and sold homes with great flurry. At the same time, credit card debt increased as well. Securitization, which until that time had produced great benefits in the residential housing market, aided both sides of the bubble.

By creating constant liquidity flow for mortgage lenders, the GSEs brought the revolving credit concept to the mortgage market. When private label securitizations followed, they added to the liquidity generated. Traditionally, a bank made mortgages and kept them on its books until the loans were paid off. Now, it would securitize them, receive cash, and be free to create more mortgages. The only discipline to prevent a bank from creating mortgages with loose lending standards was the requirements of the agencies: they would only purchase mortgages made using their own guidelines regarding down payments, mortgage insurance, and the like. When agencies were not involved or if they relaxed their standards, the process was subject to serious stress.

Revolving mortgage credit had a disastrous effect on the market once the mortgage-for-all idea became institutionalized. The contagion spread directly from the questionable creditworthiness of the borrowers to the agencies and securitizers that sold the mortgage-backed securities to bondholders. Many foreign investors, including European banks, sovereign wealth funds, and hedge funds held these mortgage-related bonds, lured by the higher than average bond yields they produced. When the contagion of defaults began to spread, it hit all sectors with equal force. The problem continued because the ARM re-settings were spread over time, depending on when the mortgages were originally made. This ensured that the subprime crisis would take several years to work its way through the system.

A major problem that began appearing after 2003 was the widespread use of the alternate mortgage product, or AMP. These were mortgages with enticingly low initial interest payments, often deferring principal repayments for several years. The AMPs tended to lull the mortgage holder into believing he had been given a low interest rate bargain rather than a mortgage that was due for recalibration at a later date, often with unpleasant consequences. The Government Accountability Office (GAO) examined the trend and concluded, "Mortgage statistics show that lenders offered AMPs to less creditworthy and less wealthy borrowers than in the past. Some of these recent borrowers may have more difficulty refinancing or selling their homes to avoid higher monthly payments, particularly in an interest-rate environment where interest rates have risen or if the equity in their homes fell because they were making only minimum monthly payments or home values did not increase."[10] Despite the warnings, no action was taken.

The residential mortgage market began suffering problems well before the subprime crisis began in August 2007. By mid-2007, over one million mortgages were in default and the number was rising. The GAO noted that rising interest rates were the main cause. The problems were being experienced mostly by homeowners with adjustable rate mortgages of some sort. The marginal rise in short-term rates in 2004 and 2005 put pressure on the ARMs and their subsequent re-fixing rates rose. The rise in rates and the defaults also shed light on many industry practices that had gone unnoticed. Shoddy lending practices, poor or no income verification, and poor loan documentation all contributed to the problem, the GAO noted.[11] The agency went on to say that the interest rate situation made more foreclosures likely in late 2007 and 2008, a prediction that came true.

The role that securitization played in the credit market crisis and the financial collapse that followed cannot be underestimated. It was acknowledged that many of the subprime mortgages should never have been created in the first instance, but securitization still made them possible. How was it possible that the poor could have been granted mortgages when they had no income other than a welfare check? Why had lending standards become so lax? As with credit cards, home loans were being granted and then immediately securitized. The original lenders did not retain them on their books, so their interest in them was momentary at best. And since they did not keep them, they had little reason to conform to decent lending standards. The loans would be the bondholders' problem, not theirs. Through these substantial cracks in the system, subprime mortgages gained a toehold in the market, which later became a foothold. Fifteen years before, $300 billion was the size of all new mortgages created, mostly of a decent credit quality. Now it was the size of the weaker part of the market alone.[12]

Once the pools of mortgages were assembled to support a bond, the rating agencies rated them on the basis of the collateral. Many bonds were rewarded with the highest ratings available despite the fact that they were backed by mainly subprime loans. When the credit market crisis began in the late summer of 2007 many of the bonds quickly dropped in value or were severely marked down, presenting investors with losses or illiquid securities. Questions quickly arose concerning the reasons they were assigned such high credit ratings in the first place, but it appeared that the rating agencies were under the same pressure as the firms that documented the mortgage loans were in the securitization process. Too many transactions had forced them to adopt shortcuts in order to keep up with the volume of business and the shortcuts overlooked vital information that would have caused the new bonds to be assigned a lower rating. In the great rush to create as many new securities as possible, lack of oversight contributed significantly to the credit market crisis.

Of more concern was the fact that subprime originations had increased from less than 5 percent of mortgages made in 2001 to more than 13 percent by 2007. The biggest jump occurred from 2003 to 2004 when the number more than doubled. Alternate-A originations (medium-grade mortgages) showed similar increases. Their numbers almost quadrupled from 2003 to 2005. This activity was accompanied by record amounts of mortgage-related bonds issued. Agency bonds were accompanied by collateralized mortgage obligations (CMOs) and collateralized debt obligations (CDOs), a CDO being a structured vehicle made up of subprime and Alt-A mortgages and sliced into tranches in much the same fashion as CMOs. A wide range of investors bought them, ranging from the banks themselves to foreign banks eager to earn the marginally higher yield the bonds offered. Many, such as thrift institutions, bought them precisely because they were mortgage related. While these banks thought they were diversifying risk, they were not freeing themselves from mortgage-related risk but only counterparty risk.

The whole process surrounding securitization was central to the problem. As the GAO observed, "Data on private label securitized loans show significant increases from 2000 to 2006 in the percentage of mortgages with higher loan to value ratios (the amount of the loan divided by the value of the home), adjustable interest rates, limited or no documentation of borrower income or assets, and deferred payment of principal or interest."[13] But not all originators of subprime mortgages were clearing their balance sheets with private label bonds. Countrywide Financial was one of the major sellers of subprime mortgages and offloaded a great many of them to Fannie Mae, although buying them was clearly beyond the agency's orbit.

Residential mortgage statistics in the United Kingdom displayed a pattern similar to that in the United States. The time frame was different, however. The mortgage explosion in Britain began in 1996 and carried forward to 2007. New mortgage loans expanded to over a million per year in 1997 and remained over a million per year until 2007. The peak year was 2002 when 1.396 million new loans were made. The total value of the loans expanded equally, with £60.6 billion created in 1997, increasing to over £157 billion by 2006. This pales in comparison with the United States, which created $20 trillion beginning in 2000, continuing until mid-2008. The United Kingdom created a total of slightly over £1 trillion during that period.[14]

Of those mortgages made, fixed rates were in the minority until recently. Traditionally, lending in the United Kingdom was done on an adjustable basis, with fixed rate mortgages the exception rather than the rule. But securitization still played a large role in funding U.K. mortgages despite the fact that the corporate bond market in Britain literally had been defunct for twenty years before the recent boom began. In 1996, only 19 percent of the mortgages were fixed, but by 2007 the percentage had risen to 75 percent. Unlike in the United States, many residential mortgage loans were made by traditional building societies rather than by commercial banks. Among the lenders, building societies led the way with six of the top ten lenders. The credit market crisis also affected them badly. By the end of 2008, three of them had been forced either to merge with a stronger partner or be supported by the U.K. Treasury. This was a pattern similar to that in the United States, where three of the top mortgage lenders required assistance from regulators in 2008 and two of them were thrift institutions, the equivalent of building societies.[15]

The U.K. market resembled the U.S. market more in broad outline than in function or size. Room for building new residential housing units existed in the United States on a much greater scale than in Britain. Housing units were also larger in the United States on average and cheaper per square foot. And Britain went through real estate boom and bust cycles about every fifteen years, in contrast to the United States, which had not witnessed a serious downturn after World War II with the exception of the early 1990s. The sharp increase in mortgage borrowing in Britain did share a common trait with the United States, however. When British lenders discovered securitization, they took to it with a vengeance. Mortgage lenders in the United Kingdom made more use of the securitization market than any country other than the United States.[16] Between 2000 and 2007, total European securitization of all sorts of assets stood at €2.44 trillion. Of the residential mortgage-backed securities (MBSs) created, the United Kingdom accounted for about 75 percent. Government agencies like Fannie Mae or Freddie Mac did not exist in Europe or Britain so the securitization market was private label. Many of the bonds were covered, however.

Credit-card-backed ABSs were also much more popular in the United Kingdom than elsewhere in Europe. Over 30 percent of all credit-card-backed ABSs originated in the United Kingdom, where credit card use had become increasingly popular. Following Britain, Spain and Germany were second and third in using securitization, although their total numbers were much smaller than those in the United Kingdom over the time period.[17] It should be noted that the European version was covered; that is, the bonds had recourse to the original borrower, unlike the private label securitizations in the United States.

The deregulated financial environment had a direct and positive effect on the mortgage boom. High interest rates were not the primary cause of the crisis that developed in the late summer of 2007. However, they served as a secondary cause because higher rates were associated with higher risk and because of securitization bond investors sought those collateralized mortgage-related securities yielding more than traditional conventional MBSs. That led them to CMOs backed by subprime and Alt-A mortgages even though yields were relatively low in historic terms.

Securitization also had many benefits for residential mortgages that were recognized outside the United States and Britain. In the mid-2000s, businesses in all the developed European countries had entered the securitization market. In addition to the major members of the European Union, borrowers in Russia, Turkey, the Czech Republic, Ukraine, and Kazakhstan all issued securitized bonds in varying degrees.[18] Russia was the largest issuer in this group. The major securitized borrowing area for European and non-European countries was residential real estate. The credit card phenomenon was less of an influence in parts of Europe and Asia and was slower to develop.

Much of the European version was covered; that is, the bonds had recourse to the original borrower, unlike the private label securitizations in the United States. They followed a German instrument developed in the eighteenth century called *pfandbrief*, a bond that was collateralized by mortgages but remained on the balance sheet of the borrower, which was obligated to cover any shortfall if a problem developed among the mortgage payers. Although *pfandbriefen* were private obligations, they provided the model upon which the GSEs were based.[19] But the non-American uses of mortgage-backed securities never produced the collision of consumption and housing debt witnessed in the United States.

A revealing characteristic of cannibal consumption became painfully apparent during the credit market crisis when the default rate on homes had more of a significant economic effect than credit card defaults. Why were homeowners willing to default on their homes and abandon them while continuing to maintain their credit card payments? This clearly was a reversal of past behavior when the home was considered worth saving first, not last. Consumers seemed to be unclear about the effects of rising interest rates but certainly seemed to understand how to react to extreme adversity. It generally was assumed that if a mortgage went into default, the lenders had legal recourse to the home but not to other assets of the borrower. Not so with credit cards. If a card went into default, the credit card company did have recourse to other assets. When push came to shove, consumers apparently knew which resource to preserve while letting the other fail. But this general assumption was not always correct. The process varied within the states, and in many cases the states provided remedies to the lenders, including deficiency judgments, allowing access to other assets of borrowers and the ability to garnish wages; in other words, treating defaulted home loans in much the same fashion as defaulted credit card balances. Once considered the family castle, the home nevertheless became another casualty of credit cards, if only by being treated relatively lightly by borrowers when compared to consumer credit. This phenomenon provided a lasting testimony to the power of consumer credit.

Credit Card *Alterum Tantum*

In the mortgage market, high rates of interest were not prevalent during the 1990s and 2000s and did not cause the financial crisis beginning in 2007. Mortgage rates followed the yield curve for Treasury securities, so rates remained low except for the lower-quality mortgages. But their rates were low in historic terms, despite the adjustments made to unrealistically low AMPs or exotic adjustables. Adjustable mortgages may have helped erode the usury laws but did not necessarily mean high, punitive rates of interest. The same could not be said for credit cards, however.

As the credit card phenomenon grew after 1975, credit providers recognized that consumers treated their cards gingerly; defaulting on payments was only a last resort when all other avenues had failed. As long as a customer made a payment each month, lenders were willing to accept payment without the prospect of the debt being paid in full in the foreseeable future. When cards were first introduced, payment was expected in full at the next billing cycle. Then credit terms that amortized outstanding balances over a three-year repayment period were introduced. Monthly statements based their required payment amounts on the three-year repayment, which would be paid off in slightly less than three years if the customer faithfully followed the repayment schedule. But the requirements of securitization soon clouded the issue. When card companies began selling credit card receivables to securitizers, longer terms were preferred to shorter ones. If a bond were based on three-year card receivables and the customers actually paid off their balances slightly early, the bond holders receiving those payments would experience prepayment risk. That sort of risk had always been a problem for investors in the mortgage assistance agencies' obligations; the bonds purchased were paid off early as homeowners retired their mortgages before the final payment was due, in some cases much earlier.

In order to ensure that credit card ABSs lasted at least as long as their maturity dates, the card companies encouraged customers to make a minimum monthly payment that was less than the one suggested by the three-year amortization schedule. The lesser minimum extended the life of the loan substantially. For instance, if a customer owed $5,000 on a card charging 14 percent annually, the monthly payment based on a three-year amortization schedule would be $179 per month (one of thirty-six equal payments at an annual rate of 14 percent); however, the credit card company might set the minimum at 2 percent of that amount, or $100. That would be the minimum required by the lender to keep the account in good order. The interest on this card balance if paid at the three-year rate would be $58.33 per month. But if the minimum payment were chosen, then only $41.67 would go to paying the principal, meaning that it would take much longer to pay off the loan. And interest is always due on the unpaid amount, so it is in the card companies' interest for customers to pay the minimum only.

If the minimum payment were chosen, it would take the borrower 351 months to pay off this loan, adding $6,555 in interest to the bill. If the interest rate were to change, then the payoff period would be longer. At 16 percent, it would take 428 months and add $9,328 in interest charges. Although consumers are aware of the implications of paying only the minimum, there was surprisingly little said about the practice except to warn them that it was not fulfilling their financial obligation to themselves. Other than requiring lenders to state the annual percentage rate (effective rate) for consumers on their bills, no federal regulation existed to control rates. Once the *Marquette* decision was reached by the Supreme Court state usury laws became even weaker as lenders were allowed to choose their locales rather than abide by state usury ceilings.

The growth in consumer credit in the United States was dramatic after the introduction of credit cards. At year end 2008, consumer credit outstanding stood at $1.45 trillion, with $892 billion being credit cards. Forty years before, it stood at $85 billion, with only $2.1 billion outstanding in the form of revolving credit cards.[20] Approximately 75 percent of the credit card debt was securitized in 2008; none was in 1968. The spread between the card lenders' cost of funds (commercial paper rates) and the amount charged to cardholders was large, allowing securitizers to sell ABSs collateralized by card receivables quite easily. Default rates on outstanding cards were low relative to other consumer loans (around 3 percent) and the lenders usually sold those balances to collectors for a few pennies on the dollar.

The paradox the card companies presented in their lending activities was clear. While creating easy credit on the one hand, they naturally wanted tough laws on the other to protect themselves against the problems they created. Credit card lenders were especially fearful of customers declaring bankruptcy to avoid paying their balances. In 1999, they mounted an intensive lobbying campaign against reform of the bankruptcy laws of 1978. The lenders wanted fewer people to be able to declare personal bankruptcy and finally imposed their will on Congress not to make the current law broader or more liberal.

In 2004, Chapter 7 and 13 bankruptcies accounted for 30 percent of card charge-offs. Consumer bankruptcies numbered 1.56 million in 2004, down from 1.625 million in 2003. Then Congress reformed the bankruptcy code in 2005, twenty-seven years after the last reform was passed. The original critics of the 1978 legislation appeared to be correct. The code was being used to avoid excessive credit card debt. In the months leading to the new law becoming effective in October 2005, personal bankruptcy filings soared and with them credit card defaults. Before the act, filings averaged about 1.6 million per year. After the law became effective, they declined by 1 million cases.[21] While it may be argued that the new law inflated the numbers before October 2005, they began to rise again even under the new code after a brief respite. Part of the phenomenon can be attributed to publicity. The new law was widely covered by the print and broadcast media. Every major radio and television station, magazine and newspaper ran stories on its eventual arrival so many debtors knew of its potential consequences and the short time in which they had to act.

The Bankruptcy Abuse Protection and Consumer Protection Act of 2005 required filers to get bankruptcy counseling and increased the amount of court fees. The *Nilson Report* analyzed the numbers before and after the act took effect and the numbers appeared to confirm critics' greatest fears. The code of 1978 had been used by credit card abusers who filed for bankruptcy rather than pay their debts. Before the new act, Chapter 7 filings averaged about 1.14 million per year and $41,000 each, causing a loss to lenders of $23.5 billion. After the act, the number of filings fell to 349,000 in 2006 for an average of $58,000 each and a total loss of $10.26 billion.[22]

Chapter 13 filings were similar. Before the act, the average number of filings was 428,000, which immediately dropped to 248,000 in 2006. The average amount of a filing increased from $30,000 to $78,000, representing losses of $8.4 billion to $12.6 billion for the creditors. The law created a means test for those filing under Chapter 7, so the increase in Chapter 13 filings was not unusual. Several assumptions made about bankrupts also were confirmed by the results.

Most people filing under Chapter 7 had few assets to liquidate, so little was lost by wiping the slate clean. Others were clever enough to hide them so that it appeared that little was left to satisfy creditors in the courts. A procedure employed by credit collection agencies also seemed to be known to those in arrears on their cards. Collectors would not pursue a person in arrears who was unemployed. When many of those individuals did find employment, they then often filed for Chapter 13 to protect their assets immediately from the collectors who would pursue them again.

In the forty years since they were introduced, credit cards and their other plastic cousins such as prepaid cards and debit cards have proved to be the most successful financial innovation in American history. The numbers they have produced are staggering. At the end of 2007, customers used bank-issued credit cards to pay for $4.34 trillion worth of purchases worldwide, with the Americans and Europeans accounting for 75 percent. In order to achieve that, over 64.5 billion transactions occurred, with Americans accounting for almost half of them. Over 2.38 billion cards exist with slightly over 1 billion in use in the United States alone. That represents three credit cards for every person in the United States whether the persons actually have a card or not. In mid-2008, $954 billion in revolving consumer credit was outstanding in the United States, as was $1.6 trillion of non-revolving credit, for a total of $2.55 trillion. This did not include home equity loans. Of the revolving credit, statistics suggest that around 60 percent of credit card bills are not paid fully when the first bill arrives and the balance is financed on a revolving basis.[23]

Interest Rate Arbitrage

For years since World War II, Wall Street and the City of London had known and practiced what became known as the "carry trade." The process was simple: it involved borrowing cheap money and buying higher-yielding assets. The surfeit of cheap money produced by many central banks in the early 2000s made this type of investing particularly easy. Usually, the technique was used domestically, but then it expanded internationally once markets became more global. The concept was profitable as long as no barriers existed to moving funds internationally at quick notice.

The larger the spread between borrowed money and the asset yield, the greater the arbitrage profit. Borrowing and investing in the same currency was usually the norm in the carry trade, but when hedge funds entered the picture in the early 2000s the game plan began to change. If a currency with a low interest rate could be borrowed, sold, and reinvested in another currency area promising a higher return, then the carry trade would be exported easily. In the early 2000s, Icelandic bonds yielded almost 9 percent while major currencies could be borrowed between 1 and 3 percent. The Japanese yen had the lowest borrowing cost. That could increase the carry to a full 8 percent (800 basis points).

The only risk involved was currency risk. The spread was appetizing but could be deceiving if currency values changed. At returns double the average Treasury bond yield, the trade was considered worth the risk, however. Hedge funds began borrowing yen in order to sell it for Icelandic krona with which they would buy Icelandic government bonds. If done in large volume, the trades paid off well. The Japanese authorities were not inclined to intercede because the yen were borrowed outside Japan, providing little incentive to intervene.

The strategy worked well for a while but began to unravel during the subprime crisis. Carry trades by hedge funds helped bring Iceland to its financial knees in 2008 as the country teetered on the verge of bankruptcy. As the yen began to appreciate and the krona weakened, money was transferred out of Iceland as quickly as it had arrived. The key ingredient in the carry trade was that the currency borrowed remained at the same exchange rate or moved lower in value. But the credit market crisis helped push the yen to all-time highs against other major currencies and the krona. Once it became apparent that currency risk threatened profitable carry trades, money began to flee. Government bond prices slumped and so too did the investments made in Icelandic banks and industry, all of which began to totter on the brink of bankruptcy as carry trade money left the country. Criticizing the government for emulating American and British economic policies that produced a highly leveraged consumer lifestyle, one Icelandic bank depositor noted, "There's so much anger in the society now because of what has happened, we're witnessing the death of Reaganism-Thatcherism. We have to go back to our older values. The free market is not doing what it's supposed to be doing."

The Collapse of the Credit Markets

The credit market crisis of 2007 quickly became the most discussed market collapse since the South Sea Bubble and the crash of 1929. Often described as a bubble created by inflated asset values and excessive leverage, it actually was a great pyramid of debt instruments stacked on top of each other the like of which had not been seen since the fall of the Insull empire in the early 1930s but on a larger and much more complicated scale. Once crucial portions of the pyramid collapsed, the entire structure was doomed to failure. In this respect, it resembled the South Sea Bubble and bore striking similarities to 1929.

At the very bottom of the pyramid were residential mortgages. Above them were consumer loans; above both of them were financial market instruments that employed them through securitization and arbitrage. On the next level were financial institutions that created the instruments and earned their profits from them. Many banks had created many of these instruments and convinced regulators that they posed no threat to the financial system since they were hedging instruments. Once the banks began using highly leveraged instruments of their own creation as regulatory capital, it soon would become apparent that a new sort of bubble had been created, built on a foundation of poorly rated debt and credit risk arbitrage.

Since the financial deregulation of 1999, other non-bank regulators were having an effect upon banking institutions, underlining the importance of the shadow banking system and the piecemeal, but important, effect that regulators could have on it. Banking regulators were not alone in relaxing previously established standards. The SEC also encouraged deregulation by making one of the most crucial decisions in its history in favor of the securities houses under its control. In 2004, the chief executives of the four major investment banks prevailed on the SEC to relax its capital requirements on them by 50 percent, effectively allowing them to double their leverage. Effectively, this let them establish leverage ratios of forty to one from twenty to one, an enormous increase in margined capital. This helped the investment banks underwrite even more mortgage-related securities. The move inadvertently complemented the Fed's relaxing of capital requirements in accordance with the guidelines of the Bank for International Settlements and proved to be the major force behind the credit market debacle as a result.

At the beginning of the crisis, an instrument unknown outside of financial circles became the first victim of the deflating bubble. Financial engineers had created special investment vehicles (SIVs) several years before in order to create a type of carry trade that could be used as a funding source. These vehicles were pools funded by commercial paper with the proceeds invested in medium-term obligations such as CDOs and other asset-backed securities (ABSs). Their liabilities were short-term while their assets were medium-term on average. The assets were purchased on margin, enhancing the gains for the pools. These mismatched instruments gained in popularity between 2004 and 2007, tripling in asset size. Before the crisis began, thirty-six SIVs existed, holding around $400 billion in assets. Although only a small amount of the assets were invested in subprime mortgages, values began to drop in 2007 and investors began to liquidate, forcing several of the SIVs to liquidate or restructure, including hedge funds run by the investment bank Bear Stearns.[24] The repercussions were felt quickly. Several public pension funds and employee funds faced liquidity problems when asset values fell and were unable to meet demands for cash temporarily, not unlike the crisis caused in Orange County, California two decades before.

The problems with SIVs helped precipitate the financial crisis and underlined some of its fundamental problems. Special investment vehicles raised funds to purchase mortgage-related and other fixed income assets from the commercial paper market, relying on it as a constant source of funds. Although the market had existed in the United States for 150 years, it had become more popular as a source of funds since the 1970s, when credit card issuers began to use it as a source with which to purchase card receivables from merchants. The card loans made to consumers, when combined with the commercial paper market, became the first part of the shadow banking system after World War II. Most of these activities fell outside the realm of federal banking regulators. When SIVs were developed, they relied on instruments created by the shadow system, including CDOs and private label mortgage securities. Since some of the CDOs also included derivative products such as credit default swaps, the soundness of the entire SIV concept depended upon a normal financial environment with few if any extraneous shocks to the system as a whole. If the soundness of the system were shaken, these sorts of instruments would be the first adversely affected.

Not clear at the time was the exposure of banking institutions to instruments created by the shadow system. This became evident when the investment bank Bear Stearns began suffering problems in the winter of 2008. Normally, an investment bank experiencing financial problems was somewhat isolated from the banking system as a whole before the deregulatory legislation in 1999. But in the nine intervening years, Bear Stearns, like other securities firms, had engaged in many commercial banking activities on the wholesale level and was also a packager of private label mortgage securities. It also ran several hedge funds, selling participations in them to investors. These hedge funds failed in the summer of 2007 and its costs began to rise in the repo-market where it obtained much of its short-term funding. When the bank finally requested assistance, the Federal Reserve intervened, reminiscent of Long-Term Capital Management. It was the first time the central bank propped up a securities dealer until a buyer could be found. In a hastily arranged takeover, J. P. Morgan Chase intervened and purchased the stock of the ailing bank with the approbation of the Fed. Ben Bernanke, the chairman of the Fed, later remarked, "Our view was that the Fed had to act because its [Bear Stearns'] failure would have brought down that [repo] market, which would have had implications for other firms."[25] This was important because the firm was recognized as a primary dealer in Treasury securities by the Fed; Bear Stearns was one of the firms with which the Fed conducted its monetary policy in the money market.

The downfall of Bear Stearns was caused by its exposure to the mortgage market. Its balance sheet was highly leveraged and most of its funding was short-term in nature, exposing it to demands for funds at short notice. The financial world was split in its opinion about the rescue. Some claimed that the bank should have been allowed to fail; the financial system needed a shock of that nature to correct its ills. Others argued for a more lenient treatment from the Fed; few argued that the path taken was correct. Secretary Henry Paulson of the Treasury presided over the financial crisis and relied on the black swan as an explanation for the travails of the bank. "There was no playbook for responding to a once or twice in a hundred year event," he remarked, emphasizing instead the obligation of the Treasury to remedy the problem.[26] Similar comments were made by former Fed chairman Alan Greenspan. The links—risky and otherwise—between the markets were overlooked.

As the number of subprime mortgage defaults increased, pressure was put on the banks originally making the loans as well as the securitizers. One fact, which had not been given much thought before, became clear as the crisis unfolded. Securitized bond obligations, especially those for mortgages, always were assumed to carry the guarantee of the original lending institution in the event the collateral pool somehow failed. This was the implicit guarantee provided by the federal government for Freddie Mac and Fannie Mae obligations. They had been successful for decades. Another implicit assumption arose—that all securitized bonds were in the same legal position. But that was not the case with private label residential CMOs in particular. The investor had no recourse to the original lender. If the pool defaulted fully or partially, the losses stopped with investors. The lenders had no obligation to support them.

Wall Street had sold the private label residential mortgage securities for some years under the description that such collateralized bonds were "bankruptcy remote." This emphasized the opposite side of investor risk by seeking to assure investors that if the issuer went bankrupt they would be protected by the collateral. If the original lending bank filed for bankruptcy, investors would be protected because the securitized collateral belonged to them and were not general obligations of the failed institution. But the other side of that argument was not discussed clearly: if the pool failed the original lender had no obligation to support it because the mortgages were no longer its assets. Structured finance originally was devised to help financial institutions shed assets through securitization. The technique was a risk mitigation technique. Once the assets were gone, the lender wanted nothing more to do with them. If it did, it would not have employed securitization in the first place. The U.S. government's implicit guarantee of the GSEs was an anomaly: without it the agencies would never have been successful. And the U.S. Treasury had never been in the position of having to bail out a mortgage assistance agency. The housing market had been too resilient since World War II.

Once the agencies began to drift from their securitization model, their balance sheets and income statements came under serious stress. For several years prior to the financial crisis they had been purchasing subprime mortgages from lenders. When the foreclosures began, the crisis hit the agencies as well as investors because the agencies had to make up any interest shortcomings in the pools of outstanding bonds. They had been purchasing these mortgages from large lenders that made subprime and Alt-A mortgages their specialty. Two lenders, notably Countrywide Savings and Washington Mutual, both failed during the crisis. The same fate befell Fannie Mae and Freddie Mac after it became clear that the implicit government guarantee discussed for years on Wall Street was becoming explicit.

In the summer of 2008, the shares of many financial institutions, including Fannie and Freddie, came under severe pressure and began to fall precipitously. Both agencies lost most of their market capitalization and had to be put into receivership by the Treasury until their finances could be sorted out. The occasion marked the third postwar default of a GSE since the Farm Credit System needed to be restructured twenty years before as the result of a farm crisis. The savings and loan crisis, about the same time as the farm problem, also required a federal agency, the Federal Home Loan Bank Board, to be restructured. But the seizure of the mortgage agencies' operations was the largest in the hundred-year history of federal agencies.

The nature of the agencies came into question and the mercantilist analogy was drawn again as the extent of their losses became better known. Although placed in receivership, the two agencies continued to perform their normal operations and supported the residential housing market. Their borrowing costs remained low as the implicit guarantee of the Treasury ensured that they were able to continue borrowing despite the fact that their equity capital was gone. But the guarantee costs to the Treasury meant that no further funds would be available to other institutions that might run into financial difficulties.

After organizing a hasty resolution to Bear Stearns' problems, there was an assumption that the Fed and the Treasury would not let a major financial institution fail during the crisis. The concept of "too big to fail" became the catchword of the period as most market participants believed that institutions with sizable assets could not technically fail because of their importance to the economy. Criticism arose because this was an implicit acknowledgment that the taxpayers would have to underwrite an institution's lending policies regardless of soundness. This was the most recent application of the idea of moral hazard that had been discussed in the United States since the FDIC was created in 1933. In this case, the hazard far exceeded the insurable amounts of deposits and included the entire asset base of large institutions.

Since the collapse of Bear Stearns, rumors of financial difficulties had surrounded Lehman Brothers, one of Wall Street's oldest and best-known investment banks. Also an active participant in the money market and a primary dealer, Lehman was a packager of CMOs and a major participant in the swap market. It also had a major exposure to the real estate market in addition to its underwriting activities. Despite attempts to shore up its balance sheet, Lehman's problems climaxed in September 2008 when it requested assistance from the Fed so that it could continue in business. The central bank responded in much the same way as it had in previous crises: it sought a buyer for Lehman among the banking community.

Following the deregulation of 1999, Lehman also had become very large, possessing assets of over $600 billion. No other bank came forward as a buyer and as a result Lehman filed for bankruptcy several days later. The filing was the largest in U.S. history and caused great confusion in the markets, which were expecting a bailout or successful resolution of some sort. The swap market, especially the market for credit default swaps (CDSs), suffered as well, having an indirect effect at other banks in the system since CDSs were included in bank capital and any deterioration in their value would mean an immediate deterioration at a crucial juncture for many banking institutions.

The market for fixed income derivatives suffered a worse shock when the Treasury agreed to bail out the insurer AIG after failing to intervene on behalf of Lehman Brothers. The company, the world's largest insurer, was on the verge of collapse mainly because of its activities in the swap market, not its traditional insurance business. Many banks had entered the insurance business through the back door by conducting swaps on a large scale and AIG had extended its activities through swaps. In both cases, financial institutions were extending themselves into businesses that did not require a license in which to operate.[27] The Financial Crisis Inquiry Commission established to examine the causes of the crisis concluded that "the inconsistency of federal government decisions in not rescuing Lehman after having rescued Bear Stearns and the GSEs, and immediately before rescuing AIG, added to uncertainty and panic in the financial markets."[28]

The result of the crisis was a sharp downturn in residential mortgage credit. Consumer credit declined slightly, from $2.55 trillion in 2007 to $2.477 trillion in 2009. During that time, credit card use continued to increase while non-revolving credit declined slightly.[29] The number of new residential mortgage originations fell from $2.7 trillion in 2006 to $1.5 trillion in 2008, recovering to $2 trillion in 2009.[30] This trend affected the number of new corporate bonds being issued since many of the SEC registrations during that time period were for asset-backed securities. It also revealed how much the capital markets had been preoccupied with mortgage-related securities. In 2007, $2.2 trillion worth of new corporate bonds were issued by U.S. corporations, declining to $861 billion in 2008 and $947 billion in 2009.[31] During the same period, private label residential mortgage securitizations collapsed, leaving most of the market for new issues to the GSEs. Since the capital markets had been preoccupied with mortgages, when the market began to decrease the bubble had been removed from the economy and economic activity slowed considerably.

Both consumer credit and residential mortgage credit suffered during the crisis, but the residential mortgage market fared worse. The number of mortgage foreclosures rose dramatically to the point where over one hundred thousand new foreclosures were being recorded monthly from 2008 through 2011.[32] The number of mortgage originations that did occur after 2008 masked the fact that many of the foreclosed homes were sold at bargain prices to new owners or that some homeowners refinanced their existing debt.

The crisis also added impetus to a trend that had been developing since the early 2000s. By 2010, debit card use was almost equaling credit card use by consumers who were attempting to reduce their indebtedness by paying for consumption purchases up front rather than charging them.[33] The number of credit card defaults rose to record heights nevertheless. By 2010, the default rate was almost 10 percent, three times the ordinary rate assumed by card lenders.[34] One of the great ironies of the commoditization of credit was found in what card lenders called the "default rate." In trade terms this was not the rate of cardholders who did not pay their bills but rather the interest rate applied to those who violated the card companies' collection policies in some manner. If a payment was received late, the companies increased the interest rate of the account to as much as 30 percent to reflect the increased risk they felt they were exposed to by the cardholder. Access to further credit was not denied, but a higher price was exacted for it. But even the higher rates could not make up for the shortfall created by the collapse of the securitization market.

In the fall of 2008, Congress passed emergency legislation referred to as the Troubled Assets Relief Program (TARP), which allowed the Treasury to purchase financial assets in the market in order to help stabilize asset prices. In addition, the Federal Reserve announced its Commercial Paper Funding Facility, which allowed it to purchase commercial paper in the market so that interest rates would remain low rather than increase, reflecting the skepticism of institutional investors about conditions in the money market, especially after the collapse of Lehman Brothers. After the crisis began, many investors avoided commercial paper, potentially leading to a collapse in the availability of consumer credit. This operation helped provide support for the many credit card lenders that funded their activities in the money market, ensuring a continued supply of short-term funds for consumer lenders but in reduced amounts. Interest rates on commercial paper fell to low levels, reflecting the Fed's accommodative monetary policy during the crisis. But lenders were quick to increase their own rates to cardholders, claiming increased counterparty and credit risk. The rise in card rates brought a reaction from legislators and consumers, many of whom claimed the lenders were charging usurious rates at a time of otherwise low interest rates. Usury again was claimed after decades of remaining in the background of discussions about financial markets that emphasized less regulation rather than more.

One Last Time

As the financial crisis lingered, usury again became an issue both in the states and in Washington, DC. Thirty-four states had usury laws on their books that capped consumer interest at 36 percent and a dozen others had laws regulating payday lenders. Most of these laws were legacies from the movement to raise usury ceilings in the 1920s. Many of the usury laws exempted banks and applied only to finance companies or other lenders. The bank exemptions were designed to avoid conflict with the usury ceiling embedded in the National Bank Act of 1864. In reality, the *Marquette* decision prevailed as far as banks were concerned.

The rates of interest charged by lenders generally prompted attempts in Congress to intervene by passing a usury ceiling of 36 percent, applicable to all lenders. Some attempts were made to cap rates even lower at institutions that received TARP money from the Treasury.[35] Other attempts were made to lower the maximum lending rate to a specific spread over a bank's costs of funds in the marketplace. Despite the attempts, the prevailing consensus was that limiting interest rates during a financial crisis was not helpful to lenders and could lead to an even further diminution of credit in the markets than was already the case since the banks had become extremely cautious in their lending policies. The credit crisis produced a tightening of lending standards and higher consumer interest rates; the latter increased to compensate banks for the default risks found in the mortgage and consumer lending markets.

The home foreclosure crisis plus predatory practices by credit card lenders led Congress to create a new consumer protection agency among many other reforms when the Dodd-Frank Wall Street Reform Act was passed in

2010. Building on several prior actions of the Federal Reserve, the new law sought to protect consumers against precipitous interest rate increases by credit card lenders, but it made no mention of the actual rates of interest that could be charged as previous bills sought. From an emotive perspective, usury ceilings were appealing but would not be included in legislation. If the Fed had been able to set rates on consumer loans such action would have been inconsistent with its management of the money supply and float, which relied on using monetary aggregates to control interest rates rather than the other way around. It appeared that interest rate ceilings were still viewed as static, considered only by populists and non-market-oriented activists.

Despite attempts in Congress and elsewhere to resurrect the usury ceiling debates, no prohibition of the practice was included in the Dodd-Frank law. The free market ideology prevailed again in this instance and the functions of the Fed under Regulation Z were left intact. Customers were free to borrow as they wished as long as lenders made an attempt to inform them of the effective rate of interest being charged under the consumer lending act of 1968. The extent of the credit market crisis did not have any immediate effect on the ancient debate, suggesting that it was no longer a viable concept in a world of commoditized credit. The idea that central bank regulators could manage the monetary aggregates successfully appeared to make usury an outdated term, with the exception of criminal usury.

After decades of denying that usury was relevant to the American financial system, passing mention of it was still made in Dodd-Frank, although the mention was a far cry from what supporters wished. According to the law, there was "no authority to establish a usury limit" in the new law without a specific act of Congress.[36] This was included to maintain the line of demarcation between national banks and others, in order to prevent jurisdictional conflicts between the states' banking prerogatives and federal banking law. If a national usury law was to be passed, it would have to be done by Congress and not imposed by a federal agency that was part of the Dodd-Frank reforms. One notable Wall Street law firm commented on this part of the act, "Some members of Congress may attempt to amend the Act to include additional substantive provisions. For example, the Act's prohibition on the establishment of a national usury limit and the preservation of a national bank's ability to export interest rates may be revisited in the future, especially given that they arguably are in tension with other goals of the Act."[37]

When market economies developed, static ideas like usury were assumed to have outlived their usefulness. Yet the debate and the use of the term survived; its inclusion in the Dodd-Frank law along with hundreds of more contemporary terms and practices demonstrated that the idea was alive and well although in a state of semi-hibernation. The idea that usury prohibitions were a cornerstone of natural law theory had long since dissolved, replaced by the attractions of modern consumer society and the dictates of economic growth, which had become public policy in the twentieth century. But excessive interest, whether in nominal terms or real terms created by compounding, still prevailed. Ironically, nominal rates charged to consumers during the financial crisis after 2007 were similar to the rates charged by Brutus or those paid by Edward III. The development of market economies created a set of business and corporate interest rates that conformed to the dictates of supply and demand in the market, but consumption loan rates remained a thorny problem as they have since antiquity. The persistence of pawn shops remains a testament to the tacit acceptance of high rates, disguised by the lenders as an occasional credit facility made available to the working class.

Albert Einstein reputedly once remarked that compound interest was the eighth wonder of the world. Richard Price recognized that fact as well, although the political will to use it to uselful public purposes often was lacking in the eighteenth century as it has been in the twenty-first. In its long history, consumer interest has remained remarkably the same despite subtle changes in calculations and lending policies over the years. On the long-term planning side, it had been put to more positive use through the use of annuities and pension planning. Interest, and especially compound interest, has remained one of the major socioeconomic issues for the last three thousand years, but the intricacies of the calculations have remained mostly a mystery to all except finance specialists and bankers. Unlike the other major cornerstones of natural law or economic theory, it remains the one practice that contains both positive and negative elements, with the former winning out over the latter. In the Middle Ages, it was considered a necessary evil, a means of survival as well as a way forward. Today, it remains a price worth paying because it demonstrates the ebullience and the optimism of the human condition.

Understanding interest and borrowing as part of the natural law tradition helps underscore both the seriousness and the ambiguity that debt has occupied in banking and finance for three thousand years. Over the centuries debt has become a central issue that, despite modern advances in the theory and practice of finance, continues to maintain its grip on modern society much as it did in the ancient and medieval worlds. As a practice, it has changed remarkably little and the effects of abusing it can be as volatile today as they were at anytime in the past. Until the debt crisis of 2008, it was incorrectly assumed that excessive borrowing could be controlled and managed without incident. Miscalculations have proved to be part of the tradition as well.

Early Interest Rate Tables and Calculations

Simon Stevin

S imon Stevin's interest rate tables, first published in 1582, were discount, or present value tables, and included the future value of an annuity as well. Table 1 presents the table for 6 percent interest, from the French edition of his *Tables of Interest* published in 1625. In Column 1 is the number of time periods, or years. Column 2 contains the present value of 10 million units at 6 percent, while Column 3 is the compound, or future, value of the discounted value in Column 2, considered as an annuity for the same time period (also at 6 percent). Decimal points were omitted in both examples and the reader was assumed to realize that discounting involved amounts less than one while compounding involved amounts greater than one. Factors in Column 2 are all less than 1.0 while factors in Column 3 are greater than 1.0. All factors assume semi-annual compounding or discounting.

Table 1. Stevin's Interest Rate Table for 6 Percent Interest

1	2	3
1	9433962	9433962
2	8899964	18333926
3	8396192	26730118
4	7920936	34651054

5	7472581	42123635
6	7049605	49173240
7	6650571	55823311
8	6274124	62097935
9	5918985	68016920
10	5583948	73600868
11	5267875	78868743
12	4968983	83838436
13	4688390	88526826
14	4423009	92949835
15	4172650	97122485
16	3936462	101058947
17	3713643	104772590
18	3503437	108276027
19	3305129	111581156
20	3118046	114699202
21	2941553	117640755
22	2275050	120415805
23	2617971	123033777
24	2469785	125503562
25	2329986	127833548
26	2198100	130031648
27	2073679	132105327
28	1956301	134061628
29	1845567	135907195
30	1741101	137648296

Source: Simon Stevin, *L'arithmetique de Simon Stevin de Bruges: Reueue* corrigee et augmentee de plusieurs traictez et annotations par Albert Girard* (Leiden: De l'imprimerie des Elzeviers, 1625).

James Hodder

Figure 1 shows a facsimile of Hodder's interest rate table, from the first American edition of his book published in 1719. The rate selected here is 6 percent. To determine the interest (at 6 percent) on 36 pounds over twenty years, multiply the 36 pounds by the figure to the right of the 20 (in the column on the left), the figure being 3 pounds, 4 shillings, 1 pence, and 2 farthings. Since the English and Americans did not adopt the Gregorian calendar until 1750, his answer has to be adjusted (shortened) by ten days per year in order to be consistent with a similar calculation used in Stevin's table. Otherwise, the calculation assumes 20 shillings to a pound, 240 pence to a pound, and 4 farthings in a pence, or 960 farthings per pound.

l.	*s.*	*d.*	*q.*	
1	1	01	02	1	The Table is fo plain,
2	1	02	05	2	that I fuppofe it needs
3	1	03	09	3	very little Demonftrati-
4	1	05	03	0	on; I fhall therefore on-
5	1	06	09	0	ly give you one or two
6	1	08	04	1	Examples.
7	1	10	00	3	
8	1	11	01	2	As,
9	1	13	09	1	
10	1	15	09	3	If you would know
11	1	17	11	2	what 36 *l.* comes to In-
12	2	00	02	3	tereft upon Intereft for
13	2	02	07	3	20 Years.
14	2	05	02	2	Look againft Number
15	2	07	11	0	20 in the firft Column,
16	2	10	09	2	and you will find what
17	2	13	10	0	the Intereft upon Intereft
18	2	17	00	3	of 1 *l.* comes to for that
19	3	00	05	3	time. Then fay, by the
20	3	04	01	2	Rule of Three,
21	3	07	11	2	

Figure 1. Hodder's interest rate table. From James Hodder, *Hodder's Arithmetick* (Boston: J. Franklin, 1719).

Edmund Halley

Figure 2 shows an annuities entry, including a reference to Halley's tables, published in an early edition of the *Encyclopedia Britannica*.

III. *Life Annuities.*

THE value of annuities for life is determined from obfervations made on the bills of mortality. Dr Halley, Mr Simpfon, and Monf. de Moivre, are gentlemen of diftinguifhed merit in calculations of this kind.

Dr Halley had recourfe to the bills of mortality at Breflaw, the capital of Silefia, as a proper ftandard for the other parts of Europe, being a place pretty central, at a diftance from the fea, and not much crowded with traffickers or foreigners. He pitches upon 1000 perfons all born in one year, and obferves how many of thefe were alive every year, from their birth to the extinction of the laft, and confequently how many died each year, as in the firft of the following tables: which is well adapted to Europe in general. But in the city of London, there is obferved to be a greater difparity in the births and burials than in any other place, owing probably to the vaft refort of people thither, in the way of commerce, from all parts of the known world. Mr Simpfon, therefore, in order to have a table particularly fuited

Figure 2. An annuities entry from *Encyclopedia Britannica*, 1773.

fuited to this populous city, pitches upon 1280 perfons all born in the fame year, and records the number remaining alive each year, till none were in life.

Dr Halley's table on the bills of mortality at Breflaw.

Age.	Perf. liv.	A.	Perf. liv.	A.	Perf. liv.	A.	Perf. liv.
1	1000	24	573	47	377	70	142
2	855	25	567	48	367	71	131
3	798	26	560	49	357	72	120
4	760	27	553	50	346	73	109
5	732	28	546	51	335	74	98
6	710	29	539	52	324	75	88
7	692	30	531	53	313	76	78
8	680	31	523	54	302	77	68
9	670	32	515	55	292	78	58
10	661	33	507	56	282	79	49
11	653	34	499	57	272	80	41
12	646	35	490	58	262	81	34
13	640	36	481	59	252	82	28
14	634	37	472	60	242	83	23
15	628	38	463	61	232	84	20
16	622	39	454	62	222	85	15
17	616	40	445	63	212	86	11
18	610	41	436	64	202	87	8
19	604	42	427	65	192	88	5
20	598	43	417	66	182	89	3
21	592	44	407	67	172	90	1
22	586	45	397	68	162	91	0
23	579	46	387	69	152		

Mr Simpfon's table on the bills of mortality at London.

It may not be improper in this place to obferve, that however perfect tables of this fort may be in themfelves, and however well adapted to any particular climate, yet the conclufions deduced from them muft always be uncertain, being nothing more than probabilities, or conjectures drawn from the ufual period of human life. And the practice of buying and felling annuities on lives, by rules founded on fuch principles, may be juftly confidered as a fort of lottery or chance-work, in which the parties concerned muft often be deceived. But as eftimates and computations of this kind are now become fafhionable, we fhall here give fome brief account of fuch as appear moft material.

From the above tables the probability of the continuance or extinction of human life is eftimated as follows.

1. The probability that a perfon of a given age fhall live a certain number of years, is meafured by the proportion which the number of perfons living at the propofed age has to the difference between the faid number and the number of perfons living at the given age.

Thus, if it be demanded, what chance a perfon of 40 years has to live feven years longer ? from 445, the number of perfons living at 40 years of age in Dr Halley's table, fubtract 377, the number of perfons living at 47 years of age, and the remainder 68, is the number of perfons that died during thefe 7 years ; and the probability or chance that the perfon in the queftion fhall live thefe 7 years is as 377 to 68, or nearly as 5¾ to 1. But, by Mr Simpfon's table, the chance is fomething lefs than that of 4 to 1.

2. If the year to which a perfon of a given age has an equal chance of arriving before he dies, be required, it may be found thus : Find half the number of perfons living at the given age in the tables, and in the column of age you have the year required.

Thus, if the queftion be put with refpect to a perfon of 30 years of age, the number of that age in Dr Halley's table is 531, the half whereof is 265, which is found in the table between 57 and 58 years ; fo that a perfon of 30 years has an equal chance of living between 27 and 28 years longer.

3. By the tables, the premium of infurance upon lives may in fome meafure be regulated.

Thus, The chance that a perfon of 25 years has to live another year, is, by Dr Halley's table, as 80 to 1 ; but the chance that a perfon of 50 years has to live a year longer is only 30 to 1. And, confequently, the premium for infuring the former ought to be to the premium for infuring the latter for one year, as 30 to 80, or as 3 to 8.

Prob. I. To find the value of an annuity of 1 l. for the life of a fingle perfon of any given age.

Monf. de Moivre, by obferving the decreafe of the probabilities of life, as exhibited in the table, compofed an algebraic theorem or canon, for computing the value of an annuity for life; which canon I fhall here lay down by way of

Rule. Find the complement of life ; and, by the tables, find the value of 1 l. annuity for the years denoted by the faid complement ; multiply this value by the amount

amount of 1 l. for a year, and divide the product by the complement of life; then subtract the quot from 1; divide the remainder by the interest of 1 l. for a year; and this last quot will be the value of the annuity sought, or, in other words, the number of years purchase the annuity is worth.

EXAMP. What is the value of an annuity of 1l. for an age of 50 years, interest at 5 per cent.

```
         86
         50 age given.
         36 complement of life.
```

By the Tables, the value is, 16.5468
Amount of 1 l. for a year,   1.05
```
                    827340
                    165468
```

Complement of life, 36)17.374140(.482615
From unity, viz. 1.000000
Subtract   .482615
Interest of 1l. .05).517385(10.3477, value sought.

By the preceding problem is constructed the following table.

The value of 1 l. annuity for a single life.

Age.	3 per c.	3½ per c.	4 per c.	4½ per c.	5 per c.	6 per c.
9=10	19.87	18.27	16.88	15.67	14.60	12.80
8=11	19.74	18.16	16.79	15.59	14.53	12.75
7=12	19.60	18.05	16.64	15.51	14.47	12.70
- 13	19.47	17.94	16.60	15.43	14.41	12.65
6=14	19.33	17.82	16.50	15.35	14.34	12.60
15	19.19	17.71	16.41	15.27	14.27	12.55
16	19.05	17.59	16.31	15.19	14.20	12.50
5=17	18.90	17.46	16.21	15.10	14.12	12.45
18	18.76	17.33	16.10	15.01	14.05	12.40
19	18.61	17.21	15.99	14.92	13.97	12.35
4=20	18.46	17.09	15.89	14.83	13.89	12.30
21	18.30	16.96	15.78	14.73	13.81	12.20
22	18.15	16.83	15.67	14.64	13.72	12.15
23	17.99	16.69	15.55	14.54	13.64	12.10
3=24	17.83	16.56	15.43	14.44	13.55	12.00
25	17.66	16.42	15.31	14.34	13.46	11.95
26	17.50	16.28	15.19	14.23	13.37	11.90
27	17.33	16.13	15.04	14.12	13.28	11.80
28	17.16	15.98	14.94	14.02	13.18	11.75
29	16.98	15.83	14.81	13.90	13.09	11.65
30	16.80	15.68	14.68	13.79	12.99	11.60
2=31	16.62	15.53	14.54	13.67	12.88	11.50
32	16.44	15.37	14.41	13.55	12.78	11.40
33	16.25	15.21	14.27	13.43	12.67	11.35
34	16.06	15.05	14.12	13.30	12.56	11.25
35	15.86	14.89	13.98	13.17	12.45	11.15
36	15.67	14.71	13.82	13.04	12.33	11.05
37	15.46	14.52	13.67	12.90	12.21	11.00
38	15.29	14.34	13.52	12.77	12.09	10.90
1=39	15.05	14.16	13.36	12.63	11.96	10.80
40	14.84	13.98	13.20	12.48	11.83	10.70

The value of 1 l. annuity for a single life.

A.	3 per c.	3½ per c.	4 per c	4½ per c.	5 per c.	6 per c.
41	14.63	13.79	13.02	12.33	11.70	10.55
42	14.41	13.59	12.85	12.18	11.57	10.45
43	14.19	13.40	12.68	12.02	11.43	10.35
44	13.96	13.20	12.50	11.87	11.29	10.25
45	13.73	12.99	12.32	11.70	11.14	10.10
46	13.49	12.78	12.13	11.54	10.99	10.00
47	13.25	12.56	11.94	11.37	10.84	9.85
48	13.01	12.36	11.74	11.19	10.68	9.75
49	12.76	12.14	11.54	11.00	10.51	9.60
50	12.51	11.92	11.34	10.82	10.35	9.45
51	12.26	11.69	11.13	10.64	10.17	9.30
52	12.00	11.45	10.92	10.44	9.99	9.20
53	11.73	11.20	10.70	10.24	9.82	9.00
54	11.46	10.95	10.47	10.04	9.63	8.85
55	11.18	10.69	10.24	9.82	9.44	8.70
56	10.90	10.44	10.01	9.61	9.24	8.55
57	10.61	10.18	9.77	9.39	9.04	8.35
58	10.32	9.91	9.52	9.16	8.83	8.20
59	10.03	9.64	9.27	8.93	8.61	8.00
60	9.73	9.36	9.01	8.69	8.39	7.80
61	9.42	9.08	8.75	8.44	8.16	7.60
62	9.11	8.79	8.48	8.19	7.93	7.40
63	8.79	8.49	8.20	7.94	7.68	7.20
64	8.46	8.19	7.92	7.67	7.43	6.95
65	8.13	7.88	7.63	7.39	7.18	6.75
66	7.79	7.56	7.33	7.12	6.91	6.50
67	7.45	7.24	7.02	6.83	6.64	6.25
68	7.10	6.91	6.75	6.54	6.36	6.00
69	6.75	6.57	6.39	6.23	6.07	5.75
70	6.38	6.22	6.06	5.92	5.77	5.50
71	6.01	5.87	5.72	5.59	5.47	5.20
72	5.63	5.51	5.38	5.26	5.15	4.90
73	5.25	5.14	5.02	4.92	4.82	4.60
74	4.85	4.77	4.66	4.57	4.49	4.30
75	4.45	4.38	4.29	4.22	4.14	4.00
76	4.05	3.98	3.91	3.84	3.78	3.65
77	3.63	3.57	3.52	3.47	3.41	3.30
78	3.21	3.16	3.11	3.07	3.03	2.95
79	2.78	2.74	2.70	2.67	2.64	2.55
80	2.34	2.31	2.28	2.26	2.23	2.15

The above table shews the value of an annuity of one pound for a single life, at all the current rates of interest; and is esteemed the best table of this kind extant, and preferable to any other of a different construction. But yet those who sell annuities have generally one and a half or two years more value, than specified in the table, from purchasers whose age is 20 years or upwards.

Annuities of this sort are commonly bought or sold at so many years purchase; and the value assigned in the table may be so reckoned. Thus the value of an annuity

William Webster

Figure 3 presents a sample of William Webster's widely used interest rate tables, first published in 1634. It uses pounds and pence rather than decimals, so it needs to be converted to be compared with continental tables such as Stevins's.

Compound Intereſt direct at 8 per Centum.

The yearly increaſe of an annuity of 10 l, and ſo of any annuitie or yearly paiment to 31 yeares at Compound intereſt after 8 *per Centum*: Neceſſary for all ſuch as forbeare, or are to receive recompence for any ſuch paimēts detained. *Fractions are part of pence.*

yeares	l s d	yeares	l s d
1	10.00.0	17	337.10. 0 9/25
2	20.16.0	18	374.10. 0 9/25
3	32.09.3 9/25	19	414.09. 2 10/25
4	45.01.2 16/25	20	457.12. 4 11/25
5	58.13.3 20/25	21	504.04. 6 18/25
6	73.07.2 5/25	22	554.11. 3 22/25
7	89.04.6 17/25	23	608.18. 7 14/25
8	106.07.3 21/25	24	667.12.11 1/25
9	124.17.6 3/25	25	731.01. 1 21/25
10	144.17.3 17/25	26	799.10.10 9/25
11	166.09.1 3/25	27	873.10. 1 6/25
12	189.15.5	28	953.07. 8 14/25
13	214.19.0 12/25	29	1039.13. 1 14/25
14	242.02.11 17/25	30	1132.16. 6 24/25
15	271.10.4 21/25	31	1233.07. 6 8/25
16	303.04.10 3/25		

Figure 3. Interest rate table from William Webster, *Webster's Tables* (London: M. Flesher for Nicolas Bourne, 1634).

Isaac Newton

Figure 4 shows the problem concerning compound interest posed by Isaac Newton; the problem was published in 1720. In contemporary terms, it solves for the compound rate of interest that would be better known as the yield to maturity for the annuity. It is one of the early attempts at solving for the rate.

PROBLEM XVI. If an annual Penfion of the [Number of] Pounds *a*, to be paid in the five next following Years, be bought for the ready Money *c*, to find what the Compound Intereft of 100 *l. per Annum* will amount to ?

Make 1 — *x* the Compound Intereft of the Money *x* for a Year, that is, that the Money 1 to be paid after one Year is worth *x* in ready Money ; and, by Proportion, the Money *a* to be paid after one Year will be worth *ax* in ready Money, and after 2 Years [it will be worth] *axx*, and after 3 Years *ax*³, and after 4 Years *ax*⁴, and after 5 Years *ax*⁵. Add thefe 5 Terms, and you'll have *ax*⁵ + *ax*⁴ + *ax*³ + *axx* + *ax* = *c*, or *x*⁵ + *x*⁴ + *x*³ + *x*² +

$x = \frac{c}{a}$ an Æquation of 5 Dimenfions, by Help of which when *x* is found by the Rules to be taught hereafter, put *x* : 1 :: 100 : *y*, and *y* — 100 will be the Compound Intereft of 100 *l. per Annum.*

It is [will be] fufficient to have given thefe Inftances in Queftions where only the Proportions of Quantities are to be confider'd, without the Pofitions of Lines : Let us now proceed to the Solutions of Geometrical Problems.

Figure 4. The problem of compound interest as posed by Newton. From Isaac Newton, *Universal Arithmetick: or, A Treatise of Arithmetical Composition and Resolution*, translated by Raphson (London: J. Senex, 1720).

Notes

Chapter 1

1. See Benjamin Nelson, *The Idea of Usury: From Tribal Brotherhood to Universal Otherhood*, 2nd ed. (Chicago: University of Chicago Press, 1969), chap. 1.

2. E. Neufeld, "The Rate of Interest and the Text of Nehemiah 5.11," *Jewish Quarterly Review* 44 (1954): 196.

3. *The Twelve Tables*, Table 8, 18A. See Yale Law School, *The Avalon Project*, http://avalon.yale.edu.

4. Although simple interest ruled the day, many borrowers had to take out a new loan to pay an older one, effectively paying interest on two loans so that compound interest was present although not intended by lenders. See William Smith, William Wayte, and G. E. Marindin, editors, *A Dictionary of Greek and Roman Antiquities*, 3rd ed. (London: John Murray, 1901), 836.

5. *Twelve Tables*, Table 8, 18B where a usurer, if condemned, was liable for quadruple damages while a thief was liable only for double damages.

6. See Reinhard Zimmerman, *The Law of Obligations: The Roman Foundations of the Civilian Tradition* (Oxford: Clarendon Press, 1996), 167–168.

7. Cicero attempted to act as a mediator between Brutus's agent and the Cypriots who owed him money. But the agent, Scaptius, would not agree to take 1 percent per month as interest on the loan, despite the fact that the Cypriots offered to put it on deposit in a temple for safekeeping. He demanded 4 percent instead. Cicero was unable to get the two parties to agree. He wrote that "all present cried that Scaptius was as shameless as could be for refusing to be satisfied with one percent compound interest . . . but I regarded him as shameless rather than stupid, for either he was dissatisfied with one percent on good security, or he hoped for four percent on doubtful security See Marcus Tullius Cicero, *Selected Letters*, translated by P. G. Walsh (Oxford: Oxford University Press, 2008), letter 60, p. 132.

8. S. G. Vesey-Fitzgerald, "Dam Dupat—Alterum Tantum," *Journal of Comparative Legislation and International Law* 7 (1925): 176.

9. Plato, *The Laws*, in *The Dialogues of Plato*, translated by Benjamin Jowett (Oxford: Clarendon Press, 1953), 742 c.

10. Aristotle, *Politics*, translated by Ernest Barker (New York: Oxford University Press, 1962), x, 4.

11. First Council of Nicaea, Canon 17, in *Decrees of the Ecumenical Councils*, edited by Norman P. Tanner (Washington, DC: Georgetown University Press, 1990), 1: 14.

12. R. W. Carlyle, and A. J. Carlyle, *A History of Mediaeval Political Theory in the West* (Edinburgh: William Blackwood, 1903), 1: 79ff.

13. Canon 12 of the Council of Carthage and Canon 36 of the Council of Aix.

14. Justinian, *The Institutes*, translated by J. B. Moyle, 5th edition (Oxford: Clarendon Press, 1913), Title IV, p. 47.

15. Ferdinand Mackeldey, *Handbook of the Roman Law*, translated by Moses Dropsie (Philadelphia: T. and J. W. Johnson and Co., 1883), 305–306.

16. "*The Constitutions of Leo*," Title IV, in *The Civil Law*, translated by C. P. Scott, vol. 17 (Cincinnati: Central Trust Co., 1912).

17. Isaac Disraeli, *Curiosities of Literature*, 1st series (New York: William Pearson and Co., 1835), 7.

18. From the "Laws of King Liutprand," in Katherine Fisher Drew, *The Lombard Laws* (Philadelphia: University of Pennsylvania Press, 1973), 151.

19. Robert S. Lopez, *The Commercial Revolution of the Middle Ages, 950–1350* (Cambridge: Cambridge University Press, 1976), 61.

20. Magna Carta, chap. 10. The original Lombards, who first invaded northern Italy in the late sixth century, developed a series of written laws based in part on Justinian's code. But there was no mention of usury in their early barbarian laws. After they were defeated by Charlemagne in 774, they became part of the Frankish kingdom. Later, the term "lombard" became generic for moneylender. Most lombards in northern Europe from the thirteenth century originally were pawnbrokers.

21. S. P. Scott, translator, *Forum Judicum* (*Visigothic Code*) (Boston: Boston Book Company, 1910), book 5, chap. 8.

22. Sidney Homer and Richard Sylla, *A History of Interest Rates*, 4th edition (Hoboken, NJ: John Wiley and Sons, 2005), 100.

23. See John T. Noonan, "Gratian Slept Here: The Changing Identity of the Father of the Systematic Study of Canon Law," *Traditio* 35 (1979): 145–172.

24. John T. Noonan, *The Scholastic Analysis of Usury* (Cambridge, MA: Harvard University Press, 1957), 101–102.

25. Carlyle and Carlyle, *Mediaeval Political Theory*, 1: 79.

26. Edwin S. Hunt and James M. Murray, *A History of Business in Medieval Europe, 1200–1550* (Cambridge: Cambridge University Press, 1999), 73.

27. See Lopez, *The Commercial Revolution of the Middle Ages*, 73–75; and Jonathon B. Baskin and Paul J. Miranti, *A History of Corporate Finance* (Cambridge: Cambridge University Press, 1997), 38.

28. Thomas Aquinas, *Summa Theologica*, translated by Fathers of the English Dominican Province (New York: Benziger Brothers, 1948), Q. LXVII, Article 2:7.

29.   Homer and Sylla, *A History of Interest Rates*, 89.

30.   Tanner, *Decrees*, 200.

31.   Diana Wood, *Medieval Economic Thought* (Cambridge: Cambridge University Press, 2002), 162.

32.   W. J. Ashley, *An Introduction to English Economic History and Theory* (New York: G. P. Putnam's Sons, 1894), 149.

33.   Tanner, *Decrees*, 223.

34.   Walter Ullmann, *A History of Political Thought: The Middle Ages* (London: Penguin, 1965), 82.

35.   Gustav Cassel, *The Nature and Necessity of Interest* (reprint; New York: Kelley and Millman, 1957), 3.

36.   Tanner, *Decrees*, 265.

37.   Francis Plowden, *A Treatise upon the Law of Usury and Annuities* (London: J. Butterworth, 1797), chap. 4, p. 125.

38.   Quoted in R. H. Tawney, *Religion and the Rise of Capitalism* (London: Penguin, 1938), 42.

39.   Tanner, *Decrees*, 299.

40.   See Ashley, *English Economic History and Theory*, 150.

41.   *Dialogue of the Exchequer*, II.x., in Joseph Jacobs, *The Jews of Angevin England: Documents and Records* (London: G. P. Putnam's Sons, 1893), 49–51.

42.   Jacques LeGoff, *Your Money or Your Life: Economy and Religion in the Middle Ages*, translated by Patricia Ranum (New York: Zone Books, 1990), 44.

43.   Leonardo Pisano Fibonacci, *Liber Abaci*, translated by Laurence E. Sigler (New York: Springer-Verlag, 2003), 404.

44.   Fibonacci, *Liber Abaci*, 438. Fibonacci also developed a theory of numbers that has become known as the Fibonacci sequence. In this sequence, a number is the sum of the two numbers preceding it. For example, in the sequence 0, 1, 1, 2, 3, 5, 8, 13, 21, each number, beginning with the second occurrence of 1, is the sum of the two preceding it. This type of sequence has been used by securities and currency traders attempting to find a rationale for pricing financial instruments in the secondary markets. As the chain of numbers grows longer, dividing a number by the one preceding it yields 1.619, the famous golden ratio of the Middle Ages, described in detail by Luca Pacioli.

45.   This is a standard shorthand used in compound interest problems to determine how long it takes to double one's money. The rate of interest is divided into 72 and the answer is the number of periods. For instance, 72 divided by 9 percent would mean that money would double in eight years.

46.   Quoted in Sidney Z. Ehler and John B. Morrall, *Church and State through the Ages* (London: Burns and Oates, 1954), 92.

47.   Henry Charles Lea, *The Inquisition of the Middle Ages*, abridged by Margaret Nicholson (New York: Macmillan, 1961), 693.

48.   Eleanor Ferris, "The Financial Relations of the Knights Templars to the English Crown," *American Historical Review* 8 (1902): 6.

49.   See Raymond de Roover, "The Scholastics, Usury, and Foreign Exchange," *Business History Review* 41 (1967): 257–271.

50.   Ehler and Morrall, *Church and State*, 22.

51.   See Lea, *The Inquisition*, 701ff.; and Noonan, *Scholastic Analysis*, 171n.

52. Tanner, *Decrees*, 385–386.

53. See Desmond Seward, *The Monks of War: The Military Religious Orders* (London: Penguin, 1972), chap. 12.

54. The execution made de Molay into something of a martyr and he remains the "patron saint" of the Freemasons, a fraternal society founded in the early eighteenth century and linked by some to the Templars. Others trace the Masons directly from the Templars, claiming no break in the order of succession.

55. See Raymond de Roover, *The Medici Bank: Its Organization, Management, Operations, and Decline* (New York: New York University Press, 1948), 82–83 for an example of the mechanics of dry exchange. Also, Homer and Sylla, *A History of Interest Rates*, 75–76.

56. Thomas Aquinas, *Selected Political Writings*, translated by J. G. Dawson (Oxford: Basil Blackwell, 1959), 173.

57. *Summa Theologica*, Q. LXXVII, Article 1.

58. Aquinas, *Selected Political Writings*, 175.

59. Aquinas, *Summa Theologica*, Q. LXXVII, Article 1:3.

60. Aquinas, *Summa Theologica*, Q. LXXVII, Article 1:7.

61. See Leon Poliakov, *Jewish Bankers and the Holy See: From the Thirteenth to the Seventeenth Century* (New York: Routledge and Kegan Paul, 1977), pp. 26–27.

62. Aquinas, *Selected Political Writings*, 85.

63. Jacobs, *The Jews of Angevin England*, xvii.

64. Dan Michel, *Ayenbite of Inwyt*, edited by Richard Morris (London: Early English Text Society, 1866), 35, 44. The *Ayenbite*, translated as the *Remorse of Conscience*, is quoted in modern English in Ashley, *English Economic History and Theory*, 163.

65. Dan Michel, *Ayenbite of Inwyt*, 35, 44.

66. See A. P. d'Entreves, *Natural Law* (London: Hutchinson, 1951), chap. 1.

67. Gratian, *The Treatise on the Laws* (Decretum 1–20), translated by Augustine Thompson (Washington, DC: Catholic University of America Press, 1993), 3.

68. Anwar Iqbal Qureshi, *Islam and the Theory of Interest* (Lahore, Pakistan: Sh. Muhammad Ashraf, 1946), 42; and Samuel Pufendorf, *Of the Law of Nature and Nations* (Oxford, 1712), book 5, chap. 7, p. 405.

Chapter 2

1. Bernardo Davanzati, *A Discourse upon Coins*, translated by John Toland (London: Awnsham and John Churchil, 1696) from the original 1588 edition. Early ideas about the quantity of money available in an economy led to what later became known as quantity theory, although in the Renaissance the idea was more clearly related to debasement than inflation.

2. Quoted in Jerah Johnson, "The Money = Blood Metaphor, 1300–1800," *Journal of Finance* 21 (1966): 119.

3. Davanzati, *Discourse*.

4. Norman P. Tanner, editor, *Decrees of the Ecumenical Councils* (Washington, DC: Georgetown University Press, 1990), 6: 626–627.

5.   Lucas Pacioli *Ancient Double-Entry Bookkeeping: Lucas Pacioli's Treatise*, translated by John B. Geisbeek (Houston: Schloars Book Co., 1914), p. 73.

6.   Natalie Zemon Davis, "Sixteenth Century French Arithmetics on the Business Life," *Journal of the History of Ideas* 21 (1960): 23.

7.   Geoffrey Chaucer, *The Canterbury Tales*, translated into modern English by Neville Coghill (London: Penguin, 1951).

8.   See Humbert O. Nelli, "The Earliest Insurance Contract—A New Discovery," *Journal of Risk and Insurance* 39 (1972): 2.

9.   Thomas Aquinas, *Summa Theologica*, translated by Fathers of the English Dominican Province (New York: Benziger Brothers, 1948), Q. LXVII, Article 1: 3.

10.   Justinian, *The Institutes*, translated by J. B. Moyle, 5th edition (Oxford: Clarendon Press, 1913), title IV.

11.   Edwin W. Kopf, "The Early History of the Annuity," *Proceedings of the Casualty Actuarial Society* 12 (1927): 233.

12.   Raymond de Roover, *The Rise and Decline of the Medici Bank, 1397–1494* (New York: Norton, 1966), 16.

13.   Leon Poliakov, *Jewish Bankers and the Holy See: From the Thirteenth to the Seventeenth Century*, translated by Miriam Kochan (New York: Routledge and Kegan Paul, 1977), 74–75.

14.   Ephraim Russell, "The Societies of the Bardi and the Peruzzi and Their Dealings with Edward III," in *Finance and Trade Under Edward III*, edited by George Unwin (Manchester: Frank Cass and Co., 1918), 130.

15.   De Roover, *The Rise and Decline of the Medici Bank*, 15.

16.   See Tim Parks, *Medici Money: Banking, Metaphysics, and Art in Fifteenth Century Florence* (New York: Norton, 2005).

17.   De Roover, *The Rise and Decline of the Medici Bank*, 124.

18.   De Roover, *The Rise and Decline of the Medici Bank*, 374.

19.   Roland H. Bainton, *Here I Stand: A Life of Martin Luther* (New York: New American Library, 1955), 184.

20.   Max Weber, *The Protestant Ethic and the Spirit of Capitalism*, translated by Talcott Parsons (New York: Charles Scribner's Sons, 1958), 38.

21.   "Usury, a Dialogue on Interest," in Gerald Strauss, translator, *Manifestations of Discontent in Germany on the Eve of the Reformation* (Bloomington: Indiana University Press, 1971), 110–113.

22.   Quoted in Conrad Henry Moehlman, "The Christianization of Interest," *Church History* 3 (1934): 9–10.

23.   Benjamin Nelson, *The Idea of Usury: From Tribal Brotherhood to Universal Otherhood*, 2nd edition (Chicago: University of Chicago Press, 1969), 75–76.

24.   Moehlman, "The Christianization of Interest," 11.

25.   Quoted in Nelson, *The Idea of Usury*, 84.

26.   Quoted in Donald O. Wagner, "Coke and the Rise of Economic Liberalism," *Economic History Review* 6, no. 1 (1935): 33.

27.   Thomas Wilson, *A Discourse Upon Usury*, edited with an introduction by R. H. Tawney (reprint, New York: Augustus M. Kelley, 1965), 163.

28.   Statutes of Apparel, announced at Greenwich, June 15, 1574; 16 Elizabeth 1.

29. D. L. Thomas and N. E. Evans, "John Shakespeare in the Exchequer," *Shakespeare Quarterly* 35 (1984).

30. *The Merchant of Venice*, act 1, scene 3, edited by John Dover Wilson (Cambridge: Cambridge University Press, 1958).

31. Carolus Molinaeus, *A Treatise on Contracts and Usury*, in Arthur Eli Monroe, editor, *Early Economic Thought* (New York: Gordon Press, 1975), 114–115. Raymond de Roover noted that the casuistry displayed by the Scholastics over topics such as usury did little to enhance their reputation in academic and legal circles and their other intellectual achievements suffered as a result. See Raymond de Roover, "The Scholastics, Usury, and Foreign Exchange," *Business History Review* 41 (1967): 271.

32. Wilson, *A Discourse upon Usury*, 87.

33. Wilson, *A Discourse Upon Usury*, 155.

34. Roger Fenton, *A Treatise of Usurie* (London: William Aspley, 1612), 73.

35. Robert Filmer, *Quaestio Quodlibetica* (London: Humphrey Moseley, 1653), 26.

36. Filmer, *Quaestio Quodlibetica*, 113.

37. Francis Bacon, *The Essays, or Counsels Civil and Moral* (Indianapolis: Bobbs Merrill, 1905), 179.

38. Jean Bodin, "Reply to the Paradoxes of Malestroit Concerning the Dearness of All Things and the Remedy Thereof," in *Early Economic Thought*, edited by Arthur Eli Monroe (New York: Gordon Press, 1975), 130.

39. Quoted in Monroe, *Early Economic Thought*, 136.

40. Sidney Homer and Richard Sylla, *A History of Interest Rates*, 4th edition (Hoboken, NJ: John Wiley and Sons, 2005), 132.

41. Hugo Grotius, *The Rights of War and Peace*, translated by A. C. Campbell (New York: M. Walter Dunne, 1901), book 2, chap. 12, para. 20.

42. Grotius, *The Rights of War and Peace*, book 2, chap. 12, p. 76.

43. Samuel Pufendorf, *Of the Law of Nature and Nations* (Oxford: 1710), book 5, chap. 7, p. 406.

44. John Milton, "In Salmasii Hundredam," cited in Merritt Hughes, *John Milton, Complete Poems and Major Prose* (New York: Odyssey Press, 1957), 160.

45. Homer and Sylla, *A History of Interest Rates*, 131.

46. Jonathan B. Baskin and Paul J. Miranti, *A History of Corporate Finance* (Cambridge: Cambridge University Press, 1997), 71.

47. Quoted in Monroe, *Early Economic Thought*, 171.

48. Homer and Sylla, *A History of Interest Rates*, 76.

49. Edwin S. Hunt and James S. Murray, *A History of Business in Medieval Europe, 1200–1550* (Cambridge: Cambridge University Press, 1999), 208.

Chapter 3

1. Robert Wallace, *Various Prospects of Mankind, Nature, and Providence* (London: A. Millar, 1761; reprint, New York: A. M. Kelley, 1969), 6. Citations refer to the 1969 edition.

2.   Edwin W. Kopf, "The Early History of the Annuity," *Proceedings of the Casualty Actuarial Society* 12 (1927): 244–245.

3.   Coffee houses also contributed to a famous London exchange. Lloyds of London, the insurance exchange, was founded in 1688 at Edward Lloyd's coffee house in London, and it became a place where individuals (or "names") could subscribe to maritime insurance syndicates, as is the practice today. Coffee incidentally was reputedly first drunk in Britain during the English Civil War when a young member of Balliol College, Oxford named Nathanael Konopios brewed the first cup, unwittingly beginning what would become a long tradition.

4.   Edmund Halley, "An Estimate of the Degrees of Mortality in Mankind" (1693), reprinted in *The World of Mathematics*, vol. 3, edited by James Newman (Toronto: General Publishing Co., 1956), 1440.

5.   Peter Bernstein, *Against the Gods: The Remarkable Story of Risk* (New York: John Wiley and Sons, 1998), 87.

6.   John Graunt, *Bills of Mortality*, reprinted in *The World of Mathematics*, vol. 3, edited by James Newman (Toronto: General Publishing Co., Inc., 1956), 1428.

7.   J. B. C. Murray, *The History of Usury from the Earliest Time to the Present* (Philadelphia: J. B. Lippincott, 1866), 50.

8.   Statute, 12 Charles II.

9.   Quoted in Nigel Stirk, "Arresting Ambiguity: The Shifting Geographies of a London Debtors' Sanctuary in the Eighteenth Century," *Social History* 25 (2000): 316.

10.   34, 35 Henry VIII, cap. 4.

11.   Josiah Child, *Brief Observations Concerning Trade and Interest of Money* (London: Elizabeth Calvert and Henry Mortlock, 1668).

12.   3 George I, cap. 8.

13.   A. Andreades, *History of the Bank of England*, translated by Christabel Meredith (London: F. S. King and Son, 1909), 55.

14.   A sunset clause is purposely built into financial legislation to allow a trial period for the law under question before it is made permanent. It is found in both English and American financial legislation.

15.   Daniel Defoe, *The Villainy of Stock Jobbers* (London: n.p., 1701), 26.

16.   Andreades, *History*, 121.

17.   *Applebees' Weekly Journal*, August 27, 1720.

18.   Andreades, *History*, 133.

19.   *Earl of Chesterfield v. Janssen*, 2 Ves Sen. 141; and Sybil Campbell, "The Economic and Social Effect of the Usury Laws in the Eighteenth Century," *Transactions of the Royal Historical Society* 16 (1933): 199.

20.   Kopf, "The Early History," 259; and *The Law Times*, May 8, 1879 in the case of *Lawley v. Hooper*, p. 305.

21.   John A. Bolles, *A Treatise on Usury and the Usury Laws* (Boston: James Munroe, 1837), 19. This author concluded that the Massachusetts law was meant to apply to members of the same church or community group, following the ancient Hebrew tradition.

22.   Murray, *The History of Usury*, 70ff. In his history, Murray discusses the relevance of the laws of the colonizing country on the laws in the colony. He discusses at some length the fact that native American Indians had no laws about borrowing and

were considered not tied to the land but only migrants wandering the countryside, so the laws of England prevailed, not those of any other authority. This discussion also demonstrates the relationship of the maximum interest rate with permanent, fixed (or immobile) property, which became prevalent in the eighteenth century.

23.   See Robert E. Wright, *Hamilton Unbound: Finance and the Creation of the American Republic* (New York: Praeger, 2002), 20–26.

24.   William Blackstone, *Commentaries on the Laws of England*, edited by William Carey Jones (San Francisco: Bancroft-Whitney, 1916), book 2, chap. 30.

25.   An example of Stevin's early tables can be found in the Appendix.

26.   Montesquieu, *The Spirit of the Laws*, translated by Thomas Nugent (London: J. Nourse and P. Vaillant, 1773), 79 (book 22, chap. 20).

27.   Montesquieu, *The Spirit of the Laws*, 121 (book 22, chap. 19).

28.   The yields on the consols remained well below the official usury ceiling rates for most of the eighteenth century. See Sidney Homer and Richard Sylla, *A History of Interest Rates*, 4th edition (Hoboken, NJ: John Wiley and Sons, 2005), 157.

29.   Quoted in the *Anti-Jacobin Review*, December 1, 1806, p. 457.

30.   Quoted in the *Anti-Jacobin Review*, December 1, 1806, p. 458.

31.   David Hume, *Essays: Moral, Political, and Literary*, edited by Eugene F. Miller (Indianapolis: Liberty Fund, 1987), ii, iv, 6.

32.   Adam Smith, *The Wealth of Nations* (London: T. Nelson and Sons, 1852), 146 (book II, 4, 14).

33.   Joseph Hume Francis, *History of the Bank of England* (Chicago: Euclid Publishing Co., 1888), 39.

34.   Isaac Newton, *Universal Arithmetick: or, A Treatise of Arithmetical Composition and Resolution*, translated by Raphson (London: J. Senex, 1720), 84.

35.   A. Smith, *The Wealth of Nations*, 175.

36.   A. Smith, *The Wealth of Nations*, 147.

37.   *Morning Post and Daily Advertiser*, July 18, 1791.

38.   *St. James's Chronicle*, March 20, 1792.

39.   In 1790, Alexander Hamilton adopted the idea of the U.S. government selling tontines in order to reduce the national debt. His ideas were based upon those discussed in Britain, including those of Price, through Pitt. See Robert M. Jennings, Donald F. Swanson, and Andrew P. Trout, "Alexander Hamilton's Tontine Proposal," *William and Mary Quarterly* 45 (1988): 107–115.

40.   Quoted in Carl B. Cone, "Richard Price and Pitt's Sinking Fund of 1786," *Economic History Review* 4 (1951): 243.

41.   See *New Encyclopedia* (London: Vernor, Hood, and Sharpe, 1807), 720.

42.   Cone, "Sinking Fund," 244.

43.   Richard Price, *Observations on the Importance of the American Revolution* (Dublin: L. White et al., 1785), 11

44.   *Public Advertiser*, January 4, 1777.

45.   Quoted in James Birch Kelly, *A Summary and History of the Law of Usury* (London: Richard James Kennett, 1835), 176.

46.   Philip Ziegler, *The Sixth Great Power: A History of One of the Greatest of All Banking Families, the House of Barings, 1762–1929* (New York: Knopf, 1988), 214. The author also notes that British government financing and its allegiances would have been very different if Barings had been of Jewish origin rather than German since it

would have created a totally different network of bankers with whom they would have to had done business.

47.   This sort of action was referred to as a *qui tam* action and originally was listed as *Smith qui tam v. Prager*. See, for instance, *Bells Weekly Messenger*, July 17, 1796, p. 96 for a summary.

48.   Jeremy Bentham, *In Defence of Usury*, 4th edition (London: Payne and Foss, 1818), 38.

49.   Bentham, *Defence*, 39.

50.   Bentham, *Defence*, letter 9.

51.   Quoted in John Ashton, *The Dawn of the XIXth Century in England*, 5th edition (London: T. Fisher Unwin, 1806), 17.

52.   Ashton, *Dawn*, 17. The basket included an income tax, which was added in the last ten years of the time period, adding substantially to the overall cost increase.

Chapter 4

1.   Bruce H. Mann, *Republic of Debtors: Bankruptcy in the Age of American Independence* (Cambridge, MA: Harvard University Press, 2002), 102.

2.   On discharging a debt under the bankruptcy laws, see David A. Skeel, *Debt's Dominion: A History of Bankruptcy Law in America* (Princeton, NJ: Princeton University Press, 2001), 6–7, 98–99.

3.   Mann, *Republic of Debtors*, 223.

4.   Henry Thornton, *An Enquiry into the Nature and Effects of the Paper Credit of Great Britain* (Philadelphia: James Humphreys, 1807), 243.

5.   *The Times*, May 24, 1816.

6.   David Ricardo, *The Works and Correspondence of David Ricardo*, edited by Piero Sraffa and M. H. Dobb, vol. 5, *Speeches and Evidence 1815–1823* (Indianapolis: Liberty Fund, 2005), April 12, 1821.

7.   Ricardo, *Works and Correspondence*, vol. 5, June 17, 1823.

8.   *The Times*, June 25, 1847.

9.   Commons Debates, "Usury Laws Repeal Bill," HC Deb February 27, 1824, vol. 10 cc551–71.

10.   3, 4 Victoria, cap. 110.

11.   E. W. Brabrook, "Friendly Societies and Similar Institutions," *Journal of the Statistical Society of London* 38 (1875): 197. A mutual society was a bank essentially owned by its depositors, meaning that the amount of deposit for each saver was at risk in the event of failure. As a result, the lending policies of mutuals needed to be prudent so that the deposit base was as safe as possible.

12.   17, 18 Victoria, cap. 88.

13.   *The Times*, July 15, 1870, p. 10.

14.   *The Times*, February 17, 1819.

15.   James Connery, *The Reformer, or an Infallible Remedy to Prevent Pauperism and Periodical Returns of Famine* (London: J. Murray, 1836), 57.

16.   Cited in the *New York Daily Times*, May 13, 1852.

17.   Lawrence M. Friedman, *A History of American Law*, 3rd edition (New York: Touchstone Press, 2005), 412.

18.   Cited in John Whipple, *Stringent Usury Laws: The Best Defense against Hard Times* (Boston: Dayton and Wentworth, 1855), 3.

19.   Whipple, *Usury Laws*, 3.

20.   The *Webster's Dictionary* of 1828 had an entry for *anatocismus*, but it was one of the last times the word would be found in an American dictionary. The *Palgrave Dictionary of Political Economy* still listed it in the 1894 edition. The term survives in the *Oxford English Dictionary*.

21.   Whipple, *Usury Laws*, 5.

22.   *New-York Daily Times*, October 5, 1854.

23.   Whipple, *Usury Laws*, 9–10. The governor's position is borne out by more recent studies. See Howard Bodenhorn, "Usury Ceilings and Bank Lending Behavior: Evidence from Nineteenth Century New York," National Bureau of Economic Research Working Paper 11734 (2005). and Hugh Rockoff, "Prodigals and Projecture: An Economic History of Usury Laws in the United States from Colonial Times to 1900," National Bureau of Economic Research Working Paper 9742 (2003).

24.   Whipple, *Usury Laws*, 35.

25.   *Joshua Balme v. Henry Wornbough*, 1862.

26.   John Duer, *The Law and Practice of Marine Insurance* (New York: John S. Voorhies, 1845), 2.

27.   National Banking Act, 1864, Section 30.

28.   U.S. Senate, "Report of the Secretary of the Treasury in Answer to a Resolution of the Senate Calling for the Amount of American Securities Held in Europe and Other Foreign Countries, on the 30th June 1853," Executive Document No. 42, 33rd Congress, 1st Session, 1854.

29.   Quoted in Ellis Paxton Oberholtzer, *Jay Cooke: Financier of the Civil War* (Philadelphia: George W. Jacobs Co., 1907), 81.

30.   "Living without pay or die," Oberholtzer, *Jay Cooke*, 104.

31.   April 8, 1863.

32.   *The World*, May 20, 1863.

33.   Quoted in Henrietta Larson, *Jay Cooke, Private Banker* (Cambridge, MA: Harvard University Press, 1936), 165.

34.   Samuel Wilkeson, *How Our National Debt May Be a National Blessing* (Philadelphia: M'Laughlin Brothers, 1865), 10.

35.   *The Defiance Democrat*, July 22, 1865. The newspaper referred to the actual author of the pamphlet, Samuel Wilkeson, as Cooke's hired "Bohemian."

36.   Richard Henry Dana Jr., *Speech in the House of Representatives of Massachusetts, February 14, 1867, on the Repeal of the Usury Laws* (New York: Cowan, McClure and Co., 1872), 20.

37.   Reprinted in *The World*, March 4, 1873.

38.   *New York Times*, January 8, 1873.

39.   *Historical Statistics of the United States*, Table CJ 713–722.

40.   Karl Marx and Friedrich Engels, *Capital*, translated by Samuel Moore and Edward Aveling (Moscow: Progress Publishers, 1971), 3: 599.

41.   Marx and Engels, *Capital*, 3: 600.

42.   *The Times*, August 4, 1869.

43.   Henry Clews, *Twenty Eight Years in Wall Street* (New York: Irving Publishing, 1888), 99–100.

44. *The Times*, October 15, 1868.

45. National Federation of Remedial Loan Associations, *Bulletin* 1 (1912): 20.

46. For non-farm workers. *Historical Statistics of the United States*, Table Ba 4280.

47. *The World*, January 27, 1895.

48. Arthur H. Ham, *The Chattel Loan Business* (New York: Russell Sage Foundation, 1909), 37.

49. *Samuel v. Newbold*, cited in Joseph Bridges Matthews and George Frederick Spear, *The Money-Lenders Act, 1900* (London: Sweet and Maxwell, 1908), 4–5.

50. Matthews and Spear, *Money-Lenders Act*, 8–9.

51. Justice L. J. Vaughn Williams in *Poncione v. Higgins*, cited in Joseph Bridges Matthews, *The History of Money-Lending, Past and Present: Being a Short History of the Usury Laws in England* (London: Sweet and Maxwell, 1906), 36.

52. J. Adriance Bush, *The National Bankruptcy Act of 1898* (New York: Banks Law Publishing Company, 1899), 63.

Chapter 5

1. John Maynard Keynes, *The Economic Consequences of the Peace* (Boston: Harcourt Brace and How, 1920), 21.

2. Gustav Cassel, *The Nature and Necessity of Interest* (London: Macmillan, 1903), 181.

3. U.S. Treasury, *Annual Report*, 1918, p. 70.

4. Quoted in *The Magazine of Wall Street*, June 9, 1917.

5. Keynes, *The Economic Consequences of the Peace*, 165–166.

6. U.S. Department of Commerce, *Historical Statistics of the United States: Colonial Times to 1957* (Washington, DC: Government Printing Office, 1957), Series X 415–422.

7. *New York Times*, May 1, 1922.

8. *Historical Statistics of the United States*, edited by Susan Carter, Scott Gartner, Michael Haines, Alan Olmstead, and Richard Sutch (New York: Cambridge University Press, 2006), Series D 603–617.

9. U.S. Department of Commerce, *Historical Statistics*, Series X 415–422.

10. Quoted in the *New York Times*, May 13, 1928.

11. See Arthur Ham, *The Campaign against the Loan Shark* (New York: Russell Sage Foundation, 1928).

12. See Wendy A. Woolson, *In Hock: Pawning in America from Independence through the Great Depression* (Chicago: University of Chicago Press, 2010).

13. *New York Times*, July 16, 1911.

14. *New York Times*, April 2, 1928.

15. *New York Times*, May 19, 1928.

16. *New York Times*, April 28, 1928.

17. William J. Morgan, quoted in the *Capital Times* (Madison, Wisconsin), May 28, 1931.

18. Michael Perino, *The Hellhound of Wall Street* (New York: Penguin Press, 2010), 124.

19. Marcus Gleisser, *The World of Cyrus Eaton* (New York: A. S. Barnes, 1965), 43.

20. Forest McDonald, *Insull* (Chicago: University of Chicago Press, 1962), 287.

21.   McDonald, *Insull*, 287.

22.   U.S. Senate, "Stock Exchange Practices Report," Senate Report 1455, Senate Banking Committee, 73rd Congress, 2nd session (1934): testimony of Samuel Insull Jr., February 16, 1933, p. 362.

23.   U.S. Senate, "Stock Exchange Practices," 1515.

24.   Quoted in U.S. Senate, "Stock Exchange Practices," 87.

25.   Irving Fisher, *The Theory of Interest* (New York: Macmillan, 1930), part 1, chap. 2, 4.

26.   Frederick Macaulay, *Some Theoretical Problems Suggested by the Movements of Interest Rates, Bond Yields and Stock Prices in the United States since 1856* (Washington, DC: National Bureau of Economic Research, 1938).

27.   Lawrence R. Samuel, *Freud on Madison Avenue: Motivation Research and Subliminal Advertising in America* (Philadelphia: University of Pennsylvania Press, 2010), 36ff.

28.   *Historical Statistics*, Series Cd 153–263.

29.   Robert Manning, *Credit Card Nation: The Consequences of America's Addiction to Debt* (New York: Basic Books, 2000), 85.

30.   See David Caplovitz, *Consumers in Trouble: A Study of Debtors in Default* (New York: Free Press, 1974).

31.   Franco Modigliani and Merton H. Miller, "The Cost of Capital, Corporation Finance, and the Theory of Investment," *American Economic Review* 48 (1958): 261–297.

32.   Harry Markowitz, "Portfolio Selection," *Journal of Finance* 7 (1952): 77–91.

33.   William F. Sharpe, "Capital Asset Prices: A Theory of Market Equilibrium under Conditions of Risk," *Journal of Finance* 19 (1964): 425–442.

34.   Edward I. Altman, "Financial Ratios, Discriminant Analysis and the Prediction of Corporate Bankruptcy," *Journal of Finance* 24 (1968): 589–609.

35.   Quoted in the *New York Times*, December 18, 1967.

36.   *Oakland Tribune*, August 3, 1969.

37.   *New York Times*, February 5, 1980.

38.   *Marquette National Bank of Minneapolis v. First of Omaha Service Corp.*, No. 77-1265, December 18, 1978, 439 U.S. 299.

39.   *New York Times*, April 2, 1989.

40.   Teresa Sullivan, Elizabeth Warren, and Jay Lawrence Westbrook, *As We Forgive Our Debtors: Bankruptcy and Consumer Credit in America* (New York: Oxford University Press, 1989), 76.

41.   Traditionally, if credit card defaults did not exceed 3–4 percent of the total outstanding, the card companies considered their overall lending risk minimal.

42.   Securitization is now a template process, using the same essential procedure regardless of the assets being securitized. The lender gathers loans it made recently and sells them to a pooler, who in turn uses them as collateral for a bond. The cash flows from the pool of loans now support the bond interest and principal repayment.

43.   This point originally was made by Thomas H. Stanton, *Government Sponsored Enterprises: Mercantilist Companies in the Modern World* (Washington, DC: AEI Press, 2002).

44.   Federal Reserve Board, *Statistical Release*, G. 19; www.federalreserve.gov/releases.

Chapter 6

1.   Discounting future cash flows at low rates of interest produces a greater present value for comparison purposes than discounting at high rates of interest.

2.   The interest rates were quoted on this bid-offer basis and changed by the minute, quoted by deposit dealers at the London banks. The rates were money market rates, and not a stated bank rate of lending, such as the American prime rate.

3.   *New York Times*, October 17, 1971. The prime rate had been used by banks since the early 1930s as a way of describing the lowest possible interest rate charged to a prime business borrower. It was calculated as a specific spread over commercial paper rates but was not changed frequently, leading to complaints that it was an inflexible interest rate.

4.   Morgan Guaranty Trust, *World Financial Markets*, 1978–1979; and World Bank, *World Debt Tables, 1980–81*.

5.   Quoted in Federal Deposit Insurance Corporation, *An Examination of the Banking Crises of the 1980s and Early 1990s* (Washington, DC: Federal Deposit Insurance Corporation, 1997), 26.

6.   Federal Deposit Insurance Corporation, *The Banking Crises*, 240.

7.   *Federal Reserve Statistical Release*, six-month LIBID; www.federalreserve.gov/releases.

8.   Anthony Sampson, "So Give Credit Where Credit Is Due," *New York Times*, January 10, 1982.

9.   Federal Deposit Insurance Corporation, *The Banking Crises*, 246.

10.   Alan Garcia, address to Peruvian Congress, July 28, 1985, quoted in Jackie Roddick, *Dance of the Millions: Latin America and the Debt Crisis* (London: Latin American Bureau, 1988), 169.

11.   Roddick, *Dance*, 46.

12.   Quoted in Roddick, *Dance*, 48.

13.   *New York Times*, July 5, 1983.

14.   Continuous interest refers to interest charged on the most frequent basis available given the capacity of calculators or computers to perform the calculation. Ordinarily, it means interest compounded daily.

15.   World Bank, *World Debt Tables, 1990–91*.

16.   Federal Deposit Insurance Corporation, *The Banking Crises*, 207.

17.   *New York Times*, January 18, 1985.

18.   Federal Reserve Board, *Flow of Funds Accounts*, Table D.1, Z.1, December 9, 2010.

19.   The Treasury allowed the stripping of its bonds after Congress officially passed a bill called the Separate Trading of Registered Interest and Principal of Securities Program (STRIP) in 1984. It would not permit the Treasury to issue new zero coupon bonds, however. The national debt still was funded with traditional coupon bonds, which then could be stripped by official primary dealers recognized by the Fed.

20.   Giles Jacob, *A New Law Dictionary*, 6th edition (London: Henry Lintot, 1750).

21.   The requirement was calculated as capital as a percentage of loans on the books of a bank.

22.   Event risk refers to a risk incurred by a bond borrower when a one-off event affects its credit rating adversely, such as a take-over attempt, or an unforeseen lawsuit or some other type of unanticipated liability.

23.   *New York Times*, February 7, 1985.

24.   For reporting purposes, the notional amount of a swap is reported on the books as a contingent liability. Although the notional amount only reflects the amount that the actual cash flows use as a hypothetical principal amount, it is the only viable method of reporting the amount of ultimate exposure of the swap itself.

25.   Philippe Joiron, *Big Bets Gone Bad: Derivatives and Bankruptcy in Orange County* (San Diego: Academic Press, 1995), 2.

26.   Joiron, *Big Bets*, 102.

27.   Joiron, *Big Bets*, 9.

28.   A credit rating of BBB or better. Below that level, bonds were considered "high yield," or junk.

29.   Texas International's issue defaulted ten years later when the company declared bankruptcy and the bonds sank to 20 percent of their original issue price.

30.   The Depository Institutions Act was an amendment to the DIDMCA passed two years before, effectively speeding up the deregulation of interest rates, especially among savings institutions.

31.   Ivan F. Boesky, *Merger Mania* (New York: Holt, Rinehart and Winston, 1985), 90.

32.   Boesky, *Merger Mania*, 102.

33.   George Anders, *Merchants of Debt: KKR and the Mortgaging of American Business* (New York: Basic Books, 1992), 179.

34.   Carmen M. Reinhart and Kenneth S. Rogoff, *This Time Is Different: Eight Centuries of Financial Folly* (Princeton, NJ: Princeton University Press, 2009), 61.

35.   Abbigail Chiodo and Michael Owyang, "A Case Study of a Currency Crisis: The Russian Default of 1998," Federal Reserve Bank of St. Louis, *Review* (November/December 2002): 11.

36.   As Rinehart and Rogoff demonstrated, the number of Latin American sovereign defaults, along with many others of middle-income countries, was much greater than might be imagined in the period 1970–2008. See Reinhart and Rogoff, *This Time Is Different*, 23.

37.   Some of Argentina's Brady bonds were restructured in 2010 as the government sought to restructure some of the country's maturing debt, extending maturities for another ten years by issuing new bonds to be exchanged for the old.

38.   *New York Times*, February 12, 1990.

39.   *New York Times*, January 6, 2002.

Chapter 7

1.   For an account of the events leading to Nixon's address in which the link between the dollar and gold was severed, see Robert Solomon, *The International Monetary System, 1945–1976* (New York: Harper and Row, 1977), 180ff.

2.   Koran 3:130, quoted in Anwar Iqbal Qureshi, *Islam and the Theory of Interest* (Lahore, Pakistan: Sh. Muhammad Ashraf, 1967), 42. The same passage is translated in the Oxford translation of the Koran by A. J. Arberry as "O believers, devour not usury, doubled and redoubled, and fear you God."

3.   Qureshi, *Islam and the Theory of Interest*, xix.

4.   Quoted in Mahmoud A. El-Gamal, *Islamic Finance: Law, Economics, and Practice* (Cambridge: Cambridge University Press, 2006), 140.

5.   Quoted in El-Gamal, *Islamic Finance*, 141.

6.   Sh. Wahba Al Zuhayli, "The Juridical Meaning of Riba," in Abdulkader Thomas, *Interest in Islamic Economics: Understanding Riba* (London: Routledge, 2006), 28–29.

7.   El-Gamal, *Islamic Finance*, 62.

8.   Ibrahim Warde, *Islamic Finance in the Global Economy* (Edinburgh: Edinburgh University Press, 2000), 148.

9.   When screening equity for inclusion in one of the Islamic equity indexes, compliers usually adopt one of these two approaches. The *Financial Times* uses accounts receivables to total assets while Dow Jones uses market capitalization. The Accounting and Auditing Organization for Islamic Financial Institutions uses accounts receivables to total assets in its calculations.

10.   *New York Times*, January 28, 1986.

11.   John Foster, *BBC News*, December 11, 2009.

12.   Quoted in *Daily Mail*, February 17, 2008.

13.   El-Gamal, *Islamic Finance*, 14.

14.   Tarik M. Yousef, "The Murabaha Syndrome in Islamic Finance: Laws, Institutions and Politics," in *The Politics of Islamic Finance*, edited by Clement M. Henry and Rodney Wilson (Karachi, Pakistan: Oxford University Press, 2005), 63ff. As the author demonstrates, the share of *murabaha* financing in Islamic banking in the 1990s was about 50 percent while the total of all mark-up instruments, including *murabaha*, was about 75 percent.

15.   Henry and Wilson, *The Politics of Islamic Finance*, 7.

16.   *Allroya*, June 2, 2010.

17.   *IMF Survey*, September 2007; and *Financial Times*, December 12, 2010.

18.   El-Gamal, *Islamic Finance*, 113–114.

19.   *Daily Mail*, February 17, 2008. That description would have applied to a *murabaha sukuk*, not an *ijara*, if the term "switched" meant the transfer of ownership.

20.   Quoted in *Sukuk.me*, December 15, 2009.

21.   John Ferry, "Scuppered by *Sukuk*," *Risk* 23 (2010): 90.

22.   Gross national income per capita.

23.   Grameenfo.org.

24.   Muhammad Yunus, *Banker to the Poor: Micro-Lending and the Battle against World Poverty* (New York: PublicAffairs, 1999), 49–50.

25.   Annual report, Grameen Bank, 2011.

26.   Grameen-info.org.

27.   *The Hindu Business Line*, January 15, 2011. The company SKS attracted a $12 million investment from Sequoia Capital, one of the larger U.S. hedge funds.

28.   National Public Radio, December 31, 2010.

29.   *The Economic Times* (India), March 17, 2011.

30.   Federal Deposit Insurance Corporation, *FDIC Survey of Unbanked and Underbanked Households* (Washington, DC: Federal Deposit Insurance Corporation, 2009), 10–11.

31.   FDIC, *Survey*, 15–45.

32.   FDIC, *Survey*, 30.

33.   U.S. Small Business Administration, *Small Business and Micro Business Lending in the United States, for Data Years 2007–2008* (Washington, DC: U.S. Small Business Administration, 2009).

34.   M. Richardson, "Increasing Microlending Potential in the United States through a Strategic Approach to Regulatory Reform," *Journal of Corporation Law* 34 (2009): 929ff.

Chapter 8

1.   Council of Mortgage Lenders; cml.org.uk.

2.   Myron S. Scholes, "Crisis and Risk Management," *American Economic Review* 90 (2000): 18.

3.   The Fed enacted rules to control float in the 1970s. In 1980, the Depository Institutions Deregulation and Monetary Control Act allowed the Fed to begin charging banks for float. That, along with faster electronic processing and the decline of check use, has reduced float to only about 10 percent of its levels in the 1970s, despite growth in the money supply.

4.   Alan Greenspan and James Kennedy, "Sources and Uses of Equity Extracted from Homes," *Finance and Economics Discussion Series* 20, Federal Reserve Board (2007): 23.

5.   The term "cannibal consumption" was originally used in Charles R. Geisst, *Collateral Damaged: The Marketing of Consumer Debt to America* (New York: Bloomberg Press, 2009).

6.   *Historical Statistics of the United States*, edited by Susan Carter, Scott Gartner, Michael Haines, Alan Olmstead, and Richard Sutch (New York: Cambridge University Press, 2006), table Dc653–669—Housing units, by occupancy and ownership.

7.   MortgageDaily.com.

8.   The maximum rate, or a cap, a homeowner can pay on a mortgage is accompanied by a minimum rate, known as a floor. These boundaries conform to bond and options features used to create what is known as a "collar," the difference or spread between them. The collar is the range of uncertainty between interest rates to which the lender of the mortgage is immune. Conversely, it is the range to which the mortgage payer is exposed at the same time.

9.   Before the Taxpayer Relief Act of 1998, the only way to gain an exemption on the amount of capital gain made on a home sale was to roll over the proceeds into a new residence of equal or greater value than the old one.

10.   Government Accountability Office, "Alternative Mortgage Products: Impact on Defaults Remains Unclear, but Disclosure of Risks to Borrowers Could Be Improved," September 20, 2006.

11. Government Accountability Office, "Information on Recent Default and Foreclosure Trends for Home Mortgages and Associated Economic and Market Developments," October 2007, 24.

12. MortgageDaily.com.

13. Government Accountability Office, "Information on Recent Default and Foreclosure Trends," 26.

14. Council of Mortgage Lenders, cml.org.uk.

15. Northern Rock became the first official casualty of the subprime crisis on either side of the Atlantic and had to be bailed out by the U.K. Treasury several months before its American counterparts were given assistance by the U.S. Treasury and the Federal Reserve.

16. Association for Financial Markets in Europe, afme.eu.

17. Afme.eu.

18. Asian Securitization Forum, asian-securitization.com.

19. Unlike *pfandbriefen*, the GSE borrowings were off balance sheet.

20. Federal Reserve Board, *Statistical Release*, various issues, all sources and types of lenders, federalreserve.gov/releases.

21. MortgageDaily.com.

22. *Nilson Report*, various issues, 2006, Nilsonreport.com.

23. *Nilson Report*, various issues.

24. Financial Crisis Inquiry Commission, *The Financial Crisis Inquiry Report* (New York: PublicAffairs, 2011), 252–253.

25. Financial Crisis Inquiry Commission, *Report*, 291.

26. Henry Paulson speaking at the Ronald Reagan Presidential Library, U.S. Fed News Service, Washington, DC, November 20, 2008.

27. Banks operating in swaps were imitating insurance companies but were not required to have insurance licenses. The same unlicensed extension of their business was realized by traditional insurance companies that engaged in swaps because it enabled them to diversify their activities into areas not usually associated with insurance.

28. Financial Crisis Inquiry Commission, *Report*, 343.

29. Federal Reserve Board, *Statistical Release*, December 2008 and 2010.

30. Mortgage Bankers Association, *Mortgage Origination Estimates*, February 2011.

31. Federal Reserve Board, *Statistical Release*, December 2009 and 2010.

32. RealtyTrac.com, various issues.

33. *Nilson Report*, various issues.

34. *Nilson Report*, various issues.

35. Notably, two bills introduced in 2009. The Protecting Consumers from Unreasonable Credit Rates Act (HR 1608) proposed establishing a national usury rate cap of 36 percent while the Interest Rate Equity Act (HR 1610) proposed capping credit card interest rates from institutions receiving TARP money at 18 percent.

36. United States Congress, House of Representatives, "Dodd-Frank Wall Street Reform Act," HR 4173, p. 628, 1027(o).

37. Skadden, Arps, Slate, Meagher, and Flom, *The Dodd-Frank Act: Commentary and Insights* (New York: privately published, 2010), 187.

Bibliography

Primary Sources and Translations

Aquinas, Thomas. *Selected Political Writings*. Translated by J. G. Dawson. Oxford: Basil Blackwell, 1959.

Aquinas, Thomas. *Summa Theologica*. Translated by Fathers of the English Dominican Province. New York: Benziger Brothers, 1948.

Aristotle. *Nicomachean Ethics*. Translated by Martin Ostwald. Indianapolis: Bobbs-Merrill, 1962.

Aristotle. *Politics*. Translated by Ernest Barker. New York: Oxford University Press, 1962.

Ashton, John. *The Dawn of the XIXth Century in England*. 5th edition. London: T. Fisher Unwin, 1806.

Azo of Bologna. *Summa on the Codex and Institutes of Justinian*. Bologna, Italy, 13th–14th century. MS, Bodleian Library, Oxford.

Bacon, Francis. *The Essays, or Counsels Civil and Moral*. Indianapolis: Bobbs-Merrill, 1905.

Bagehot, Walter. *Lombard Street: A Description of the Money Market*. New York: Scribner, Armstrong and Co., 1877.

Baily, Francis. *Tables for the Purchasing and Renewing of Leases*. London: W. J. and J. Richardson, 1802.

Benbrigge, John. *Usura Accommodata*. London: Nathaniel Brookes, 1646.

Bentham, Jeremy. *In Defence of Usury*. 4th edition. London: Payne and Foss, 1818.

Blackstone, William. *Commentaries on the Laws of England.* Edited by William Carey Jones. San Francisco: Bancroft-Whitney, 1916.

Blaxton, John. *The English Usurer: Or, Usury Condemned.* Reprint, Amsterdam: Theatrum Orbis Terrarum, 1974.

Boler, James, and Michael Sparke. *The Money Monger, or Usurer's Almanacke.* London: William Jones, 1626.

Bodin, Jean. "Reply to the Paradoxes of Malestroit Concerning the Dearness of All Things and the Remedy Thereof." In *Early Economic Thought*, edited by Arthur Eli Monroe. New York: Gordon Press, 1975.

Bush, J. Adriance. *The National Bankruptcy Act of 1898.* New York: Banks Law Publishing Company, 1899.

Chaucer, Geoffrey. *The Canterbury Tales.* Translated into modern English by Neville Coghill. London: Penguin, 1951.

Child, Josiah. *Brief Observations Concerning Trade, and Interest of Money.* London: r Elizabeth Calvert and Henry Mortlock, 1668.

Cicero, Marcus Tullius. *"De La Publica" and "De Legibus."* Translated by C. W. Keyes. Cambridge, MA: Harvard University Press, 1970.

Cicero, Marcus Tullius. *Selected Letters.* Translated by P. G. Walsh. Oxford: Oxford University Press, 2008.

Clews, Henry. *Twenty Eight Years in Wall Street.* New York: Irving Publishing, 1888.

Connery, James. *The Reformer, or an Infallible Remedy to Prevent Pauperism and Periodical Returns of Famine.* London: J. Murray, 1836.

Culpeper, Thomas. *Tract against Usurie.* London: Christopher Wilkinson, 1668.

Dana, Richard Henry, Jr. *Speech in the House of Representatives of Massachusetts, February 14, 1867, on the Repeal of the Usury Laws.* New York: Cowan, McClure and Co., 1872.

Davanzati, Bernardo. *A Discourse upon Coins.* Translated by John Toland. London: Awnsham and John Churchil, 1696.

Defoe, Daniel. *The Villainy of Stock Jobbers.* London: n.p., 1701.

Drew, Katherine Fisher. *The Laws of the Salian Franks.* Philadelphia: University of Pennsylvania Press, 1991.

Drew, Katherine Fisher. *The Lombard Laws.* Philadelphia: University of Pennsylvania Press, 1973.

Duer, John. *The Law and Practice of Marine Insurance.* New York: John S. Voorhies, 1845.

Ehler, Sidney Z., and John B. Morrall. *Church and State through the Ages.* London: Burns and Oates, 1954.

Federal Deposit Insurance Corporation. *An Examination of the Banking Crises of the 1980s and Early 1990s.* Washington, DC: Federal Deposit Insurance Corporation, 1997.

Federal Deposit Insurance Corporation. *FDIC National Survey of Unbanked and Underbanked Households.* Washington, DC: Federal Deposit Insurance Corporation, December 2009.

Fenton, Roger. *A Treatise of Usurie.* London: William Aspley, 1612.

Fibonacci, Leonardo Pisano. *The Book of Squares.* Translated by Laurence Sigler. Boston: Academic Press, 1987.

Fibonacci, Leonardo Pisano. *Liber Abaci.* Translated by Laurence Sigler. New York: Springer-Verlag, 2003.

Filmer, Robert. *Quaestio Quodlibetica.* London: Humphrey Moseley, 1653.

Financial Crisis Inquiry Commission. *The Financial Crisis Inquiry Report.* New York: Public Affairs, 2011.

Fisher, Irving. *The Rate of Interest.* New York: Macmillan, 1907.

Fisher, Irving. *The Theory of Interest.* New York: Macmillan, 1930.

Government Accountability Office. "Alternative Mortgage Products: Impact on Defaults Remains Unclear, but Disclosure of Risks to Borrowers Could Be Improved." September 20, 2006.

Government Accountability Office. "Credit Cards: Customized Minimum Payment Disclosures Would Provide More Information to Customers but Impact Could Vary." April 2006.

Government Accountability Office. "Credit Cards: Increased Complexity in Rates and Fees Heightens Need for More Effective Disclosures to Consumers." September 2006.

Government Accountability Office. "Information on Recent Default and Foreclosure Trends for Home Mortgages and Associated Economic and Market Developments." October 2007.

Grahame, James. *Defence of Usury Laws, and Considerations on the Probable Consequences of Their Projected Repeal.* Edinburgh: A. Constable, 1817.

Gratian. *The Treatise on Laws* (Decretum 1–20). Translated by Augustine Thompson. Washington, DC: Catholic University of America Press, 1993.

Graunt, John. *Bills of Mortality.* Reprinted in *The World of Mathematics,* vol. 3, edited by James Newman. Toronto: General Publishing Co., 1956.

Grotius, Hugo. *The Rights of War and Peace.* Translated by A. C. Campbell. New York: M. Walter Dunne, 1901.

Halley, Edmund. "An Estimate of the Degrees of Mortality in Mankind." Reprinted in *The World of Mathematics,* vol. 3, edited by James Newman. Toronto: General Publishing Co., 1956.

Historical Statistics of the United States. Edited by Susan Carter, Scott Gartner, Michael Haines, Alan Olmstead, and Richard Sutch. New York: Cambridge University Press, 2006.

Hodder, James. *Hodder's Decimal Arithmetick: Or, a Plain and More Methodical Way of Teaching the Said Art.* London: Thomas Rooks, 1671.

House of Commons. *Parliamentary Debates.* Hansard 1803–2005. London, 2010.

Hughes, Merritt. *John Milton, Complete Poems and Major Prose.* New York: Odyssey Press, 1957.

Hume, David. *Essays: Moral, Political, and Literary.* Edited by Eugene F. Miller. Indianapolis: Liberty Fund, 1987.

Jacob, Giles. *A New Law Dictionary.* 6th edition. London: Henry Lintot, 1750.

Justinian. *Annotated Justinian Code.* Translated by Fred H. Blume. University of Wyoming, 1920–52.

Justinian. *The Institutes.* Translated by J. B. Moyle. 5th edition. Oxford: Clarendon Press, 1913.

Keynes, John Maynard. *The Economic Consequences of the Peace.* New York: Harcourt Brace and Howe, 1920.

Leo XIII, Pope. *Rerum Novarum: Encyclical on the Condition of the Working Classes.* London: Catholic Truth Society, 1983.

Locke, John. *The Conduct of the Understanding.* London: Scott, Webster, and Geary, 1838.

Marx, Karl, and Friedrich Engels. *Capital.* Translated by Samuel Moore and Edward Aveling. Moscow: Progress Publishers, 1971.

Matthews, Joseph Bridges, and George Frederick Spear. *The Money-Lenders Act, 1900.* London: Sweet and Maxwell, 1908.

Michel, Dan. *Ayenbite of Inwyt.* Edited by Richard Morris. London: Early English Text Society, 1866.

Molinaeus, Carolus. *A Treatise on Contracts and Usury.* In *Early Economic Thought*, edited by Arthur Eli Monroe. New York: Gordon Press, 1975.

Monroe, Arthur Eli, editor. *Early Economic Thought.* New York: Gordon Press, 1975.

Montesquieu. *The Spirit of the Laws.* Translated by Thomas Nugent. London: J. Nourse and P. Vaillant, 1773.

Morgan Guaranty Trust. *World Financial Markets.* 1978–1979.

Mun, Thomas. *England's Treasure by Foreign Trade.* London: Thomas Clark, 1664.

National Association of Remedial Loan Associations. *Bulletin* 1, no. 1 (July 1912).

New Encyclopedia. 23 volumes. London: Vernor, Hood, and Sharpe, 1807.

Newman, James R. *The World of Mathematics*. Toronto: General Publishing Co., 1956.

Newton, Isaac. *Universal Arithmetick: or, A Treatise of Arithmetical Composition and Resolution*. Translated by Raphson. London: J. Senex, 1720.

Pacioli, Lucas. *Ancient Double-Entry Bookkeeping: Lucas Pacioli's Treatise*. Translated by John B. Geisbeek. Houston: Scholars Book Co., 1914.

Paterson, W., editor. *The Practical Statutes of the Session 1854*. London: John Crockford, 1854.

Pitt, Moses. *The Cry of the Oppressed*. London: Moses Pitt, 1691.

Plato. *Dialogues*. Translated by Benjamin Jowett. Oxford: Clarendon Press, 1953.

Plowden, Francis. *A Treatise upon the Law of Usury and Annuities*. London: J. Butterworth, 1797.

Price, Richard. *Observations on the Importance of the American Revolution*. Dublin: L. White et al., 1785.

Pufendorf, Samuel Baron. *Of the Law of Nature and Nations*. Oxford, 1710.

Ricardo, David. "Letters on the Sinking Fund from David Ricardo to Francis Place." *Economic Journal* 3, no. 10 (June 1893): 289–293.

Ricardo, David. *The Works and Correspondence of David Ricardo*. Edited by Piero Sraffa and M. H. Dobb. Vol. 5, *Speeches and Evidence 1815–1823*. Indianapolis: Liberty Fund, 2005.

Scott, S. P., translator. *The Civil Law*. Cincinnati: Central Trust Company, 1912.

Scott, S. P., translator. *Forum Judicum (The Visigothic Code)*. Boston: Boston Book Company, 1910.

Sherlock, William. *The Charity of Lending without Usury*. London: William Rogers, 1690.

Smith, Adam. *The Wealth of Nations*. London: T. Nelson and Sons, 1852.

Smith, H. *A Preparative to Marriage; Of the Lord's Supper; Of Usury*. Reprint, Amsterdam: Theatrum Orbis Terrarum, 1975.

Smith, William, William Wayte, and G. E. Marindin, editors. *A Dictionary of Greek and Roman Antiquities*. 3rd edition. London: John Murray, 1901.

Stevin, Simon. *L'arithmetique de Simon Stevin de Bruges: Reueue® corrigee et augmentee de plusieurs traictez et annotations par Albert Girard*. Leiden: De l'imprimerie des Elzeviers, 1625.

Strauss, Gerald, translator. *Manifestations of Discontent in Germany on the Eve of the Reformation*. Bloomington: Indiana University Press, 1971.

Tanner, Norman P., editor. *Decrees of the Ecumenical Councils*. Washington, DC: Georgetown University Press, 1990.

Thornton, Henry. *An Enquiry into the Nature and Effects of the Paper Credit of Great Britain.* Philadelphia: James Humphreys, 1807.

U.S. House of Representatives. "Dodd-Frank Wall Street Reform and Consumer Protection Act." 111th Congress, 2nd session, January 5, 2010.

U.S. House of Representatives, Committee on Banking, Finance, and Urban Affairs, Subcommittee on Financial Institutions Supervision, Regulation, and Insurance. *To Extend Regulation Q: Hearing before the Subcommittee on Financial Institutions Supervision, Regulation, and Insurance of the Committee on Banking, Finance, and Urban Affairs.* 95th Congress, February 7, 1977. Washington, DC: Government Printing Office.

U.S. Department of Commerce. *Historical Statistics of the United States: Colonial Times to 1957.* Washington, DC: Government Printing Office, 1957.

U.S. Senate. "Report of the Secretary of the Treasury in Answer to a Resolution of the Senate Calling for the Amount of American Securities Held in Europe and Other Foreign Countries, on the 30th June 1853." Executive Document no. 42, 33rd Congress, 1st session, 1854.

U.S. Senate. "Stock Exchange Practices Report." Senate Report 1455, Senate Banking Committee, 73rd Congress, 2nd session (1934).

U.S. Small Business Administration. *Small Business and Micro Business Lending in the United States, for Data Years 2007–2008.* Washington, DC: U.S. Small Business Administration, 2009.

Wallace, Robert. *Various Prospects of Mankind, Nature, and Providence.* London: A. Millar, 1761. Reprint, New York: A. M. Kelley, 1969.

Ward, John, *Clavis Usurae; Or, a Key to Interest, Both Simple and Compound.* London: William Taylor, 1710.

Webster, William. *Webster's Tables.* London: M. Flesher for Nicolas Bourne, 1634.

Whipple, John. *Stringent Usury Laws: The Best Defense against Hard Times.* Boston: Dayton and Wentworth, 1855.

Wilkeson, Samuel. *How Our National Debt May Be a National Blessing.* Philadelphia: M'Laughlin Brothers, 1865.

Wilson, Thomas. *A Discourse upon Usury.* Edited by R. H. Tawney. Reprint, New York: Augustus M. Kelley, 1965.

World Bank. *World Debt Tables, 1990–91.* Washington, DC: World Bank, 1992.

Secondary Sources

Altman, Edward I. "Financial Ratios, Discriminant Analysis and the Prediction of Corporate Bankruptcy." *Journal of Finance* 24 (1968): 589–609.

Anders, George. *Merchants of Debt: KKR and the Mortgaging of American Business.* New York: Basic Books, 1992.

Andreades, A. *History of the Bank of England.* Translated by Christabel Meredith. London: F. S. King and Son, 1909.

Armstrong, Lawrin D. *Usury and Public Debt in Early Renaissance: Lorenzo Ridolfi on the Monte Comune.* Toronto: Pontifical Institute of Mediaeval Studies, 2003.

Ashley, William J. *An Introduction to English Economic History and Theory.* New York: G. P. Putnam's Sons, 1894.

Austin, Peter E. *Baring Brothers and the Birth of Modern Finance.* London: Pickering and Chatto, 2007.

Bainton, Roland H. *Here I Stand: A Life of Martin Luther.* New York: New American Library, 1955).

Bar, Karl Ludwig von. *A History of Continental Criminal Law.* Translated by Thomas Bell. Boston: Little Brown, 1916.

Barber, Malcom. *The Trial of the Templars.* Cambridge: Cambridge University Press, 1978.

Baskin, Jonathan B., and Paul J. Miranti. *A History of Corporate Finance.* New York: Cambridge University Press, 1997.

Bellomo, Manlio. *The Common Legal Past of Europe.* Washington, DC: Catholic University of America Press, 1995.

Bellot, Hugh H. L., and R. James Willis. *The Law Relating to Unconscionable Bargains with Money Lenders.* London: Stevens and Haynes, 1897.

Berger, Adolph. "Encyclopedic Dictionary of Roman Law." *Transactions of the American Philosophical Society* 43 (1953): 333–809.

Bernstein, Peter L. *Against the Gods: The Remarkable Story of Risk.* New York: John Wiley and Sons, 1996.

Bird, Edward J., Paul A. Hagstrom, and Robert Wild. "Credit Card Debts of the Poor: High and Rising." *Journal of Policy Analysis and Management* 18 (1999): 125–134.

Block, Kenneth M., and Jeffrey B. Steiner. "Usury: Voiding Criminally Usurious Loans under the Civil Usury Law." *New York Law Journal* 228 (2002): 1–3.

Blydenburgh, Jeremiah W. *A Treatise on the Law of Usury.* New York: John S. Voorhees, 1844.

Bodenhorn, Howard. "Usury Ceilings and Bank Lending Behavior: Evidence from Nineteenth Century New York." National Bureau of Economic Research Working Paper 11734, 2005.

Bolles, John A. *A Treatise on Usury and the Usury Laws.* Boston: James Munroe, 1837.

Brabrook, E. W. "Friendly Societies and Similar Institutions." *Journal of the Statistical Society of London* 38 (1875): 185–214.

Brundage, James A. *Medieval Canon Law.* New York: Longman, 1995.

Caldor, Lendel. *Financing the American Dream: A Cultural History of Consumer Credit.* Princeton, NJ: Princeton University Press, 1999.

Campbell, Sybil. "The Economic and Social Effect of the Usury Laws in the Eighteenth Century." *Transactions of the Royal Historical Society* 16 (1933): 197–210.

Campbell-Kelly, Martin, Mary Croarken, Raymond Flood, and Eleanor Robson. *The History of Mathematical Tables: From Sumer to Spreadsheets.* New York: Oxford University Press, 2003.

Caplovitz, David. *Consumers in Trouble: A Study of Debtors in Default.* New York: Free Press, 1974.

Carlyle, R. W., and A. J. Carlyle. *A History of Mediaeval Political Theory in the West.* Edinburgh: William Blackwood, 1903.

Cary, M., and H. H. Scullard. *A History of Rome.* 3rd edition. London: Macmillan, 1975.

Caskey, John. *Fringe Banking: Check-Cashing Outlets, Pawnshops, and the Poor.* New York: Russell Sage Foundation, 1996.

Cassel, Gustav. *The Nature and Necessity of Interest.* London: Macmillan, 1903.

Center for Medieval and Renaissance Studies. *The Dawn of Modern Banking.* New Haven, CT: Yale University Press, 1979.

Chiodo, Abbigail, and Michael Owyang. "A Case Study of a Currency Crisis: The Russian Default of 1998." Federal Reserve Bank of St. Louis, *Review* (November/December 2002): 7–17.

Choudhury, M. A., and U. A. Malik. *The Foundations of Islamic Political Economy.* London: Macmillan, 1992.

Cochrane, Charles Norris. *Christianity and Classical Culture.* New York: Oxford University Press, 1957.

Comyn, Robert Buckley. *A Treatise on the Law of Usury.* Philadelphia: J. S. Littell, 1834.

Cone, Carl B. "Richard Price and Pitt's Sinking Fund of 1786." *Economic History Review* 4 (1951): 243–251.

Davis, Natalie Zemon. "Sixteenth Century French Arithmetics on the Business Life." *Journal of the History of Ideas* 21 (1960): 18–48.

D'Entreves, A. P. *Natural Law*. London: Hutchinson, 1951.

de Roover, Raymond. *The Medici Bank: Its Organization, Management, Operations, and Decline*. New York: New York University Press, 1948.

de Roover, Raymond. *Money, Banking, and Credit in Mediaeval Bruges: Italian Merchant Bankers, Lombards, and Money Changers—A Study in the Origins of Banking*. Cambridge, MA: Medieval Academy of America, 1948.

de Roover, Raymond. *The Rise and Decline of the Medici Bank, 1397–1494*. New York: Norton, 1966.

de Roover, Raymond. "The Scholastics, Usury, and Foreign Exchange." *Business History Review* 41 (1967): 257–271.

Disraeli, Isaac. *Curiosities of Literature*. 1st series. New York: William Pearson and Co., 1835.

Divine, Thomas F. *Interest: An Historical and Analytical Study in Economics and Modern Ethics*. Milwaukee, WI: Marquette University Press, 1959.

Eichengreen, Barry, and Peter H. Lindert, editors. *The International Debt Crisis in Historical Perspective*. Cambridge, MA: MIT Press, 1989.

El-Gamal, Mahmoud A. *Islamic Finance: Law, Economics, and Practice*. Cambridge: Cambridge University Press, 2006.

Ellis, Diane. "The Effect of Consumer Interest Rate Deregulation on Credit Card Volumes, Charge-Offs, and the Personal Bankruptcy Rate." *Bank Trends*, Federal Deposit Insurance Corporation, Division of Insurance, Bank Trends—Analysis of Emerging Risks in Banking (March 1998): 98–105.

English, Edward D. *Enterprise and Liability in Sienese Banking, 1230–1350*. Cambridge, MA: Medieval Academy of America, 1988.

Evans, David S., and Richard Schmalensee. *Paying with Plastic: The Digital Revolution in Buying and Borrowing*. Cambridge, MA: MIT Press, 1999.

Ferris, Eleanor. "The Financial Relations of the Knights Templars to the English Crown." *American Historical Review* 8 (1902): 1–17.

Ferry, John. "Scuppered by *Sukuk*." *Risk* 23 (2010): 90–92.

Fichtenau, Heinrich. *The Carolingian Empire*. Translated by Peter Munz. Oxford: Oxford University Press, 1957.

Finn, Margot. *The Character of Credit: Personal Debt in English Culture, 1740–1914*. Cambridge: Cambridge University Press, 2007.

Fischer, Michael J. "Pacioli on Business Profits." *Journal of Business Ethics* 25 (2000): 299–312.

Francis, Joseph Hume. *History of the Bank of England*. Chicago: Euclid Publishing Co., 1888.

Friedman, Lawrence M. *A History of American Law*. 3rd edition. New York: Touchstone Press, 2005.

Fryde, E. B., and Edward Miller. *Historical Studies of the English Parliament*. Cambridge: Cambridge University Press, 1970.

Geisst, Charles R. *Collateral Damaged: The Marketing of Consumer Debt to America*. New York: Bloomberg Press, 2009.

George, S. *A Fate Worse Than Debt*. London: Penguin, 1988.

Gleisser, Marcus. *The World of Cyrus Eaton*. New York: A. S. Barnes, 1965.

Goetzmann, William N., and K. Geert Rouwenhorst. *The Origins of Value: The Financial Innovations That Created Modern Capital Markets*. New York: Oxford University Press, 2005.

Goldstine, Herman H. *A History of Numerical Analysis: From the Sixteenth through the Nineteenth Century*. New York: Springer-Verlag, 1977.

Gordon, Barry. *Economic Analysis before Adam Smith: Hesiod to Lessius*. London: Macmillan, 1975.

Grammp, William. "The Controversy over Usury in the Seventeenth Century." *Journal of European Economic History* 10 (1981): 671–695.

Grassby, Richard. *The Business Community of Seventeenth Century England*. Cambridge: Cambridge University Press, 2002.

Greenspan, Alan and James Kennedy. "Sources and Uses of Equity Extracted from Homes." *Finance and Economics Discussion Series* 20, Federal Reserve Board (2007): 1–49.

Ham, Arthur H. *The Campaign against the Loan Shark*. New York: Russell Sage Foundation, 1912.

Ham, Arthur H. *The Chattel Loan Business*. New York: Russell Sage Foundation, 1909.

Hammond, Bray. *Banks and Politics in America from the Revolution to the Civil War*. Reprint, Princeton, NJ: Princeton University Press, 1991.

Haskins, Charles Homer. *The Renaissance of the Twelfth Century*. Cambridge, MA: Harvard University Press, 1927.

Hawkes, David. *The Culture of Usury in Renaissance England*. London: Palgrave Macmillan, 2010.

Hendrick, Burton J. *The Story of Life Insurance*. New York: McClure, Phillipps, and Co., 1907.

Henry, Clement, and Rodney Wilson. *The Politics of Islamic Finance*. Karachi, Pakistan: Oxford University Press, 2005.

Hidy, Ralph W. *The House of Baring in American Trade and Finance*. Cambridge, MA: Harvard University Press, 1949.

Homer, Sidney, and Richard Sylla. *A History of Interest Rates*. 4th edition. Hoboken, NJ: John Wiley and Sons, 2005.

Hourani, Albert. *A History of the Arab Peoples*. Cambridge, MA: Belknap Press, 1991.

Hudson, Michael. "The Mathematical Economics of Compound Interest: A 4,000 Year Overview." *Journal of Economic Studies* 27 (2004): 344–360.

Hunt, Edwin S., and James M. Murray. *A History of Business in Medieval Europe, 1200–1550*. Cambridge: Cambridge University Press, 1999.

Hunter, W. A. *A Systematic and Historical Exposition of Roman Law*. London: Sweet and Maxwell, 1897.

Iqbal, Munawar, and Philip Molyneux. *Thirty Years of Islamic Banking: History, Performance, and Prospects*. Basingstoke: Palgrave Macmillan, 2005.

Jacobs, Joseph. *The Jews of Angevin England: Documents and Records*. London: G. P. Putnam's Sons, 1893.

Jennings, Robert M., Donald F. Swanson, and Andrew P. Trout. "Alexander Hamilton's Tontine Proposal." *William and Mary Quarterly* 45 (1988): 107–115.

Johnson, Jerah. "The Money = Blood Metaphor, 1300–1800." *Journal of Finance* 21 (1966): 119–122.

Joiron, Philippe. *Big Bets Gone Bad: Derivatives and Bankruptcy in Orange County*. San Diego: Academic Press, 1995.

Jones, Norman. *God and the Moneylenders: Usury and the Law in Early Modern England*. Oxford: Blackwell, 1989.

Jones, W. J. *The Foundations of English Bankruptcy: Statutes and Commissions in the Early Modern Period*. Philadelphia: American Philosophical Society, 1979.

Kamen, Henry. *The Spanish Inquisition*. New York: New American Library, 1965.

Katz, Alyssa. *Our Lot: How Real Estate Came to Own Us*. New York: Bloomsbury Press, 2009.

Kelly, James Birch. *A Summary and History of the Law of Usury*. London: Richard James Kennett, 1835.

Kerridge, Eric. *Usury, Interest, and the Reformation*. Aldershot, England: Ashgate, 2002.

Kopf, Edwin W. "The Early History of the Annuity." *Proceedings of the Casualty Actuarial Society* 13 (1927): 225–266.

Kroos, Herman E., editor. *Documentary History of Banking and Currency in the United States.* New York: Chelsea House, 1983.

Larson, Henrietta. *Jay Cooke, Private Banker.* Cambridge, MA: Harvard University Press, 1936.

Lea, Henry Charles. *The Inquisition of the Middle Ages.* Abridged by Margaret Nicholson. New York: Macmillan, 1961.

LeGoff, Jacques. *The Birth of Purgatory.* Chicago: University of Chicago Press, 1981.

LeGoff, Jacques. *Your Money or Your Life: Economy and Religion in the Middle Ages.* Translated by Patricia Ranum. New York: Zone Books, 1990.

Levy, David. "Adam Smith's Case for Usury Laws." *History of Political Economy* 19, no. 3 (1987): 387–400.

Lidington, D. R. "Parliament and the Enforcement of the Penal Statutes: The History of the Act 'In Restraint of Common Promoters.'" *Parliamentary History* 2 (1989): 302–328.

Lopez, Robert S. *The Commercial Revolution of the Middle Ages, 950–1350.* Cambridge: Cambridge University Press, 1976.

Macaulay, Frederick. *Some Theoretical Problems Suggested by the Movements of Interest Rates, Bond Yields and Stock Prices in the United States since 1856.* Washington, DC: National Bureau of Economic Research, 1938.

Mackeldey, Ferdinand. *Handbook of the Roman Law.* Translated by Moses Dropsie. Philadelphia: T. and J. W. Johnson, 1883.

Mann, Bruce. *Republic of Debtors: Bankruptcy in the Age of American Independence.* Cambridge, MA: Harvard University Press, 2002.

Manning, Robert D. *Credit Card Nation: The Consequences of America's Addiction to Debt.* New York: Basic Books, 2000.

Markowitz, Harry. "Portfolio Selection." *Journal of Finance* 7 (1952): 77–91.

Matthews, Joseph Bridges. *The Law of Money-Lending, Past and Present: Being a Short History of the Usury Laws in England.* London: Sweet and Maxwell, 1906.

McDonald, Forest. *Insull.* Chicago: University of Chicago Press, 1962.

McKeever, Kent. "A Short History of Tontines." *Fordham Journal of Corporate and Financial Law* 15 (2010): 491–521.

Michell, H. *The Economics of Ancient Greece.* Cambridge: W. Heffer and Sons, 1940.

Modigliani, Franco, and Merton H. Miller. "The Cost of Capital, Corporation Finance, and the Theory of Investment." *American Economic Review* 48 (1958): 261–297.

Moehlman, Conrad Henry. "The Christianization of Interest." *Church History* 3 (1934): 3–15.

Mommsen, Theodore. "Der Zinswucher des M. Brutus." *Hermes* 34 (1899): 145–150.

Mueller, Reinhold C. *The Venetian Money Market: Banks, Panics, and the Public Debt, 1200–1500.* Baltimore: Johns Hopkins University Press, 1997.

Munro, John H. "The Medieval Origins of the Financial Revolution: Usury, Rentes, and Negotiability." *International History Review* 25 (2003): 505–562.

Murray, J. B. C. *The History of Usury from the Earliest Time to the Present.* Philadelphia: J. B. Lippincott, 1866.

Neal, Larry. *The Rise of Financial Capitalism: International Capital Markets in the Age of Reason.* Cambridge: Cambridge University Press, 1990.

Nelli, Humbert O. "The Earliest Insurance Contract—A New Discovery." *Journal of Risk and Insurance* 39 (1972): 215–220.

Nelson, Benjamin. *The Idea of Usury: From Tribal Brotherhood to Universal Otherhood.* 2nd edition. Chicago: University of Chicago Press, 1969.

Neufeld, E. "The Rate of Interest and the Text of Nehemiah 5.11." *Jewish Quarterly Review* 44 (1954): 194–204.

Noonan, John T. "Gratian Slept Here: The Changing Identity of the Father of the Systematic Study of Canon Law." *Traditio* 35 (1979): 145–172.

Noonan, John T. *The Scholastic Analysis of Usury.* Cambridge, MA: Harvard University Press, 1957.

Oberholtzer, Ellis Paxton. *Jay Cooke: Financier of the Civil War.* Philadelphia: George W. Jacobs Co., 1907.

Parks, Tim. *Medici Money: Banking, Metaphysics, and Art in Fifteenth Century Florence.* New York: Norton, 2005.

Perino, Michael. *The Hellhound of Wall Street.* New York: Penguin Press, 2010.

Poitras, Geoffrey. *The Early History of Financial Economics, 1478–1776.* Northampton, MA: Edward Elgar, 2000.

Poliakov, Leon. *Jewish Bankers and the Holy See: From the Thirteenth to the Seventeenth Century.* Translated by Miriam Kochan. New York: Routledge and Kegan Paul, 1977.

Prestwich, Michael. "Early Fourteenth Century Exchange Rates." *Economic History Review* 32 (1979): 470–482.

Qureshi, Anwar Iqbal. *Islam and the Theory of Interest.* Lahore, Pakistan: Sh. Muhammad Ashraf, 1967.

Raban, Sandra. *England under Edward I and II: 1259–1327.* Oxford: Blackwell, 2000.

Reinhart, Carmen, and Kenneth S. Rogoff. *This Time Is Different: Eight Centuries of Financial Folly.* Princeton, NJ: Princeton University Press, 2009.

Richardson, M. "Increasing Microlending Potential in the United States through a Strategic Approach to Regulatory Reform." *Journal of Corporation Law* 34 (2000): 923–942.

Rockoff, Hugh. "Prodigals and Projecture: An Economic History of Usury Laws in the United States from Colonial Times to 1900." National Bureau of Economic Research Working Paper 9742 (2003).

Roddick, Jackie. *The Dance of the Millions: Latin America and the Debt Crisis.* London: Latin American Bureau, 1988.

Rolnick, Arthur J., François R. Velde, and Warren E. Weber. "The Debasement Puzzle: An Essay on Medieval Monetary History." *Journal of Economic History* 56 (1996): 789–808.

Roseveare, Henry. *The Financial Revolution, 1660–1760.* London: Pearson, 1991.

Runciman, Steven. *A History of the Crusades.* New York: Harper and Row, 1964.

Russell, Ephraim. "The Societies of the Bardi and the Peruzzi and Their Dealings with Edward III." In *Finance and Trade Under Edward III,* edited by George Unwin. Manchester: Frank Cass and Co., 1918.

Rutterford, J. "From Dividend Yield to Discounted Cash Flow: A History of UK and US Equity Valuation Techniques." *Accounting, Business and Financial History* 14 (2004): 115–149.

Ryan, Franklin Winton. *Usury and Usury Laws.* Boston: Houghton Mifflin, 1924.

Sachs, Jeffrey D., editor. *Developing Country Debt and the World Economy.* Chicago: University of Chicago Press, 1991.

Samuel, Lawrence R. *Freud on Madison Avenue: Motivation Research and Subliminal Advertising in America.* Philadelphia: University of Pennsylvania Press, 2010.

Schevill, Ferdinand. *The Medici.* New York: Harper and Row, 1949.

Scholes, Myron S. "Crisis and Risk Management." *American Economic Review* 90 (2000): 17–22.

Seward, Desmond. *The Monks of War: The Military Religious Orders.* London: Penguin, 1972.

Sharpe, William F. "Capital Asset Prices: A Theory of Market Equilibrium under Conditions of Risk." *Journal of Finance* 19 (1964): 425–442.

Shatzmiller, Joseph. *Shylock Reconsidered: Jews, Moneylending, and Medieval Society.* Berkeley: University of California Press, 1990.

Skadden, Arps, Slate, Meagher, and Flom. *The Dodd-Frank Act: Commentary and Insights.* New York: privately published, 2010.

Skeel, David A. *Debt's Dominion: A History of Bankruptcy Law in America.* Princeton, NJ: Princeton University Press, 2001.

Solomon, Robert. *The International Monetary System, 1945–1976.* New York: Harper and Row, 1977.

Stanton, Thomas H. *Government Sponsored Enterprises: Mercantilist Companies in the Modern World.* Washington, DC: AEI Press, 2002.

Stasavage, David. *Public Debt and the Birth of the Democratic State: France and Great Britain, 1688–1789.* Cambridge: Cambridge University Press, 2003.

Stirk, Nigel. "Arresting Ambiguity: The Shifting Geographies of a London Debtors' Sanctuary in the Eighteenth Century." *Social History* 25 (2000): 316–329.

Sullivan, Theresa A., Elizabeth Warren, and Jay Lawrence Westbrook. *As We Forgive Our Debtors: Bankruptcy and Consumer Credit in America.* New York: Oxford University Press, 1989.

Sullivan, Teresa, Elizabeth Warren, and Jay Lawrence Westbrook. *The Fragile Middle Class: Americans in Debt.* New Haven, CT: Yale University Press, 2000.

Tawney, R. H. *Religion and the Rise of Capitalism.* London: Penguin, 1969.

Thomas, Abdulkader S. *Interest in Islamic Economics: Understanding Riba.* New York: Routledge, 2006.

Thomas, D. L., and N. E. Evans. "John Shakespeare in the Exchequer." *Shakespeare Quarterly* 35 (1984): 125–137.

Thorne, Samuel, William F. Dunham, Philip Kurland, and Ivor Jennings. *The Great Charter.* New York: Pantheon, 1965.

Ullmann, Walter. *A History of Political Thought: The Middle Ages.* London: Penguin, 1965.

Unwin, George, editor. *Finance and Trade under Edward III.* Manchester: Frank Cass and Co., 1918.

Vesey-Fitzgerald, S. G. "Dam Dupat—Alterum Tantum." *Journal of Comparative Legislation and International Law* 7 (1925): 171–178.

Wagner, Donald O. "Coke and the Rise of Economic Liberalism." *Economic History Review* 6, no. 1 (October 1935): 30–44.

Warde, Ibrahim. *Islamic Finance in the Global Economy*. Edinburgh: Edinburgh University Press, 2000.

Weber, Max. *The Protestant Ethic and the Spirit of Capitalism*. Translated by Talcott Parsons. New York: Charles Scribner's Sons, 1958.

Whiteside, D. T. *The Mathematical Papers of Isaac Newton, 1664–1666*. Cambridge: Cambridge University Press, 1967.

Williams, Brett. *Debt for Sale: A Social History of the Credit Trap*. Philadelphia: University of Pennsylvania Press, 2004.

Wood, Diana. *Medieval Economic Thought*. Cambridge: Cambridge University Press, 2002.

Woolson, Wendy A. *In Hock: Pawning in America from Independence through the Great Depression*. Chicago: University of Chicago Press, 2010.

Wright, Robert E. *Hamilton Unbound: Finance and the Creation of the American Republic*. New York: Praeger, 2002.

Wright, Robert E. *One Nation under Debt: Hamilton, Jefferson, and the History of What We Owe*. New York: McGraw-Hill, 2008.

Yergin, Daniel. *The Prize: The Epic Quest for Oil, Money, and Power*. New York: Simon and Schuster 1991.

Yunus, Muhammad. *Banker to the Poor: Micro-Lending and the Battle against World Poverty*. New York: PublicAffairs, 2009.

Yunus, Muhammad. *Creating a World without Poverty: Social Business and the Future of Capitalism*. New York: PublicAffairs, 2007.

Ziegler, Philip. *The Sixth Great Power: A History of One of the Greatest of All Banking Families, the House of Barings, 1762–1929*. New York: Knopf, 1988.

Zimmerman, Reinhard. *The Law of Obligations: The Roman Foundations of the Civilian Tradition*. Oxford: Clarendon Press, 1996.

Index

Acknowledgments

I would like to thank John Rilling and Patrick Horner for reading parts of the manuscript and making valuable comments. I also benefited greatly from discussions with Jeff Horn about the role of usury and usury laws in eighteenth-century France. Manhattan College provided invaluable assistance through the generosity of the Ambassador Charles A. Gargano Chair of Global Economics and Finance, allowing me to rummage through archives in Oxford, Bologna, and Milan. And Elizabeth Hanrahan provided excellent research assistance.